The ASTD Reference Guide to

WORKPLACE LEARNING AND PERFORMANCE:
Present and Future Roles and Competencies

THIRD EDITION

Volume I

William J. Rothwell and Henry J. Sredl

Human Resource Development Press

AMERICAN SOCIETY
FOR TRAINING AND
DEVELOPMENT

Third Edition of The ASTD Reference Guide to Workplace Learning and Performance:
Present and Future Roles and Competencies

Library of Congress Cataloging in Publication Data

Sredl, Henry, J., 1935–
    The ASTD Reference Guide to Workplace Learning and Performance:
    Present and Future Roles and Competencies

    Includes bibliographies and indexes.
    1. Employees, Training of—Handbooks, manuals, etc. 2. Personnel management—Handbooks, manuals, etc. I. Rothwell, William J., 1951– .
II. American Society for Training and Development. III. Title.
HF5549.5T7S657 1991, 658.3'124 86-26006

ISBN 0-87425-582-1 (v.1)
ISBN 0-87425-583-X (v.2)

Production services by Anctil Virtual Office
Editorial services by Suzanne Bay
Cover design by Eileen Klockars

Dedication

This book is dedicated to our wives,
Marcelina Rothwell and Rowena Sredl.

Contents

PART 3: Reviewing and Selecting Performance-Improvement Strategies

APPENDICES

Exhibits

CHAPTER 3

CHAPTER 4

CHAPTER 5

CHAPTER 6

CHAPTER 7

CHAPTER 11

CHAPTER 12

CHAPTER 13

CHAPTER 14

CHAPTER 15

CHAPTER 16

PREFACE TO THE THIRD EDITION

Workplace Learning and Performance (WLP) is carried out by many people—HRD practitioners, line managers, hourly workers, training and development professionals, Organization Development professionals, employment counselors, economic development officials, operating managers, supervisors, in-house career development professionals, school-to-work coordinators, educators, and school guidance counselors. While job titles vary, people who perform WLP work share certain work *roles* (activities), *outputs* (results of what they do), *competencies* (qualities that help them achieve results), and *ethical standards* (notions of right and wrong). All these factors are affected by emerging trends.

People who perform WLP work devote their time and attention to the broad goals of:

1. Helping individuals, groups, and organizations anticipate or adapt to change;
2. Increasing individual, group, and organizational performance; and
3. Improving the quality of life at work.

They achieve these goals through many learning and organizational *interventions* (change efforts). A *learning intervention* is any activity requiring learning from individuals, groups, or organizations. Examples of learning interventions include (among others) employee development, employee education, and training. An *organizational intervention* is any activity requiring the management of the organization to change the work environment in which people perform. Organizational interventions can include making changes to employee selection systems, reward or incentive systems, job design, organizational design, tools and equipment, or any other issues affecting what people do and how they perform, and any changes made to the work setting in which they carry out their work.

The publication in 1983 of the research-based competency study *Models for Excellence*, sponsored by The American Society for Training and Development (ASTD) and carried out under the leadership of Patricia McLagan, increased general awareness of the importance of roles, work outputs, and competencies. That study was later updated, substantially revised, and expanded in 1989 in a four-volume work entitled *Models for HRD Practice,* published by The American Society for Training and Development.

More recent competency studies of the field have also been conducted since the second edition of this book was published in 1992. They include: *ASTD Models for Human Performance Improvement: Roles, Competencies, Outputs* by William Rothwell (1996); *ASTD Models for Learning Technologies: Roles, Competencies, and Outputs* by George Piskurich and Ethan Sanders (1998); and, most recently, *ASTD Models for Workplace Learning and Performance: Roles, Competencies, and Outputs* by William Rothwell, Ethan Sanders, and Jeff Soper (1999), all published by The American Society for Training and Development. *ASTD Models for Workplace Learning and Performance* is the only study in this group to provide a recent and comprehensive re-examination of the field in light of the emerging trends affecting it.

The Purpose of This Book

The ASTD Reference Guide, third edition, is intended to serve as a companion to *ASTD Models for Workplace Learning and Performance,* just as the first edition of this book was a companion to *Models for Excellence,* and the second edition was a companion to *Models for HRD Practice.* Simply stated, the purpose of this book is to provide a context for the Workplace Learning and Performance (WLP) field, to expand on the roles and competencies described in *ASTD Models for Workplace Learning and Performance,* and to provide WLP professionals, operating managers, academicians, students, and other interested readers with the resources for enacting those roles and demonstrating those competencies. While *ASTD Models for Workplace Learning and Performance* focuses primarily on what WLP professionals *do,* this book provides background information on the WLP field and guides the reader to many references to the literature of the WLP field. Prospective and practicing WLP professionals, line managers, and others should find this book useful as a desk reference. Academicians should find this book suitable as a textbook for undergraduate and graduate courses in WLP. Students and those interested in professional WLP work should find this book useful as a broad introduction to the field.

The Organization of the Book

This book is organized into seven parts. Parts I, II, and III are contained in Volume I.

Part I describes the context of WLP by furnishing key definitions and a status report on WLP as it is practiced today, and explains the historical evolution of the field.

Part II focuses on the WLP field. It reviews some previous competency studies of the WLP field, highlights the results of *ASTD Models for Workplace Learning and Performance,* advises readers about planning professional careers in WLP, reviews ethical issues associated with WLP work, and notes key trends likely to affect the field.

Part III reviews the range of performance-improvement strategies that may be used in organizational settings, devoting special attention to learning and organizational interventions.

Parts IV through VII are contained in Volume II. Each Chapter in the volume focuses on a single role the WLP practitioner might be expected to take on within his or her organization, as described in *ASTD Models for Workplace Learning and Performance.*

Part IV centers on the role of Manager and Analyst. Part V centers on the roles of Intervention Selector, Intervention Designer and Developer, and Intervention Implementor, and Part VI centers on the role of Change Leader and Evaluator. Part VII offers a final word about ways to develop the competencies associated with the responsibilities of a WLP professional.

About Our Authorship

If it were possible to list our names without implying a senior or junior author, we would do so. We are entirely co-equal authors. Each complements the other with his perception of life and its opportunities and challenges for HRD professionals and those they serve. This Guide would not have been possible without both of us. We deserve equal credit—or blame—for the final product.

Acknowledgments

William J. Rothwell would like to express special thanks to his graduate research assistants Xiaoli Cao, Will Hickey, Daryl Hunt, and Ning Li for their assistance in helping to track down references for the third edition. Special thanks are to be given to Xiaoli Cao for her help in alphabetizing them for easier use.

The authors would also like to express appreciation to the Board of Directors and staff of The American Society for Training and Development for supporting this project. *However, the opinions expressed in this book are the authors' own, and do not represent the official policy of ASTD or the authors' academic employers.*

William J. Rothwell
University Park, Pennsylvania

Henry J. Sredl
Corvallis, Oregon

ABOUT THE AUTHORS

WILLIAM J. ROTHWELL, Ph.D. is Professor of Human Resource Development in the Department of Adult Education, Instructional Systems and Workforce Education and Development in the College of Education on the University Park Campus of The Pennsylvania State University. He is also an active private consultant. Before arriving at Penn State in 1993, he was Assistant Vice President and Management Development Director for The Franklin Life Insurance Company and, before that, Training Director for the Illinois Office of the Auditor. He has thus worked full-time in Workplace Learning and Performance from 1979 to the present.

Dr. Rothwell has authored, coauthored, edited, or coedited numerous books. His most recent works include: Dubois, D., and Rothwell, W., *The Competency Toolkit* (Amherst, MA: HRD Press, 2000), Rothwell, W., *Building In-House Leadership and Management Development Programs* (Westport, CT: Quorum Books, 1999), Rothwell, W., Sanders, E., and Soper, J., *ASTD Models for Workplace Learning and Performance* (Alexandria, Va.: ASTD Press, 1999); Rothwell, W., *The Action Learning Guidebook: A Real-Time Strategy for Problem Solving, Training Design, and Employee Development* (San Francisco: Jossey-Bass/Pfeiffer, 1999); Rothwell, W., and Sensenig, K., eds., *The Sourcebook for Self-Directed Learning* (Amherst, MA: HRD Press, 1999); Rothwell, W., ed., *Creating, Measuring and Documenting Service Impact: A Capacity Building Resource: Rationales, Models, Activities, Methods, Techniques, Instruments.* (Columbus, OH: The EnterpriseOhio Network, 1998); Rothwell, W., and Dubois, D., eds., *In Action: Improving Human Performance* (Alexandria, Va.: The American Society for Training and Development, 1998); Rothwell, W., Prescott, R., and Taylor, M., *Strategic Human Resource Leader: How to Help Your Organization Manage the Six Trends Affecting the Workforce* (Palo Alto, Ca.: Davies-Black Publishing, 1998); Rothwell, W., ed., *In Action: Linking HRD and Organizational Strategy* (Alexandria, Va.: The American Society for Training and Development, 1998).

He has a long list of other publications to his credit. Among them: Rothwell, W., and Cookson, P., *Beyond Instruction: Comprehensive Program Planning for Business and Education* (San Francisco: Jossey-Bass, 1997); *Beyond Training and Development: State-of-the-Art Strategies for Enhancing Human Performance* (New York: AMACOM, 1996); *The ASTD Models for Human Performance Improvement* (Alexandria, VA: The American Society for Training and Development, 1996); *The Self-Directed On-the-Job Learning Workshop* (Amherst, Mass.: Human Resource Development Press, 1996); *The Just-In-Time Training Assessment Instrument* (Amherst, Mass.: Human Resource Development Press, 1996); Dubois, D., and Rothwell, W., *Developing the High Performance Workplace: Administrator's Handbook* (Amherst, Mass.: Human Resource Development Press, 1996); Dubois, D., and Rothwell, W., *Developing the High Performance Workplace: Organizational Assessment Instrument* (Amherst, Mass.: Human Resource Development Press, 1996); and *The Just-In-Time Training Administrator's Handbook* (Amherst, Mass.: Human Resource Development Press, 1996).

HENRY J. SREDL (Hank), Ph.D., is Professor Emeritus at Oregon State University in Corvallis, Oregon and President of Human Resource Associates Foundation, Inc. in Centre Harbor, New Hampshire, a private consulting firm. He has worked for over thirty years with people and people-challenges, and is a published author and member of numerous professional groups, including The American Society for Training and Development (ASTD). His previous local ASTD chapter affiliation was with the Portland Metro Chapter.

Hank's work in Eastern Europe and Asia has given him a global perspective on the issues facing HRD professionals in training and development, career development, and Organization Development.

ABOUT THE AMERICAN SOCIETY FOR TRAINING AND DEVELOPMENT

The American Society for Training and Development (ASTD) is an international organization based in Alexandria, Virginia. The largest association of Workplace Learning and Performance professionals in the U.S., ASTD's mission is to "provide leadership to individuals, organizations, and society to achieve work-related competence, performance, and fulfillment."

Vision, Mission, and Strategic Directions

Vision

- A worldwide leader in workplace learning and performance.

Mission

- We provide leadership to individuals, organizations, and society to achieve work-related competence, performance, and fulfillment.

Strategic Directions

Intensify Member Voice and Value— "Customer In"

- Engage and partner with all members and customers to understand their needs and expectations and respond with value-added solutions to strengthen learning and perform-ance in the workplace.

Create, Capture, and Provide World-Class Knowledge and Practice

- Make ASTD the preeminent and most comprehensive world-wide source of information on workplace learning and performance.

Lead through Technology

- Models and leverages technology worldwide to engage members, capture world-class knowledge, facilitate customer interaction, and deliver customized information products and services.

Shape the Industry

- Define the industry and shape its future by being the leading source of industry data, trends, and successful practices. Position ASTD as the recognized leader with current and emerging players.

Leverage ASTD's Leadership Globally

- Serve the global community by being a leading catalyst for sharing knowledge and practice worldwide.

SOURCE: http://www.astd.org/CMS/templates/template_1.html?articleid=10834

Address and Membership Information

To receive more information about ASTD, contact the Society at 1640 King Street, Box 1443, Alexandria, Virginia 22313-2043, USA. Phone: (703) 683-8100; Fax: (703) 683-8103. Visit the ASTD Web site at http://www.astd.org.

1

THE CONTEXT OF WORKPLACE LEARNING AND PERFORMANCE (WLP)

Part One comprises chapters 1 through 3. It addresses the following questions:
- How did the term *workplace learning and performance* (WLP) originate?
- Why has "workplace learning and performance" proven to be so difficult to define?
- How is "workplace learning and performance" defined in this book?
- What are some important terms in the WLP field, and what do those terms mean?
- What is the scope of WLP activities?
- Who sponsors workplace learning and performance?
- Who participates in workplace learning and performance activities?
- What is the philosophical basis of workplace learning and performance?
- How has WLP been influenced by various disciplines?

CHAPTER 1

KEY DEFINITIONS

This Chapter introduces the book, addressing such questions as these:

- How did the term *workplace learning and performance* (WLP) originate?
- Why has "workplace learning and performance" proven to be so difficult to define?
- How is workplace learning and performance defined in this book?
- What are some important terms in the WLP field, and what do those terms mean?

With the answers to these questions in mind, you should find the remainder of the book easier to understand.

WHAT IS "Workplace Learning and Performance"?

Workplace Learning and Performance: A Paradigm Shift from Human Resource Development (HRD) and Training and Development (T and D)

The term *workplace learning and performance* (WLP) is a relatively new term that describes the paradigm shift in the field once formerly referred to as *Human Resource Development* (HRD) or *Training* or *Training and Development*. (See Exhibit 1-1.) The term "workplace learning and performance" reflects more than a mere title change for those who once called themselves HRD professionals. Indeed, WLP emphasizes the *means* and *ends* sought by those in the field—*workplace learning* as a *means of achieving improved human performance in workplace settings*. Argyris succinctly explained this shift from HRD to WLP in 1994:

"Challenge your thinking about the fundamentals of your profession. In fact, prepare to reinvent yourself to be of use in the new organization—based on knowledge and measured by performance. Wake up to the shift from training to learning and the intermingling of learning with work. See how these developments will cause the trainer's role to change, to migrate to other people in the organization, and even to vanish, as learning becomes *everyone's job*. Expect vigorous debate on what learning is, where it comes from, and how it links to performance (individuals and organizations). And finally, if you cannot look critically at training, be assured that many other people can and will" (Argyris 1994).

Exhibit 1-1: Comparisons of training, HRD, and WLP

Issue	Training and Development	HRD—Human Resource Development	WLP—Workplace Learning and Performance
Definition *What does the term mean?*	Through planned learning interventions, training focuses on identifying and developing key competencies that enable employees to perform their current jobs.	*HRD* is the integrated use of training and development, organization development, and career development to improve individual, group, and organizational effectiveness (McLagan, 1989, p. 7).	*WLP* is the integrated use of learning and other interventions for the purpose of improving individual and organizational performance. It uses a systematic process of analyzing and responding to individual, group, and organizational needs. WLP creates positive, progressive change within organizations by balancing human, ethical, technological, and operational considerations.
Human Nature *What assumptions exist about people?*	People want and need to be instructed about their jobs to be productive.	People should be considered self-actualizing. Learning is key to self-actualization.	• People want to learn and develop. • People seek to achieve their potential. • Learning and performance go hand in hand by helping organizations and employees reach their goals. An organization must strike a balance between its own goals and the goals of individual employees.
Goal *What is the major goal?*	The major goal is improved knowledge, skills, and attitudes about the job.	The major goal is the integration of training and development, organization development, and career development for the purpose of achieving improved performance through planned learning.	The major goals are: • improving human performance • balancing individual and organizational needs • building knowledge capital within the organization • improving financial return.
Nature of Learning in Organizations *What principles drive learning in organizational settings?*	Learning should be focused on the job performed by the individual. The results of training should be immediate, and their relationship to the job should be readily apparent.	• Increased skill and knowledge about a particular set of tasks will lead to greater organizational effectiveness. • Pairing an individually focused intervention (such as training) with other interventions (such as organization development and career development) best facilitates learning.	• Learning interventions may or may not be appropriate for solving specific performance problems. The appropriate intervention depends on the root causes of the performance problem. • Continuous learning is an important organizational strategy because it builds the intellectual capital that is crucial to individual and organizational performance.
Trainer-Trainee Relationship *What is the desirable relationship between the trainer and the trainee?*	The focus of training and development is on making people productive in their jobs. Training seeks that end with a short-term focus; development seeks the same end with a longer-term focus. In training and development, the primary emphasis is on isolating the knowledge, skills, and attitudes that are essential to job success and on building individual knowledge, skills, and attitudes in line with those requirements. The trainer-trainee relationship is akin to the teacher-student model. The "teacher-trainer" is responsible for teaching the "student-learner" what he or she must know, do, or feel to be successful in the job.	HRD adopts an integrated approach to change through planned learning. It integrates the individually focused short-term learning initiative of training with group-focused learning initiatives (organizational development) and with longer term learning initiatives (career development) intended to prepare individuals for future work requirements. Since "training" is not the sole focus of HRD, the relationship between trainer-trainee is more complex and varies with the type of change effort and with the results sought.	WLP does not focus exclusively on learning interventions. However, workers and stakeholders have a major responsibility in planning instruction and, more importantly, in focusing on ways to support and encourage learning. Everyone has a role to play in that effort. The full-time WLP practitioner is a resource, enabling agent, and learning specialist who facilitates the process but does not take sole ownership of it. The learner has responsibility for taking initiative to pursue his or her own learning efforts. In WLP, the WLP practitioner and learner are "partners" in the learning endeavor, and both are seeking improved performance.

Exhibit 1-1: Comparisons of training, HRD, and WLP *(continued)*

Issue	*Training and Development*	*HRD—Human Resource Development*	*WLP—Workplace Learning and Performance*
Means of Motivating Learning *What motivates people to learn?*	Training and development are management responsibilities, because it is management's job to make sure that workers can perform their jobs properly. Employees are motivated to learn because they want to be successful in performing their jobs in keeping with management's requirements.	The integration of the following motivates learning: • individual motivation to learn the work through training • individual motivation to work effectively in groups • individual motivation to prepare for future career advancement.	• Organizations sponsor learning because they are aware of the competitive importance of intellectual capital; individuals are motivated to learn in response to future career goals or present work needs, problems, or performance targets. • Learning is work- and performance-focused rather than job-focused, because "jobs" may go away, but "work" seldom does.
Nature of the Field of Practice *What is the nature of the field?*	Training and development focus on planned learning events.	HRD focuses on these three-fold purposes: • giving individuals the knowledge and skills they need to perform • helping them formulate and realize career goals • interacting effectively in groups.	WLP focuses on progressive change in the workplace through learning and other performance-improvement strategies or interventions.
Governing Model *What primary model best provides guidance for the field?*	Instructional systems design (ISD)	• Instructional systems design • the action research model • various career development models	The HPI process model

SOURCE: Rothwell, W., Sanders, E., and Soper, J. (1999). *ASTD Models for Workplace Learning and Performance.* Alexandria, VA: The American Society for Training and Development, pp. 9-11. Used by permission of The American Society for Training and Development (ASTD).

Difficulties in Defining the Term

"Workplace learning and performance" is difficult to define. In fact, it shares the same definitional problem faced by its predecessors "HRD" and "T and D." Many efforts have been made over the years to define HRD, but those efforts have been largely stymied because many people have not used the term consistently. For example, some people use "HRD" to refer to government-sponsored educational or job training programs aimed at helping disadvantaged or mainstream workers. Others have used "HRD" to describe any form of education or training. Still others have used "HRD" to refer to any activity intended to increase the economic value of people as workers. No one seems to agree on a single definition, and the same problem existed for "T and D" that now exists for WLP. Since *T and D, HRD,* and *WLP* are not trademarks, registered names, or copyrighted words, confusion about their meanings will probably persist long into the future (Nadler, L. and Z. 1989).

In Patricia McLagan's 1989 study of the HRD field *Models for HRD Practice*, she identified five major reasons why efforts to define human resource development have proven fruitless (McLagan, 1989). Let us now explain why "workplace learning and performance" is so hard to define.

Reason #1: WLP is an emerging field. Relatively few educational programs have been designed specifically to prepare people for professional careers in the field. Those programs that do exist—about 300 or so, according to ASTD—are usually only found in developed nations. Most WLP professionals have earned one or more college degrees and have considerable prior work experience, but their college majors and experiences often vary widely. Moreover, few educational programs in such other fields as medicine, law, or business have adequately emphasized just how much responsibility for WLP is borne by professionals in those other fields. At present, as in the past, there is no one best way to prepare for a career in WLP, either educationally or experientially.

Reason #2: WLP is a dynamic field. WLP methods must be flexible enough for adaptation to the chaotic, fast-paced, right-sized, competitive work environments that characterize today's business, government, and not-for-profit organizations—factors that contribute to the dynamic nature of the field. WLP practices are increasingly influenced by rapidly evolving work processes, instructional technology, learning research, theoretical models, and the ongoing dialogue about effective or best practices.

Reason #3: WLP relies on more than one subject matter. WLP, like HRD and T and D before it, is an applied field: It draws on theories and insights from a broad array of disciplines that include education, organization behavior, management science, industrial and individual psychology, communication, counseling, economics, sociology, general systems science, the humanities, and political and policy science. For this reason, WLP professionals have historically had difficulty identifying a common body of knowledge. This has not been a problem for other disciplines like medicine, law, or accounting.

Reason #4: WLP exists within a larger arena. WLP is focused around *any* method that can help to improve human performance. It is thus broader than traditional notions of Human Resources (HR), and encompasses any or all fields that seek to improve human capacities, particularly in workplace settings. However, it should be understood that efforts to improve human performance are affected by many other factors, in addition to the capacities of individual performers. In fact, the work environment—more so than individuals—has the greatest bearing and influence on workplace performance.

Since the publication of the first and second editions of this book, WLP has come to entail much more than simply HR at a time when the HR function itself is coming under increasing attack. In some companies, traditional HR functions have been outsourced in whole or in part because management's perception is that they do not contribute sufficiently to bottom-line results or added value. Now, more than ever, WLP and human resource professionals are being challenged to demonstrate the value of what they do in order to avoid being eliminated, outsourced, or downsized.

Reason #5: WLP is pervasive. A fifth and final reason that efforts to define WLP have proven elusive is that WLP, like HRD and Training and Development before it, has always been done by somebody. Unlike some other organizational functions, however, responsibility for WLP is not appropriately restricted to one department. Instead, responsibility for it is and should be diffused throughout organizations and even the broader society surrounding the organization. After all, everyone can—and should—play a role in improving human performance, since it cuts across organizational boundaries, layers, and functions. It is appropriately viewed as "everyone's business," but WLP professionals must take the lead in facilitating, orchestrating, and energizing the organization's efforts to enhance performance through workplace learning.

A Definition of WLP

The definition of WLP used in this book and in Rothwell, Sanders, and Soper's *ASTD Models for Workplace Learning and Performance* is somewhat unique. (See Exhibit 1-2.) That definition deserves elaboration, because it is the focus of this book.

Exhibit 1-2: A definition of workplace learning and performance

---

Workplace Learning and Performance (WLP): "The integrated use of learning and other interventions for the purpose of improving individual and organizational performance. It uses a systematic process of analyzing performance and responding to individual, group, and organizational needs. WLP creates positive, progressive change within organizations by balancing human, ethical, technological, and operational considerations."

SOURCE: Rothwell, W., Sanders, E., and Soper, J. (1999). *ASTD Models for Workplace Learning and Performance.* Alexandria, VA: The American Society for Training and Development, p. 121. Used by permission of The American Society for Training and Development.

Integrated is a noteworthy word in this definition. It means that performance-improvement interventions are not isolated efforts for improvement: they are integrated, because they require individual learning as well as organizational action and support. Interventions can be classified as either *learning* interventions or *organizational* (sometimes called management) interventions, but to be most effective in effecting change, these interventions should be used together—that is, they should be integrated.

WLP *uses a systematic process of analyzing performance and responding to individual, group, and organizational needs* known as the *Human Performance Improvement (HPI) process.* It is important to understand that the HPI process is used by WLP professionals much as the Instructional Systems Design (ISD) model is used by instructional designers, and the Action Research Model (ARM) is used by Organization Development practitioners. (All three of these models will be described later in this book.) The HPI Process entails: analyzing performance; seeking to determine the cause(s) of human performance problems or improvement opportunities;

selecting the appropriate interventions to address the problems (or satisfy the needs); implementing the interventions, following through to ensure that they are implemented in line with desired goals; and evaluating results.

Finally, as the definition explains, *WLP creates positive, progressive change within organizations by balancing human, ethical, technological, and operational considerations.* Progressive change means improvements in performance, but such performance improvements should not be bought at the expense of people. WLP professionals have an important obligation to seek an ethical balance among many human, ethical, technological, and operational considerations.

WHAT IS THE SCOPE OF WLP?

The above-described definition of WLP warrants further elaboration to clarify the scope of WLP. Let's begin with a look at a few important terms: learning, performance, management or organizational intervention, learning intervention, training, education, development, organization development, career development, and knowledge management. Every WLP professional seeking to be effective must understand what these terms mean.

To understand their interrelationships, bear in mind three points from the outset: First, all these activities involve change. Second, all activities, different as they may be, are ways to improve performance. Third, realize that individuals can make only six types of job movements in any organization: *in* (entry), *out* (termination), *up* (promotion), *down* (demotion), *across* (lateral movement), or *progress in place* (increasing technical proficiency in present job duties, job enrichment, exploration of new possibilities, or changes in individual capabilities, performance, or potential) (Haire, 1968). Every one of these movements affects organizational as well as individual performance. Of course, work can also be accomplished without making changes with people. For example, the work can be *outsourced* (moved in whole or in part out of the organization through use of vendors or contingent/temporary workers), *simplified* (that is, work processes can be streamlined), or *insourced* (accomplished with help from other organizational groups).

"People" movements of any kind imply change, and individuals must prepare themselves for change through a combination of organizational and learning interventions. *Training* helps individuals prepare for movements in or out of jobs or their current work. *Employee Education* prepares individuals for movements up, down, or across the organization's hierarchy. *Employee Development* contributes to individual growth and to individuals as vehicles for organizational learning. *Career Development* helps individuals turn their career goals into realities and helps organizations meet their future HR needs. *Organization Development* helps individuals, groups, and organizations change their ways of solving problems and making decisions.

What Is Learning?

Learning refers to a change process based on the acquisition of new knowledge, skills, or attitudes. While in the strictest sense of the term only individuals can learn, much attention in recent years has focused around team-oriented, group-oriented, or organizationally-oriented learning in which groups or organizations acquire and retain the knowledge, skills, or attitudes of their members.

Learning can occur in any setting, however. *Workplace learning* is any learning that occurs in (or for) the workplace. *On-the-job learning* occurs on the job. *Near-the-job learning* occurs in settings close by the workplace or job setting and one special category of it occurs in "vestibule training." *Off-the-job learning* occurs away from the setting in which the work is performed. These distinctions are less important than ever because technology makes it possible to perform, and learn, work anywhere and at any time.

What Is Performance?

Improved performance is the ultimate goal sought by WLP interventions. *Performance* refers primarily, but not exclusively, to the results or outcomes of meaningful efforts. If an individual sets out to type a letter and does so successfully, then he or she has performed well. But if the same person sets out to type a letter and does not end up with a typed letter (*the letter is a work output* or *work outcome*), he or she has not performed well, regardless of reason, effort, or excuse. However, there are many reasons why that person may not have typed the letter; tracing the cause of poor performance is a first step toward finding solutions and thereby establishing the foundation for an intervention.

Some people tend to reward efforts, rather than results—or at least make excuses for failure as long as the performer made a valiant attempt with exceptional zeal. That's particularly true when the individual tried hard but failed. They might say "But I tried hard," as though effort alone should be rewarded or, at the very least, count for something. *But no effort—regardless of how intense it may be—is a substitute for results*. Understanding that point is a fundamental first step in becoming effective as a WLP professional.

One cultural practice is to confuse performance with good attitude. Performance does not necessarily mean "a good relationship with one's immediate supervisor." In fact, it is indeed possible to be highly productive and still not be especially well-liked or admired by one's immediate supervisor or peers or subordinates.

What Is an Intervention?

An *intervention* is a corrective action. It may be taken by an organization's managers, by individual workers working alone or in a group, by WLP professionals, or by any combination of these groups. Interventions might be *reactive*, intended to "fix" problems once they have surfaced, or *proactive*, intended to avert or avoid future problems. Similarly, interventions can be focused on solving problems, or focused on discovering and seizing new opportunities for performance improvement.

Let's clarify these distinctions with an example: If employees are leaving the organization, WLP professionals will seek to find out what is happening and why. What is prompting this turnover? In doing so, they are troubleshooting an existing problem. But if WLP professionals set out to improve worker retention when it is not a problem but just a good idea that will improve performance, they will be taking a proactive approach. If they set out to improve new employee orientation by taking advantage of new technology, such as Web-based training, they might be seizing new opportunities for performance improvement by slashing the unproductive breaking-in period of newcomers in a new, innovative way.

What Is an Organizational Intervention?

The world is filled with many problems, and they all stem from one of two sources—the organization, or the individual. Organizational problems stem from causes in the work setting, rather than problems with individuals. Individual problems stem from many possible causes— lack of knowledge, lack of motivation, lack of ability to learn, and so on.

An *organizational (management) intervention* calls for management action. An organizational intervention does not rely on learning as a chief driver for change, but is, instead, geared toward changing the environment or working conditions in which people carry out their work. Examples of such interventions include seeking improvements in employee-selection methods, staff-planning methods, rewards and incentives, and tools and equipment. There are, of course, a dizzyingly large number of ways by which to improve human performance that can be used in isolation or in combination with others.

Here is a simple example: If management does not supply automobile mechanics with the right tools to fix a car, then the lack of tools may cause a performance problem: the automobile mechanics will not be able to fix cars that have problems that only one kind of tool can fix. Whose fault is that? While you might argue that the mechanic could go out and buy the tools, remember that some tools are extremely expensive. It is management's responsibility to supply these tools if the organization's managers want mechanics to perform competently. Incidentally, finding fault or placing blame does not serve a useful purpose; the goal here should be to focus on solving the performance problem by taking appropriate action, rather than assigning responsibility for the cause.

Most issues in the workplace are, ultimately, the responsibility of management. Managers control how many and what kind of workers are selected, transferred, promoted, trained, and rewarded. The organization's managers even control who gets fired, what parts of an organization are to be downsized, and what work will be outsourced or handled by temporary workers. Managers also affect how the organization responds to customers and to competition, how the work is processed, and how responsibilities are allocated within the organization.

An *intervention*, then, is a correction action. An *organizational intervention* is a decisive action taken by management to address a problem or improve the potential for performance in the work setting. It is different from a learning intervention, as we will now explain.

What Is a Learning Intervention?

A *learning intervention* is an intervention that energizes change through individual, group, or organizational learning. It is thus designed to bring about performance improvement by equipping people with more knowledge or skill, or aligning their attitudes with those needed to meet or exceed customer expectations. Learning interventions may take the form of training, employee education, employee development, or organization development.

What Is Training?

Training has been defined in many different ways. In one classic definition, Leonard Nadler referred to it as "learning, provided by employers to employees, that is related to their present jobs" (Nadler, L. and Z. 1989). Lawrie defined it as a "change in skills" (Lawrie, J. 1990). Others claim that its major focus is providing basic knowledge and skills for familiar tasks tied to present jobs (Bartz et al 1989).

Training is a short-term learning intervention. It is intended to build on individual knowledge, skills, and attitudes to meet present or future work requirements. In this context, *knowledge* refers to the facts and information necessary for performing a job or task; *skills* are the abilities associated with successful performance; and *attitudes* are feelings, typically as individuals express them to others. Training helps individuals meet minimally-acceptable job requirements or refine, upgrade, and improve what they presently do. When employees finish their training, they should be able to apply it immediately.

Training can be formally planned using a systematic approach called *instructional systems design* (ISD), which is based on rigorous needs analysis, curriculum design, curriculum development, instructional delivery, and evaluation (Rothwell and Kazanas 1998). Alternatively, it can be planned informally and carried out during work activities. It is delivered off-the-job, near-the-job, or on-the-job, to individuals or to groups.

Training serves many purposes, as labels associated with it indicate.

Remedial training or *basic skills training* provides job applicants or workers with entry-level knowledge, skills, and attitudes that they should otherwise possess at the time that they are selected for a job or begin work. For instance, workers who receive training in reading, writing, and computing—basic skills that most employers expect of workers at the time they are hired—are said to receive remedial or basic skills training.

Orientation training gives workers rudimentary information about the organization, work group, or job. Employee orientation usually introduces newcomers to the organization's work rules, benefits, and facilities. Employers can also meet governmental regulations by alerting new employees to hazardous substances to which they can be exposed in the workplace.

Qualifying training overlaps with orientation training. It is designed to help individuals acquire the basic knowledge, skills, and attitudes they need to meet job requirements and carry on job-specific tasks. It is usually directed to workers in specific job categories, such as executives, managers, supervisors, sales or customer service workers, technical workers, professionals, skilled craftspersons, clerical workers, and unskilled or semi-skilled workers. Training of this type is most often organization-specific, tied to the special requirements of an organization or job. Its primary purpose is to cut the unproductive breaking-in period that newcomers normally experience if they are not told what to do or how to perform in the unique culture of one organization.

Second-chance training rectifies individual performance deficiencies. It is geared to employees who have already received qualifying training but who have not met minimum job requirements because they still do not know how to perform. Before suggesting that employees participate in second-chance training, however, their supervisors should first identify the cause of the performance problem. Training is usually appropriate for individuals only when their performance problems stem from a lack of individual knowledge, skill, or appropriate attitude—and not when they are traceable to such other possible causes as poor supervisory planning or an employee's deliberate unwillingness to perform.

Cross training prepares backup workers to perform critical activities in the absence of those normally assigned to them. For instance, a secretary trained to function as receptionist whenever a full-time receptionist is ill or vacationing is said to have been cross-trained. Cross-training is critically important in many organizations, but it is more and more difficult to do as lean-staffed, rightsized organizations struggle to function with (fewer) people whose jobs have been simultaneously enlarged and enriched.

Retraining, sometimes called *upgrading training*, updates workers so that their knowledge, skills, and attitudes keep pace with changing technology and job requirements. When an employer installs new equipment or changes work methods, people often need to be retrained.

Outplacement training is necessitated by downsizing, mergers and acquisitions, and other major disruptions of an organization's workforce. It is intended to help displaced or outplaced workers make the sometimes-traumatic transition to new jobs or careers.

What Is Employee Education?

Employee education was defined by Nadler as "learning focused on a future job" and by Lawrie as "change in knowledge." It is a vehicle for helping individuals qualify for advancement and, because it addresses career goals, it is frequently associated with Career Development activities. Usually initiated by individuals rather than by organizations, employee education is an intermediate-term learning intervention that, like training, can be carried out in many ways and for many reasons.

Remedial education is sometimes conducted on an individual's own time and away from work. It need not be tied directly to job requirements, but it does help people advance in their jobs by giving them necessary educational credentials and opportunities for personal growth. Some organizations encourage employees to earn a General Education Diploma (GED), the equivalent of a high school diploma and one form of remedial education.

Qualifying education provides individuals with the educational credentials necessary for advancement in their careers. Tuition reimbursement programs offered by many employers encourage qualifying education, as does an organization's sponsorship of the burgeoning number of industry-sponsored or professional certification or accreditation programs (these sometimes satisfy college-credit requirements). Certification programs include such widely different designations as CPA (Certified Public Accountant), CLU (Certified Life Underwriter), CDP (Certified Data Processor), and SPHR (Senior Professional in Human Resources).

Continuing education, conducted on or off the work site, helps individuals keep abreast of changes in their occupations or professions, though not necessarily how those changes affect them on their jobs, which is addressed by upgrading training. Some occupations require professionals to complete an established number of continuing education hours each year to retain their state licenses; public school teaching, accounting, insurance, real estate, law, medicine, nursing, and engineering professions in many states have such requirements. However, continuing education requirements vary widely, a cause for concern for WLP professionals who help employees in one organization comply with the widely differing continuing education requirements of various occupations.

What Is Employee Development?

Nadler defined *development* as "learning experiences, provided by employer to employees, that are not job-related." Lawrie defined it as "a change in attitudes or values." Development is a long-term learning intervention that is usually focused on stimulating new ideas. It may also serve as a tool for developing an organization or group through individual development.

Like training and education, development may be carried out in many ways.

Individually-initiated developmental experiences involve little or no prompting from others. One study determined that, on average, adults spend 700 hours a year at learning projects (Tough 1979), usually as a means of helping them cope with current life or work problems (Knowles 1984). Research reveals that some learning experiences are key to individual development, though they are not always recognized as such at the time they occur (Lindsey et al 1987). In one sense, any effort made by an individual to investigate something new can be considered a development experience. Examples might include learning a foreign language in anticipation of an overseas trip, reading a book about card games to improve individual playing ability, or mastering rudimentary leadership skills by heading up a charity drive.

Organizationally-initiated developmental experiences are prompted by the employer, usually represented by the individual's immediate supervisor or manager. Managers might, for instance, deliberately develop their employees by: giving them short-term project assignments to stimulate insight, sending them off-site to participate in specialized programs, rotating them to other jobs or functions within the organization for extended periods, coaching them on-the-spot about special problems, or providing them with opportunities to receive structured feedback through assessment centers or multi-rater, full-circle development questionnaires. Lombardo and Eichinger identified 88 ways to develop individuals while they are doing their current job assignments (Lombardo and Eichinger 1989).

Jointly-initiated developmental experiences strike a balance between individually-initiated and organizationally-initiated developmental experiences. For instance, an individual may volunteer for a special assignment as a means of gaining new insight into a problem, and the individual's immediate supervisor might approve such an assignment during working hours to facilitate development. Some organizations even provide competitive entry to special developmental programs, such as allowing an employee to spend a year as a visiting faculty member at a university, take a year or two off with full pay for graduate study at a university, or even rotate on full salary to a supplier or distributor organization.

What Is Career Development?

Career Development has a two-fold purpose of providing direction and purpose for an individual's career, while at the same time ensuring that an organization has an appropriate supply of human resources to meet present and future demands.

Many specialized terms are associated with Career Development. One definition of *career* is "the sequence of a person's work-related activities and behaviors and associated attitudes, values, and aspirations over the span of one's life." *Career planning* can be defined as "a deliberate process for becoming aware of self, opportunities, constraints, choices, and consequences; identifying career-related goals; and "career pathing" or programming work, education, and related developmental experiences to provide the direction, timing, and sequence of steps to attain a specific career goal." *Career management* might mean "an ongoing process of preparing, implementing, and monitoring career plans undertaken by the individual alone or in concert with the organization," and *Career Development* as "the outcomes of actions on career plans. The outcomes that are pursued may be based on the needs of the organization and/or the individual" (Storey, 1979).

Career Development comprises both individually-oriented career planning and organizationally-oriented career management. Career planning helps individuals identify future job or occupational opportunities inside or outside their organizations; career management helps organizations identify the numbers and kinds of people needed to meet future work requirements.

Organizations facilitate individual career-planning activities by making available self-study career-planning workbooks, offering career-planning workshops to employees, or encouraging management career-coaching or mentoring of employees. Organizations conduct career-management activities by identifying replacements for a few key positions as a form of disaster planning (*replacement planning*), identifying successors for key positions (*succession planning*), or extending planning to all positions in an organization (*human resource planning*). To handle career development effectively, organizations must conduct career management while also encouraging employees to conduct their own career planning.

What Is Organization Development?

Organization Development (OD) is associated with long-term change efforts directed toward individuals, groups, and organizations; it is intended to change or improve decision-making, problem-solving, and group or organizational culture. French and Bell, in what has become one classic definition of organization development, described OD as "a top management-supported, long-range effort to improve an organization's problem-solving and renewal processes, particularly through a more effective and collaborative diagnosis and management of organizational culture emphasizing formal work team, temporary team, and intergroup culture, with the assistance of a consultant-facilitator and the use of the theory and technology of applied behavioral science, including action research" (French and Bell, 1984). Beckhard, in another classic definition, characterized OD as "an effort (1) planned, (2) organization-wide, and (3) managed from the top, to (4) increase organization effectiveness and health through (5) planned interventions in the organization's 'processes,' using behavioral-science knowledge" (Beckhard 1969). Bennis has called OD "a response to change, a complex educational strategy intended to change the beliefs, attitudes, values, and structure of organizations so that they can better adapt to new technologies, markets, and challenges, and the dizzying rate of change itself" (Bennis 1969). Some authorities regard OD as a broad field that encompasses training, education, development, and career development activities (Schmuck and Miles 1971).

OD interventions, meaning "planned change efforts," vary in scope and purpose. They may be directed toward changing an organization, one or more work groups, a pair or a triad, an individual's role, or an individual. OD can address performance problems having to do with organizational, intergroup, intragroup, or individual goals, plans, communication, culture, climate, leadership, authority, problem-solving, decision-making, conflict/cooperation, role definitions, and other issues. These performance problems can be addressed by *modes of intervention* such as training, education, development, process consultation, data feedback, problem-solving, planning, OD task forces, and technostructural activities. Other OD interventions are possible as well.

While OD may focus on different problems and use varying modes of intervention, it relies on a common model for problem-solving and change to guide its efforts. This is called the *action research model (ARM)*. The term was coined by John Collier and first used in a change effort by Kurt Lewin (French and Bell 1984).

OD is based on several important assumptions. These include the following: People want to belong to a work group; individual feelings affect group performance as much as facts do; leaders cannot see to the needs of everyone in a group all the time; openness and interpersonal trust are essential to group performance; most groups function far less effectively than they are capable of; and that a willingness to see others as creative and useful can be a self-fulfilling prophecy. OD interventions often have high success rates, though those successes are seldom widely-publicized (Golembiewski 1990).

What Is Knowledge Management?

Knowledge management is a way of managing where 1) the knowledge of the organization is explicitly considered in strategy, policy, procedure, and activities in the organization; and 2) where performance is linked directly to the organization's tangible and intangible intellectual assets. *Knowledge management* is thus defined as "the process and methods of collecting, organizing, and disseminating intellectual capital." *Intellectual capital* is defined as "an organization's knowledge that is composed of human capital, structural capital, and customer capital" (Rothwell, W., Sanders, E., and Soper, J. 1999). It is the essence of what makes an organization competitive, productive, profitable, and performance-oriented. The reason? Annie Brooking says that the third-millennium enterprise is productive in an information age precisely because management understands that "its work-force is valuable because of what it knows. Good training is an asset, as it maintains the work-force and its know-how" (Brooking 1996). WLP professionals are interested in enhancing the management of knowledge in their organizations, and increasing and retaining investments in intellectual capital.

CHAPTER 2

Sponsors and Participants of Workplace Learning and Performance (WLP)

This Chapter paints the landscape of Workplace Learning and Performance as it is today. It addresses two simple questions:

1. Who sponsors WLP?
2. Who participates in WLP?

All organizations undertake WLP efforts, of course, though the nature and extent of those efforts may differ. After all, WLP can be a byproduct of experience in doing work-related activities. All organizations, then, play some role in building intellectual capital and creating an infrastructure that contributes to productivity and high performance. Some organizations set about building intellectual capital as a key part of their mission, and devote much time and attention to doing that. Other organizations do not set about building intellectual capital in any planned, systematic way.

WHO SPONSORS WLP?

Workplace learning can be conducted or coordinated by any one of a large number of groups or entities. They include public and private elementary and secondary schools, post-secondary schools, other sources of postsecondary education (the military and apprenticeship programs), colleges or universities, government-funded training programs, training vendors, and employer-sponsored programs. (See Exhibit 2-1, which provides a picture to show the many sponsors of WLP.) In the first section of Chapter Two, we will briefly review these sponsors and describe the role they play; in the second section, we will focus on who receives training and what kind of training they receive. The intent of this Chapter, then, is to summarize the present status of WLP.

Exhibit 2-1: The sponsor wheel*

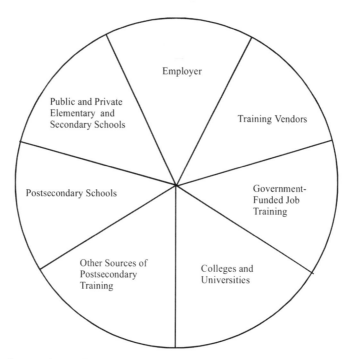

* Note: This Exhibit shows the major sponsors of Workplace Learning and Performance. While they are shown in equal proportions, some contribute more that others—as the text explains.

SOURCE: Bassi, L., and Van Buren, M. (1999). *The 1999 ASTD State of the Industry Report.* [A supplement to Training and Development Magazine.] Alexandria, VA: The American Society for Training and Development, p. 5. Used by permission of ASTD. All rights reserved.

Public and Private Elementary and Secondary Schools

The role of public and private elementary and secondary schools in building American society cannot be overemphasized. Aside from communicating important democratic principles to youngsters, schools provide basic knowledge in English (reading and writing), history, mathematics, and physical and social science—the foundation for subsequent academic achievement and preparation for employment. However, they serve another purpose, perhaps equally important: they instill in young people a work ethic that produces self-disciplined, hard-working workers (Nasaw 1979). Public and private elementary and secondary schools in other countries serve similar functions.

Considering the monumental task confronting them since the beginning of universal education, U.S. schools are highly efficient and effective. Yet they are frequently and widely criticized for churning out illiterates and semi-literates, permitting dropout rates to skyrocket, and failing to prepare students to meet the growing challenges of present and future workplaces. Violence in U. S. schools has also recently surged to the forefront of national and international attention. The response of many political leaders to these problems has been a call for experimentation and new ways to approach education—including the use of charter schools and vouchers that would transfer public funds to private schools selected by individual families. Some parents have responded to the criticisms by assuming responsibility for their children's educations through home schooling.

The challenge we now face is to find more and better ways for business, government, and not-for-profit organizations to work cooperatively with primary and secondary educational institutions through school-to-work programs and other efforts to improve the quality of education. There are many ways that employers can work with the schools; these partnerships pose unique challenges and are not as simple to perform successfully as they may seem, but they *can* make important contributions toward improving the quality of education in the U. S. Each employer organization should consider, during its strategic planning process, how it can contribute to improving education and thereby help to build the societal infrastructure within which the employer's organization functions, not to mention its future workforce!

Postsecondary Schools

Postsecondary schools serve the needs of the many people who are unwilling—or financially unable—to attend four-year colleges and universities to prepare themselves for a career. These include community colleges and technical schools, non-collegiate vocational schools, the military, and employers.

Community colleges and vocational and technical schools dominate postsecondary education, and rightly so. Employers consistently report that they are very influential in helping their organizations meet their future needs.

Military and apprenticeship programs are two other sources of postsecondary training. The military has provided qualifying training to millions of people not part of the U. S. workforce, and many young people who are unable to afford college or other vocational preparation opt for military enlistment in order to obtain marketable skills for future employment.

Apprenticeship programs sponsored by employers and unions also provide qualifying training in such skilled trades as carpentry, electrical work, and pipefitting to several hundred thousand people each year. Apprenticeship programs function much like *cooperative education,* in which planned off-the-job instruction is combined with practical on-the-job experience. Employers who are distressed with what they perceive as basic skills deficiencies among recent high school graduates are turning more and more to apprenticeship programs.

Colleges and Universities

Colleges and universities are among the most highly visible and important centers for qualifying training in this country. As the mean age of the U. S. population increases, colleges and universities have been experiencing an influx of older students returning to school for qualifying training. Many are hoping to make midlife career changes, maintain job security in the midst of widespread downsizing and outsourcing, or upgrade their educational credentials in hopes of advancing professionally in their fields. Others are hedging their bets, acquiring skills so that they can move quickly from one employer (or occupation) to another if there are dynamic changes in their workplaces. Employers continue to rely on colleges and universities as sources of future talent.

Government-Funded Job Training Programs

Government-funded job training programs are also significant sponsors of WLP. Such programs, often called *second chance training*, have traditionally rendered assistance to school dropouts, welfare recipients, the unemployed or underemployed, and individuals who were displaced due to technological changes in work processes or changes in other business conditions.

Until the passage of the Workforce Investment Act of 1998, the premier federal program to help the disadvantaged was the Job Training Partnership Act (JTPA), which worked through locally-based Private Industry Councils (PICs) and emphasized on-the-job training (OJT) in cooperation with local employers. JTPA itself replaced the Comprehensive Employment and Training Act (CETA) and the Manpower Training and Development Act (MTDA). As this book goes to press, many questions have yet to be answered about what has now become the Workforce Investment Act (WIA).

Many states also offer special employment programs to improve employment opportunities for the displaced or disadvantaged. They stimulate job creation or job placement for the purpose of economic development. These programs indicate that WLP has been widely recognized as a tool for economic development; it is also used to reduce welfare rolls, reform convicted criminals and prepare them for a productive return to the workforce, and provide qualifying or upgrading training for special groups affected by workplace changes. It need not be a financial burden to present employers: In some states, grants for employee training are available to employers who plan to upgrade the technology used in their work methods—a change that might otherwise throw many people out of work if they are not provided with special training to upgrade their skills. Some state governments also award special tax incentives or tax abatements for employer investments in other, specialized types of employee training that are necessitated by public policy.

Training Vendors

Large corporations purchase much of their employee training from external training suppliers called *vendors*. Vendors include local educational institutions, colleges and universities, former WLP professionals who have turned to consulting, or large multinational consulting firms (such as Andersen Consulting, Developmental Dimensions International, AchieveGlobal, Hay/McBer, and many others). In many cases, training vendors help employers meet specialized or temporary needs at a substantially lower cost than if they had to hire full-time WLP professionals. Training vendors are especially appropriate when the topic is a highly specialized one or is a generic need, when there is no in-house expertise, when the need is immediate, when there is a limited number of targeted employees, or when the subject matter is not proprietary, cost considerations are favorable, or the employer has a small training staff.

Vendors can perform many WLP services for organizations. A few examples: they can help employers prepare in-house training, facilitate organization development interventions, establish career development programs, deliver public seminars to which employers send employees, or publish off-the-shelf training packages for employers developing in-house instruction that can be adapted to their organization's unique needs. However, vendor choice is a critical issue that must be handled with great care: The employer should consider vendor cost, credentials, background, philosophy, delivery method, program content, and form of support before entering into an agreement.

Employer-Sponsored WLP

Employer-sponsored WLP is vast and largely invisible. It is a very important, if not the single most important, component of WLP: It is strategically positioned near the work performed by employees in a way that is not true of WLP activities sponsored by most anyone else, and it can be sustained over time. Efforts provided by vendors, on the other hand, are often short-term and only temporary.

However, employer-sponsored WLP is not nearly as widely recognized or understood by government officials or members of the general public as are, for example, economic development programs or public education. Although employer-sponsored WLP has received growing attention from government officials and the mass media in the last few years, it does not have as many impressive buildings and campuses scattered across the landscape as public educational institutions. Since it is supported solely or largely by employers, it also escapes the intense public scrutiny that tax-supported public educational institutions with popularly elected school boards readily attract. Nor is employer-sponsored WLP subject to the publicity that accompanies the processes of accrediting local public schools or auditing public job training programs. Moreover, employer-sponsored WLP is less-stringently regulated than other parts of the employer-employee relationship, though that has been changing in recent years as special employer-training requirements have been quietly added to Federal regulations such as those issued by the Occupational Safety and Health Administration (OSHA). Further, WLP professionals who work for employers are not subject, as public schoolteachers are, to state certification requirements.

However, employer-sponsored WLP activities are widespread. Employers are estimated to spend billions of dollars annually on formal (planned) job training that usually takes place on the work site (but off-the-job), and even more on informal (unplanned) training, usually taking place during work activities. These expenditures approximate 1 percent of total payroll costs, though higher expenditures by individual employers are not uncommon. The 500 largest industrial firms in the U.S., the so-called *Fortune 500* corporations, are probably best-known for their support of employer-sponsored job training. IBM alone spends close to $1 billion per year on training (Galagan 1989) and Motorola is serious enough about training to require all its employees to undergo a full week's training each year to keep their skills current (Carnevale 1990). Most *Fortune 500* firms have WLP departments or their functional equivalents.

Employers act in their own best interest to improve productivity and build intellectual capital in their organizations by sponsoring WLP efforts in their organizations. Economic data have clearly shown that human beings—not machines—have accounted for the greatest growth in national product, according to a Brookings Institute report: "Between 1929 and 1982, education prior to work was responsible for 26 percent of the expansion in the nation's productive capacity. Learning on the job contributed over half, about 55 percent, of all improvements in the nation's productive capacity. Machine capital contributed a respectable but disappointing 20 percent" (Denison 1985). What is true for the U. S. economy as a whole is also true for individuals: College-educated individuals who receive informal training on the job increase their productivity by as much as 13 percent; non-college-educated individuals increase their productivity by as much as 19 percent (Carnevale 1986). Training helps new employees identify and apply new ways to increase productivity, and career development helps employees achieve career goals while helping employers provide for a continuing source of employee talent. Organization development extends productivity improvement efforts beyond individuals in order to increase group and organizational productivity, and other learning interventions contribute to performance improvement by equipping people with what they need to know, do, and feel to perform effectively.

Employer-sponsored WLP activities are the vanguard of efforts in the U.S. against economic and technical changes, helping workers adapt as soon as possible to rapidly changing on-the-job skill requirements.

WHO PARTICIPATES IN WLP?

Participants in employer-sponsored WLP range from employees to such stakeholders as customers, clients, franchise holders, shareowners, suppliers, distributors, and vendors. (See Exhibit 2-2.) Employees participate in employer-sponsored job orientations or efforts to rectify performance deficiencies and upgrade their skills in preparation for advancement or work changes. Suppliers participate in WLP efforts when they want, for example, to ensure that their employees produce goods and services that can be used by the organizations with which they do business; distributors want their employees to know as much about the products and services they sell so they can credibly sell them and service their customers; investors want to know as much about an organization as possible to protect their investments and decide whether additional investments are warranted.

Look at Exhibit 2-2 and think about a simple example of a company. Suppose Acme Manufacturing (a fictitious firm) is the focus for the example. Acme has many possible participants for its Workplace Learning and Performance (WLP) interventions.

For example, the company might offer industry information to legislators and government officials as part of a public relations campaign to influence the laws, rules, regulations, and ordinances that affect its operations. The company might even make training courses and other WLP interventions available to government officials, who are possible participants in on-site or online learning experiences sponsored by Acme. Retailers are those that sell Acme products directly to customers. Acme might offer training or other interventions (such as reward system redesigns) to retailers so that they are more informed about Acme's products and can sell them better to customers. As a manufacturer, Acme also has suppliers—those organizations that provide Acme with raw materials and other goods or services necessary for the manufacturing process. Acme can offer training or other WLP interventions to its suppliers so that the materials Acme receives are more closely aligned to what Acme needs to use in its manufacturing process. Acme can also offer training to its stockholders—and other potential investors—to educate them about industry, company, and competitive conditions that will influence investors in making decisions to buy, sell, or maintain Acme stock. Acme can prepare training for its consumers to educate them about how to use the products made by Acme.

Employees are important possible internal participants of training or other WLP interventions sponsored by Acme. Employees may be categorized—that is, divided into specific market segments or niches—based on their divisions, departments, hierarchical levels in the chain of command, or their job categories. Exhibit 2-2 shows employees by job category. Most large firms employ executives, managers, supervisors, sales or customer service workers, technical workers (such as engineers), professionals (such as Certified Public Accountants), skilled craftspersons (such as machinists), clerical workers (such as secretaries or administrative assistants), and unskilled or semi-skilled workers (such as laborers).

Of course, it is possible to add other groups to those shown in Exhibit 2-2. For instance, Acme can choose to offer training or other WLP interventions geared to temporary workers ("temps") or to contractors or firms that receive outsourced work from Acme, such as subassembly operations.

Exhibit 2-2: The participant wheel: Who participates in WLP?

This Exhibit illustrates the diversity of participation in organizational WLP programs.

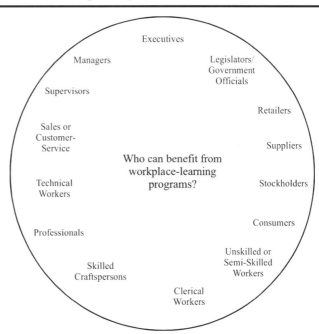

Employees as Participants

A 1995 study by the U. S. Department of Labor examined training practices across a broad spectrum of employers. That study is one of the most reliably conducted training practices in the U.S. to date—though, unfortunately, the study is not frequently updated. The study results are summarized in Exhibit 2-3, and these results paint an excellent picture of present WLP practices in the U.S. in 1995.

Exhibit 2-3: U.S. Bureau of Labor Statistics 1995 Survey of Employer-Provided Training—Employee Results

---

U.S. Bureau of Labor Statistics Reports on the Amount of Formal and Informal Training Received by Employees

Employees who work in establishments with 50 or more workers received an average of 44.5 hours of training in the period May–October 1995, according to a survey of employees conducted by the Bureau of Labor Statistics of the U.S. Department of Labor. Of these total training hours, 70 percent (31.1 hours) were spent receiving informal training, while 13.4 hours were in formal training. The survey also found that in the May–October 1995 time period, an estimated $647 per employee was spent on training, wages, and salaries, with about 65 percent of the amount spent on informal training.

The 1995 Survey of Employer-Provided Training (SEPT 95) was sponsored by the Employment Training Administration of the U.S. Department of Labor and involved two major components: (1) a survey of establishments and (2) a survey of randomly-selected employees in the surveyed establishments. In an earlier news release (July 10, 1996, USDL #96-268), BLS reported on findings from the SEPT 95 establishment survey, focusing on the amount of formal training provided and selected costs of formal training. This news release provides results from the employee survey, including information on the amount of formal and informal training received and the wage and salary cost of the time that employees spent in both formal and informal training.

Over 1,000 employees were surveyed from May through October 1995. Each employee had a personal visit-interview and provided information on his/her age, sex, race/ethnicity, occupation, education, earnings, and tenure, as well as information on his/her past training and its benefits. In addition to this background information, employees were asked to answer a series of questions on the new skills or information they learned each day over a 10-day period. Information was collected on the nature, length, and type of each learning activity. These learning activities were then categorized by BLS as either formal training, informal training, or self learning.

Training by Type and Delivery Method

While working for their current employers, 84 percent of employees received some kind of formal training and 96 percent received some kind of informal training. During the six-month survey period, employees received an average of 44.5 hours of training, of which 13.4 hours were spent in formal training and 31.1 hours in informal training. In other words, 70 percent of the training was conducted through informal instruction.

Exhibit 2-3: U.S. Bureau of Labor Statistics 1995 Survey of Employer-Provided Training—Employee Results *(continued)*

Job-Skills Training. Computer training, both formal and informal, was the most commonly received type of job-skills training. Thirty-eight percent of employees received formal computer training and 54 percent received informal training in computers while working for their current employer. Professional- and technical-skills training, management training, and sales and customer-relations training also were common types of training: Between 27 and 31 percent of employees received these types of formal training while working for their current employer. In terms of informal training, computer training was followed by production- and construction-related training, management training, sales and customer-relations training, and clerical and administrative support skills training. Between 30 and 34 percent of employees received each of these types of informal training while working for their current employer.

During May–October 1995, employees received more hours of computer training and production- and construction-related training than any other type of job-skills training. On average, employees received 11.8 hours of computer training during this period. About 5.1 hours, or 43 percent, of computer training was conducted formally, compared with an average of 30 percent for all types of training. In contrast, only 19 percent of the 10.6 hours of production- and construction-related training received was spent in formal training. Clerical, sales, and service-related training also had higher-than-average shares of training that were conducted informally.

General-skills training. Among the types of general-skills training, occupational-safety training was the most common, with 58 percent of employees receiving formal training in this area while working for their current employer. Communications, employee-development, and quality training was the next most common at 40 percent. Basic-skills training (i.e., training in elementary reading, writing, arithmetic, and English language skills) was much less common. Only 7 percent of employees received formal training and 3 percent received informal training in basic skills while working for their current employer.

In May–October 1995, employees received roughly 2½ hours of training in occupational-safety and communications, employee-development, and quality training, compared with only 18 minutes of basic-skills training. Communications, employee-development, and quality training stood out as the only type of general-skills training where the majority of the training was conducted formally rather than informally.

Training by Demographic Characteristics

Age. The youngest and oldest workers were less likely to have received formal training during the last 12 months than were workers ages 25 to 54. Similarly, the total hours of training during the May–October 1995 period were lowest for the youngest and oldest workers. Workers 24 years of age or younger and workers 55 years or older received about half as many hours of total training as prime-age workers. This general pattern is in evidence for hours of formal and informal training, but particularly for hours of formal training. The relatively low hours of formal training among the very young provides some support for the idea that employers and/or employees may be delaying their investment in training until they are sure the employment arrangement is likely to last. The low hours of training for workers 24 years or younger may also be influenced by the fact that very young workers tend to change jobs frequently and may not have settled into their chosen careers.

Exhibit 2-3: U.S. Bureau of Labor Statistics 1995 Survey of Employer-Provided Training—Employee Results *(continued)*

Sex. Men received an estimated 48 hours of training during the six-month survey period, compared with 42 hours for women. However, this difference is too small relative to the precision of the estimates to conclude that the hours of training are substantially different between men and women.

Race and Ethnicity. In general, white workers tended to receive more hours of training (48.5 hours) over the six-month period than either black (27.7 hours) or Hispanic workers (32.7 hours). While blacks received about the same number of hours of formal training as white workers, they received significantly fewer hours of informal training.

Educational Attainment. Employees with a high-school education or less were not as likely to have received formal training during the last 12 months as more educated counterparts. About 60 percent of those with a high-school diploma or less received formal training during the last 12 months, compared with 90 percent of those with a bachelor's degree or higher. Hours of training in May–October 1995 also were smallest for the least-educated group, though the differences in hours of training per employee across different educational attainment groups were not substantial.

Training by Employment Characteristics

Tenure. The number of total training hours per employee over the May–October 1995 period appears to follow a U-shaped pattern with respect to tenure with current employer. For instance, employees with fewer than two years of tenure received an average of 65 hours of training; workers with more than two years but fewer than five years at the establishment received an average of 24 hours, and those with 5–10 years of tenure received 47 hours.

Full- or Part-Time. Full-time workers (35 or more hours per week) were more likely to have received formal training in the last 12 months than were part-time workers (72 percent versus 56 percent). Similarly, during the May–October 1995 period, full-time workers received an average of 49 hours of training, versus 13 hours for part-time workers. Full-time workers received nearly five times as much informal training (34 hours for full- versus 8 hours for part-time workers) and three times as much formal training (15 hours versus 5 hours).

Occupation. Service workers are less likely than those in other occupations to have received formal training during the last 12 months. Professional and technical workers received the highest number of hours of both formal and informal training in May–October 1995. For formal training alone, there was a considerable gap between the number of hours of training received by professional and technical workers (22 hours) and the number received by employees in most other occupations, particularly managers (4 hours) and service workers (6 hours).

Earnings Quartiles. Those in the bottom quartile of the earnings distribution were less likely to receive formal training and received fewer hours of formal training than higher earners. Sixty-two percent of those in the bottom quartile received formal training in the last 12 months compared with 84 percent of those in the top quartile. Low earners received 4 hours of formal training during the six-month survey period versus 23 hours for the top quartile. For informal training, however, significant differences across earnings quartiles are not observed.

Exhibit 2-3: U.S. Bureau of Labor Statistics 1995 Survey of Employer-Provided Training—Employee Results *(continued)*

Training by Establishment Characteristics

Establishment Size. Employees in small establishments (50–99 employees) were less likely to have received formal training than those in larger ones. Some 62 percent of those in small establishments received formal training in the last 12 months, versus 73 percent of those in establishments with 100–499 employees and 71 percent in establishments with 500 or more employees. Hours of formal training per employee increased with size, ranging from 8 hours for small establishments and 17 hours for large ones (500 or more employees) between May and October, 1995. There is no clear relationship between establishment size and the hours of informal training per employee.

Industry. The amount of training received by employees ranged from a low of 34 hours per employee in wholesale trade to a high of 51 hours per employee in durable manufacturing during the six-month survey period. Industries varied in the extent to which they relied upon formal training, with the proportion of total hours of training spent in formal training spanning from a low of 12 percent for retail trade to a high of 59 percent for durable manufacturing.

Benefits. Employees at establishments providing a greater number of the selected benefits listed in our questionnaire were more likely to have received formal training during the last 12 months. For instance, 77 percent of workers in establishments with eight or more of the selected benefits received formal training in the last 12 months, versus 57 percent in establishments with fewer than four of the selected benefits.

Contract Workers. Employees in establishments that used some contract workers were more likely to have received formal training during the last 12 months than employees in establishments that did not (77 percent versus 66 percent). They also received more formal training during the six-month survey period (19 hours per employee) than employees in establishments that did not use contract workers (9 hours per employee).

Employee Turnover. A relatively small proportion of employees in high-turnover establishments received formal training in the last 12 months (61 percent compared with 75 percent for medium-turnover and 78 percent for low-turnover establishments). The amount of total training received by employees over the May–October 1995 period does not vary much on the basis of an establishment's turnover rate as measured over the three months preceding the survey date. However, workers at establishments with high rates of turnover received less formal training than those with medium or low levels.

Benefits Employees Received from Training

Among those employees who received formal training while working for their current employer, about 14 percent indicated that they received a promotion when the training was satisfactorily completed or soon thereafter, and 19 percent received a higher rate of pay or bonus. Less than one percent of trained employees indicated that they received no benefits from their formal training. The most commonly cited benefit was that employees "learned a valuable skill that improved their job performance," chosen by 78 percent of trainees.

Exhibit 2-3: U.S. Bureau of Labor Statistics 1995 Survey of Employer-Provided Training—Employee Results *(continued)*

How Formal Training Is Delivered

Classes or workshops conducted by company training personnel were the most common types of formal training activities in which employees participated; 76 percent of those receiving formal training reported this activity. This activity was followed by "classes or workshops conducted by outside trainers" and "attending lectures, conferences or seminars" at 48 and 36 percent, respectively. Only 17 percent of those who received formal training in the last 12 months indicated that they had taken courses at educational institutions.

Wage and Salary Costs of Training, by Establishment Characteristics

The wages and salaries that employees receive while in training represents an indirect cost to employers of providing training, as the time that employees spend in training is time that could have been spent working at their jobs. The value of that time can be estimated by multiplying an employee's hourly wage by the hours he/she spent in training. This measure is referred to as the wage and salary costs of training. Over the May–October 1995 period, small establishments spent $462 per employee for wage and salary costs, versus $654 for medium-sized establishments and $754 for large ones. The lower spending levels of small establishments were primarily the result of less spending on formal training. Retail trade employers spent the least per employee—$49 per employee as compared with $149 for wholesale trade (the next lowest) and $418 for mining (the highest).

An estimated total of $37 billion was spent on the indirect wage and salary costs of training during May–October 1995. Establishments with 100–499 employees accounted for the largest share of the total ($16.7 billion), compared with $14.6 billion for establishments with 500 or more employees and $5.7 billion for those with 50–99 employees. The service industry spent the most on training, $12.5 billion, primarily reflecting its large share of employment. Mining, with the smallest share of employment, accounted for the least spending, about $306 million.

Technical Note

Scope of the Survey. The data presented in this release represent the universe of employees in private establishments in the 50 states and the District of Columbia that had 50 or more employees during the fourth quarter of 1993 and were classifiable into one of the following 2-digit Standard Industrial Classifications (SIC) based on the 1987 Standard Industrial Classification Manual:

Exhibit 2-3: U.S. Bureau of Labor Statistics 1995 Survey of Employer-Provided Training—Employee Results *(continued)*

Industry	SIC code
Mining	10, 12–14
Construction	15–17
Nondurable manufacturing	20–23, 26–31
Durable manufacturing	24, 25, 32–39
Transportation and public utilities	41, 42, 44–49
Wholesale trade	50, 51
Retail trade	52–59
Finance, insurance, and real estate	60–65, 67
Services	07, 70, 72, 73, 75, 76, 78–84, 86, 87, 89.

Major Definitions and Concepts. A broad view of training is adopted in the employee portion of the 1995 Survey of Employer-Provided Training (SEPT 95). A training activity may occur any time employees are taught a skill or provided with information to help them do their jobs better. The skill or information may be learned through formal or informal training methods.

Formal training is defined in the survey as training that is planned in advance and has a structured format and defined curriculum. Examples include attending a class conducted by an employee of the company, attending a seminar given by a professional trainer, or watching a planned audio-visual presentation.

Informal training is unstructured, unplanned, and easily adapted to situations or individuals. Examples include having a co-worker show you how to use a piece of equipment or having a supervisor teach you a skill related to your job.

Job-skills training refers to training that upgrades employee skills, extends employee skills, or qualifies workers for a job.

Management training is training in supervising employees and in implementing employment practices. Examples include training in conducting employee appraisals, managing employees, resolving conflicts, following selection/hiring practices, and implementing regulations and policies.

Professional and technical skills training is training in professional areas such as engineering, nursing, accounting, science, law, medicine, training, education, and business; or in technical areas such as drafting, electronics, and medical technology.

Computer procedures, programming, and software training includes training in computer literacy, security, programming, use of standard commercial and other software, and methods for developing software applications.

Clerical and administrative support skills training is training in areas such as typing, data entry, filing, business correspondence, and administrative recordkeeping, including budget and payroll.

Sales and customer relations training is training in areas ranging from how to maintain or improve customer relations to specific selling techniques. Examples include training in how to deal with angry customers and information about specific product lines.

Exhibit 2-3: U.S. Bureau of Labor Statistics 1995 Survey of Employer-Provided Training—Employee Results *(continued)*

Service-related training includes training in the traditional service occupations—food, cleaning, protective, or personal services. Examples include training in waiting tables, preparing food, using cleaning equipment, conducting security work, providing care for children or the elderly, tailoring, and barbering.

Production- and construction-related training is training in areas such as operating or repairing machinery and equipment; manufacturing, assembling, distributing, installing, or inspecting goods; and constructing, altering, or maintaining buildings and other structures.

General-skills training refers to training that is not closely tied to specific job-related skills and/or training that is usually provided to a wide range of workers. It includes: basic skills; occupational safety; employee health and wellness; orientation; awareness; and communications, employee development, or quality training.

Basic skills training is training in elementary reading, writing, arithmetic, and English language skills, including English as a second language.

Occupational safety training provides information on safety hazards, procedures, and regulations.

Employee health and wellness training provides information and guidance on personal health issues such as stress management, substance abuse, nutrition, and smoking cessation.

Orientation training introduces new employees to personnel and workplace practices and to overall company policies.

Awareness training provides information on policies and practices that affect employee relations or the work environment, including Equal Employment Opportunity practices (EEO), affirmative action, workplace diversity, sexual harassment, and AIDS awareness.

Communications, employee development, and quality training is training in public speaking, conducting meetings, writing, time management, leadership, working in groups or teams, employee involvement, total quality management, and job reengineering.

An *establishment* is an economic unit that produces goods or services. It is usually at a single physical location and is engaged predominantly in one type of economic activity.

The list of establishment benefits included: Paid vacation, paid sick leave, healthcare plan, employee-assistance program, employee-wellness program, pension plan, profit sharing, flexible work schedules, flexible work site or telecommuting, employer-financed child care, and paid parental/family leave.

The list of establishment workplace practices included: Pay increases directly linked to mastering new skills, employee involvement in technology and equipment decisions, job redesign or reengineering, job rotation, just-in-time inventories, co-worker review of employee performance, quality circles, total quality management, and self-directed work teams.

Labor turnover is measured by computing the ratio of hires and separations in a three-month period to average employment levels.

Employment change is measured by computing the ratio of change over a three-month period to the average employment over those three months.

Exhibit 2-3: U.S. Bureau of Labor Statistics 1995 Survey of Employer-Provided Training—Employee Results *(continued)*

Data-Collection Procedures

The employee component was conducted in tandem with the employer survey. (For technical information on the employer survey, see USDL #96-268.) Two survey instruments were utilized—an employee questionnaire and an employee training log. The employee questionnaire focused on employment and demographic characteristics. Questions were included on job, employer and occupational tenure, income, weeks and hours worked, education, sex, age, race and ethnicity, marital status, and number of children. In addition, the employee questionnaire included general questions on types of training provided by the employer during the employee's tenure and in the last 12 months and on the benefits of training. The employee log collected detailed information on all training and learning activities the employee participated in over a 10-day period. The requested information on the activity included a description, its duration, who was involved, and what type of training medium was used.

Experienced field economists in the Bureau of Labor Statistics regional offices requested permission from establishment representatives to randomly sample and interview two employees. During the interview, field economists administered the employee questionnaire to the respondent using computer-assisted personal interviewing (CAPI). The field economist then collected the employee log via paper and pencil for the three-day period prior to the day of the interview and left behind a training log for the employee to complete over the next seven days and mail back to the field economist.

Sampling Procedures

The sampling frame for the employee survey was a listing (usually a payroll listing) of employees supplied by the establishment respondent. The total number of employees on the listing was required to match that reported by the establishment respondent. Field economists used a computer-generated random number program based on a simple random selection method to randomly sample two employees from all of the employees in the establishment. If one or more of the employees was unavailable, the field economists could generate up to six random numbers to try to secure the participation of two employees. For the Employee Questionnaire, each participating employee was assigned an Employee Sampling Factor equal to the total number of employees in the establishment divided by the number of participating employees in that establishment. For the Employee Training Log, each participating employee was assigned a Day Sampling Factor which was equal to the number of days in the survey's reference period (184) divided by the number of days (3 to 10) on the employee training log.

Response

Of the 1,543 establishments selected, 1,433 were eligible for survey participation (excluding those out-of-business or out-of-scope), and 1,062 participated in the employer survey.

Exhibit 2-3: U.S. Bureau of Labor Statistics 1995 Survey of Employer-Provided Training—Employee Results *(continued)*

The desired employee sample size for the employee survey was 2,866 (two employees from each of the 1,433 eligible sampled establishments). Usable employee questionnaires were collected from 1,074 employees for a response rate of 37.5 percent. Usable employee logs were collected from 1,013 employees for a response rate of 35.3 percent. Using the 1,062 establishments that participated in the employer survey as the eligible pool for employees, the number of eligible employees changes to 2,214, and the response rate changes to 50.6 percent for the employee questionnaire and 47.7 percent for the employee log.

Estimation

Missing data. Weighting class non-response adjustment procedures were used for each of the survey's instruments—the employee questionnaire and the employee training log—and account for the number of sampled establishments that did not provide any data for the instrument or provided data for only one employee. For otherwise usable instruments, a hot-deck procedure was used to impute a value for any item on the instrument for which the establishment or employee could not provide data.

Benchmarking. To increase the precision of the estimates, the weights of the usable instruments were adjusted to make the weighted occupational distribution of the instruments the same as the weighted occupational distribution in the BLS Occupational Employment Survey.

Weighting. Each of the usable employee instruments has a Final Weight associated with it. For the Employee Questionnaires, the Final Weight is the product of the Establishment Sampling Weight, Subsampling Factor, Employee Sampling Factor, Questionnaire Nonresponse Adjustments, and Questionnaire Benchmark Adjustment. For the Employee Training Log, the Final Weight is the product of the Establishment Sampling Weight, Subsampling Factor, Employee Sampling Factor, Day Sampling Factor, Log Nonresponse Adjustments, and Log Benchmark Adjustment. For technical information on weighting for the employer survey, see news release USDL #96-268.

Estimates. For this release, the population total for a variable of interest is estimated by summing, over all usable instruments, the product of an instrument's Final Weight and the instrument's value for the variable of interest. Proportions are estimated by dividing the estimated total for the variable in the numerator by the estimated population count. Rates are estimated by dividing the estimated total for the variable in the numerator by the estimated total for the variable in the denominator. For subpopulation estimates, the summation is over only the instruments that fall within the subpopulation.

Reliability of Estimates

The estimates in this release are based on a probability sample rather than a census of the population. The sample selected for the employer and employee survey was one of many possible samples, each of which could have produced different estimates that may have differed from the results obtained from a census of the population. This "sampling error" or the variation in the sample estimates across all possible samples that could have been selected is measured by the standard error. The standard error of each of the estimates given in this release was calculated using balanced repeated replication.

Exhibit 2-3: U.S. Bureau of Labor Statistics 1995 Survey of Employer-Provided Training—Employee Results *(continued)*

Percent of Employees Who Received Training, by Type of Training

	Received Formal Training		*Informal training while with current employer*
Characteristic	*While with current employer*	*Within the last 12 months*	
Total			
• All employed*	84.4	69.8	95.8
Job skills			
• Management	28.4	16.3	32.3
• Professional and technical skills	30.9	21.4	27.7
• Computer procedures, programming, and software	38.4	23.5	54.3
• Clerical and administrative-support skills	18.7	8.4	30.1
• Sales and customer relations	26.6	15.1	30.9
• Service-related	12.5	5.9	14.7
• Production and construction-related	21.0	11.3	34.1
General skills			
• Basic skills	6.7	2.3	2.9
• Occupational safety	58.0	42.8	47.7
• Communications, employee development, and quality training	40.2	22.8	32.6
• Other	3.4	1.4	.8

*Employees working in establishments of 50 or more employees.

Exhibit 2-3: U.S. Bureau of Labor Statistics 1995 Survey of Employer-Provided Training—Employee Results *(continued)*

Hours of Training per Employee by Type of Training, May–October 1995

	Hours of Training		
Characteristic	*Total*	*Formal*	*Informal*
Total			
• All employed*	44.5	13.4	31.1
Job skills			
• Management	1.7	.6	1.1
• Professional and technical skills	6.2	1.9	4.3
• Computer procedures, programming, and software	5.1	6.8	
• Clerical and administrative-support skills	3.4	.6	2.8
• Sales and customer relations	3.2	.6	2.6
• Service-related	2.1	.3	1.8
• Production and construction-related	10.6	2.0	8.6
General skills			
• Basic skills	.3	.0	.2
• Occupational safety	2.4	.6	1.8
• Communications, employee development, and quality training	2.6	1.5	1.2
• Other	.2	.2	.0

*Employees working in establishments of 50 or more employees.

Exhibit 2-3: U.S. Bureau of Labor Statistics 1995 Survey of Employer-Provided Training—Employee Results *(continued)*

Percent of Employees Who Received Training, by Selected Demographic Characteristics

Characteristic	Received Formal Training		Informal training while with current employer
	While with current employer	Within the last 12 months	
Total			
• All employed*	84.4	69.8	95.8
Age			
• 24 years and younger	81.6	63.4	100.0
• 25 to 34 years	91.3	78.5	96.9
• 35 to 44 years	88.1	74.7	97.7
• 45 to 54 years	77.9	64.7	93.7
• 55 years and over	74.4	50.7	89.9
Sex			
• Men	81.7	66.5	96.2
• Women	87.2	73.1	95.4
Race and origin			
• White	85.2	70.4	95.5
• Black	82.6	70.6	96.4
• Hispanic origin	90.8	73.7	96.9
Educational attainment			
• High school graduate or less	82.3	60.1	95.0
• Some college	79.1	67.8	96.2
• Bachelor's degree or higher	96.8	89.7	96.6

*Employees working in establishments of 50 or more employees.

Exhibit 2-3: U.S. Bureau of Labor Statistics 1995 Survey of Employer-Provided Training—Employee Results *(continued)*

Hours of Training per Employee, by Selected Demographic Characteristics, May–October 1995

Characteristic	Hours of Training		
	Total	Formal	Informal
Total			
• All employed*	44.5	13.4	31.1
Age			
• 24 years and younger	24.1	2.7	21.4
• 25 to 34 years	46.5	14.0	32.5
• 35 to 44 years	45.7	15.4	30.3
• 45 to 54 years	56.2	17.2	39.0
• 55 years and over	22.9	5.7	17.1
Sex			
• Men	47.6	12.2	35.4
• Women	41.5	14.6	26.9
Race and origin			
• White	48.5	13.6	35.0
• Black	27.7	13.8	13.9
• Hispanic origin	32.7	11.0	21.7
Educational attainment			
• High school graduate or less	35.7	10.9	24.8
• Some college	51.2	14.3	37.0
• Bachelor's degree or higher	47.9	16.1	31.8

*Employees working in establishments of 50 or more employees.

Exhibit 2-3: U.S. Bureau of Labor Statistics 1995 Survey of Employer-Provided Training—Employee Results *(continued)*

Percent of Employees Who Received Training, by Selected Employment Characteristics

	Received Formal Training		Informal training while with current employer
Characteristic	*While with current employer*	*Within the last 12 months*	
Total			
• All employed*	84.4	69.8	95.8
Usual hours worked			
• Under 35 hours	68.5	56.1	98.9
• 35 hours or more	86.6	71.6	95.4
Earnings			
• First quartile	76.7	61.8	97.9
• Second quartile	87.6	74.5	96.7
• Third quartile	77.8	62.0	92.4
• Fourth quartile	98.5	84.0	97.1
Occupation			
• Managerial and administrative	87.1	80.2	89.6
• Professional, paraprofessional, and technical	95.3	84.8	93.4
• Sales, clerical, and administrative support	89.3	72.5	97.6
• Service	70.7	49.8	93.6
• Production, construction, operations, maintenance, and material handling	80.0	66.3	98.4
Tenure with current employer			
• Up to 2 years	73.3	67.5	95.7
• More than 2, up to 5	74.8	56.8	94.0
• More than 5, up to 10	96.0	79.7	96.8
• More than 10 years	94.0	75.3	96.9

(continued)

_____

*Employees working in establishments of 50 or more employees.

Exhibit 2-3: U.S. Bureau of Labor Statistics 1995 Survey of Employer-Provided Training—Employee Results *(continued)*

Percent of Employees Who Received Training, by Selected Employment Characteristics *(concluded)*

Characteristic	Received Formal Training		Informal training while with current employer
	While with current employer	*Within the last 12 months*	
Tenure in current occupation			
• Up to 2 years	81.3	73.4	99.2
• More than 2, up to 5	87.3	68.4	91.3
• More than 5, up to 10	84.1	68.9	98.5
• More than 10 years	84.6	69.2	95.1
Tenure in current job			
• Up to 2 years	81.5	73.4	97.2
• More than 2, up to 5	80.5	59.7	91.2
• More than 5, up to 10	92.1	78.1	98.8
• More than 10 years	94.2	66.5	97.7

Exhibit 2-3: U.S. Bureau of Labor Statistics 1995 Survey of Employer-Provided Training—Employee Results *(continued)*

Hours of Training per Employee, by Selected Employment Characteristics, May–October 1995

Characteristic	Hours of Training		
	Total	*Formal*	*Informal*
Total			
• All employed*	44.5	13.4	31.1
Usual hours worked			
• Under 35 hours	12.5	4.8	7.7
• 35 hours or more	48.8	14.6	34.2
Earnings			
• First quartile	34.7	4.1	30.6
• Second quartile	42.1	11.6	30.5
• Third quartile	55.5	15.9	39.6
• Fourth quartile	43.9	22.8	21.1
Occupation			
• Managerial and administrative	26.7	4.3	22.4
• Professional, paraprofessional, and technical	61.1	22.3	38.7
• Sales, clerical, and administrative support	33.3	10.2	23.2
• Service	27.7	5.6	22.1
• Production, construction, operations, maintenance, and material handling	53.7	15.2	38.5
Tenure with current employer			
• Up to 2 years	65.3	8.9	56.5
• More than 2, up to 5	24.1	4.5	19.5
• More than 5, up to 10	46.5	19.5	27.0
• More than 10 years	41.6	21.1	20.5

(continued)

*Employees working in establishments of 50 or more employees.

Exhibit 2-3: U.S. Bureau of Labor Statistics 1995 Survey of Employer-Provided Training—Employee Results *(continued)*

Hours of Training per Employee, by Selected Employment Characteristics, May–October 1995 *(concluded)*

Characteristic	*Total*	*Formal*	*Informal*
		*Hours of Training*	
Tenure in current occupation			
• Up to 2 years	77.2	12.5	64.7
• More than 2, up to 5	29.9	7.5	22.4
• More than 5, up to 10	29.5	9.6	20.0
• More than 10 years	43.8	19.4	24.4
Tenure in current job			
• Up to 2 years	62.1	13.2	48.9
• More than 2, up to 5	24.9	4.6	20.3
• More than 5, up to 10	36.9	22.6	14.4
• More than 10 years	37.3	23.6	13.7

Exhibit 2-3: U.S. Bureau of Labor Statistics 1995 Survey of Employer-Provided Training—Employee Results *(continued)*

Percent of Employees Who Received Training, by Selected Establishment Characteristics

Characteristic	Received Formal Training		Informal training while with current employer
	While with current employer	Within the last 12 months	
Total			
• All employed[1]	84.4	69.8	95.8
Industry			
• Mining	98.0	94.7	98.8
• Construction	88.8	71.2	92.5
• Manufacturing:			
Durable goods	94.1	78.3	99.0
Nondurable goods	93.7	85.4	96.9
• Transportation, communications, and public utilities	93.2	81.4	98.1
• Wholesale trade	79.7	68.1	94.2
• Retail trade	70.0	48.8	91.4
• Finance, insurance, and real estate	91.6	87.4	96.4
• Services	84.3	70.7	97.3
Establishment size			
• 50 to 99 employees	78.9	61.6	97.1
• 100 to 499 employees	84.7	73.0	95.0
• 500 employees or more	87.7	71.0	96.1
Number of selected establishment benefits[2]			
• Fewer than 4	71.0	57.2	88.5
• 4 or 5	70.0	57.8	93.4
• 6 or 7	91.5	74.4	95.6
• 8 or more	90.3	76.5	99.7

(continued)

---

[1] Employees working in establishments of 50 or more employees.

[2] The survey questionnaire asked respondents of the establishment to select which of 11 listed benefits they provided to their employees (if any).

Exhibit 2-3: U.S. Bureau of Labor Statistics 1995 Survey of Employer-Provided Training—Employee Results *(continued)*

Percent of Employees Who Received Training, by Selected Employment Characteristics *(concluded)*

Characteristic	Received Formal Training		Informal training while with current employer
	While with current employer	*Within the last 12 months*	*Informal training while with current employer*
Number of selected establishment work practices[3]			
• 0	71.8	57.4	94.6
• 1 or 2	84.0	66.5	97.7
• 3 or 4	75.8	66.8	96.5
• 5 or 6	94.9	80.5	97.9
• 7 or more	95.0	74.6	88.9
Presence of contract employees			
• None	79.5	63.6	95.9
• Some	90.1	77.0	95.8
Turnover rate[4]			
• Low	87.4	78.0	98.0
• Medium	89.8	74.7	97.3
• High	75.5	60.7	93.2
Employment change over the last 3 months			
• Declining	82.6	70.3	98.6
• Stable	88.3	74.3	94.9
• Increasing	83.9	68.0	95.0
Part-time employment			
• None	88.1	73.5	96.7
• Some, but less than 10%	90.4	72.8	95.0
• 10 percent or more	78.3	65.8	96.1

---

[3] The survey questionnaire asked respondents of the establishment to select which of nine listed workplace practices they used at their establishment (if any).

[4] A turnover rate of less than 1.0 percent of average employment over the prior three months was defined as low, 1 to 25 percent was considered medium, and 25 percent or greater was considered high.

Exhibit 2-3: U.S. Bureau of Labor Statistics 1995 Survey of Employer-Provided Training—Employee Results *(continued)*

Hours of training per employee, by selected establishment characteristics, May–October 1995

Characteristic	Hours of Training		
	Total	Formal	Informal
Total			
• All employed[1]	44.5	13.4	31.1
Industry			
• Mining	36.1	17.2	18.9
• Construction	47.5	11.4	36.1
• Manufacturing:			
Durable goods	51.1	20.8	30.3
Nondurable goods	40.2	21.7	18.5
• Transportation, communications, and public utilities	17.6	19.7	
• Wholesale trade	33.8	8.3	25.4
• Retail trade	36.8	4.2	32.6
• Finance, insurance, and real estate	50.5	15.9	34.7
• Services	50.2	13.2	37.0
Establishment size			
• 50 to 99 employees	40.1	8.2	31.9
• 100 to 499 employees	13.5	34.5	
• 500 employees or more	16.6	26.0	
Number of selected establishment benefits[2]			
• Fewer than 4	58.4	5.9	52.6
• 4 or 5	42.5	12.8	29.7
• 6 or 7	38.7	13.9	24.8
• 8 or more	50.6	14.8	35.9

(continued)

[1] Employees working in establishments of 50 or more employees.

[2] The survey questionnaire asked respondents of the establishment to select which of 11 listed benefits they provided to their employees (if any).

Exhibit 2-3: U.S. Bureau of Labor Statistics 1995 Survey of Employer-Provided Training—Employee Results *(continued)*

Hours of Training per Employee, by Selected Employment Characteristics, May–October 1995 *(concluded)*

Characteristic	Hours of Training		
	Total	*Formal*	*Informal*
Number of selected establishment work practices[3]			
• 0	57.8	14.7	43.0
• 1 or 2	29.8	5.8	24.0
• 3 or 4	57.6	15.9	41.7
• 5 or 6	36.7	15.3	21.4
• 7 or more	49.0	19.1	29.9
Presence of contract employees			
• None	41.9	8.7	33.2
• Some	47.4	18.7	28.7
Turnover rate[4]			
• Low	46.3	27.3	19.0
• Medium	45.9	15.6	30.4
• High	41.8	7.6	34.2
Employment change over the last 3 months			
• Declining	52.0	13.3	38.6
• Stable	34.7	10.9	23.9
• Increasing	44.5	14.3	30.2
Part-time employment			
• None	57.6	14.7	42.9
• Some, but less than 10%	15.8	27.2	
• 10 percent or more	39.4	11.0	28.3

[3] The survey questionnaire asked respondents of the establishment to select which of nine listed workplace practices they used at their establishment (if any).

[4] A turnover rate of less than 1.0 percent of average employment over the prior three months was defined as low, 1 to 25 percent was considered medium, and 25 percent or greater was considered high.

Exhibit 2-3: U.S. Bureau of Labor Statistics 1995 Survey of Employer-Provided Training—Employee Results *(continued)*

Percent of Employees Receiving Benefits from Completing Formal Training Activities While Working for Current Employer*

Characteristic	Percent of Employees
Promotion received when training was satisfactorily completed	14.0
Received a higher pay rate or bonus	19.0
Completion certificate placed in file	47.9
Training was necessary for future advancement	40.1
Training was mandatory	70.0
Learned valuable skill that improved job performance	78.1
Helped employee stay current with new regulations, laws, and/or technologies	66.1
Other	2.7
No benefits	0.8

*Employees working in establishments of 50 or more employees.

Exhibit 2-3: U.S. Bureau of Labor Statistics 1995 Survey of Employer-Provided Training—Employee Results *(continued)*

Percent of Trained Employees Participating in Any of the Following Formal Training Activities within the Last 12 Months, by Selected Demographic Characteristics

Characteristic	Attended			
	Classes or workshops conducted by company personnel	*Courses conducted by outside trainer*	*Lectures, conferences or seminars*	*Educational Institutions on work time*
Total				
• All employed*	75.7	48.3	17.1	36.3
Age				
• 24 years and younger	81.1	23.4	11.4	24.6
• 25 to 34 years	79.0	44.1	15.9	30.7
• 35 to 44 years	70.9	58.6	19.6	41.7
• 45 to 54 years	74.5	52.7	20.4	43.9
• 55 years and over	78.5	38.9	7.3	27.0
Sex				
• Men	70.3	50.0	11.2	30.1
• Women	80.7	46.7	22.6	42.0
Race and origin				
• White	74.8	50.4	18.5	41.1
• Black	76.0	38.2	7.1	13.6
• Hispanic origin	85.9	41.6	12.2	17.5
Educational attainment				
• High school graduate or less	80.9	34.0	8.1	19.9
• Some college	78.1	49.0	21.5	43.9
• Bachelor's degree or higher	66.7	63.9	21.8	45.5

---

* Employees working in establishments where 50 or more employees received formal training within the last month.

Exhibit 2-3: U.S. Bureau of Labor Statistics 1995 Survey of Employer-Provided Training—Employee Results *(continued)*

Wage and Salary Costs of Training per Employee, by Selected Establishment Characteristics, May–October 1995

Characteristic	Wage and Salary Costs		
	Total Training	*Formal Training*	*Informal*
Total			
• All employed[1]	$646.9	$224.1	$422.8
Industry			
• Mining	741.9	418.0	323.8
• Construction	746.5	195.0	551.6
• Manufacturing:	815.2	346.5	468.6
Durable goods	591.9	353.8	238.1
Nondurable goods			
• Transportation, communications, and public utilities	471.3	236.8	234.5
• Wholesale trade	542.6	149.4	393.1
• Retail trade	463.4	49.1	414.2
• Finance, insurance, and real estate	878.9	235.3	643.6
• Services	718.1	252.4	465.7
Establishment size			
• 50 to 99 employees	462.0	110.2	351.8
• 100 to 499 employees	654.3	215.3	439.0
• 500 employees or more	753.5	307.5	446.0
Number of selected establishment benefits[2]			
• Fewer than 4	704.2	52.8	651.4
• 4 or 5	451.2	167.9	283.3
• 6 or 7	575.8	249.1	326.7
• 8 or more	890.0	274.3	615.7

(continued)

---

[1] Employees working in establishments of 50 or more employees.
[2] The survey questionnaire asked respondents of the establishment to select which of 11 listed benefits they provided to their employees (if any).

Exhibit 2-3: U.S. Bureau of Labor Statistics 1995 Survey of Employer-Provided Training—Employee Results *(continued)*

Wage and Salary Costs of Training per Employee, by Selected Establishment Characteristics, May–October 1995 *(concluded)*

	Wage and Salary Costs		
Characteristic	*Total Training*	*Formal Training*	*Informal*
Number of selected establishment work practices[3]			
• 0	814.0	181.2	632.8
• 1 or 2	356.1	73.7	282.5
• 3 or 4	730.6	231.3	499.3
• 5 or 6	685.4	321.9	363.5
• 7 or more	846.3	380.1	466.2
Presence of contract employees			
• None	512.8	142.0	370.8
• Some	797.1	316.1	481.0
Turnover rate[4]			
• Low	886.6	546.2	340.4
• Medium	712.4	243.4	469.0
• High	501.6	137.7	364.0
Employment change over the last 3 months			
• Declining	643.5	205.9	437.6
• Stable	528.4	184.1	344.3
• Increasing	687.1	244.9	442.2
Part-time employment			
• None	724.3	247.6	476.7
• Some, but less than 10%	651.0	253.5	397.5
• 10 percent or more	607.4	191.4	416.0

[3] The survey questionnaire asked respondents of the establishment to select which of nine listed workplace practices they used at their establishment (if any).

[4] A turnover rate of less than 1.0 percent of average employment over the prior three months was defined as low, 1 to 25 percent was considered medium, and 25 percent or greater was considered high.

Exhibit 2-3: U.S. Bureau of Labor Statistics 1995 Survey of Employer-Provided Training—Employee Results *(continued)*

Total Wage and Salary Costs of Training, by Industry and Size Class, May–October 1995 (In Thousands of Dollars)

Characteristic	Wage and Salary Costs		
	Total Training	*Formal Training*	*Informal*
Total			
• All employed[1]	$37,061,259	$12,838,575	$24,221,982
Industry			
• Mining	305,571	172,181	133,390
• Construction	1,321,935	345,217	976,718
• Manufacturing:	7,655,647	3,254,112	4,400,978
Durable goods	3,668,602	2,192,938	1,475,664
Nondurable goods			
• Transportation, communications, and public utilities	1,614,793	811,305	803,444
• Wholesale trade	1,278,848	352,234	926,614
• Retail trade	6,285,244	666,128	5,619,116
• Finance, insurance, and real estate	2,425,810	649,319	1,776,391
• Services	12,504,809	4,395,142	8,109,667
Establishment size			
• 50 to 99 employees	5,652,306	1,348,650	4,303,656
• 100 to 499 employees	16,781,558	5,521,417	11,260,007
• 500 employees or more	14,627,394	5,968,508	8,658,319

* Employees working in establishments of 50 or more employees.

SOURCE: Bureau of Labor Statistics. (1996). 1995 Survey of Employer-Provided Training-Employee Results. Washington, DC: Bureau of Labor Statistics. Published at: "http://stats.bls.gov/news.release/sept.nws.htm." For technical information: (202) 606-7386 USDL 96-515.

There are, of course, various ways by which to examine WLP. Available statistics tend to focus on training-related issues. ASTD has classified organizations according to their nature: (1) *leading edge firms* are cutting edge; (2) *benchmarking forum firms* participate in an elite group of organizations that have signed up for the benchmarking services that ASTD can provide; and (3) *benchmarking service firms* participate generally. An ambitious 1999 study sponsored by ASTD examined these organizations. The next several exhibits summarize the findings of this study in the following categories:

	Exhibit
General information:	2-4
Expenditures:	2-5
Key ratios:	2-6
Providers used:	2-7
Types of courses offered:	2-8
Use of learning technologies:	2-9
Methods of training evaluation:	2-10
Link between performance and training:	2-11

Each Exhibit is meant to be self-explanatory. However, additional information can be obtained by reading *The 1999 ASTD State of the Industry Report* (Bassi and Van Buren, 1999) and more recent updates as they are published.

Another way to examine WLP practices is to classify the jobs or occupational categories of those participating in WLP activities. Perhaps the most familiar way is to make distinctions among executives, managers, supervisors, sales or customer service workers, technical workers, professionals, skilled craftspersons, clerical workers, and unskilled or semi-skilled workers. *Executives* are the highest-level decision-makers. *Managers* oversee the work of salaried supervisors, and *supervisors* (in turn) oversee the work of hourly-paid clerical workers, sales or customer service workers, technical workers, professionals, skilled craftspersons, and/or unskilled or semi-skilled workers. *Sales or customer service workers* deal directly with the public, selling goods and services or responding to customers' needs. *Technical workers* include engineers, maintenance workers, and others whose work involves the application of technology. *Professionals* are doctors, lawyers, dentists, accountants, actuaries, and others whose work requires lengthy formal educational preparation. *Skilled craftspersons* include electricians, pipefitters, and carpenters. *Semi-skilled workers* are machine operators; *unskilled workers* are hour laborers.

More than one study has shown that executive, managerial, and supervisory personnel consistently command high priority for employer-sponsored, planned job-specific training. Other occupational groups often trail them in the number of training hours provided by employers per year. One reason that executives, managers, and supervisors receive such attention is that they are the formal leaders in their organizations: their training and development is thought to have the most ripple effect on other people.

When in-house classroom training is offered by employers, several topics are likely to be offered on a regular basis, with some variation in method of instruction. (See Exhibits 2-12 and 2-13.)

Exhibit 2-4: Company demographics

	Average Employment Size	Average Annual Payroll ($ Millions)	Percent Profit-Making
Benchmarking Service	5,147	140	65
Leading Edge	2,245	114	78
Benchmarking Forum	26,790	1,400	NA
Agriculture/Mining/Construction	1,243	49	73
Information Technology	3,778	137	87
Nondurable Manufacturing	2,949	102	91
Durable Manufacturing	2,972	104	89
Transportation/Public Utilities	4,875	121	77
Trade	39,765	712	100
Finance/Insurance/Real Estate	2,846	129	73
Services	1,534	43	43
Health Care	3,126	85	22
Government	6,578	232	0

SOURCE: Bassi, L., and Van Buren, M. (1999). *The 1999 ASTD State of the Industry Report.* [A supplement to Training and Development Magazine.] Alexandria, VA: The American Society for Training and Development, p. 5. Used by permission of ASTD. All rights reserved.

Exhibit 2-5: Training expenditure distributions

	Total Training Expenditures ($ Millions)	Wages and Salaries of Training Staff as % of Expenditures	Payments to Outside Companies as % of Expenditures	Tuition Reimburse- ments as % of Expenditures	Other Expenses as % of Expenditures
Benchmarking Service	2.0	41.4	27.1	13.3	18.3
Leading Edge	4.1	37.6	30.4	6.9	25.0
Benchmarking Forum	32.7	36.7	NA	11.6	NA
Agriculture/Mining/ Construction	0.6	31.9	40.6	8.8	19.9
Information Technology	3.9	34.0	35.3	14.2	17.2
Nondurable Manufacturing	1.0	37.6	34.8	12.8	15.2
Durable Manufacturing	1.2	32.7	35.5	15.7	15.9
Transportation/ Public Utilities	3.8	44.1	24.5	10.5	22.1
Trade	2.5	54.5	16.1	5.1	28.1
Finance/Insurance/ Real Estate	1.9	46.3	22.4	13.5	18.8
Services	1.1	34.3	26.2	16.6	22.4
Health Care	0.8	58.3	12.2	15.0	15.8
Government	2.6	46.0	26.8	15.5	14.9

SOURCE: Bassi, L., and Van Buren, M. (1999). *The 1999 ASTD State of the Industry Report.* [A supplement to Training and Development Magazine.] Alexandria, VA: The American Society for Training and Development, p. 6. Used by permission of ASTD. All rights reserved.

Exhibit 2-6: The key ratios

These seven Key Ratios provide a quick snapshot of the state of the training industry.

The numbers reveal the level of spending on training; the amount of training provided; the size of the training function; the pervasiveness of outsourcing; and the tradeoff between traditional, classroom-based training and technology-delivered training. The ASTD constructs them as ratios (or percentages) to provide statistics that are comparable across the wide variety of organizations around the world that participate in its benchmarking research. The ASTD tracks these ratios annually to demonstrate the primary trends shaping the training industry.

	Total Training Expenditure Per Employee ($)	Total Training Expenditures as % of Payroll	Percent of Employees Trained	Employee-to-Trainer Ratio	Percent of Training Time via Classroom	Percent of Training Time via Learning Technologies	Payments to Outside Companies as % of Expenditures
Benchmarking Service	649	1.8	74.3	394:1	77.6	9.1	27.1
Leading Edge	1957	4.4	83.4	97:1	77.1	11.8	30.4
Benchmarking Forum	1198	2.3	NA	312:1	66.1	NA	NA
Agriculture/ Mining/ Construction	686	1.8	79.9	429:1	86.7	8.4	40.6
Information Technology	943	2.1	70.3	283:1	76.8	11.5	35.3
Nondurable Manufacturing	588	1.7	69.8	549:1	74.3	8.5	34.8
Durable Manufacturing	488	1.6	72.9	482:1	80.1	9.1	35.5
Transportation/ Public Utilities	1004	1.9	86.5	206:1	70.0	15.8	24.5
Trade	412	1.9	69.5	743:1	68.4	7.2	16.1
Finance/ Insurance/ Real Estate	737	1.9	70.3	220:1	82.9	5.9	22.4
Services	583	2.1	72.1	434:1	76.8	8.6	26.2
Health Care	345	1.2	87.9	341:1	77.1	9.1	12.2
Government	514	1.5	70.7	635:1	85.3	7.1	26.8

SOURCE: Bassi, L., and Van Buren, M. (1999). *The 1999 ASTD State of the Industry Report.* [A supplement to Training and Development Magazine.] Alexandria, VA: The American Society for Training and Development, p. 7. Used by permission of ASTD. All rights reserved.

Exhibit 2-7: Use of other training providers

Percent of Organizations Using:	Benchmarking Service	Leading Edge	Benchmarking Forum
Non-Training Staff Employees	93	95	80
Outside Firms	77	91	90
Independent Consultants	73	85	88
Product Suppliers	60	60	77
Community Colleges	49	58	51
Other Education Institutions	54	69	67
Unions, Trade, or Professional Associations	24	25	50
Government Organizations	21	13	23

SOURCE: Bassi, L., and Van Buren, M. (1999). *The 1999 ASTD State of the Industry Report.* [A supplement to Training and Development Magazine.] Alexandria, VA: The American Society for Training and Development, p. 9. Used by permission of ASTD. All rights reserved.

Exhibit 2-8: Course types as percentage of training expenditures

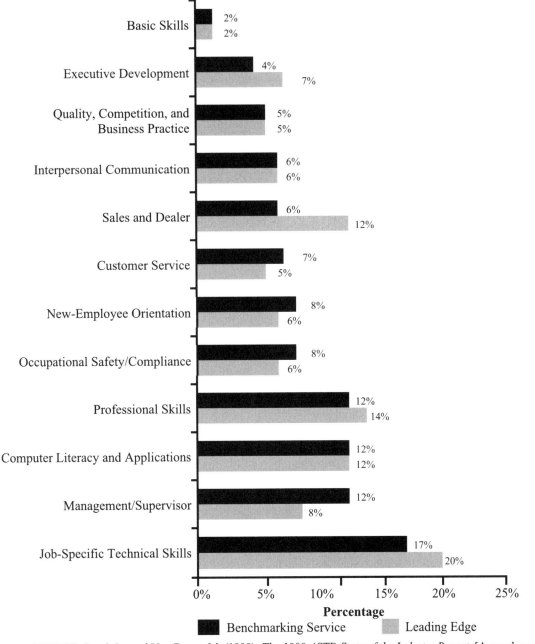

Exhibit 2-9: Use of learning technologies (1999 ASTD report)

Percent of Organizations (Courses) Using:	Benchmarking Service, 1997	Benchmarking Service, 2000	Leading Edge, 1997	Leading Edge, 2000
Presentation Methods				
CBT (Text only)	47.5 (7.2)	70.2 (14.6)	69.1 (9.3)	69.1 (15.6)
Multimedia	58.1 (12.1)	85.5 (24.5)	74.6 (11.8)	90.9 (23.8)
Interactive TV	14.3 (1.2)	38.9 (4.6)	21.8 (2.0)	41.8 (5.2)
Teleconferencing	31.4 (2.0)	61.9 (8.5)	49.1 (2.0)	70.9 (8.9)
Groupware	22.4 (3.2)	54.0 (11.0)	36.4 (2.2)	61.8 (7.7)
Virtual Reality	2.7 (0.2)	21.8 (2.7)	3.6 (0.4)	32.7 (2.7)
EPSS	14.9 (1.4)	44.7 (8.1)	21.8 (1.1)	56.4 (7.5)
Distribution Methods				
Cable TV	6.4 (0.7)	22.6 (2.6)	5.5 (0.7)	20.0 (1.9)
CD-ROMs	49.2 (4.8)	80.0 (15.7)	76.4 (7.7)	92.7 (14.1)
E-mail	33.8 (6.4)	55.7 (13.0)	40.0 (2.8)	58.2 (8.4)
Extranets	7.8 (0.8)	31.4 (4.7)	10.9 (0.3)	41.8 (3.7)
Internet	19.1 (1.7)	57.6 (9.7)	25.5 (1.8)	61.8 (7.8)

Exhibit 2-9: Use of learning technologies (1999 ASTD report) *(continued)*

Percent of Organizations (Courses) Using:	Benchmarking Service, 1997	Benchmarking Service, 2000	Leading Edge, 1997	Leading Edge, 2000
Distribution Methods *(continued)*				
Intranets	24.3 (3.3)	70.0 (17.2)	43.6 (4.0)	85.5 (19.2)
LANs	31.8 (6.4)	52.1 (12.1)'	45.5 (6.3)	56.4 (9.2)
Satellite TV	20.3 (1.2)	38.5 (4.7)	29.1 (1.5)	54.6 (4.6)
Simulators	20.6 (2.7)	32.4 (5.3)	20.0 (2.1)	36.5 (4.3)
Voicemail	14.9 (2.9)	23.7 (4.9)	10.9 (0.4)	18.2 (1.3)
Wide Area Networks	12.6 (2.4)	31.8 (7.0)	20.0 (4.1)	38.2 (8.5)
World Wide Web	18.7 (1.6)	53.1 (9.7)	25.5 (2.0)	69.1 (11.7)

SOURCE: Bassi, L., and Van Buren, M. (1999). *The 1999 ASTD State of the Industry Report.* [A supplement to Training and Development Magazine.] Alexandria, VA: The American Society for Training and Development, p. 16. Used by permission of ASTD. All rights reserved.

Exhibit 2-10: Evaluation methods

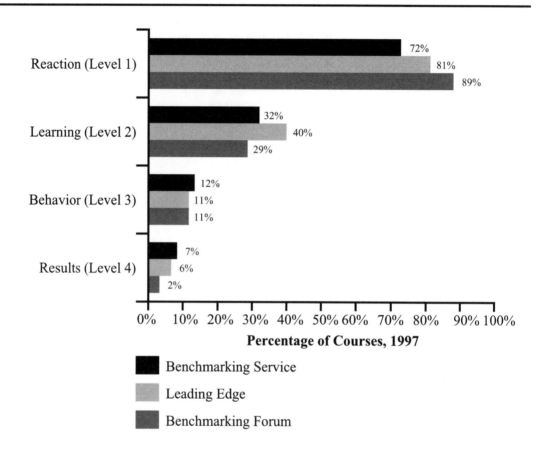

Percentage of Courses, 1997

■ Benchmarking Service

▨ Leading Edge

▨ Benchmarking Forum

SOURCE: Bassi, L., and Van Buren, M. (1999). *The 1999 ASTD State of the Industry Report.* [A supplement to Training and Development Magazine.] Alexandria, VA: The American Society for Training and Development, p. 23. Used by permission of ASTD. All rights reserved.

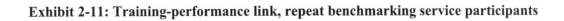

Exhibit 2-11: Training-performance link, repeat benchmarking service participants

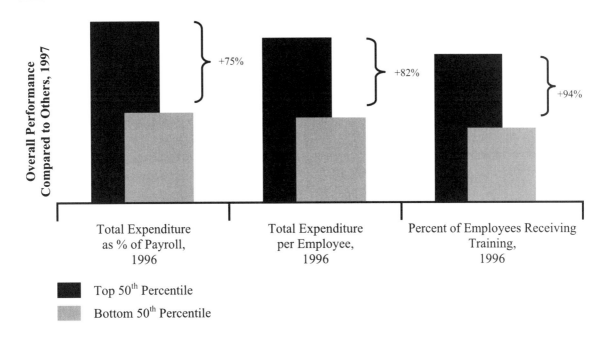

Exhibit 2-12: Specific types of training

Types of Training	% Providing This Type of Training	Designed and Delivered by		
		In-House Only (%)	Outside Only (%)	Both (%)
New-Employee Orientation	92	81	1	10
Performance Appraisals	79	58	4	17
Personal Computer	78	19	9	50
Team-Building	75	24	10	42
Leadership	75	17	13	45
Sexual Harassment	74	40	11	24
Hiring/Selection Process	71	32	12	27
Train-the-Trainer	71	20	22	29
New-Equipment Operation	71	36	4	31
Safety	69	27	3	38
Delegation Skills	66	19	12	34
Product Knowledge	66	37	2	27
Conducting Meetings	66	28	11	27
Goal-Setting	65	25	10	30
Listening Skills	64	20	9	35
Decision-Making	64	20	12	32
Managing Change	63	17	10	37
Quality Improvement	63	21	7	35
Time Management	62	18	15	29
Problem-Solving	61	20	7	35
Public Speaking/Presentation	61	15	15	31
Information Technology/MIS	60	9	18	34
Motivation	60	14	12	34
Computer Programming	58	8	27	23
Finance	57	13	16	27
Stress Management	54	15	13	26
Planning	54	20	9	26
Writing Skills	54	13	19	22
Strategic Planning	53	17	11	25
Diversity	52	19	11	23
Negotiation Skills	51	11	16	24
Creativity	48	15	13	20
Ethics	46	22	7	17
Marketing	43	10	12	21
Purchasing	40	18	12	11
Financial/Business Literacy	40	8	11	20
Substance Abuse	39	110	12	16
Outplacement/Retirement	39	16	10	13
Smoking Cessation	32	10	13	10
Reengineering	30	7	6	18
Foreign Language	22	5	12	5
Other Topics	4	1	1	2

SOURCE. "What Employers Teach." (1997). *Training, 34*(10), 55. Used by permission of Lakewood Publications.

Exhibit 2-13: Instructional methods and media

	% Using
Classroom Programs—Live	88
Workbooks/Manuals	73
Videotapes	70
Public Seminars	57
Computer-Based Training via CD-ROM	50
Audiocassettes	39
Noncomputerized Self-Study Programs	35
Case Studies	33
Role-Plays	33
Internet/WWW	31
Self-Assessment Instruments	23
Intranet/Organization's Internal Computer Network	21
Satellite/Broadcast TV	20
Games or Simulations (not computer-based)	19
Videoconferencing (to groups)	17
Teleconferencing (audio only)	11
Outdoor Experiential Programs	9
Computer-Based Games or Simulations	9
Desktop Videoconferencing	4
Virtual Reality Programs	2

Based on 1,828 responses.

SOURCE: Who Gets Trained? (1998). *Training, 35*(10), 58. Used by permission of Lakewood Publications.

Stakeholders as Participants

Relatively little is known about the participation of stakeholder groups in employer-sponsored WLP activities; far more is known about employee participation. However, organizations are clearly offering more training and other WLP activities to key stakeholders. After all, needs exist outside, as well as inside, organizations. As Rothwell and Kazanas note, "Consumers who do not know how to use a product will not buy it. Stockholders who do not know about the firm in which they have invested will not be inclined to invest more. Suppliers who remain unaware of a firm's unique production or service delivery needs will have a tough time meeting them. Retailers unfamiliar with products will not be inclined to stock them for long—and will not be knowledgeable enough to do a credible job of selling them to consumers if they do. Legislators who pass laws or government officials who create regulations will not be able to make informed decisions if they are unaware of conditions faced by business" (Rothwell and Kazanas 1994).

CHAPTER 3

The Roots of WLP:
The Historical Perspective

This Chapter focuses on the historical roots of Workplace Learning and Performance. It describes the philosophical basis of WLP, summarizes the influence of other fields, and traces how WLP has evolved.

WHAT ARE THE FORERUNNERS OF WLP?

Many beliefs commonly shared by workplace learning and performance professionals stem from a much broader philosophy. That accounts for some of the confusion about the term "WLP." However, there are several common assumptions. Most writers agree, for instance, that WLP addresses human development, change, learning, and performance improvement or performance technology—usually, but not exclusively, conducted in group or organizational settings. More recently, that includes even those who are only virtually connected to their work or who are only temporary or contingent workers.

Most writers also agree that the assumptions of WLP are normative and represent philosophical ideals. Applications may vary widely, but taken together, these assumptions are the culmination and fusion of separate developments in several disciplines.

No field of study is immune from change. In the *Structure of Scientific Revolutions*, Thomas Kuhn characterized the evolution of science itself as progressing through problem-solving activities carried out within the framework of shared theories or viewpoints (Kuhn 1962). A scientific revolution is a change in theory which, in turn, results in different ways of looking at problems. Kuhn asserted that even nonscientific fields experience such revolutions.

Nowhere is Kuhn's controversial theory perhaps more appropriate than in charting the progress of such fields influencing WLP as economics, psychology (including industrial and individual psychology and counseling), management (including organization behavior, management science, and general systems science), communication, sociology, political science (including policy analysis and evaluation research), education, and the humanities. In each case, the pendulum of thought swings from a negative to a positive view of human nature. These changes laid the foundation for a broad philosophy on which Workplace Learning and Performance is based. Exhibit 3-1 provides a picture that depicts the influence of various fields on WLP.

Exhibit 3-1: Summary of major influences on WLP

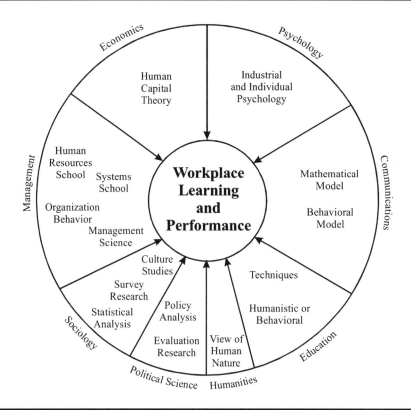

While it is not possible to trace in detail the evolution of these fields in the limited space available in this book, WLP professionals should have a grasp of how much influence these fields have exerted on WLP. For this reason, brief descriptions of their evolution and relationship to WLP are provided in the following sections:

Economics

Evolution of the Field. Economics is the study of prices, goods, markets, and human value in political contexts. Adam Smith's *Wealth of Nations* (1776) is generally considered to be the first statement of a comprehensive economic theory. From earlier writers, Smith accepted the belief that production is dependent on three key factors: land, labor, and capital. Smith likewise accepted the belief, known as the ***labor theory of value,*** that labor is the preeminent factor in production. The key to a nation's prosperity can be found in "the skill, dexterity, and judgment with which its labor is generally applied." After all, it is only through the application of labor that land or capital is rendered useful. Some later economists, most notably Karl Marx and David Ricardo, accepted but modified the Labor Theory of Value.

The early 19th-century economist J. B. Say successfully attacked the Labor Theory of Value. He maintained that "productive agencies," in combination, produced goods. Hunt expounded on Say's contention in a 1979 work: "Instead of seeing the process of production as a series of human exertions, Say asserted the existence of different "productive agencies" that combined together to produce goods. What these productive agencies were ultimately producing was 'utility'" (Hunt 1979).

Later 19th-century economists refined this view, called the ***utility theory of value.*** For example, J. S. Mill felt that capital investment and accumulation were the forces behind employment and increased productivity. Mainstream 20th-century economic theory generally assumes that capital is the preeminent factor in production, a belief shared by two key thinkers in this tradition: John Maynard Keynes and Milton Friedman.

Keynes argued that spending by government is essentially the cornerstone of full employment, and that the supply of labor has nothing to do with demand. Unlike Adam Smith and J. B. Say, who believed that markets are self-adjusting, Keynes conjectured that widespread unemployment could persist indefinitely. To counteract unemployment, he thought, government should tax and spend in a way designed to influence business activity. In short, Keynes contended that *fiscal policy* (government spending) can be used to stimulate employment or retard inflation.

Milton Friedman's views contrast with those of Keynes. To Friedman, the keys to productivity and employment are interest rates and the growth of the total supply of money available in the economy. Governmental spending intended to stimulate or retard the business cycle does not serve the best interest of long-term economic prosperity, Friedman believes. Instead, wild swings in governmental spending merely worsen economic conditions because it is the total amount of money available in the economy that determines conditions for prosperity. He believes that government ought to establish a uniform, predictable rate of increase in the total amount of money available in the economy. Since the Federal Reserve Board controls money supply in the U. S., Friedman sees the Board's actions in setting interest rates—and thereby establishing *monetary policy*—as central to the national economic health.

Beginning in the late 1950s, critics of mainstream economic theory—forerunners of what was later to be called the ***human capital school of economics***—began to question whether demand for labor is really a function of monetary or fiscal policy (Ginzberg 1958). They suggested that it is possible to regard labor as a form of capital, rather than a factor of production separate from (and driven by) it. This view has gained increasing support in the wake of perceived failures in the application of mainstream economic theory since 1964 (Carnevale 1982). The human capital school has spawned the notion that labor is a human resource, connoting the abilities and potential of people to contribute to their work not only their talents and skills, but also their creativity (Harbison 1973).

The human capacity for creating new ideas and disseminating or processing information—not the traditional economic view of labor as synonymous with physical exertion—underlies this revolutionary view of the importance of the people involved in the production process (Naisbitt 1983). National economic well-being is not a function of monetary or fiscal policy; rather, it results from long-term investment in human capital through education and training. As proof of this assertion, economists point to the coincident increase in the U. S. gross national product (GNP) and aggregate investments in education and training between 1919 and 1957 (Kendrick 1976). Human capital growth has been a major force in the growth of GNP, advocates of this theory assert.

Influence of Economics on WLP. Economics has thus evolved from Smith's 18th-century emphasis on labor to a 19th- and 20th-century emphasis on capital as preeminent in the production process. Until 1958, labor was largely considered synonymous with physical exertion. National economic well-being was considered a function of the manipulation of money through either government spending or steady growth of the money supply. The failure of mainstream economic theory since 1964 has given rise to a radically different view: *labor* as a form of capital—an asset, not an expense. While the human capital theory remains controversial, it is attracting interest, and some economists now regard people as human resources that can be developed through investment in education and training.

Economists have become increasingly aware in recent years of the influence of WLP on economic development, productivity, and individual employability. As a consequence, governmental policies in developed and developing countries are beginning to focus on WLP as a means of helping individuals become literate, prepare for employment, learn the work of organizations employing them, and upgrade individual skills resulting from technological or other changes. Unlike many other nations, however, the U. S. has not established an integrated plan known as an *industrial policy* to govern the role of human resources in national economic development.

Psychology

Evolution of the Field. Psychology is the study of the human mind, generally emphasizing the treatment of individual mental aberrations. As in economics, management, and education, any psychological theory is essentially based on a view of human nature. From that view stems a theory of how to change people. The history of psychology, like many other disciplines, is a history of changes in philosophies about human nature (Watson and Evans 1991).

Sigmund Freud is generally acknowledged to be the first modern psychological theorist. He believed that human nature is determined by unconscious drives and psychosexual occurrences during the first few years of life. Human beings are energy systems consisting of three parts: (1) *the id*, the repository of instincts; (2) *the ego*, the practical interface with the world; and (3) *the superego*, the internalized voice of societal norms and morals. Personality is largely determined in early childhood through such developmental stages as the oral, anal, and phallic stages. For Freud, an individual's psychological health is achieved by making the unconscious manifest and by strengthening the ego to withstand instinctual urges.

Freud's theory was challenged by a second wave of psychologists, known as *behaviorists.* Led by such people as B. F. Skinner, the behaviorists asserted that human nature is determined by the environment, not (as Freud believed) by unconscious drives: People are passive agents molded by their surroundings. Freud thought that psychological problems could be solved largely by helping individuals consciously recognize them. He thus assumed that attitudes and beliefs guide behavior. In contrast, the behaviorists assumed that behavior guides attitudes and beliefs—that, as a result, therapeutic psychological change can take place by altering the environment and by helping individuals act out behaviors consistent with desired change.

Beginning in the late 1950s and the early 1960s, a third wave of psychological theorists challenged the behaviorists. Known as *person-centered psychologists* and spearheaded by Carl Rogers and Abraham Maslow, they maintained that human nature is not entirely determined by the unconscious, and not entirely determined by the environment. People are not passive, as both Freudians and behaviorists implied; rather, human nature encompasses a proactive as well as a reactive side. This theory holds that people have a deep need to grow, develop, and realize their potential; therapeutic change thus results from self-awareness and self-acceptance. The psychologist becomes a mirror for clients, stimulating client insight that prompts change.

Person-centered psychology is thus fundamentally optimistic, demonstrating a deep faith in human perfectability. When applied to education or training, it places responsibility for learning squarely on the student or trainee—not on the instructor. It requires learners to focus on the present rather than the past or the future. Learners must strengthen their self-confidence, substituting self-approval for instructor approval. They must be willing to grow and learn throughout their lives, rather than stop learning just because their formal schooling comes to an end.

Twentieth-century psychology has evolved from the view that people are passive agents of their unconscious or their environment to the present view that they are active agents capable of influencing their unconscious and their environment. Exhibit 3-2 summarizes the basic assumptions of Freudian, Skinnerian, and Rogerian psychology.

Exhibit 3-2: How three major psychological theories differ

	Freudian	*Skinnerian*	*Rogerian*
Theory Name	Psychoanalysis	Behaviorism	Person-centered therapy
View of Human Nature	Passionistic	Pessimistic	Optimistic
Determinants of Human Nature	Unconscious drives and early childhood experience	Environmental Conditions	The individual's need to grow
Determinants of Human Nature	Make the unconscious conscious: strengthen the ego	Change attitudes and beliefs through behavior	Evoke greater self-awareness

Influence of Psychology on WLP. Psychology has had a profound influence on WLP. Psychologists have contributed much of what is known about human development, human learning, and organizational or group change. Moreover, WLP professionals frequently adopt the humanistic values of person-centered psychologists, who express strong faith in human adaptability and self-directedness.

Management

Evolution of the Field. Management is an activity aimed at acquiring, allocating, and using human and physical resources to achieve a goal or series of goals. A management theory is essentially a unified way of looking at the nature of people, work, and organizations. The evolution of management thought, like that of economics and psychology, has led to a new view that is consistent with the human resources philosophy.

Although management as an activity is as old as civilization, *management theory* is relatively new. Frederick Taylor (1856–1915) is generally credited with conceptualizing the first view of management to be coupled with a philosophical framework. Taylor's major work, *The Principles of Modern Management* (1911), was based on his personal experience at Bethlehem Steel in the early 1900s. Taylor and those who later followed and supported him are collectively referred to as leaders of the ***classical school of management thought.*** Taylor and his disciples espoused what they called "*scientific management*," so named because Taylor attempted to approach management in a planned, systematic, scientific way.

Taylor believed that managers should devote their attention to analyzing tasks done by workers to determine the most efficient work methods. Recognizing that different people have different talents, Taylor felt that managers should select workers carefully, to make sure that each job is filled by a person uniquely suited to do it. Workers should be sufficiently trained so they know what to do on the job and how best to do it, and managers and workers should both cooperate and should avoid bickering. Lastly, Taylor favored compensating employees based on their production rates, rather than on their seniority or other factors.

Taylor's work has profoundly influenced management thinking in the U. S. Subsequent writers criticize Taylor for promoting a view that, in effect if not by intent, fosters the notion that workers are basically lazy. Other writers have claimed that the glowing research reports Taylor used to justify his theory were largely creative exaggerations (Wrege and Perroni 1974).

Henri Fayol (1841–1925) was writing about management theory in Europe at about the same time Frederick Taylor was writing about it in the U. S. Fayol contributed 14 widely accepted principles that are still the foundation for modern management, summarized in Exhibit 3-3. His views enhance and supplement Taylor's.

A second wave of management theorists, called the ***human relations school of management thought,*** challenged the theories of both Taylor and Fayol. From a series of experiments conducted at the Hawthorne, Illinois, facility of Western Electric between 1924 and 1932, such writers as Elton Mayo and F. J. Roethlisberger drew several important conclusions. First, they found that people are more interested in social relations with their co-workers than

Exhibit 3-3: Fayol's fourteen principles

Principle	Description
1. Division of Labor	To increase efficiency, workers should specialize in tasks for which they are best suited.
2. Authority	Managers should have authority, the right to issue orders. With authority comes responsibility for ensuring that the work is done.
3. Discipline	The organization should expect obedience from its employees, and in turn employees should expect to be treated with dignity by their employers.
4. Unity of Command	Each employee should report to only one supervisor.
5. Unity of Direction	Each activity of an organization should have one leader and one plan.
6. Subordination of Personal Interests	Management must ensure that decisions are made from a rational standpoint and not solely to placate self-interested individuals or groups.
7. Remuneration	People should be paid in order to motivate them.
8. Centralization	The issuing of orders creates a degree of centralization in all organizations. However, it is possible to increase employee autonomy (decentralization) or decrease it (centralization).
9. The Scalar Chain	Authority is hierarchical and must be made explicit. In other words, it must be clear who reports to whom.
10. Order	All materials and all activities should be kept where they are appropriate.
11. Equity	Employees should be treated justly.
12. Stability of Tenure	People resources should be planned for.
13. Initiative	Managers should encourage workers to be enthusiastic about their work.
14. Esprit de Corps	Management should encourage harmony and discourage destructive conflict within the organization.

SOURCE: Adapted from Wren, D. (1979). *The Evolution of Management Thought* (2nd ed.). New York: Wiley.

they are in making money. Hence, Taylor's assumption that workers will produce more if rewarded for higher individual production had practical limitations when applied to intact work groups. Second, the researchers asserted that people are more responsive to the feelings of their work group than to management attempts to control them. Social relationships will heavily influence how employees perform their work; organizations, therefore, are influenced as much by human feelings and morale as they are by the logic of efficiency and effectiveness. From these research conclusions, advocates of the ***human relations school*** made practical admonitions to managers: Help workers feel accepted by their work groups; persuade employees to accept decisions, using influence rather than power; and listen to people for expressions of feelings as well as facts.

Critics of the Human Relations School have pointed out that this theory merely gives the illusion that management is interested in employee concerns—that workers are only made to *feel* good and useful, not *be* good and useful. Later researchers have seriously questioned the way the Hawthorne studies were conducted: Some critics have suggested that the researchers' conclusions were inaccurate or fallacious due to flawed research methodology.

Post–1950s Management Theories

Two schools of management thought have dominated thinking in the U. S. since the early 1960s: the general systems school and the human resources school.

Ludwig von Bertalanffy is commonly considered the first person to use the term ***general systems theory,*** in 1937; subsequent writers, including Kenneth Boulding and Norbert Wiener, refined the theory. Early behavioral scientists, basing their work on the assumptions of human relations, concluded that organizations are social *systems* composed of interacting, interrelated, and interdependent parts. *Closed systems* do not depend on their surroundings for vital supplies or other resources; *open systems* depend entirely on their surroundings.

A classic description of General Systems Theory applied to human interaction can be found in the work of Donald Katz and Robert Kahn (Katz and Kahn 1978). They have noted ten common characteristics of open systems. Those characteristics are summarized in Exhibit 3-4.

According to open systems theory, then, organizations are totally dependent on the larger environment in which they operate. The manager is in charge of a *subsystem*, a part within the organizational system. The system is, in turn, part of a larger *suprasystem*, such as the industry of which the organization is a part, the national or international economy, or the nation's culture. Work is viewed as a transformation process that is value-neutral, meaning neither good nor bad in its own right. Individuals in open systems enact *roles*, and indeed the organization is a *system of roles* that regulates member behavior and interpersonal relations. Organizational roles, the parts played by people, result from a complex interplay of environmental and organizational factors, role expectations established and sent by others, personal attributes, work group relations, and interpretations of the role made by the person in it.

Exhibit 3-5 depicts an organization as an open system.

Exhibit 3-4: Characteristics of open systems

Characteristics of Open Systems	Description
1. Importation of Energy	Open systems, like organizations, import energy from the environment and depend on the environment for such resources/inputs as people, supplies, finances, and information.
2. Throughput	Open systems transform inputs through work processes or methods.
3. Output	Open systems expel the inputs they transformed during throughtput into the surrounding environment.
4. Cycle of events	Exchanges between the environment and the organization have a pattern.
5. Negative entropy	Open systems experience a tendency, natural to all organizations, to lose energy and disintegrate.
6. Information input, negative feedback, and the coding process	Open systems receive information in the form of inputs, regulate their operations, and code the information received based on signals to which members of the organization are attuned.
7. The steady state and dynamic homeostasis	The rate of exchange—that is, the general amount of energy expended in receiving inputs, transforming them, and expelling them as outputs—remains relatively constant, in a steady state. The result is dynamic homeostasis, meaning that an even level of activity is attained and preserved in an organization.
8. Differentiation	Open systems are characterized by a movement from general to specialized functions, meaning that there is a tendency for duties or activities to be allocated to different groups or individuals.
9. Integration and Coordination	Open systems are characterized by integrative forces that counter differentiation to achieve unity. Coordination assures uniform functioning within the system.
10. Equifinality	Open systems are capable of reaching the same state through many different ways.

SOURCE: Katz, D. and Kahn, R. (1978). *The Social Psychology of Organizations* (2nd ed.). New York: Wiley. Used by permission of the publisher.

Exhibit 3-5: The organization as an open system

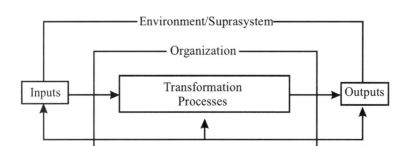

While the systems view has exerted an important influence on management thinking in the U. S., another school of thought has also had a major impact. Highly philosophical, the ***human resources school of management thought*** first gained prominence during the recession of 1957–1958 (Wren 1979). Extending beliefs of the human relations school, advocates of the human resources school make several assumptions: First, they believe that individuals are by nature creative, and deserve greater self-direction and responsibility than they are typically given in most organizations. Second, individuals are capable of much greater usefulness to their work groups and co-workers than management typically recognizes or takes advantage of. Third, work is as natural as play. Indeed, people want to work, because work is a vehicle for self-expression and creativity. Fourth, effective leadership consists of making employee potential manifest. Managers should work toward unlocking employee talents and creativity, pushing responsibility for decision-making to the lowest levels possible. Fifth, organizations are too often structured so as to interfere with, rather than nourish, employee creativity. For instance, organization charts, job descriptions, and other trappings of bureaucracy too often limit individual ability to act. Employees should instead be encouraged, and even empowered, to make suggestions, take action, and apply their creativity. Sixth, power in organizations should consist more of influencing employees than exacting obedience through rewards or punishments. Above all, managers should exemplify and model qualities prized by the organization. Seventh and finally, organizational goals and individual needs are not inherently at odds; rather, they are capable of integration.

Critics have attacked advocates of the general systems and human resources schools of management thought for promising more than they have delivered. General systems theory is accused of making organizations appear mechanistic; human resources theory is accused of providing norms but no guidelines for applying them. However, both schools have exerted a profound influence on WLP.

Exhibit 3-6 summarizes the four major management theories.

Exhibit 3-6: The organization as an open system

	THEORIES			
	Scientific Management	*Human Relations*	*Systems Theory*	*Human Resources*
Theorist	Frederick Taylor	Elton Mayo	Katz and Kahn	Chris Argyris
View of Human Nature	Economic/ Pessimistic	Social	Dramatic (roles)	Creative
Motivation	Money	Feelings	Expectations	Needs
View of Organizations	Mechanistic (like a machine)	Social	Systems	Restrictive to individuals
Nature of work	A necessary evil	A forum for group relations	A transforma-tion process	A vehicle for self-expression and creativity

Influence of Management on WLP. WLP efforts are carried out, more often than not, in organizational settings. They are thus influenced heavily by how managers view the role of management itself and how they view their organization's role in supporting knowledge-management and intellectual capital, organization development, career development, employee development, employee education, and employee training.

Communication

Evolution of the Field. Communication has to do with the sharing of information and emotions. It is associated with the exchange of meaning, usually through symbols. Organizational communication occurs within an organizational structure. Communication is the basic process from which all management and learning functions stem.

Every school of management thought has made key assumptions about the com-munication process. Classical management, for instance, emphasized the role of manager as information link between employees and higher-level authority. Fayol believed that the *scalar chain*, meaning the differing levels of authority in organizations, should be preserved by encouraging workers to communicate only with immediate superiors, unless they are specifically granted permission to communicate with higher authority. The **human relations school** first recognized the important effect that feelings, interpersonal trust, and openness can have on the flow of information from superiors and co-workers. The **human resources school** recognizes that employees, as well as managers, are potentially important sources of information. As a result, it stresses two-way communication. Finally, **general systems theory** stresses the value of information as a vital input for organizations.

Communication experts use special terms that deserve definition. *Upward communication* refers to messages directed up the scalar chain. *Downward communication* means messages or orders directed down the scalar chain. *Lateral communication* means messages directed to those of equal status or authority. *The sender* is the source of a message; *the medium* is the means by which a message is sent; *transmission* is the process of sending a message. *Noise* means anything that distorts the sending, transmission, or reception of a message. *The receiver* is the recipient of messages. *Feedback* is the process of determining whether the message is received. *Formal communication* is information that travels along steps in the scalar chain; *informal communication* is information that travels between and among friends, including rumors spread by way of the grapevine. Finally, a *communication model* is a simplified depiction of the communication process.

There are three major schools of communication theory: Mathematical (or Cybernetic), Behavioral, and Transactional (Pace 1983). Advocates of ***mathematical theory*** view the communication process as mechanical, resembling the relationship between a radio transmitter and receiver. Shannon and Weaver's model (see Exhibit 3-7) is perhaps the best-known of this type. Messages are encoded from a source, sent through a medium, and decoded by a receiver. Noise distorts messages, much as static affects radio reception. The mathematical theory is powerfully descriptive, making the communication process easy to understand.

Exhibit 3-7: Shannon and Weaver's mathematical communication model

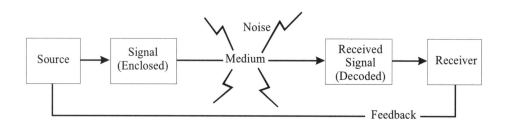

SOURCE: Adapted from Shannon, C., and Weaver, W. (1949). *The Mathematical Theory of Communication.* Urbana, IL: University of Illinois Press.

In contrast, advocates of the ***behavior theory*** regard communication as a process indistinguishable from the determinants of behavior. Berlo's model (see Exhibit 3-8) represents this theory. Senders are affected by their skills of expression, attitudes about the message and receivers, personal knowledge, and the social system. The message consists of content and medium, while the channel may be a stimulus to any or all senses. Receivers and senders are affected by their communication skills, attitudes about the message and the sender, personal knowledge, and the social system.

Exhibit 3-8: Berlo's behavioral communication model

SOURCE	MESSAGE	CHANNEL	RECEIVER
Skills and Attitudes	Media Content	The Five Senses	Skills and Attitudes

SOURCE: Adapted from Berlo, D. (1960). *The Process of Communication.* New York: Holt, Rinehart & Winston.

Advocates of **transactional theory** stress the interactive nature of the communication process. Both sender and receiver have three ego states: parent, adult, and child. (See Exhibit 3-9.) The parent ego state represents the internalized values of a person's parents. It is moralistic. The adult state is highly rational. The child state represents a person's childhood. It is spontaneous, impulsive, creative, and manipulative. Communication is only effective when the same or complementary ego states of sender and receiver speak to each other; communication is ineffective when a message directed to one ego state is answered with a message directed to an incompatible ego state. For example, the comment "If I were you, I'd go to school" is moralistic in tone and is thus the kind of statement made by the parent ego state to the receiver's child ego state. An appropriate response from the message receiver would be a comment from the child ego state, such as "I wanted to do something else." An inappropriate response would be a remark directed to the wrong ego state, like "Why do you care what I do?" ("Why" indicates the adult ego.) Transactional communication emphasizes the importance of feelings and the interactive nature of meanings in social contexts.

Exhibit 3-9: Transactional communication model

Sender   Receiver

(P)   (P) Parent

(A)   (A) Child

(C)   (C) Adult

Influence of Communication on WLP. Modern communication theory, having evolved from a rather limited and even mechanistic view to a view that stresses the importance of human interaction, has emphasized the psychological and symbolic meanings of the communication process.

WLP has been influenced, to a significant degree, by theories of organizational communication. After all, instruction is a form of communication, and learning most often occurs through the communication process. Moreover, *what* is learned and *how* it is applied in organizational settings are influenced by communication within and between groups and individuals.

Sociology

Evolution of the Field. Sociology is the study of human behavior in social contexts. It bears the same relationship to the study of groups, organizations, and societies that psychology bears to the study of individuals. Sociology has historically focused on customs, rites, rituals, and other meaning-laden interactions between people.

Sociology stemmed from various attempts by eighteenth and nineteenth century moral philosophers to bring scientific methods to the study of society. Chief among them was August Comte (1798–1857), who is generally credited with founding sociology. In his *System of Positive Polity or Treatise on Sociology* (1875), Comte sought to apply scientific methods to the study of society, an approach now called ***positivism.*** He based his terminology and principles for the new discipline on biology. By doing so, he built the framework for the discipline on the analogy that societies function like organisms—an approach called ***functionalism.***

Comte's views were subsequently revised by the Englishman Herbert Spencer (1820–1903) and Spencer's followers. Spencer accepted Comte's positivistic, functionalistic views. Enjoying enormous popularity as an early prophet of the Industrial Revolution, he posited that societies and organisms both become more complex and specialized as they increase in size. His views planted the seeds for ***social darwinism,*** the deterministic belief that only the fittest human beings and societies survive in competition with others.

Early twentieth-century sociology was also deterministic in focus, stemming in part from the influence of social darwinism. Human societies develop in similar ways, it was argued, no matter how different their circumstances or environments. Sociologist Emile Durkheim pointed out that groups develop a collective psychology different from individuals acting independently. To understand such "social facts" as rituals requires collective, not individual, analysis and insight. Any change to a social fact, as sociologists A. R. Radcliffe-Brown and Bronislaw Malinowski later posited, leads to other societal changes. The reason: "social facts" in any society are inherently interrelated.

Beginning in the late 1930s, the deterministic slant of nineteenth century sociology began to erode as Talcott Parsons mounted an impressive argument in favor of the systematic analysis of social phenomena. Parsons, acting in the tradition of Comte, sought to construct a grand theory of social action that would explain how and why society functions. While his own views about society have since been criticized as too static, he was successful in emphasizing the importance of *theory building,* and thereby provided a means by which sociology could evolve through systematic study.

However dated Parsons' prose in his classic *The Social System* (1951) may seem today, his work toward developing a grand, all-encompassing theory laid the foundation in many respects for present-day organizational studies. For instance, Parsons conceived of *cultures* as *systems of interaction.* He pointed out that **norms**—unspoken beliefs and guides to action—regulate the behavior of individuals while in groups and other social settings. When individuals enter a new culture and confront new norms, they undergo a socialization process in which they become attuned to the new setting by internalizing the collective beliefs and values of group members. *Norms* provide stability to society and (indeed) are structures from which much societal control of member behavior is often exerted. Social change, Parsons believed, was evolutionary and resulted from social conflict and pressure for increasing differentiation (*specialization of parts*) and integration (*collective and dependent interaction of parts*).

Sociologists since Parsons have scoped their efforts more modestly. Robert Merton began this delimiting process, believing that a search for a grand theory of societies was too ambitious. He believed that sociologists should instead seek explanations at lower levels than grand theory, what he called "theories of the middle range." A better approach than grand theorizing, Merton argued, was to begin with simple descriptions of "what is happening" in a social setting. Examinations of the reasons (causes) for existing conditions begin with descriptions of what they are.

Present-day sociology has been typified by more expansive theorizing than in its earliest days. Sociologists have recently focused attention on interactions between society and individuals (a school of sociological thought called **interactionism**), on perceptions of individual reality as derived internally rather than externally (a school of thought called **phenomenology**), and with everyday methods used by individuals to search for knowledge about self and society (a school of sociological thought called **ethnomethodology**).

Influence of Sociology on WLP. WLP professionals owe a significant debt to sociologists. Much of what is known today about the study of *organizational culture* and *individual socialization,* which excited new interest after publication of *In Search of Excellence* and *Corporate Cultures* in 1982, stems from sociological theory. In addition, sociologists pioneered the application of interviews, surveys, and other methods of social data-gathering that are widely used by WLP professionals in assessing learning needs and identifying problems in intragroup and intergroup functioning. Sociologists also pioneered the application of statistics to the study of social issues, and their techniques are still widely used in analyzing data gathered through interviews, surveys, and observations.

Political Science

Evolution of the Field. Political Science is the systematic study of government and its processes. Sometimes distinguished from political philosophy, which is the examination of governmental ideas, political science is more often directed toward the study of governmental institutions. Its roots can be traced to Aristotle, early sociologists such as August Comte, and modern behavioral psychologists.

Beginning in the 1920s and extending into the 1950s, political science was dominated by the thinking of such writers as Arthur Bentley, Charles E. Merriam, Graham Wallas, and Harold Lasswell. Bentley focused attention on groups rather than on the state and on human beliefs and behavior rather than institutions of government; Merriam dramatized the importance of power in political matters; Wallas championed the use of quantitative methods in political study; and Lasswell brought the unique perspective of Freudian psychology to political analysis.

Beginning in the 1960s, some political scientists started to question, if not utterly reject, the discipline's longstanding love affair with empiricism (scientific method), arguing that it led to a deterministic and often falsely rational explanation of political events that are not always driven exclusively by rational considerations of self-interest. They longed for a value-free political science, one not burdened by normative perspectives about appropriate ideas or methods for studying political phenomena.

Political scientists have more recently centered their attention around such issues as power, government, political processes, political decision-making, policy analysis, policy formulation, and policy evaluation. Of special interest has been the influence of what C. Wright Mills calls the *power elite*. The power elite consists of individuals who, by virtue of money, position, or other factors, exert greater-than-average influence on political decision-making.

Influence of Political Science on WLP. Political science's influence on WLP is that it provides a systematic basis for the study of politics and power. Quite often, though not always, politics involves groups operating out of self-interest, whether in government or in organizations. As a result, the form, mission, goals, and structure of organizations are not necessarily based on what is best for the organization; rather, they may be negotiated and, to some extent, based on the self-serving interests of key individuals and groups. Each organization is governed by a *dominant coalition*, much like a power elite, that enforces its will through the control of rewards and punishments of other organizational members.

Historically, WLP professionals have been politically naïve when compared to savvy operating managers. While there is some evidence that WLP professionals are becoming more canny about organizational and governmental politics as they affect human change and learning issues, one result of the political naïveté of WLP professionals has been that ill-advised but politically popular interventions have been undertaken in some organizations. That may change as a consequence of more streetwise political action by WLP professionals.

Education

Evolution of the Field. Education can be understood as the study of knowledge, skills, attitudes, and values. It is also the means by which important information and values are transmitted to members of a culture. It is one vehicle for enculturating and socializing individuals into their societies. Education figured prominently in human culture from earliest times—in ancient Egypt, Mesopotomia, China, India, and the Central and South American cultures of the Mayans, Aztecs, and Incas.

The ancient Greeks and Romans viewed education as means of awakening the human spirit. Philosophy commanded highest priority because it taught the contemplation of truth and beauty, considered the greatest good. Education, for the Greeks, was not equated with career preparation. Indeed, the Greeks considered work distasteful, a matter best left to slaves. For the ancients, then, the purpose of education was to instill appreciation for the arts and the skills of governance.

Education also figured in cultures outside the Western tradition, flourishing in the Islamic world of Spain during the European Dark Ages. European universities were created during the Middle Ages and the Renaissance, beginning in the twelfth century, and the thinking of the ancients on educational matters was put into formal doctrine. Of course, agriculture was the dominant industry at that time, and relatively few people could read or write; the few who did were mostly priests, and they were (of course) all men.

Essentially, three forms of educational preparation emerged in Western society and persisted from the Middle Ages until well after the Industrial Revolution swept across Europe in the nineteenth century. A child's schooling was dependent on social station. First-born males of aristocratic birth were schooled as gentlemen, and many attended universities. To obtain a baccalaureate degree, students devoted four years to the study of the classical *trivium*, consisting of Latin grammar, logic, and rhetoric. An advanced degree required an additional three years devoted to the study of the classical *quadrivium*, consisting of arithmetic, geometry, astronomy, and music. Men of aristocratic birth, but not first-born, were apprenticed to study the "professions": medicine, law, or the military. Males of nonaristocratic birth whose families had more money and higher social standing than peasants were apprenticed to such trades as weaving and metal-working.

The need for unskilled labor increased during the Industrial Revolution in the 18th century as peasants migrated from the agrarian countryside to the industrialized cities. The remnants of feudal society gradually crumbled, giving way to a new class of wealthy industrialists who modeled the schooling of their children on earlier aristocratic practices. They believed that success came as a result of hard work and proper morals; education soon became a means of instilling proper morality and communicating societal values to undisciplined youth.

Early in the 20th century, many industrial nations instituted mandatory education. In the United States, the campaign for public schools was led by reformers, but it was heavily funded by business. Education was seen as a means by which to socialize young people to the dominant values of society—the Protestant work ethic—and to make them docile, morally-disciplined workers.

Education has long been touted in the U.S. as the key to upward social mobility. The *Horatio Alger myth* that poor people can get rich in America through hard work eventually came to mean that the poor can become successful by educating themselves or their children appropriately. It has been related to the American dream of material success earned through hard work. Since there is a correlation between the amount of education and the inclination to seek more, it is likely that the growing interest in workplace learning comes as a result of a more educated post–World War II labor force. The reason: workplace training—especially when it is employer-sponsored—facilitates promotion and occupational mobility.

In the 1960s, researchers began to study adult teaching and learning as a discipline distinct from the study of children's learning. Stimulated by third wave psychology and the human resource school of management thought, writers such as Houle, Knowles, and Tough suggested that adults simply learn in ways different from children. A new term was coined— ***androgogy,*** meaning those activities intended to help adults learn. It differed from ***pedagogy,*** meaning activities intended to help children learn. Exhibit 3-10 summarizes major differences between them.

Exhibit 3-10: How pedagogy and androgogy differ

Topic	*Pedagogy*	*Androgogy*
The learner	Dependent	Independent
Role of the learner experience	Unimportant; a nuisance	Essential, because learning occurs through the pooling of the learner's experience
Motivation to learn	External to the learner; dictated by society	Internal to the learner; dictated by personal/ career needs
Orientation to learn	Subject-matter is arranged logically	Process-oriented; oriented around problems and arranged psychologically

Influence of Education on WLP. It is not easy to trace the influence of education on WLP. Suffice it to say, however, that the nature of this influence can be categorized in two ways.

First, education has often influenced what kind of performance-improvement interventions are undertaken in organizations. Since many WLP professionals are grounded in education, they naturally think of learning interventions before others. For instance, the basic skills deficiencies of high school and college graduates must often be addressed and rectified by employers. If those deficiencies are not rectified by employers, then they must often be addressed by governmental programs that facilitate the employment of the economically disadvantaged.

Second, education has often influenced the form of WLP activities. Everyone often automatically expects that planned learning activities like training should be offered in classroom settings and handled like formal schooling. In reality, of course, classroom training is only one of many ways to promote learning. In fact, these days it may be more expensive, and not necessarily as efficient in light of emerging instructional technologies.

The Humanities

Evolution. The humanities comprise studies that are primarily concerned with imagination, human values, and the human spirit. Examples of such studies include linguistics, literature, history, philosophy, archeology, the fine arts, and foreign languages. While the humanities are commonly associated with certain disciplines or subjects, they can also be conceptualized as studies celebrating the imagination of humankind. They are in this way very different from the natural and social sciences.

The term **humanism** is originally derived from the writings of the ancient Roman orator Cicero, who used it to refer to ideal education and an appreciation for humanity. Humanism as a philosophy was revived by St. Augustine in the Middle Ages, who also used it to refer to an outline for education. The term gradually fell into disuse until the fifteenth century, when it came to distinguish those who directed their attention to human (or secular) studies, rather than divine (or religious) studies. Humanism flourished after the discovery of the writings of the ancient Greeks and Romans, and its influence was widely felt during the Age of Reason in eighteenth-century Europe.

In the nineteenth and twentieth centuries, humanistic studies gradually became differentiated from scientific studies. Some humanistic thinkers viewed science as essentially amoral. Scientists were seen as pursuing knowledge with reckless disregard of the human consequences of what they learned. Humanists, on the other hand, brought questions of morals, ethics, and values to human experience and human existence. They directed their attention to fundamental questions about the meaning of human existence and the critique of existing human conditions. In this respect humanists differ from scientists, who seek meaning in physical phenomena.

Some observers believe that it is inappropriate to associate the humanities with any specific subject matter; rather, they believe it is more appropriate to associate the humanities with the studies of language and criticism. Humanists are frequently concerned with evaluating art and nature, often using previous human authority as the basis for evaluation; scientists, in contrast, are concerned with determining the parameters of nature.

Influence of the Humanities on WLP. The influence of the humanities on WLP has been one of method, not so much one of subject matter. WLP professionals frequently find themselves playing devil's advocate in order to challenge the status quo in their organizations, refusing to accept matters uncritically. They raise questions such as these: Why does the organization do what it does? What are the consequences of management actions and decisions on employees and customers? How well is the organization responding to social issues as well as to work issues? In many cases, WLP professionals are the only ones who bring up questions of values, ethics, and morals about organizational practices. That is an important but very lonely role, one that rarely brings flashy rewards. Yet it often helps to nudge organizations along the path of social progress and increased responsiveness to employee and societal needs.

HOW DID WLP EVOLVE?

Before the Twentieth Century

WLP has a long and venerable tradition, stretching back to the earliest times. Its evolution is, of course, closely linked to the evolution of job training, Organization Development, career development, government-sponsored work programs, and other influences. These have been treated in detail by other writers (Houle 1972 and Tough 1979). What follows is a brief synopsis of historical developments.

"As early as 1800 BC.," note Carnevale, Gainer, and Villet, "the Babylonian Code of Hammurabi laid out rules governing the transferring of skills from one generation to another, from artisans to youth" (Carnevale et al 1990). The ancient Egyptians, Greeks, and Romans also focused their attention on formalized work-based apprenticeship programs (U.S. Dept. of Labor, Employment and Training Administration 1987).

Employers in eighteenth and nineteenth century Europe at the beginning of the Industrial Revolution had to manage an unskilled, illiterate workforce. They coped with shortages of trained laborers by reducing the skills needed on jobs (job simplification) and by using highly directive, frequently autocratic, management methods. Almost all workplace learning before 1900 was on-the-job training, which seemed to meet the needs of employers as long as jobs were relatively uncomplicated and did not require extended training periods.

During the Twentieth Century

As industry developed in the U. S. and in Europe, the old apprenticeship system and informal on-the-job training methods proved increasingly inadequate. They were gradually replaced in larger, progressive organizations by factory schools—essentially early training centers intended to teach skilled trades. Hoe and Company established one of the first in 1872, and several others were founded over the next 20 years.

Along with the factory school came two other developments: the YMCA started to offer trade training (as early as 1892), and efforts were made early in the 20th century to establish cooperative education. In cooperative education, students alternate between school and work, thus combining theory with practical experience. During the same period, the U.S. Congress created the nation's system of Land Grant colleges, later a source of college-trained labor.

Relatively little was done about employee training during the early years of the 20th century, despite the widespread acceptance of the classical school of management thought and Frederick Taylor's scientific management theory, which emphasized its importance. Even severe shortages of skilled labor during World War I did little to stimulate interest in widespread and systematically planned employer-sponsored work-based learning, and the Depression years made it easy for employers to pick and choose among experienced workers. There was no need to sponsor training for inexperienced workers or poor performers.

It was World War II that awakened a new interest in training. Indeed, initiatives begun during and immediately after that war have had a profound impact on today's workforce. Three major initiatives were begun: (1) *The J programs* included Job Instruction Training (JIT) which emphasized human relations and gave first- and second-line supervisors instruction in how to train. JIT was so successful that it was followed by: Job Methods Training (JMT), Job Safety Training (JST), and Program Development Training (PDT); (2) *The Engineering, Science, and Management War Training program (ESMWT)*, designed to meet the need for college-trained workers for technical and managerial work; and (3) *The GI Bill*. Immediately following World War II, this program stimulated the development of higher education by providing funds for war veterans to attend college.

It was also immediately after World War II that the seeds were also sown for what was later to be recognized as Organization Development (OD). OD grew from three major historical elements. The first is laboratory research, based on unstructured small-group sessions where participants learn about themselves, others, and the nature of group processes. From a 1946 workshop led by such important people as Kurt Lewin, Kenneth Benne, and Ronald Lippitt, researchers found that learning about group functioning appeared to take place more readily through feedback rather than lectures. In 1947, several of the original researchers held the first T-group session ("T" stands for "training"). It was the precursor of modern T-group training in which strangers meet for about one week in a series of lectures and small, unstructured sessions to explore group dynamics. T-group methods were used as early as the late 1950s in settings where participants knew one another.

The second major element of OD is survey-guided development, using attitude-survey results to produce an impetus for organizational change. The work of Rensis Likert figures prominently: Likert discovered that attitude surveys were a waste of time unless managers and subordinates used the results to jointly plan organizational improvement.

The third major element of OD is action research, a model for problem-solving and change. Though the term was coined by John Collier, Kurt Lewin was the first to use it in an organizational change effort. Sometimes called the "basis" of OD, it consists of a clearly identifiable sequence of activities.

OD has historically been based on certain important assumptions:
- People want to belong to a work group.
- Individual feelings affect group performance as much as facts.
- Leaders cannot see to the needs of everyone in a group all the time.
- Openness and interpersonal trust are essential to group performance.
- Most groups function far less effectively than they are capable of.
- The willingness to see others as creative and useful can be a self-fulfilling prophecy.

Career development has been a more recent addition to WLP. Its historical roots can be traced to the establishment of the U. S. Job Service in the 1930s, intended to facilitate worker placement in the external labor market. Over the last decade, the term "career development" has been used to refer to the effort to facilitate worker utilization and job satisfaction in internal labor markets; workers are helped to identify specific needs for training and education that will satisfy their career objectives and provide the organization with a way to improve the pool of promotable and skilled labor.

A summary of historical influences leading up to and culminating in Workplace Learning and Performance is provided in Exhibit 3-11.

Exhibit 3-11: Workplace learning and performance time line

1770:   The industrial revolution begins.

1772:   Josiah Wedgwood, an English potter and the creator of Wedgwood ware, experiments with industrial quality control.

1800s: The Industrial Revolution moves work from the individual, family, or small group to the emerging corporate organization. Training people to work at specific tasks becomes a necessity.

1809:   The Masonic Grand Lodge of New York, under De Witt Clinton, establishes vocational training facilities.

1830:   Columbia University establishes a new curriculum for young men "employed in business and mercantile establishments."

1862:   The Morill Act, signed by U.S. President Abraham Lincoln, establishes land-grant agricultural and mechanical colleges. County extension agents begin to train farmers to improve productivity.

1872:   Hoe and Company of New York opens one of the first factory schools.

1880:   Christopher Langdell introduces the case method at Harvard Law School.

1883:   A German adult educator coins the term "androgogy," referring to adult learning.

1906:   The National Society for the Promotion of Industrial Education is formed.

1910:   J. L. Moreno introduces role play and psychodrama in Vienna, Austria.

1911:   Frederick W. Taylor publishes *The Principles of Scientific Management.*

1916:   Henri Fayol declares that the work of managers is to plan, organize, coordinate, and control.

1917:   Charles R. Allen uses the "show, tell, do, check" method to train 50,000 shipyard workers.

1920s: Unions set up their first training programs for employees. Bell Labs introduces total quality management (TQM) and statistical quality control.

1924:   Joseph M. Juran begins his work on managing quality.

1925:   Mary Parker Follett develops "The Law of the Situation" emphasizing human factors in management and recommending joint business planning between leaders and subordinates.

1926:   *The Meaning of Adult Education*, by Eduard C. Lindeman, challenges the notion that the pedagogical model of education is appropriate for adults.

1927:   The Hawthorne Experiments at the Western Electric Plant in Cicero, Illinois reveal the influences of physical and psychological factors on productivity.

Exhibit 3-11: Workplace learning and performance time line *(continued)*

1931:	Professor Erwin H. Schell initiates the M.I.T. Executive Development program—the first "away-from-company" program for executives.
1933:	The Wagner-Peyser Act creates the U.S. Employment Service.
1936:	Dale Carnegie publishes *How to Win Friends and Influence People.*
1938:	U.S. President Franklin D. Roosevelt signs an executive order stating that the government, as an employer, should provide training for its employees.
1940:	The first train-the-trainer programs for supervisors are developed by the Training Within Industry Service of the War Manpower Commission. Known as "J" programs, they cover job instruction training, job relations training, job methods training, and job safety training.
1942:	Peter Drucker publishes his first book, *The Future of Industrial Man: A Conservative Approach.*
1942:	The American Society for Training Directors (ASTD) is formed on April 2, 1942 at a meeting of the American Petroleum Institute in New Orleans, Louisiana. Fifteen training directors hold their first meeting on January 12, 1943, in Baton Rouge.
1943:	Abraham Maslow publishes *A Theory of Human Motivation.*
1944:	The G.I. Bill of Rights is signed, making grants and loans for college available to U.S. military personnel.
1945:	ASTD publishes the first issue of *Industrial Training News*, a quarterly publication that is eventually to become *Training & Development* magazine.
1946:	Kurt Lewin first experiments with group dynamics at the Connecticut Interracial Commission.
1947:	National Training Laboratories conducts its first session in human-relations training, also known as sensitivity training or T-group training.
1947:	*Industrial Training News* changes its name to *Journal of Industrial Training* and becomes a bimonthly periodical.
1950:	American quality experts Joseph M. Juran and W. Edwards Deming go to Japan as advisors on the reconstruction of Japanese industry.
1951:	*Total Quality Control,* by A. V. Feigenbaum, is published.
1951:	ASTD opens its first permanent office in Madison, Wisconsin, the hometown of Russell Moberly, the secretary-treasurer who was keeping all its records.
1952:	ASTD membership reaches 1,600. There are 32 ASTD chapters across the country.
1953:	B.F. Skinner's *Science and Human Behavior* is published, introducing the idea of behavior modification.
1954:	*Journal of Industrial Training* changes its name to *The Journal of the American Society of Training Directors.*
1956:	IBM opens the first residential executive-development facility at Sands Point on Long Island, New York.

Exhibit 3-11: Workplace learning and performance time line *(continued)*

1958:   Responding to the USSR's launch of Sputnik, the U.S. government signs the National Defense Education Act.

1959:   ASTD's *Journal of Industrial Training* changes its name to *Training Directors Journal* and publishes Donald L. Kirkpatrick's article establishing four levels of evaluation for training: reaction, learning, behavior, and results.

1959:   The U.S. Chamber of Commerce introduces the Action Course in Practical Politics. Corporate trainers are responsible for this popular effort, which encourages employees to be active in political parties.

1960:   Douglas M. McGregor's *The Human Side of Enterprise* is published, describing Theory X and Theory Y as opposing viewpoints of people's fundamental perceptions of work.

1961:   *Sloan Management Review* publishes Edgar H. Schein's "Management Development as a Process of Influences."

1961:   ASTD begins the publication of *Training Research Abstracts*, later incorporated into *Training & Development Journal.*

1962:   Congress votes into law the Manpower Development and Training Act (MDTA).

1962:   The National Society for Performance and Instruction is formed.

1962:   The National Testing Service publishes the Myers-Briggs psychological type indicator.

1964:   ASTD changes its name to the American Society for Training and Development.

1966:   *Training Directors Journal* changes its name to *Training and Development Journal.*

1967:   McGraw-Hill publishes the first edition of *ASTD's Training and Development Handbook.*

1968:   ASTD membership reaches 7,422. There are 65 chapters.

1968:   The term "Human Resource Development" is coined by Leonard Nadler during a class he is teaching at George Washington University in Washington, D.C.

1970:   The NTL Institute for Behavioral Science announces it will build "the world's first university devoted entirely to applied behavioral science."

1970:   The new U.S. Occupational Safety and Health Administration mandates safety education and training for workers.

1971:   *Management Science* publishes Henry Mintzberg's "Managerial Work: Analysis from Observation," describing managerial work in terms of 10 roles, and challenging Henri Fayol's 1916 definition.

1972:   ASTD and U.S. State Department (AID) sponsor the first international training and development conference in Geneva, Switzerland. Two hundred people from six continents attend.

Exhibit 3-11: Workplace learning and performance time line *(continued)*

1973: The International Federation of Training and Development Organizations is formed, with ASTD's assistance, through a grant from the Agency for International Development.

1973: The federal Comprehensive Employment and Training Act (CETA) is enacted. CETA provides public service employment and subsidized on-the-job training for the disadvantaged.

1973: Malcolm Knowles's *The Adult Learner: A Neglected Species* is published.

1974: *Changing Supervisor Behavior,* written by A. P. Goldstein and M. Sorcher, is published, linking behavioral modeling to training.

1975: ASTD opens a branch office in Washington, D.C.

1978: ASTD membership reaches 15,323; chapters number 110.

1978: Section 127 of the Revenue Act of 1978 is enacted. The law excluded from taxable income employer-sponsored educational assistance for any type of course.

1978: Following ASTD's efforts in Congress, the Employee Education Assistance IRS exemption is approved.

1978: International Society for Performance Improvement publishes Thomas Gilbert's book titled *Human Competence.*

1978: ASTD publishes its first study of competencies: *Study of Professional Training and Development Roles and Competencies*, by Pinto and Walker.

1981: ASTD moves its headquarters from Madison, Wisconsin, to Washington, D.C.

1981: Kenneth Blanchard and Spencer Johnson publish *The One Minute Manager.*

1982: Tom Peters and Robert Waterman publish *In Search of Excellence.*

1983: The National Commission on Excellence in Education publishes *A Nation at Risk.*

1983: The Job Training Partnership Act is enacted. The U.S. Congress passes this act to provide training and employment assistance to disadvantaged and dislocated workers.

1983: McLagan's and McCullough's competency study *Models for Excellence* is published by ASTD.

1983: ASTD publishes monographs *Human Capital* and *Investment and Employee Training,* outlining economic data to prove that economic growth and prosperity depend on investing in training.

1984: ASTD implements a new governance structure, resulting in a new leadership direction for the Board of Directors and the creation of a Board of Governors to look at the future.

1985: ASTD publishes *Jobs for the Nation,* describing the impact of training on the U.S. economy.

1986: ASTD succeeds in getting the U.S. Congress to approve a National Job Skills Week.

Exhibit 3-11: Workplace learning and performance time line *(continued)*

1987:   George S. Odiorne publishes *The Human Side of Management.*

1987:   ASTD launches a new national conference on technical and skills training.

1987:   The Malcolm Baldrige National Quality Award is established.

1987:   ASTD establishes a research function and receives a $750,000 grant from the U.S. Department of Labor; research grants to ASTD will reach almost $3 million by 1993.

1987:   The Hudson Institute publishes *Workforces 2000: Work and Workers for the 21ˢᵗ Century,* by William B. Johnston and Arnold H. Packer. Based on research funded by the U.S. Department of Labor, the report spurs business and government leaders to reevaluate workforce-related policies.

1988:   ASTD membership reaches 24,500. There are 150 chapters.

1989:   ASTD publishes its first competency study, *Models for HRD Practice,* in which Patricia McLagan defines the field of human resource development.

1990:   ASTD and the U.S. Department of Labor publish *The Learning Enterprise* by Anthony P. Carnevale and Leila J. Gainer, as well as the more comprehensive *Training in America: The Organization and Strategic Role of Training,* by Carnevale, Gainer, and Janice Villet. Both works establish the size and scope of the training enterprise in the United States.

1990:   ASTD launches a new magazine, *Technical & Skills Training.*

1990:   Peter M. Senge publishes *The Fifth Discipline: The Art and Practice of the Learning Organization.*

1990:   *HRD Quarterly* research journal is jointly published by ASTD, Jossey-Bass, and University of Minnesota.

1991:   ASTD publishes *America and the New Economy* by ASTD's chief economist, Anthony Patrick Carnevale, establishing the economic link between learning and performance.

1991:   *Training & Development Journal* becomes *Training & Development.* Circulation tops 34,000 worldwide.

1992:   ASTD establishes its Benchmarking Forum.

1992:   ASTD's Public Policy Council is created.

1993:   U.S. President Bill Clinton creates the Office of Work-Based Learning within the U.S. Department of Labor.

1994:   ASTD launches ASTD On-Line, an electronic information-access service.

1994:   ASTD holds its 50ᵗʰ annual and first international conference in Anaheim, California.

1994:   Goals 2000: Educate America Act and School-to-Work Opportunities Act are enacted. Goals 2000 provides federal funds to states and local school districts to improve education. School-to-Work provides federal funds to create systems to help youths make the transition from school to work.

Exhibit 3-11: Workplace learning and performance time line *(continued)*

1996:   ASTD publishes *ASTD Models for Human Performance Improvement*, a competency study by William J. Rothwell.

1997:   ASTD publishes *Responding to Workplace Change: A National Vision for a System for Continuous Learning* by Mary McCain and Cynthia Pantazis. The report outlines national recommendations to improve federal employment and training programs and establish a system of continuous learning for all Americans.

1998:   ASTD launches "The Virtual Community" on its Web site (www.astd.org). This service allows ASTD members the chance to network, share, and locate information via the Web.

1998:   ASTD begins offering the six-course series "Human Performance in the Workplace."

1998:   The Workforce Investment Act is enacted. ASTD successfully works with Congress to enact a new federal job training reform law that enables states and local governments to develop customer-driven employment and training systems.

1998:   ASTD publishes *ASTD Models for Learning Technologies* by George M. Piskurich and Ethan S. Sanders.

1998:   ASTD and the Society for Applied Learning Technologies begin co-sponsoring the "Interactive Multimedia" conferences.

1998:   After 18 years of serving as ASTD president, Curtis E. Plott retires from ASTD and Laura Liswood replaces him as the new president.

1999:   ASTD publishes *ASTD Models for Workplace Learning and Performance* by William J. Rothwell, Ethan S. Sanders, and Jeffrey Soper.

2

THE WLP PROFESSIONAL AND THE PRACTICE OF WORKPLACE LEARNING AND PERFORMANCE

Part Two comprises Chapters 4 through 8. It addresses the following questions:
- Why is there need for a competency study of WLP work?
- What competency studies of WLP work have been performed?
- What is the background of *ASTD Models for Workplace Learning and Performance*?
- What are the various components of *ASTD Models*?
- How can the results of *ASTD Models* be summarized?

This Part also covers the steps one can take to enter the field of Workplace Learning and Performance. The following areas will be addressed:
- What are the steps involved in planning a career in WLP?
- How can people explore careers in the WLP field?
- How can an individual establish career goals, assess personal strengths and weaknesses, prepare an individual career plan, implement the career plan, secure a first job in the WLP field, and choose a career path?

The WLP professional will be challenged to uphold ethical and professional standards. The following concerns will be addressed:

- Why are values and ethics important?
- What special ethical issues affect WLP work?
- What special ethical dilemmas confront WLP professionals?
- What forces are likely to affect the WLP field in the future, and thus affect the competencies of WLP professionals?

CHAPTER 4

The Quest for Meaning: Competency Studies of Workplace Learning and Performance

In this Chapter we turn our attention to early views about work in workplace learning and performance. More specifically, we shall discuss the need for studies that describe or prescribe WLP work—and fields related to it—and we will summarize several of them. This Chapter, then, lays the groundwork for reviewing the most recent and comprehensive competency study of WLP yet performed, *ASTD Models for Workplace Learning and Performance*—hereafter abbreviated simply as *ASTD Models*, the subject of Chapter Five.

WHY IS THERE A NEED FOR A COMPETENCY STUDY OF WLP WORK?

There is a growing perception among many executives, managers, and employees that if any nation is to meet the competitive challenges of the world marketplace in the future, more attention must be paid to *all* methods of improving organizational, group, and individual performance. Every nation needs a workforce in the future that can learn and perform.

Workplace Learning and Performance is a crucial component in any effort to improve a nation's ability to meet present and future challenges. As part of this effort, WLP professionals and managers must identify appropriate roles to play, sharpen their competencies to enact those roles, and devote increasing attention to achieving results (outputs). A competency study is useful because it helps clarify the range of roles that can be played and the competencies and outputs associated with successful practice.

As McLagan pointed out in *Models for HRD Practice* (1989), a competency study can be used "for organization design, staffing, staff assessment and development, performance management, assurance of ethical conduct, career advising, and Organization Development." WLP professionals can use it in their own "job design, performance management, career planning, professional development, documentation of accomplishments, competency assessment, and ethics self-assessment." Academicians can use it "for course curricula, learner assessment, research agendas, student advising, and faculty management and development" (McLagan 1989).

WHAT COMPETENCY STUDIES OF WLP HAVE BEEN DONE?

For many years, substantial attention has been devoted to the competencies appropriate for successful performance in WLP and in other fields related to human performance improvement. While space in this book does not allow for a comprehensive treatment of all those competency studies or a historical perspective that traces the field's development through those studies, it is possible to summarize a few important competency studies that have helped to define, shape, and advance the field that has been variously called Training and Development (T & D), Human Resource Development (HRD), and (now) Workplace Learning and Performance. Competency studies are important because they are research-based descriptions of what WLP professionals must know or do to perform their work successfully. What follows is a brief summary of earlier studies sponsored by the Ontario Society for Training and Development, the American Society for Training and Development, the International Society for Performance Improvement, the International Board of Standards for Training, Performance and Instruction, the Organization Development Institute, and the Society for Human Resource Management.

The Ontario Society for Training and Development (OSTD)

In 1976, the Ontario Society for Training and Development (OSTD) began work to identify core competencies for trainers. The resulting study, entitled *Competency Analysis for Trainers: A Personal Planning Guide,* identified four professional roles—instructor, designer, manager, and consultant. The OSTD study provided professionals with role descriptions and a weighted bibliography for each role. It also described activity areas associated with the four roles. Those areas included administration, communication, course design, evaluation, group dynamics, learning theory, human resource planning, person/organization interface, instruction, materials and equipment management, and needs analysis. The purpose of the study was to provide professionals with a tool to appraise jobs, identify and organize individual strengths, and prepare resumes organized around knowledge, skills, and abilities. The model was updated in 1986 (Gilley and Eggland 1989).

The American Society for Training and Development (ASTD)

ASTD has sponsored, in all, six studies of the field: The first was entitled *A Study of Professional Training and Development Roles and Competencies,* published in 1978. This was followed by *Models for Excellence,* published in 1983; *Models for HRD Practice,* published in 1989; *ASTD Models for Human Performance Improvement,* published in 1996; *ASTD Models for Learning Technologies,* published in 1998; and the most recent work, *ASTD Models for Workplace Learning and Performance.*

A Study of Professional Training and Development Roles and Competencies

One forerunner of WLP, *A Study of Professional Training and Development Roles and Competencies,* was the first empirical study of the training and development field (Pinto and Walker 1978). The project was led by Patrick Pinto and James Walker. Based on the results of a survey of 3,000 Training and Development professionals, it identified and categorized 14 major T & D activities: (1) analyzing and diagnosing needs; (2) determining appropriate training approaches; (3) designing and developing programs; (4) developing material resources; (5) managing internal resources; (6) managing external resources; (7) developing and counseling individuals; (8) preparing job/performance-related training; (9) conducting classroom training; (10) developing groups and organizations; (11) conducting research on training; (12) managing working relationships with managers and clients; (13) managing the training and development function; and (14) managing professional self-development. The study linked 104 related, minor activities to these 14 major activities.

Models for Excellence

Models for Excellence, the second ASTD-sponsored competency study, was published in 1983. Spearheaded by Patricia McLagan as Volunteer Study Director, the project identified 15 key roles or functions performed in T & D, culminating with the publication of *Models for Excellence*. Also identified were 31 competency or knowledge areas and 102 work outputs (results) of the application of the competencies. The training and development roles identified in the study were: evaluator; group facilitator; individual development counselor; instructional writer; instructor; manager of training and development; marketer; media specialist; needs analyst; program administrator; program designer; strategist; task analyst; theoretician; and transfer agent. Competencies identified in the study included adult learning understanding, audiovisual skill, career development knowledge, competency identification skill, computer competence, cost-benefit analysis skill, counseling skill, data reduction skill, delegation skill, facilities skill, feedback skill, futuring skill, group process skill, industry understanding, intellectual versatility, library skills, model building skill, negotiation skill, objectives preparation skill, organization behavior understanding, organization understanding, performance observation skill, personnel and HR field understanding, presentation skills, questioning skill, records management skill, relationship versatility, research skills, training and development field understanding, training and development techniques understanding, and writing skills. *Models for Excellence* was the basis for the first edition of this book; it also became the foundation for a third ASTD-sponsored competency study—*Models for HRD Practice*, completed in 1989.

Models for HRD Practice

Models for HRD Practice was the basis for the second edition of this book, and its description of Human Resource Development (HRD) provided a broader focus than earlier competency studies of the field. HRD was defined by the study as "the integrated use of training and development, organization development, and career development to improve individual, group, and organizational effectiveness. Those three areas use development as their primary process, and are the focal point of this study" (McLagan 1989). The study results were compiled after numerous meetings and several rounds of questionnaires to over 800 experts in the HRD field. The results were published in five related volumes: *The Models; The Research Report; The Manager's Guide; The Practitioner's Guide*; and (separately issued) *The Academic Guide*.

It was its focus on HRD—rather than training and development—that distinguished *Models for HRD Practice* from its predecessor, *Models for Excellence*. HRD was placed in the larger context of Human Resources, because other HR areas were (according to the study) likely to influence and in turn be influenced by HRD efforts.

Models for HRD Practice listed 11 HRD roles, 35 competencies, and 74 work outputs. The roles identified were: (1) *Researcher*: The role of identifying, developing, or testing new information (theory, research, concepts, technology, models, hardware, and so on) and translating the information into implications for improved individual or organizational performance; (2) *Marketer*: The role of marketing and contracting for HRD viewpoints, programs, and services; (3) *Organization Change Agent*: The role of influencing and supporting changes in organization behavior; (4) *Needs Analyst*: The role of identifying ideal and actual performance and performance conditions, and determining causes of discrepancies; (5) *Program Designer*: The role of preparing objectives, defining content, and selecting and sequencing activities for a specific intervention; (6) *HRD Materials Developer*: The role of producing written or electronically mediated instructional materials; (7) *Instructor/Facilitator*: The role of presenting information, directing structured learning experiences, and managing group discussion and group process; (8) *Individual Career Development Advisor*: The role of helping individuals to assess personal competencies, values, and goals and to identify, plan, and implement development and career actions ; (9) *Administrator*: The role of providing coordination and support services for the delivery of HRD programs and services; (10) *Evaluator*: The role of identifying the impact of an intervention on individual or organizational effectiveness; (11) *HRD Manager*: The role of supporting and leading a group's work, and linking that work with the total organization (McLagan 1989).

The competencies identified in *Models for HRD Practice* are shown in Exhibit 4-1; the work outputs associated with the work of the HRD practitioner are shown in Exhibit 4-2.

McLagan's 1989 study remains the preeminent competency study of HRD, though the field itself has since changed and has moved beyond HRD. McLagan's seminal study prompted numerous follow-up studies, which are summarized in the pages that follow.

Exhibit 4-1: Competencies of the HRD practitioner identified in *Models for HRD Practice*

Technical Competencies (*Functional knowledge and skills*)	1. *Adult-Learning Understanding:* knowing how adults acquire and use knowledge, skills, attitudes; understanding individual differences in learning
	2. *Understanding of Career Development Theories and Techniques:* knowing the techniques and methods used in career development; understanding their appropriate uses
	3. *Competency-Identification Skill:* identifying the knowledge and skill requirements of jobs, tasks, and roles
	4. *Computer Competence:* understanding and/or using computer applications
	5. *Electronic Systems Skill:* having knowledge of functions, features, and potential applications of electronic systems for the delivery and management of HRD (such as computer-based training, tele-conferencing, expert systems, interactive video, satellite networks)
	6. *Facilities Skill:* planning and coordinating logistics in an efficient and cost-effective manner
	7. *Objectives-Preparation Skill:* preparing clear statements that describe desired outputs
	8. *Performance-Observation Skill:* tracking and describing behaviors and their effects
	9. *Subject Matter Understanding:* knowing the content of a given function or discipline being addressed
	10. *Understanding of Training and Development Theories and Techniques:* knowing the theories and methods used in training; understanding their appropriate use
	11. *Research Skill:* selecting, developing, and using methodologies such as statistical and data-collection techniques for formal inquiry

Exhibit 4-1: Competencies of the HRD practitioner identified in *Models for HRD Practice (continued)*

Business Competencies
(*Having a strong management, economics, or administration base*)

12. *Business Understanding:* knowing how the functions of a business work and relate to each other; knowing the economic impact of business decisions

13. *Cost-Benefit Analysis Skill:* assessing alternatives in terms of their financial, psychological, and strategic advantages and disadvantages

14. *Delegation Skill:* assigning task responsibility and authority to others

15. *Industry Understanding:* knowing the key concepts and variables such as critical issues, economic vulnerabilities, measurements, distribution channels, inputs, outputs, and information sources that define an industry or sector

16. *Organization-Behavior Understanding:* seeing organizations as dynamic, political, economic, and social systems that have multiple goals; using this larger perspective as a framework for understanding and influencing events and change

17. *Understanding of Organization Development Theories and Techniques:* knowing the techniques and methods used in organization development; understanding their appropriate use

18. *Organization Understanding:* knowing the strategy, structure, power networks, financial position, and systems of a specific organization

19. *Project-Management Skill:* planning, organizing, and monitoring work

20. *Records-Management Skill:* storing data in an easily retrievable form

Exhibit 4-1: Competencies of the HRD practitioner identified in *Models for HRD Practice (continued)*

Interpersonal Competencies (*Having a strong communication base*)	21. *Coaching Skill:* helping individuals recognize and understand personal needs, values, problems, alternatives, and goals
	22. *Feedback Skill:* communicating information, opinions, observations, and conclusions so that they are understood and can be acted on
	23. *Group-Process Skill:* influencing groups so that tasks, relationships and individual needs are addressed
	24. *Negotiation Skill:* securing win-win agreements while successfully presenting a special interest in a decision
	25. *Presentation Skill:* presenting information orally so that an intended purpose is achieved
	26. *Questioning Skill:* gathering information from stimulating insight in individuals and groups through use of interviews, questionnaires, and other probing methods
	27. *Relationship-Building Skill:* establishing relationships and networks across a broad range of people and groups
	28. *Writing Skill:* preparing written material that follows generally accepted rules of style and form, is appropriate for the audience, is creative, and accomplishes its intended purpose
Intellectual Competencies (*Knowledge and Skills related to thinking*)	29. *Data Reduction Skill:* scanning, synthesizing, and drawing conclusions from data
	30. Information Search Skill: gathering information from printed and other recorded sources; identifying and using information specialists and reference services and aids

---

Exhibit 4-1: Competencies of the HRD practitioner identified in *Models for HRD Practice (continued)*

Intellectual Competencies
(*Knowledge and skills related to thinking*) (concluded)

31. *Intellectual Versatility:* recognizing, exploring, and using a broad range of ideas and practices; thinking logically and creatively without undue influence from personal biases

32. *Model Building Skill:* conceptualizing and developing theoretical and practical frameworks that describe complex ideas in understandable, usable ways

33. *Observing Skill:* recognizing objectively what is happening in or across situations

34. *Self-Knowledge:* knowing one's personal values, needs, interests, style, and competencies and their effects on others

35. *Visioning Skill:* projecting trends and visualizing possible and probable futures and their implications

---

SOURCE: McLagan, P. *(1989). The Models.* Alexandria, VA.: The American Society for Training and Development, 1989, pp. 43–45. (© 1989 by The American Society for Training and Development, Alexandria, VA. Reprinted by permission of ASTD.)

Exhibit 4-2: Work outputs of HRD practitioners

---

1. Concepts, Theories, or Models of Development or Change
2. HRD Research Articles
3. Research Designs
4. Data Analysis and Interpretations
5. Research Findings, Conclusions, and Recommendations
6. Information on Future Forces and Trends
7. Positive Image for HRD Products, Services, and Programs
8. Plans to Market HRD Products, Services, and Programs
9. HRD Promotional and Informational Material
10. Marketing and Sales Presentations
11. Contracts or Agreements to Provide Service
12. Sales/Business Leads

Exhibit 4-2: Work outputs of HRD practitioners *(continued)*

13. Teams
14. Resolve Conflicts for an Organization or Group
15. Changes in Group Norms, Values, Culture
16. Designs for Change
17. Client Awareness of Relationships within and around the Organization
18. Plans to Implement Organization Change
19. Implementation of Change Strategies
20. Recommendations to Management Regarding HRD Systems
21. Strategies for Analyzing Individual or Organization Behavior
22. Tools to Measure Individual, Work Group, or Organizational Performance Discrepancies
23. Recommendations for Needed Change in Individual, Work Group, or Organizational Performance
24. Definitions and Descriptions of Desired Individual or Group Performance
25. Program/Intervention Objectives
26. Program/Intervention Designs
27. Graphics
28. Video-Based Material/Live Broadcasts
29. Audio-Based Material
30. Computer-Based Material
31. Print-Based Learner Material
32. Job Aids
33. Instructor/Facilitator Guides
34. Hardware/Software Purchasing Specifications
35. Advice on Media Use
36. Learning Environment
37. Presentations of Material
38. Facilitations of Structured Learning Events
    (such as case studies, role plays, games, simulations, tests)
39. Facilitations of Group Discussions
40. Facilitation of Media-Based Learning Events
    (such as videotapes, films, audiotapes, teleconferences, computer-assisted instruction)
41. Test Delivery and Feedback
42. Group Members' Awareness of Their Own Group Process
43. Feedback to Learners
44. Individual Action Plans for Learning Transfer
45. Individuals with New Knowledge, Skills, Attitudes
46. Professional Counseling or Referrals to Third Parties
47. Career Guidance and Advice
48. Feedback on Development or Career Plans
49. Support for Career Transitions

Exhibit 4-2: Work outputs of HRD practitioners *(continued)*

50. Transfer of Development or Career Planning Skills to the Learner
51. Provision of Career-Development Resources
52. Behavior Change from a Counseling/Advising Relationship
53. Individual Career Assessments
54. Facility and Equipment Selections
55. Facility and Equipment Schedules
56. Records of Programs and Clients
57. Logistical Support and Service to Program Participants
58. On-Site Program Support and Staff Management
59. Functioning Equipment
60. Evaluation Designs and Plans
61. Evaluation Instruments
62. Evaluation Findings, Conclusions, Recommendations
63. Evaluation Processes
64. Evaluation Feedback
65. Work Direction and Plans for HRD Staff
66. Performance Management for HRD Staff
67. Resource Acquisition and Allocation for HRD
68. Linkage of HRD to Other Groups/Organizations
69. HRD Budgets and Financial Management
70. HRD Department Work Environment
71. HRD Department Strategy
72. HRD Department Structure
73. HRD Long-Range Plans
74. HRD Policy

SOURCE: McLagan, P. (1989). *The Models.* Alexandria, VA: The American Society for Training and Development, pp. 18–20 (©1989 by The American Society for Training and Development, Alexandria, VA. Reprinted by permission of ASTD.)

ASTD Models for Human Performance Improvement

ASTD Models for Human Performance Improvement was a research-based study of the Human Performance Improvement (HPI) process. One important feature of this study is that the HPI process can be carried out by anyone—HRD professionals, line managers, employees, suppliers, distributors, and any other group or individual who cares about improving human performance. *ASTD Models for Human Performance Improvement* was thus not a competency study limited to HRD or WLP professionals alone. Its implications are broader.

The study defined *Human Performance Improvement* (HPI) as "the systematic process of discovering and analyzing important human performance gaps, planning for future improvements in human performance, designing and developing cost-effective and ethically justifiable interventions to close performance gaps, implementing the interventions, and evaluating the financial and nonfinancial results." The *HPI process model*, introduced in this study, was defined as "a six-step model that describes key steps in conducting human performance improvement work" (Rothwell 1996). The steps in the HPI process model include:

- *Step 1. Performance analysis*: The first step involves "identifying and describing past, present, and future human performance gaps."
- *Step 2. Cause analysis*: "The root causes of a past, present, or future performance gap are identified."
- *Step 3. Selection of Appropriate Interventions*: "Here people who do human performance work consider possible ways to close past, present, or possible future performance gaps by addressing their root cause(s)."
- *Step 4. Implementation*: In this step, "people who do human performance improvement work help the organization prepare to install an intervention."
- *Step 5. Change Management*: "During this step, people who do human performance improvement work should monitor the intervention as it is being implemented."
- *Step 6. Evaluation and Measurement*: "At this point, those conducting human performance improvement work take stock of the results achieved by the intervention."

In this competency study, the roles of those who perform HPI work are tied to the HPI process model. There are four roles: (1) *Analyst*: "conducts troubleshooting to isolate the cause(s) of human performance gaps and identifies areas in which human performance can be improved"; (2) *Intervention specialist*: "selects appropriate interventions to address the root cause(s) of performance gaps"; (3) *Change manager*: "ensures that interventions are implemented in ways consistent with desired results and that they help individuals and groups achieve results"; and (4) *Evaluator*: "assesses the impact of interventions and follows up on changes made, actions taken, and results achieved in order to provide participants and stakeholders with information about how well interventions are being implemented (Rothwell 1996).

ASTD Models for Human Performance Improvement also listed 38 competencies and 95 terminal and enabling outputs linked to the work of HPI practitioners.

ASTD Models for Learning Technologies

ASTD Models for Learning Technologies was a research-based study that directed attention to the impact of changing technology on the roles of HRD professionals. Its focus was thus narrower than its predecessors. Its purpose was not to examine all the roles, competencies, and outputs of T & D, HRD, or WLP professionals. Instead, it examined how traditional roles, competencies, and outputs are influenced by new, emerging, and cutting-edge technologies.

ASTD Models for Workplace Learning and Performance

ASTD Models for Workplace Learning and Performance re-examined the role of HRD professionals—now called WLP professionals—after a ten-year hiatus following the sweeping examination of the field in *Models for HRD Practice* (1989). In one sense, it can be thought of as an update of that earlier study that considered the revolutionary changes brought about by HPI and learning technologies. (This study is treated in more depth in the next chapter.)

The International Society for Performance Improvement (ISPI)

The International Society for Performance Improvement (ISPI), formerly called the National Society for Performance and Instruction (NSPI), formed a task force in 1980 to investigate the competencies of professionals (Gilley and Eggland 1989). In 1981, NSPI's task force joined forces with a parallel task force established by the Association for Educational Communications and Technology (AECT), which had also been established to examine competencies for the field. The joint NSPI/AECT task force was eventually dissolved, but its work continued under the auspices of a not-for-profit corporation called the International Board of Standards for Training, Performance, and Instruction (IBSTPI).

The International Board of Standards for Training, Performance, and Instruction (IBSTPI)

IBSTPI is a 15-member Board that was formed in 1984. According to IBSTPI, the Board "considers itself a service organization to professionals, consumers, managers, educators, researchers, and vendors in the training and performance improvement field. IBSTPI provides these groups with competencies for effective practice, research information, curriculum guides, assessment tools, and training. To date, IBSTPI has developed and disseminated competencies for the professional instructional/training designer, a bibliographic reference, competencies for instructors, a code of ethics, competencies for training managers, and supporting materials. The Board continues to be engaged in ongoing research into new standards, advances in the technology, and measurement systems." More recently, it has turned its attention to the professional certification of trainers.

Competencies for the roles of instructional design, instructor, and manager, identified by IBSTPI in three separate studies, are presented in Exhibit 4-3 (Foshay 1986). Two of those competency studies have become the basis for books (Rothwell and Kazanas 1998).

The Organization Development Institute (ODI)

Many studies have been undertaken to examine the competencies, skills, or other requirements necessary for success in OD. Several have been published in *Training and Development Journal* and included under References.

Exhibit 4-3: Competencies of instructional designers, instructors, and training managers

Instructional Designer	Instructor	Training Manager
1. Determine projects that are appropriate for instructional design	1. Analyze course materials and learner information	1. Assess organizational, departmental, and program needs
2. Conduct a needs assessment	2. Assure preparation of the instructional site	2. Develop plans for the department and programs
3. Assess the relevant characteristics of learners/trainees	3. Establish and maintain instructor credibility	3. Link human performance to the effectiveness of the enterprise
4. Analyze characteristics of a setting	4. Manage the learning environment	4. Apply instructional design and development principles
5. Perform job, task, and/or content analysis	5. Demonstrate effective communication skills	5. Assure the application of effective training principles
6. Write statements of performance objectives	6. Demonstrate effective presentation skills	6. Evaluate the instructional design, development, and delivery function
7. Develop the performance measurements	7. Demonstrate effective questioning skills and techniques	7. Apply the principles of performance management to own staff
8. Sequence the performance objectives	8. Respond appropriately to learners' needs for clarification or feedback	8. Think critically when making decisions and solving problems
9. Specify the instructional strategies	9. Provide positive reinforcement and motivational incentives	9. Assure actions are consistent with goals and objectives
10. Design the instructional materials	10. Use instructional methods appropriately	10. Adapt strategies and solutions
11. Evaluate the instruction/training	11. Use media effectively	11. Produce effective and efficient solutions
12. Design the instructional management system	12. Evaluate learner performance	12. Develop and sustain social relationships

Exhibit 4-3: Competencies of instructional designers, instructors, and training managers *(continued)*

Instructional Designer	Instructor	Training Manager
13. Plan and monitor instructional design projects	**13.** Evaluate delivery of instruction	**13.** Provide leadership
14. Communicate effectively in visual, oral, and written form	**14.** Report evaluation information	**14.** Use effective interpersonal communication techniques
15. Interact effectively with other people	**15.** Communicate effectively orally and in writing	
16. Promote the use of instructional design		

SOURCE: International Board of Standards for Training, Performance, and Instruction. Used by permission.

ODI, a nonprofit educational association, was organized in 1968. An ODI committee directed its attention to identifying the competencies of OD professionals. ODI has also prepared a competency test for OD professionals wishing to become "Registered OD Consultants" (RODC). A book is already based on ODI's competency study of Organization Development (Rothwell, Sullivan, and McLean, eds., 1995).

The Society for Human Resource Management (SHRM)

The Society for Human Resource Management (SHRM) has sponsored several HR studies that focus on all HR activities, not solely WLP-related activities based on human development and learning.

Several studies have been sponsored by the Human Resource Certification Institute (HRCI), affiliated with SHRM, to examine the "body-of-knowledge" requirements for HR practitioners as a foundation for the SHRM-affiliated certification program leading to the designations PHR (Professional in Human Resources) and SPHR (Senior Professional in Human Resources). Through this process, the researchers have been able to identify relationships between subdisciplines of HR.

Another study was conducted by Tom Lawson to review "current and emerging trends in business today, characterize the evolving role of the human resource (HR) function in response to these trends, and describe the competencies critical to the success of today's and tomorrow's HR leaders." Lawson and his team met and interviewed more than 50 Human Resource practitioners and more than 20 Chief Executive Officers from various organizations. The aim was "to define and describe the senior-level HR professional and determine from both a CEO and HR practitioner perspective the competencies required of superior HR leaders." (Lawson 1990) The result was a competency profile of required skills/capabilities of operating unit and corporate level HR professionals and the HR function itself. Lawson's study is unique in that it brings to bear senior management's view of HR practice on the competencies necessary for success in the field.

CHAPTER 5

An Overview of the Roles, Competencies, and Work Outputs of WLP Work in *ASTD Models for Workplace Learning and Performance*

In this Chapter, we shall address two questions: (1) What is the background of *ASTD Models for Workplace Learning and Performance*? (2) How can the key results of this competency study be summarized?

USES FOR *ASTD MODELS FOR WORKPLACE LEARNING AND PERFORMANCE*

In 1997, the ASTD Board of Directors authorized a new competency study to update the Society's understanding of the field (Rothwell, Sanders, and Soper 1999). The focus of the study was workplace learning and performance (WLP), a term that better reflected the changing nature of the field than the term HRD. The purpose of the study was to:

- Define workplace learning and performance (WLP)
- Summarize key points about learning and performance
- Review the origins of WLP
- Provide a model of WLP
- Describe the present and future roles, competencies, and outputs necessary for successful workplace learning and performance

The culmination of this work was entitled *ASTD Models for Workplace Learning and Performance* (hereafter abbreviated simply as *ASTD Models*). It distinguishes training and HRD from WLP and thereby dramatizes the paradigm shifts that have influenced thinking about the field in recent years.

The Models serves numerous purposes for various stakeholder groups. Those purposes are listed in Exhibit 5-1.

Exhibit 5-1: Uses for ASTD models for workplace learning and performance

Audience for *ASTD Models*	Possible Uses for *ASTD Models*
WLP practitioners	• Preparation for entry into WLP work
	• Preparation for assumption of more responsibility in WLP or broader responsibility for WLP work
	• Design or organization of work tasks
	• Career planning
	• Personal or professional development
	• Recording of personal or professional accomplishments
WLP managers	• Introduction of line managers and top managers to WLP—and to their roles in building, sustaining, and increasing the impact of intellectual capital
	• Linking of WLP to the organization's strategic plan, objectives, and competitive approaches
	• Educating line managers and top managers about possible expanded roles for WLP professionals in the organization
	• Reexamination of the mission of the WLP function
	• Reexamination of staffing requirements of the WLP function
	• Assessment and development of WLP staff members
	• Establishment of the basis for an organization-specific code of ethics for those performing WLP work
	• Offering career advice and guidance to WLP staff members and others

Exhibit 5-1: Uses for ASTD models for workplace learning and performance *(continued)*

Audience for *ASTD Models*	Possible Uses for *ASTD Models*
Line managers	• Education about their possible roles in performing WLP work
	• Education about contributions that WLP can make to the organization and to the line managers' areas of responsibility
	• Preparation for coaching their full-time and part-time employees to take more active roles in learning and development as they perform their work
Workers/learners	• Education about their possible roles in WLP
	• Education about the contributions that WLP can make to the organization and to the workers' or learners' areas of responsibility
	• Preparation for coaching co-workers to take more active roles in their own learning and development, with the goal of improved performance in mind
Academics	• Conducting needs assessment for academic programs in WLP or related fields
	• Conducting academic program reviews
	• Establishment of academic program curricula
	• Development of course curricula
	• Establishment of a research agenda
	• Advising of students
	• Personal and professional development
	• Application of WLP principles to academic institutions

SOURCE: Rothwell, W., Sanders, E., and Soper, J. (1999). *ASTD Models for Workplace Learning and Performance*. Alexandria, VA: The American Society for Training and Development, p.112. Used by permission of The American Society for Training and Development.

HOW CAN *ASTD MODELS FOR WORKPLACE LEARNING AND PERFORMANCE* BE SUMMARIZED?

ASTD Models presents the detailed results of the research study. First, it places the WLP field within the context of many functions. *ASTD Models* summarizes the roles, competencies, and work outputs of WLP practitioners. Key definitions are reprinted from *ASTD Models* in Exhibit 5-2. They follow definitions provided in the earlier *ASTD Models for HRD Practice*.

Exhibit 5-2: Definitions of key terms used in *ASTD Models*

Competency	"An area of knowledge or skill that is critical for producing key outputs. Competencies are internal capabilities that people bring to their jobs; capabilities which may be expressed in a broad, even infinite, array of on-the-job behaviors" (McLagan, 1989, p. 77).
Ethical Issues	"Key areas of ethical challenge that WLP practitioners frequently face" (McLagan, 1989, p. 119).
Output	"A product or service that an individual or group delivers to others, especially to colleagues, customers, or clients" (McLagan, 1989, p. 77).

SOURCE: Rothwell, W., Sanders, E., and Soper, J. (1989). *ASTD Models for Workplace Learning and Performance*. Alexandria, VA: The American Society for Training and Development, pp. 119–120.

Roles

People are hired into jobs or positions. Often, a *job description* outlines what they are to do; a *job specification* describes the education, experience, or other requirements necessary to qualify for the job. (ASTD has published sample job descriptions for WLP.) Employee performance appraisals measure, over some time period, how well an individual is performing job duties.

While job descriptions summarize what people do, they do not tell the whole story. How people approach their jobs is a question of role, the part played by an individual in the context of the environment, organization, and work group. *Roles* are thus ways individuals carry out their jobs. Role theory occupies a central place in the social sciences and has influenced sociology, psychology, and anthropology. Values guide what roles are accepted and, in part, how they are carried out.

See Exhibit 5-3 for a classic model that represents the nature of a role. In this model, the environment is everything outside the organization, and the organization is a system of roles. Each person in it plays multiple parts. *Role senders* are people dealing with someone filling a role. They have expectations about the role and behaviors appropriate for it. *Role receivers* are those cast in the role, much like actors or actresses in theatrical productions. *Individual variables* are based on physiological, psychological, environmental, and motivational factors. Work group/interpersonal relations concern small group contexts in which a role is enacted.

Exhibit 5-3: A model for understanding roles

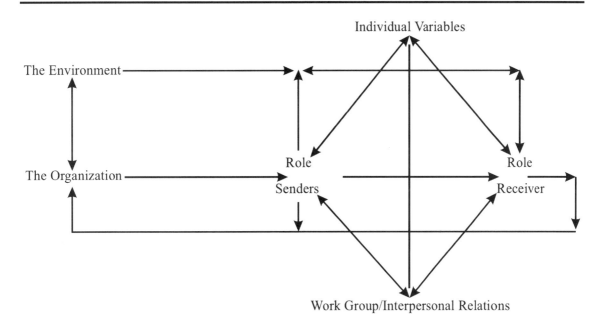

SOURCE: Katz, D. and Kahn, R. (1978). *The Social Psychology of Organizations*. New York: John Wiley & Sons. Used by permission of the publisher.

Though the model may appear complicated, it is not difficult to understand. Anybody working in an organization is both role sender and role receiver. Individual behavior in a role is influenced by the environment, the organization, role senders, role receivers, individual variables, and work group/interpersonal relations.

The environment creates demands on the organization and may create demands on roles within it. For example, if a new law is passed regulating an industry, it may exert special pressures on legal staff (who interpret it) and on those directly affected by it. Court decisions on affirmative action, family medical leave, and other changes may create special pressures on Human Resource managers and those who make hiring decisions.

Each organization has its own culture, norms, and values, and they influence role enactment. In one organization, for instance, people might have one idea about the role of accountant, but people in other organizations might have different ideas about this role.

Role senders send messages to role receivers. They expect certain behaviors from anyone occupying a position and do not expect other behaviors. Expectations stem from past dealings with people occupying similar positions. A production manager may have a set of expectations about the role of WLP professional, for example. When an WLP professional acts consistently with those expectations, the production manager is satisfied. If behavior differs from the expectation, the manager may comment on appropriate role behavior and thus send a message about it. Role enactment is also influenced by role receivers, who occupy roles. They receive messages from others about how they should behave. Their actions—that is, role behaviors—are messages that show how they perceive their role and interpret role messages from others. Individual variables influence both role senders and receivers. For example, differences in innate talents cause people to differ in how they enact a role. Finally, work group and interpersonal relations also affect both role senders and receivers. An individual's status and interpersonal skills may influence how well a role can be enacted. Similarly, relationships between groups may influence role perceptions. This model is useful in clarifying how and why people act in an organizational setting.

ASTD Models lists seven roles of WLP professionals. The roles are listed and defined in Exhibit 5-4.

Exhibit 5-4: Roles of the WLP professional

Role	Description
Manager	Plans, organizes, schedules, monitors, and leads the work of individuals and groups to attain desired results; facilitates the strategic plan; ensures that WLP is aligned with organizational needs and plans; and ensures accomplishment of the administrative requirements of the function.
Analyst	Troubleshoots to isolate the causes of human performance gaps or identifies areas for improving human performance.
Intervention Selector	Chooses appropriate interventions to address root causes of human performance gaps.

Exhibit 5-4: Roles of the WLP professional *(continued)*

Role	Description
Intervention Designer and Developer	Creates learning and other interventions that help to address the specific root causes of human performance gaps. Some examples of the work of the intervention designer and developer include serving as instructional designer, media specialist, materials developer, process engineer, ergonomics engineer, instructional writer, and compensation analyst.
Intervention Implementor	Ensures the appropriate and effective implementation of desired interventions that address the specific root causes of human performance gaps. Some examples of the work of the intervention implementor include serving as administrator, instructor, organization development practitioner, career development specialist, process re-design consultant, workspace designer, compensation specialist, and facilitator.
Change Leader	Inspires the workforce to embrace the change, creates a direction for the change effort, helps the organization's workforce to adapt to the change, and ensures that interventions are continuously monitored and guided in ways consistent with stakeholders' desired results.
Evaluator	Assesses the impact of interventions and provides participants and stakeholders with information about the effectiveness of the intervention implementation.

SOURCE: Rothwell, W., Sanders, E., and Soper, J. (1999). *ASTD Models for Workplace Learning and Performance*. Alexandria, VA: The American Society for Training and Development, p. 43.

Outputs of WLP Work

Rothwell, Sanders, and Soper (1999) define an *output* (or *work output*) as "a product or service that an individual or group delivers to others, especially to colleagues, customers, or clients." It is the result—tangible or intangible—of WLP work. *ASTD Models* supplies sample work outputs only, since it is difficult to guess what the possible outputs of future WLP work may become. Sample outputs from the study are listed in Exhibit 5-5.

Exhibit 5-5: Sample outputs of WLP work by role

Role	Sample Outputs
Manager: Plans, organizes, schedules, and leads the work of individuals and groups to attain desired results; facilitates the strategic plan; ensures that WLP is aligned with organizational needs and plans; and ensures the accomplishment of the administrative requirements of the function	• WLP plans for the organization or unit • Strategies that align WLP efforts to organizational and individual needs • Work plans for WLP efforts • Plans to secure the human talent to carry out WLP efforts • Objectives that support desired business results
Analyst: Conducts troubleshooting to isolate the causes of human performance gaps or identifies areas for the improvement of human performance	• Analytical methods that uncover the root causes of performance gaps • Results of assessment • Reports to key stakeholders of individual, group, or organizational change efforts about directions of such efforts • Reports to executives that highlight the relationship between human performance and financial performance
Intervention Selector: Selects appropriate WLP and non-WLP interventions to address root causes of human performance gaps	• Recommendations to others about selecting interventions to address or avert problems, or seize opportunities • Recommendations to others about ways to combine interventions • Assessments of the expected impact of interventions • Objectives for interventions that are aligned with desired business results

Exhibit 5-5: Sample outputs of WLP work by role *(continued)*

Role	Sample Outputs
Intervention Designer and Developer: Designs and develops interventions that help to address the specific root causes of human performance gaps and that effectively complement other WLP or non-WLP interventions targeted at achieving similar results	• Intervention designs • Action plans for interventions • Lists of stakeholders and participants for interventions • Links intervention design to business objectives
Intervention Implementor: Ensures the appropriate and effective implementation of desired interventions to address the specific root causes of human performance gaps in a manner that effectively complements other WLP or non-WLP interventions targeted at achieving similar results	• Plans and schedules for implementing interventions • Facilitation methods that will deliver the intervention appropriately • Consulting services • Contributions to business goals and objectives • Measurable return-on-investment
Change Leader: Inspires the workforce to embrace the change, creates a direction for the change effort, helps the organization's workforce to adapt to the change, and ensures that interventions are continuously monitored and guided in ways consistent with stakeholders' desired results.	• Revised implementation plans that reflect changes in the original intervention strategy • Periodic reports to key stakeholders of interventions about their progress • Written illustrations of successful implementation cases.
Evaluator: Assesses the impact of interventions and follows up on changes made, actions taken, and results achieved in order to provide participants and stakeholders with information about the effectiveness of intervention implementation.	• Reports that show the evaluation results • Recommendations for future WLP interventions • Reports that determine if intervention results caused a positive impact on business objectives

SOURCE: Rothwell, W., Sanders, E., and Soper, J. (1999). *ASTD Models for Workplace Learning and Performance*. Alexandria, VA: The American Society for Training and Development, p. 61. Used by permission of The American Society for Training and Development. All rights reserved.

Present and Future Competencies for WLP Work

McLagan defines a *competency* as "an area of knowledge or skill that is critical for producing key outputs. Competencies are internal capabilities that people bring to their jobs; capabilities which may be expressed in a broad, even infinite, array of on-the-job behaviors" (McLagan 1989). *The Models* lists competencies for WLP work, as shown in Exhibit 5-6. They are related to roles in Exhibit 5-7. The perceived current and future importance of the competencies, as identified by the various groups participating in *ASTD Models*, are listed in Exhibits 5-8, 5-9, 5-10, and 5-11.

Exhibit 5-6: Competencies for WLP

Analytical Competencies	Description
Analytical Thinking	Clarifying complex issues by breaking them down into meaningful components and synthesizing related items
Analyzing Performance Data	Interpreting performance data and determining the effect of interventions on customers, suppliers, and employees
Career-Development Theory and Application	Understanding the theories, techniques, and appropriate applications of career development interventions used for performance improvement
Competency Identification	Identifying the skills, knowledge, and attitudes required to perform work
Intervention Selection	Selecting performance-improvement strategies that address the root cause(s) of performance gaps, rather than treating symptoms or side effects
Knowledge Management	Developing and implementing systems for creating, managing, and distributing knowledge
Model Building	Conceptualizing and developing theoretical and practical frameworks that describe complex ideas
Organization-Development Theory and Application	Understanding the theories, techniques, and appropriate applications of organization development interventions as they are used for performance improvement
Performance Gap Analysis	Performing "front-end analysis" by comparing actual and ideal performance levels in the workplace; identifying opportunities and strategies for performance improvement

Exhibit 5-6: Competencies for WLP *(continued)*

Analytical Competencies	Description
Performance Theory	Recognizing the implications, outcomes, and consequences of performance interventions in order to distinguish between activities and results
Process Consultation	Using a monitoring and feedback method to continually improve the productivity of work groups
Reward-System Theory and Application	Understanding the theories, techniques, and appropriate application of reward-system interventions used for performance improvement
Social Awareness	Seeing organizations as dynamic political, economic, and social systems
Staff-Selection Theory and Application	Understanding the theories, techniques, and appropriate applications of staff-selection interventions used for performance improvement
Standards Identification	Determining what constitutes success for individuals, organizations, and processes
Systems Thinking	Recognizing the interrelationship among events by determining the driving forces that connect seemingly isolated incidents within the organization; taking a holistic view of performance problems in order to find root causes
Training Theory and Application	Understanding the theories, techniques, and appropriate applications of training interventions used for performance improvement
Work Environment Analysis	Examining the work environment for issues or characteristics that affect human performance; understanding characteristics of a high-performance workplace
Workplace Performance, Learning Strategies, and Intervention Evaluation	Continually evaluating and improving interventions before and during implementation
Business Competencies	**Description**
Ability to See the "Big Picture"	Identifying trends and patterns that are outside the normal paradigm of the organization

Exhibit 5-6: Competencies for WLP *(continued)*

Business Competencies	Description
Business Knowledge	Demonstrating awareness of business functions and how business decisions affect financial and nonfinancial work results
Cost/Benefit Analysis	Accurately assessing the relative value of performance-improvement interventions
Evaluation of Results against Organizational Goals	Assessing how well workplace performance, learning strategies, and results match organizational goals and strategic intent
Identification of Critical Business Issues	Determining key business issues and forces for change, and applying that knowledge to performance-improvement strategies
Industry Awareness	Understanding the current and future climate of the organization's industry, and formulating strategies that respond to that climate
Knowledge Capital	Measuring knowledge capital and determining its value to the organization
Negotiating/Contracting	Organizing, preparing, monitoring, and evaluating work performed by vendors and consultants
Outsourcing Management	Ability to identify and select specialized resources outside of the organization; identifying, selecting, and managing technical specifications for these specialized resources
Project Management	Planning, organizing, and monitoring work
Quality Implications	Identifying the relationships and implications among quality programs and performance
Interpersonal Competencies	**Description**
Communication	Applying effective verbal, nonverbal, and written communication methods to achieve desired results
Communication Networks	Understanding the various methods through which communication is achieved
Consulting	Understanding the results that stakeholders desire from a process and providing insight into how they can best use their resources to achieve goals

Exhibit 5-6: Competencies for WLP *(continued)*

Interpersonal Competencies	Description
Coping Skills	Dealing with ambiguity and stress resulting from conflicting information and goals; helping others deal with ambiguity and stress
Interpersonal Relationship Building	Effectively interacting with others in order to produce meaningful outcomes

Leadership Competencies	Description
Buy-in/Advocacy	Building ownership and support for workplace initiatives
Diversity Awareness	Assessing the impact and appropriateness of interventions on individuals, groups, and organizations
Ethics Modeling	Modeling exemplary ethical behavior and understanding the implications of this responsibility
Goal Implementation	Ensuring that goals are converted into efficient actions; getting results despite conflicting priorities, lack of resources, or ambiguity
Group Dynamics	Assessing how groups of people function and evolve as they seek to meet the needs of their members and of the organization
Leadership	Leading, influencing, and coaching others to help them achieve desired results
Visioning	Seeing the possibilities of "what can be" and inspiring a shared sense of purpose within the organization

Technical Competencies	Description
Adult Learning	Understanding how adults learn and how they use knowledge, skills, and attitudes
Facilitation	Helping others to discover new insights
Feedback	Providing performance information to the appropriate people

Exhibit 5-6: Competencies for WLP *(continued)*

Technical Competencies	Description
Intervention Monitoring	Tracking and coordinating interventions to assure consistency in implementation and alignment with organizational strategies
Questioning	Collecting data via pertinent questions asked during surveys, interviews, and focus groups for the purpose of performance analysis
Survey Design and Development	Creating survey approaches that use open-ended (essay) and closed style questions (multiple choice and Likert items) for collecting data; preparing instruments in written, verbal, or electronic formats
Technological Competencies	**Description**
Computer-Mediated Communication	Understanding the implication of current and evolving computer-based electronic communication
Distance Education	Understanding the evolving trends in technology-supported delivery methods and the implications of separating instructors and learners in time and location
Electronic Performance Support Systems	Understanding current and evolving performance support systems and their appropriate applications
Technological Literacy	Understanding and appropriately applying existing, new, or emerging technology

SOURCE: Rothwell, W., Sanders, E., and Soper, J. (1999). *ASTD Models for Workplace Learning and Performance.* Alexandria, VA: The American Society for Training and Development, p. 53–56. Used by permission of The American Society for Training and Development. All rights reserved.

Exhibit 5-7: WLP roles and associated competencies

Competencies	Roles						
	Manager	Analyst	Intervention Selector	Intervention Designer and Developer	Intervention Implementor	Change Leader	Evaluator
Analytical Competencies							
Analytical Thinking	X	X				X	X
Analyzing Performance Data			X	X		X	X
Career-Development Theory and Application	X		X	X		X	
Competency Identification	X	X					
Intervention Selection			X	X			
Knowledge Management	X		X	X		X	
Model Building		X		X		X	
Organization-Development Theory and Application	X		X	X		X	
Performance Gap Analysis	X	X	X				X
Performance Theory	X	X	X	X		X	X
Process Consultation	X				X	X	
Reward-System Theory and Application	X		X	X		X	
Social Awareness	X	X				X	
Staff-Selection Theory and Application	X		X			X	
Standards Identification	X	X		X		X	X
Systems Thinking	X	X	X	X		X	X
Training Theory and Application			X	X	X	X	

Exhibit 5-7: WLP roles and associated competencies *(continued)*

Competencies	Roles						
	Manager	Analyst	Intervention Selector	Intervention Designer and Developer	Intervention Implementor	Change Leader	Evaluator
Work Environment Analysis	X	X				X	X
Workplace Performance, Learning Strategies, and Intervention Evaluation				X	X	X	X
Business Competencies							
Ability to See the "Big Picture"	X	X				X	X
Business Knowledge	X	X				X	
Cost/Benefit Analysis	X		X				X
Evaluation of Results against Organizational Goals	X					X	X
Identification of Critical Business Issues	X	X	X			X	
Industry Awareness	X	X	X	X		X	
Knowledge Capital	X					X	X
Negotiating/Contracting	X						
Outsourcing Management	X		X			X	
Project Management	X			X		X	
Quality Implications	X	X	X			X	X
Interpersonal Competencies							
Communication	X	X	X	X	X	X	X
Communication Networks	X	X	X	X	X	X	X

Exhibit 5-7: WLP roles and associated competencies *(continued)*

Competencies	Roles						
	Manager	Analyst	Intervention Selector	Intervention Designer and Developer	Intervention Implementor	Change Leader	Evaluator
Consulting	X		X		X	X	
Coping Skills	X	X			X	X	
Interpersonal Relationship-Building	X	X	X	X	X	X	X
Leadership Competencies							
Buy-in/Advocacy	X		X		X	X	
Diversity Awareness	X		X	X	X	X	
Ethics Modeling	X	X	X	X		X	
Goal Implementation	X					X	
Group Dynamics	X	X			X	X	
Leadership	X					X	
Visioning	X					X	
Technical Competencies							
Adult Learning			X	X	X	X	
Facilitation	X				X	X	
Feedback	X					X	X
Intervention Monitoring					X	X	X
Questioning		X					X
Survey Design and Development		X		X			

Exhibit 5-7: WLP roles and associated competencies *(continued)*

Competencies	Roles						
	Manager	Analyst	Intervention Selector	Intervention Designer and Developer	Intervention Implementor	Change Leader	Evaluator
Technological Competencies							
Computer-Mediated Communication	X		X	X	X	X	
Distance Education			X	X			
Electronic Performance Support Systems			X	X	X		
Technological Literacy	X	X	X	X	X	X	X

Exhibit 5-8: WLP practitioners' perceptions of current and future top-ranked competencies

Practitioners *Current*: Top-Ranked Competencies			Practitioners *Future*: Top-Ranked Competencies		
Rank	*Competency*	*Mean*	*Rank*	*Competency*	*Mean*
1	Communication	(4.17)	1	Competency Identification	(4.52)
2	Competency Identification	(4.13)	2	Technological Literacy	(4.51)
3	Leadership	(4.10)	3	Leadership	(4.48)
4	Analytical Thinking	(4.09)	*4	Communication	(4.44)
5	Interpersonal Relationship-Building	(3.97)	*5	Intervention Selection	(4.44)
*6	Feedback	(3.92)	6	Analytical Thinking	(4.43)
*7	Intervention Selection	(3.92)	*7	Industry Awareness	(4.38)
*8	Industry Awareness	(3.92)	*8	Performance Gap Analysis	(4.38)
9	Adult Learning	(3.91)	9	Ability to See the "Big Picture"	(4.37)
10	Performance Gap Analysis	(3.90)	*10	Evaluation of Results against Organizational Goals	(4.34)
			*11	Knowledge Management	(4.34)

Key:
"*" Indicates a tie. Either competency could be in the higher or lower ranking.

Note: An 11th ranking was added to the "future" side of this table, due to a tie for 10th place.

SOURCE: Rothwell, W., Sanders, E., and Soper, J. (1999). *ASTD Models for Workplace Learning and Performance*. Alexandria, VA: The American Society for Training and Development, p. 72. Used by permission of The American Society for Training and Development. All rights reserved.

Exhibit 5-9: Expert WLP practitioners' perceptions of current and future top-ranked competencies

Experts *Current*: Top-Ranked Competencies			Experts *Future*: Top-Ranked Competencies		
Rank	*Competency*	*Mean*	*Rank*	*Competency*	*Mean*
1	Analytical Thinking	(4.44)	1	Leadership	(4.66)
2	Leadership	(4.38)	*2	Technological Literacy	(4.58)
3	Interpersonal Relationship-Building	(4.24)	*3	Systems Thinking	(4.58)
*4	Facilitation	(4.20)	4	Visioning	(4.52)
*5	Communication	(4.20)	5	Identification of Critical Business Issues	(4.52)
6	Performance Gap Analysis	(4.16)	6	Knowledge Management	(4.52)
7	Buy-in/Advocacy	(4.14)	7	Interpersonal Relationship-Building	(4.52)
*8	Visioning	(4.12)	8	Analytical Thinking	(4.48)
*9	Identification of Critical Business Issues	(4.12)	9	Buy-in/Advocacy	(4.46)
10	Systems Thinking	(4.04)	10	Ability to See the "Big Picture"	(4.42)

Key:

"*" Indicates a tie. Either competency could be in the higher or lower ranking.

SOURCE: Rothwell, W., Sanders, E., and Soper, J. (1999). *ASTD Models for Workplace Learning and Performance*. Alexandria, VA: The American Society for Training and Development, p. 77. Used by permission of The American Society for Training and Development. All rights reserved.

Exhibit 5-10: Line manager responses: Competency rankings in order of difference*

Competency Name [Competency Grouping]	Current Rank (Mean)	Future Rank (Mean)	Mean Difference (Mean)
Computer-Mediated Communication [Technological]	22 (3.65)	6 (4.32)	(+.67)
Distance Education [Technological]	44 (3.26)	22 (3.91)	(+.65)
Electronic Performance Support Systems [Technological]	45 (3.22)	33 (3.73)	(+.51)
Technological Literacy [Technological]	23 (3.65)	15 (4.09)	(+.44)
Negotiating/Contracting [Business]	49 (3.17)	40 (3.59)	(+.42)
Knowledge Management [Analytical]	18 (3.78)	10 (4.18)	(+.40)
Knowledge Capital [Business]	39 (3.35)	31 (3.73)	(+.38)
Outsourcing Management [Business]	51 (3.00)	48 (3.36)	(+.36)
Analyzing Performance Data [Analytical]	37 (3.48)	29 (3.77)	(+.29)
Social Awareness [Analytical]	50 (3.09)	47 (3.38)	(+.29)
Workplace Performance, Learning Strategies, and Intervention Evaluation [Analytical]	27 (3.59)	25 (3.86)	(+.27)
Business Knowledge [Business]	21 (3.65)	20 (3.91)	(+.26)
Adult Learning [Technical]	36 (3.48)	32 (3.73)	(+.25)
Evaluation of Results against Organizational Goals [Business]	33 (3.57)	27 (3.82)	(+.25)

* Competencies are listed in order of their difference means. "Computer-Mediated Communication," the competency with the highest difference mean, appears at the top of the list; "Distance Education," which has the second highest difference mean, appears second, and so forth.

Exhibit 5-10: Line manager responses: Competency rankings in order of difference* *(continued)*

Competency Name [Competency Grouping]	Current Rank (Mean)	Future Rank (Mean)	Mean Difference (Mean)
Organization Development Theory and Application [Analytical]	43 (3.30)	42 (3.55)	(+.25)
Survey Design and Development [Technical]	42 (3.30)	43 (3.55)	(+.25)
Systems Thinking [Analytical]	30 (3.57)	26 (3.82)	(+.25)
Ability to See the "Big Picture" [Business]	4 (4.26)	2 (4.50)	(+.24)
Identification of Critical Business Issues [Business]	7 (4.14)	5 (4.38)	(+.24)
Leadership [Leadership]	3 (4.26)	1 (4.50)	(+.24)
Model Building [Analytical]	52 (2.86)	52 (3.10)	(+.24)
Industry Awareness [Business]	19 (3.74)	18 (3.96)	(+.22)
Communication Networks [Interpersonal]	24 (3.61)	28 (3.82)	(+.21)
Cost/Benefit Analysis [Business]	20 (3.65)	23 (3.86)	(+.21)
Coping Skills [Interpersonal]	32 (3.57)	30 (3.77)	(+.20)
Intervention Monitoring [Technical]	48 (3.17)	50 (3.36)	(+.19)
Project Management [Business]	13 (3.96)	14 (4.14)	(+.18)
Consulting [Interpersonal]	31 (3.57)	34 (3.73)	(+.16)
Diversity Awareness [Leadership]	40 (3.32)	44 (3.48)	(+.16)

Exhibit 5-10: Line manager responses: Competency rankings in order of difference* *(continued)*

Competency Name [Competency Grouping]	Current Rank (Mean)	Future Rank (Mean)	Mean Difference (Mean)
Staff-Selection Theory and Application [Analytical]	35 (3.52)	36 (3.68)	(+.16)
Training Theory and Application [Analytical]	41 (3.30)	45 (3.46)	(+.16)
Analytical Thinking [Analytical]	8 (4.13)	7 (4.27)	(+.14)
Goal Implementation [Leadership]	11 (4.00)	13 (4.14)	(+.14)
Quality Implications [Business]	46 (3.22)	49 (3.36)	(+.14)
Interpersonal Relationship-Building [Interpersonal]	10 (4.04)	12 (4.18)	(+.14)
Buy-in/Advocacy [Leadership]	24 (3.91)	17 (4.00)	(+.09)
Facilitation [Technical]	16 (3.87)	19 (3.96)	(+.09)
Performance Gap Analysis [Analytical]	9 (4.09)	11 (4.18)	(+.09)
Process Consultation [Analytical]	25 (3.61)	35 (3.68)	(+.07)
Questioning [Technical]	26 (3.61)	37 (3.68)	(+.07)
Reward-System Theory and Application [Analytical]	34 (3.52)	39 (3.59)	(+.07)
Work Environment Analysis [Analytical]	28 (3.57)	38 (3.64)	(+.07)
Intervention Selection [Analytical]	2 (4.35)	4 (4.41)	(+.06)
Communication [Interpersonal]	6 (4.17)	8 (4.23)	(+.06)

Exhibit 5-10: Line manager responses: Competency rankings in order of difference* *(continued)*

Competency Name [Competency Grouping]	Current Rank (Mean)	Future Rank (Mean)	Mean Difference (Mean)
Performance Theory [Analytical]	38 (3.35)	46 (3.41)	(+.06)
Standards Identification [Analytical]	5 (4.17)	9 (4.23)	(+.06)
Group Dynamics [Leadership]	47 (3.22)	51 (3.27)	(+.05)
Feedback [Technical]	12 (3.96)	16 (4.00)	(+.04)
Visioning [Leadership]	17 (3.83)	24 (3.86)	(+.03)
Career-Development Theory and Application [Analytical]	29 (3.57)	41 (3.59)	(+.02)
Competency Identification [Analytical]	1 (4.44)	3 (4.46)	(+.02)
Ethics Modeling [Leadership]	15 (3.91)	21 (3.91)	(0)

Exhibit 5-11: Competency groupings: Means by respondent group

Group	Total Current and Future	Analytical	Technical	Leadership	Business	Interpersonal	Technological
Practitioners	C = 3.59 F = 4.10 D = .51*	C = 3.56 F = 4.07 D = .51*	C = 3.72 F = 4.06 D = .34	C = 3.71 F = 4.13 D = .42	C = 3.49 F = 4.04 D = .55*	C = 3.77 F = 4.20 D = .43	C = 3.43 F = 4.25 D = .82**
Experts	C = 3.69 F = 4.11 D = .42	C = 3.67 F = 4.08 D = .41	C = 3.64 F = 3.81 D = .17	C = 3.96 F = 4.27 D = .31	C = 3.61 F = 4.09 D = .48	C = 3.94 F = 4.26 D = .32	C = 3.35 F = 4.27 D = .92**
Line managers	C = 3.65 F = 3.85 D = .20	C = 3.65 F = 3.80 D = .15	C = 3.57 F = 3.71 D = .14	C = 3.78 F = 3.88 D = .10	C = 3.61 F = 3.87 D = .26	C = 3.79 F = 3.95 D = .16	C = 3.45 F = 4.01 D = .56*
Total Average	C = 3.64 F = 4.02 D = .38	C = 3.63 F = 3.98 D = 35	C = 3.64 F = 3.86 D = .22	C = 3.82 F = 4.09 D = .27	C = 3.57 F = 4.00 D = .43	C = 3.83 F = 4.14 D = .31	C = 3.41 F = 4.18 D = .77**

Key:

C = [current] Average, mean score of all *current* competencies within a competency grouping, divided by the number of competencies within the grouping.

F = [future] Average, mean score of all *future* competencies within a competency grouping, divided by the number of competencies within the grouping.

D = (Difference) The future score minus the current score within each cell.

Total Current and Future (column) = Average of all 52 competencies within a respondent group, added together and divided by the total number of competencies (52)

Total Average (row) = The current or future competency grouping average of all three respondent groups, added together and then divided by 3. The difference scores in this row are calculated within the cell.

* = Significant increase of above 10% (>.50) between current and future scores

** = Significant increase of above 15% (>.75) between current and future scores

What do the results of the study mean? The important point to understand is that, as the field has moved from T and D to HRD to WLP, the focus of attention and the results sought have changed. Traditional trainers direct their attention to an activity (training) and seek to equip learners with what they must know or do to perform their work. HRD practitioners direct their attention to several activities (T and D, OD, and Career Development) and seek to achieve improved performance through one or more learning interventions. But WLP professionals seek performance improvement as the end and work backward, from problem identification and cause analysis, to draw on a range of hundreds of possible interventions to rectify human performance problems that stem from individual or organizational causes.

SUMMING UP

WLP professionals must work within an organizational context. In small organizations, they may need to adopt some, if not all, of the WLP roles described in this chapter. In larger organizations, their roles may be more specific. In most cases, however, no WLP professional will function in only one role capacity at all times, nor will they apply all the competencies of WLP work at all times.

CHAPTER 6

Career Planning for WLP Work

WLP professionals are often responsible for helping other people recognize and develop their potential. Thus, it is reasonable to expect that those who perform WLP work should be able to recognize and develop their own potential and improve their own performance. This Chapter briefly describes one way to think of personal career planning, providing a mental map of steps in career planning for prospective or experienced WLP professionals.

STEPS IN CAREER PLANNING FOR WLP

Think of career planning for WLP as a process consisting of several clearly identifiable steps: (1) exploring careers in WLP; (2) establishing career goals, objectives, and strategies by clarifying the WLP role (or roles) desired and typical entry-level requirements; (3) assessing personal strengths and weaknesses relative to the goals/objectives and the typical entry-level requirements; (4) preparing an individual career plan to qualify, over time, for an WLP role or roles; (5) implementing the individual career plan, modifying it as requirements change to take advantage of opportunities in the field; (6) evaluating career progress periodically, relative to the career plan; and (7) taking steps to upgrade the knowledge, skills, and abilities relative to changing career goals/objectives and changing job/occupational requirements. These steps are described at length in this Chapter.

EXPLORING CAREERS IN WLP

Begin career planning for WLP by collecting as much information as possible about the field. After all, it will be difficult to establish career goals without knowing about the field or career prospects in it. Though exploration is particularly important for those who have never worked in WLP, experienced professionals are also well-advised to remain current about career prospects in the field. We suggest you gather career information by:

- Analyzing the careers, personality characteristics, and attitudes of WLP professionals
- Reading about the field
- Talking to others about their careers
- Participating in professional associations
- Monitoring the Internet and Web sites relevant to WLP
- Gaining relevant experience through paid or unpaid internships, or volunteer work

Finally, draw conclusions from your investigations—and discuss them with others—so you will have a realistic assessment about what it takes to enter the WLP field, progress successfully in it, and (if necessary) move out of it.

Analyzing Careers, Personalities, and Attitudes of WLP Professionals

One way to explore careers in WLP is to analyze what is known about the backgrounds, personalities, and attitudes of those already working in the field. While future job requirements may not call for exactly the same skills as in the past, information about the careers and personalities of experienced WLP professionals can evoke valuable insights about desirable academic majors, work experiences, and personality characteristics for entry and progress in the field.

However, relatively little information is available on these subjects. However, some information is available about Human Resource practitioners, a group to which many WLP practitioners are aligned. A 1991 study of 3,050 people from all industries, sponsored by the consulting firm Personnel Decisions, Inc. and reported in the May/June 1991 issue of ASTD's *National Report on Human Resources,* found that 24 percent of HR managers majored in social science, 4 percent in medicine, 9 percent in English literature, 3 percent in physical science, and 2 percent in technical fields such as engineering." A 1997 study done for the Society for Human Resource Management revealed the following statistics about practitioners in the Human Resources field:

- *"Total Number of HR Professionals*: Between 1984 and 1996, the total number of HR professionals increased from 440,000 to 538,000—a 22 percent change. In contrast, all managerial and professional specialty occupations grew by 46 percent over the same period, from 24,858,000 to 36,497,000."
- *"Total Number of HR Professionals by Sex*: In 1984, 46.8 percent of the profession was male and 53.4 percent was female. By 1996, males represented 37.5 percent of the profession and females 62.5 percent. Women comprise a significantly higher percentage of the HR profession (62.5 percent) than they do of all managerial and professional specialty occupations as a whole (48.6 percent) or of the total workforce (46.2 percent)."
- *"Total Number of HR Professionals by Race and Hispanic Origin*: In 1984, the racial breakdown of the HR profession was 88.6 percent white, 10.0 percent black, and 3.6 percent Hispanic origin. In 1996, the figures were 83.8 percent white,

13.2 percent black, and 5.4 percent Hispanic origin. According to the data, in 1996 blacks were better represented in the HR profession (13.2 percent) than they were in all managerial and professional specialty occupations (7.4 percent) or in the total workforce (10.7 percent). In the same year, Hispanics were better represented in HR (5.4 percent) than in all managerial and professional specialty occupations (4.5 percent), but comprised a lower percentage in HR than in the total workforce (9.2 percent). (Please note: data was not available for other ethnic minority groups. Percentages do not total 100 percent because Hispanic origin may be white or black)."

- *"HR Professionals by Age*: In 1996, the breakdown of the HR profession by age was as follows:

20 to 24 years:	16.9%
25 to 34 years:	26.0%
35 to 44 years:	29.7%
45 to 54 years:	26.2%
55 to 64 years:	18.9%
65 years and over:	11.9%"

- *"HR Professionals by Employment Sector*: In 1984, 69.5 percent of HR professionals were employed in the private sector, 28.4 percent by the public sector, and 2.0 percent were self-employed. In 1996, 74.2 percent were private-sector workers, 22.9 percent were government employees, and 4.1 percent were self-employed."

- *"Median Weekly Earnings of Full-Time HR Professionals*: The median weekly earnings (in constant 1983 dollars) of full-time HR professionals are declining. For personnel and labor relations managers, for example, median weekly earnings in 1983 were $490.00. Earnings climbed to $601.00 by 1987, then began a steady decline to $455.00 in 1995, the latest year for which figures were available. Earnings for personnel, training, and labor relations specialists followed a similar pattern— $414.00 in 1983, peaking at $445.00 in 1987 and falling to $399.00 by 1995."

- *"Median Weekly Earnings by Sex*: According to the data, male HR professionals, on average, earn a higher weekly wage than their female counterparts. In the personnel, training, and labor relations specialist category, the median weekly earnings of men in 1995 were $452.00. For women, they were $380.00. For the personnel and labor relations manager category, data was not available after 1989, but in 1989, the median weekly earnings of males were $730.00 versus $418.00 for women."

- *"Unemployment Rate*: The unemployment rate for personnel and labor relations managers was 3.4 percent in 1984. The rate peaked at 5.4 percent in 1992, decreasing to 1.5 percent in 1996. For personnel, training, and labor relations specialists, the unemployment rate has fluctuated between 2.2 percent and 4.7 percent between 1984 and 1996. In 1996, the rate for those in this category was 2.7 percent, slightly higher than that for all managerial and specialty occupations (2.3 percent)."

Think about the information presented above. (Remember that WLP professionals are a slightly different group that overlaps with, but is not exactly identical to, the information about HR professionals presented above. No statistics are available about WLP professionals specifically.) Ponder this information and then consider this question: *Why do WLP professionals seem to represent such varied academic preparations and work backgrounds?* Answering that question is important, because it can yield valuable clues about appropriate competencies that entry-level WLP professionals should bring to their jobs.

One way to account for the wide variations in academic preparations and work experiences is simply that WLP professionals work in many different organizations and enact many roles and role combinations. There is no one entry-level job into the WLP field; rather, there are many. Nor do all organizations place the same demands on WLP professionals; consequently, not all entry-level WLP jobs require precisely the same role profile. Appropriate academic preparation and work experience varies, as well. Examples of possible entry-level positions include classroom instructor, instructional designer, training coordinator, audiovisual specialist, and Web-based training specialist. Further variations may result from the unique nature of a specific job, WLP practices in different industries, and expectations of the managers in one organization. For instance, "classroom instructors" might deliver training in general subject areas—such as management or sales—or in technical areas such as computers or accounting, or even about an organization's products. Some preparation in the subject matter and/or previous experience in the organization or industry might be required. Hence, variations in the backgrounds of individual WLP professionals are not surprising, but frequently much more is required than just one college course or a short seminar in training and development.

Employers might well be looking for an individual who has had significant exposure to the organization's industry, previous experience in WLP, and appropriate academic credentials for a job opening. (See American Society for Training and Development listings in Reference section.) In addition, employers might have specific expectations about appropriate traits or characteristics of WLP professionals for their organizations.

Information about the personalities and attitudes of experienced WLP professionals is just as difficult to find as information about their careers. One 1989 study examined the psychological profiles of excellent trainers (Leach 1991). A questionnaire was mailed to the training directors of Fortune 500 companies; 204 of 500 were returned. The training directors were instructed on the questionnaire to provide information about the demographic, personal, and interpersonal characteristics of "the best trainer in their organization." The results of the survey revealed that these excellent trainers differ from the general population in 20 of 21 categories. Generally speaking, they are perceived to be interested in others, capable of interacting effectively with others, and more creative than most people (Leach 1991). Many have tacit beliefs about what they do that affects their work (Watkins 1990).

Reading About WLP

A second way to explore career opportunities in WLP is to read local newspapers and WLP-related professional journals with care. Scan classified advertisements in local papers or Web sites for positions in WLP for several months. The job positions will vary, so it will be necessary to focus on descriptions of work duties. Common job positions listed in newspapers or on the web include trainers, staff development specialists, personnel trainers, job career counselors, employee development specialists, management development specialists, and Organization Development specialists. Note carefully the job requirements and, for the sake of future job hunting, also note the employers listing these openings. It is a good bet that an employer listing one WLP opening will also have others. Those employers are good prospects to approach for other positions in WLP—or at least for information about future prospects in the field.

In addition, explore career opportunities in the WLP field by subscribing to journals related to Human Resources Management or WLP. If nothing else, go to the library to review them occasionally. If you are seriously interested in a career in WLP, read them to gather career information about the field, and watch for current openings listed in the classified advertisements. Note also the names and addresses of any specialized placement firms in WLP or HR that appear in those journals. (There are several.) It will be useful to keep track of this information if you ever plan to do a job search for a WLP position. *The most important journals in WLP and related fields are listed in Appendix A.*

Talking to Others About WLP

A third way you can explore career opportunities in WLP is by talking to people who are presently employed in the field. Find them by contacting large local employers or attending meetings of a local chapter of a professional association, such as the American Society for Training and Development. Once you have identified a few WLP professionals, call them or arrange to meet them.

Plan to ask them some questions that will help you explore opportunities in the WLP field. Here are a few you might consider:

- How did you first enter the WLP field?
- How did you prepare yourself for WLP work?
- What did you do before you worked in WLP?
- What do you *like most* about working in WLP? Why?
- What do you *like least* about working in WLP? Why?
- What knowledge, skills, or previous experience would be helpful in your job that you do not presently possess?
- How can an individual acquire such knowledge, skills, or experience?
- What colleagues of yours would you recommend me to talk with about a career in WLP?

- What college courses, short seminars, or other learning experiences would be especially helpful to acquire the skills necessary to get a WLP job and then succeed in the job?
- What books or other references would you specifically recommend to someone interested in an WLP career?
- In what direction do you see your career headed? Why?
- Where do you feel the WLP field is headed, and what can potential job-seekers do to prepare to take advantage of those opportunities?

Try to meet several experienced WLP professionals with different job titles who work in different organizations and industries. Cultivate a network of these contacts over time. Be sure, too, to mention your interest in WLP to friends and acquaintances, since they might know of opportunities in their organizations and can link you to the right people to discuss careers in WLP.

Joining Professional Associations

A fourth way you can explore career opportunities in WLP is by joining professional associations. *(See the list of professional associations listed in Appendix B.)* Make it a point to attend local Chapter meetings and, if possible, national conferences, so you can meet and network with WLP professionals. Take that opportunity to pose questions about the field, the careers of people you meet, and future career prospects in the WLP field.

Monitoring the Internet and Web Sites Relevant to WLP

A fifth way you can find out about career opportunities in WLP is to monitor internet sites and Web sites relevant to WLP. That way, you can even find out about the profession as it is practiced internationally. *Use the list presented in Appendix C to find some relevant Internet and Web sites that help you learn more about the field and about career opportunities in it.*

Gaining Relevant Experience in WLP

A sixth way you can explore career opportunities in WLP is by gaining experience relevant to it. For instance, participate in paid or unpaid learning experiences or internships focused on WLP; volunteer to assist with WLP work in a local business; enlist the support of your supervisor to volunteer for WLP-related assignments on a full-time or part-time job; or join voluntary associations—charities, community groups, even political campaigns—and ask for work that will yield WLP experience.

If you have appropriate academic credentials or work experience, volunteer to teach a class at a local community or senior college. Many colleges want qualified part-time faculty with skills in specific areas. You will sharpen your presentation skills (what trainers call *platform skills*) in this way. You can also volunteer to lead self-help groups, like those found in many churches or synagogues. Experience of this kind helps you develop group-facilitation skills.

There are undoubtedly other ways to learn about WLP and acquire relevant experience. Examine the list of roles, work outputs, and competencies of the WLP field, described in Chapter 5. Prepare a list of ways you can learn more about each one and gain relevant experience on or off your present job or while you are in school. Be imaginative about what you can do!

ESTABLISHING CAREER GOALS, OBJECTIVES, AND STRATEGY

Defining Terms

A *career goal* is a general, desired career result to be achieved. It can be expressed as work outputs you wish to be able to produce, quality requirements related to work outputs you wish to be able to meet, competencies you wish to add or develop, roles you wish to add or develop, job titles you wish to hold, or a career direction you wish to pursue. Career goals are typically expressed without specific reference to timing. To cite a few examples, see Exhibit 6-1.

Exhibit 6-1: Examples of career goals

Career Goal Linked To:	*Description of Career Goal:*
Work outputs	"I want to be able to do marketing and sales presentations related to WLP."
Quality requirements related to work outputs	"I want to be able to meet the quality requirements in my organization associated with marketing and sales presentations."
Competencies	"I want to improve my facilitation skills."
Roles to learn or improve	"I want to be able to enact the role of analyst."
Job title to be achieved	"I would eventually like to be named Chief Learning Officer."
Career direction to be pursued	"I want to start out in WLP at the corporate headquarters, then move to the field as a corporate WLP specialist, and finally move back to the corporate headquarters in a field other than WLP."

Some individuals prefer to think of their career goals in terms of the supervisor to whom they will report, the type of organization for which they will work, working conditions or industry in which they will ply their trade, or the type of personal needs that their jobs will satisfy.

A *career objective* is related to, but is more specific than, a career goal. It is a specific result to be achieved within a predetermined time. To convert the career goals listed in the previous paragraph to career objectives, simply add a *timetable* (when will the goal be achieved?) and a *way to measure achievement* (how will the goal's accomplishment be measured?).

A *career strategy* is a means by which to achieve career goals and objectives. It is a direction—a series of steps to be taken—to achieve one's career goals and objectives. To devise a career strategy for a goal or objective, simply answer this question: *How will the goal or objective be achieved*? Strategies can include pursuing additional education, gaining relevant work experience, or gaining relevant experience through off-the-job activities.

Establishing Career Goals, Objectives, and Strategy

Establish your career goals, objectives, and strategy by using the information you acquired through the exploration stage. Then work on articulating those goals, objectives, and strategy. As part of this process, reflect on your personal values and career or job preferences. Do that by answering the questions posed in Exhibit 6-2. Record your answers on a separate sheet.

Exhibit 6-2: Reflecting on personal values and career/job preferences: Questions to consider

Question	Notes
1. *(Industry)* In what industry or industries would you like to work? Are there any in which you would not like to work?	
2. *(Organization)* In what type of organization would you like to work? Are there any in which you would not like to work? Think about each of the following: **a.** *Organizational purpose.* Would you feel most comfortable pursuing profits (business/industry) or serving other people (government/non-profit)? Why?	

Exhibit 6-2: Reflecting on personal values and career/job preferences: Questions to consider *(continued)*

---

    b. *Culture.* Would you prefer a strict hierarchy of authority (military), somewhat strict (business/government), or not at all strict (university/self-employed consultant)? To what extent do you want a say in decisions affecting you?

    c. *Size.* How large or small an organization would you prefer to work in? For what reasons?

---

3. *(Supervisor)* For what kind of person would you like to work? For what kind of person would you not like to work? Describe your view of the ideal supervisor. Then describe the least ideal or least challenging supervisor. Explain your reasoning for each description.

---

4. *(Location)* Where do you most want to work? Where do you least want to work? Focus your thinking on:

    a. *Region of the world.* How amenable would you be to residing in a country outside the U.S.?

    b. *Region of the country.* Do you have preferences for certain states or regions? If so, which ones—and why?

    c. *Population density.* Would you prefer to work in a large city, a medium-sized one, a suburb, or a small town? What are your reasons?

Exhibit 6-2: Reflecting on personal values and career/job preferences: Questions to consider *(continued)*

5. *(Workplace Learning and Performance [WLP] Department)* In what type of WLP department would you most want to work? Least want to work? Focus on:

 a. *Size.* How important would it be to you to run a one-person WLP department? Be one of two people in WLP? Be part of a team of three or more?

 b. *State-of-the-Art.* Would you like to begin with a WLP department that is: somewhat behind the times, state-of-the-art, or ahead of the times? How important is it to be in a WLP department that is current? Why?

 c. *Relationships.* Some WLP departments struggle for cooperation and support. Would you prefer to work in one where support from other parts of the organization is strong, mediocre, or weak? Why?

 d. *Trainees.* Whom do you want to serve: Employees? Customers? Franchise holders? Suppliers? What are your preferences, and what are your reasons for them?

6. In what type of job do you want to work, at present? What types of jobs would you want to avoid? Think about:

Exhibit 6-2: Reflecting on personal values and career/job preferences: Questions to consider *(continued)*

a. *Job specifications.* For what kind of WLP job are you qualified now? Why do you think so? What special knowledge, skill, or experience do you offer an employer that others do not?

b. *Task responsibilities.* What kind of WLP work can you do now? What kind do you wish to qualify to do in the future? Would you prefer to enact most of the roles outlined in *ASTD Models for Workplace Learning and Performance*—or only some of them? Which ones interest you most? Least? What accounts for your interests?

c. *Salary.* What is the absolute minimum salary you would accept? How willing would you be to accept a less-than-competitive salary at present, with the possibility of rapid advancement? How willing would you be to accept a higher-than-competitive salary at present with little possibility for advancement?

d. *Growth potential.* How important is it to you to develop your skills through your job assignments? Could you accept a boring job? Could you accept a job for which you would need to struggle to meet expectations?

Exhibit 6-2: Reflecting on personal values and career/job preferences: Questions to consider *(continued)*

---

    e. *Flexibility*. How important is it
    to you to have flexibility in how
    you approach work tasks?
    Could you tolerate a job
    offering limited flexibility?

ASSESSING PERSONAL STRENGTHS AND WEAKNESSES RELATIVE TO CAREER GOALS AND OBJECTIVES

A *career strength* contributes to realization of a career goal or preference; a *career weakness* impedes that realization.

Look carefully at your answers to the questions in Exhibit 6-2. Focus particularly on those that concern the kind of job or work that you want. Then consider: What are your strengths and weaknesses relative to that job? How well-prepared are you at this time to be hired for the job or work you want?

To help you assess your career strengths and weaknesses in order to identify areas for your future development, consider how well you are equipped to demonstrate the competencies associated with WLP work. Then get feedback from several people about areas that you might need to develop. Ask them to work with you to identify areas for future development that are linked to your career goals, objectives, and strategy. Then draw your own conclusions from the activity by taking an inventory of your career strengths and weaknesses. If you wish, use the self-assessment CD-ROM that is printed with *ASTD Models for Workplace Learning and Performance* to do a self-assessment and get some suggestions for your future development. To be successful, you should become a self-directed learner like the kind of person described in *The Sourcebook for Self-Directed Learning* (Rothwell and Sensenig, eds. 1999).

PREPARING AN INDIVIDUAL CAREER PLAN

What is an Individual Career Plan?

An *Individual Career Plan* (ICP), which can be considered synonymous with an Individual Development Plan (IDP), sets forth your career goals, objectives, strategies, strengths, and weaknesses. Its purpose is to help you identify (1) what WLP role or roles for which you wish to qualify over time; (2) what competencies you need to acquire, strengthen, or otherwise develop; and (3) what you can use or do to help you qualify for the roles and/or acquire, strengthen, or otherwise develop competencies. For an individual preparing a career plan, there are no "right" or "wrong" goals, objectives, strategies, strengths, weaknesses, or means for developing competencies. For the individual, "right" means whatever will work to meet career goals and objectives. For a WLP Manager, however, there might well be various "right" or "wrong" individual career goals in the context of organizational and departmental needs to be considered. "Right" means whatever matches up to the organizational or departmental requirements.

Ideally, the preparation of an individual career plan should be a joint undertaking of individuals and their immediate supervisors. It can also benefit from the input of a mentor. It should take into account the individual's unique learning style, and it should result from a meaningful dialogue focusing on both individual career goals/objectives and organizational/departmental needs.

Resources for Building WLP Competencies

As part of preparing an individual career plan, be sure to clarify the *means* by which you can acquire, strengthen, or develop the competencies you identified.

Here are a few specific actions you can take: (1) Acquire work experience relevant to the competency or competencies you wish to develop; (2) Enroll in formal or informal educational programs; (3) Enroll in training programs; (4) Read about the subject; (5) Network with others who are proficient and observe them applying a competency, or ask them to describe in detail what they do.

Depending on the competencies you wish to acquire, some of these approaches may work better than others. For example, it is relatively easy and often effective to observe and then try to imitate a good classroom instructor as part of an effort to develop group-process skill; however, it is not too useful to watch an instructional writer in an effort to develop writing skill. So you should give some thought to choosing an appropriate method for developing each competency in line with your career goals and objectives.

IMPLEMENTING THE INDIVIDUAL CAREER PLAN

To implement the individual career plan, take action to *develop yourself.*

Gaining Experience Relevant to the Competency

If you are enrolled in a college WLP program, you might be able to acquire relevant work experience through an internship, part-time paid or unpaid employment, or summer work.

Be sure to take advantage of any opportunities. Do not depend on a college professor to take the initiative for you. Rather, take the initiative yourself. Find a willing employer who can give you relevant WLP experience.

If you are not a student but would like to have a career in WLP, there are other steps you can take.

First, try to gear your present job around short-term assignments that will help you acquire or develop the competencies you need. Volunteer to do training, write instructional materials, prepare visual aids, or take on other tasks linked to the competencies you are trying to acquire or develop. Above all, build support from your supervisor. It can also be very helpful to identify one or more mentors or sponsors who can help you achieve your career goals and develop necessary competencies.

Second, use the same methods to acquire or build competencies that you already used to explore career opportunities. For instance, join voluntary associations—charities, community groups, industry education committees, professional societies, or even political campaigns. Ask for jobs that will help you acquire or develop the WLP skills you need. That should be all the easier to do if you have already volunteered to do work related to WLP while exploring career opportunities in the field.

Enrolling in Educational Programs

The American Society for Training and Development (ASTD) has prepared a *Directory of Academic Programs* that is available on computer database. (Contact ASTD National Headquarters, 1640 King Street, Alexandria, VA at phone number 703-683-8100 and/or visit the ASTD website at http:\\www.astd.org.) This *Directory* currently lists hundreds of colleges and universities offering degrees or certificates in WLP. Your local library might also have directories of accredited and nonaccredited colleges that will award graduate or undergraduate credit for life experiences in many fields—including WLP. Consult the library as well for directories of correspondence courses or external or non-traditional degree programs that allow you to learn at home on your own time.

Enrolling in Training Programs

Many colleges, universities, professional societies, and WLP vendors offer Train-the-Trainer seminars. Lasting from one day to several weeks, they are often concentrated and highly useful for learning about a specific WLP role. Some typical titles are: Effective Delivery Skills for Instructors, Preparing Instructional Materials, and Performing Needs Analysis.

Both ASTD and Lakewood Publications (the publishers of *Training*) issue annual guides to consultants, some of whom offer public seminars. If you join a professional society in WLP (an advisable move), your name will be placed on mailing lists that will bring you many brochures about specialized training. You can also access ASTD's national database of seminars on the ASTD Web site to find out what is being offered, where it is being offered, and when it is being offered. Many organizations send WLP staff off-site for such training. If you are not employed in WLP, attending such off-site training is one way (albeit sometimes an expensive one!) to meet people in the field.

Reading Independently

Many good books and articles are available on specific WLP skills. Examine the References section in the back as a starting point for building WLP competencies, since that is an important purpose of this book.

Networking with Others

You can only observe or talk to others if you create opportunities. As you pursue developmental experiences, make it a point to attend local chapter meetings of ASTD or other WLP-related organizations. Get involved, if possible. Identify people who are especially proficient in one or more competencies of special interest to you. Arrange to talk to them. In many cases they can give you advice about how to learn more. They can also show you examples of their own work and recommend developmental projects to help you acquire or build a competency.

PERIODICALLY EVALUATING CAREER PROGRESS AND MODIFYING IT TO REFLECT CHANGING CONDITIONS

It is not adequate to just establish and implement an individual career plan. You should also plan to evaluate it periodically, modifying it as necessary. Reassess the issues you addressed at the time you initially prepared the plan. Review your career plan every year at the very least, preferably during a discussion with your immediate supervisor and, when appropriate, a spouse, mentor, or significant other.

TAKING STEPS TO UPGRADE THE KNOWLEDGE, SKILLS, AND ABILITIES RELATIVE TO CHANGING CAREER GOALS/OBJECTIVES AND CHANGING JOB/OCCUPATIONAL REQUIREMENTS

Do not assume that role requirements for WLP will always remain the same or that your career goals and objectives will remain constant. Plan to develop yourself continuously; plan to re-assess your career goals and objectives as conditions change. Review the competencies expected to become more important in the future (see Chapter 5) and take special care to focus some developmental efforts on those.

GETTING YOUR FIRST JOB IN WLP

If you have never had WLP experience, the choice of a first job is important. In many ways it will influence your attitudes and help you form work behaviors that should hold you in good stead throughout your career. Moreover, it can affect your values, competencies, and even future employability. For these reasons, you should choose your first job with great care. Do not settle for just anything; rather, choose a job that will help you reach your career goals. Since it is relatively easier to move within one industry, pay special attention to the growth prospects of the occupation and industry before accepting that first job. (See Exhibits 6-3 and 6-4.)

Exhibit 6-3: Occupations with the largest job growth, 1994–2005 (*in thousands*)

Occupation	Employment Change, 1994–2005			
	1994	**Expected by 2005**	**Numerical**	**Percent**
Cashiers	3,005	3,567	562	19
Janitors and cleaners, including maids and housekeeping staff	3,043	3,602	559	18
Salespersons, retail	3,842	4,374	532	14
Waiters and waitresses	1,847	2,326	479	26
Registered nurses	1,906	2,379	473	25
General managers and top executives	3,046	3,512	466	15
Systems analysts	483	928	445	92
Home health aides	420	848	428	102
Guards	867	1,282	415	48
Nursing aides, orderlies, and attendants	1,265	1,652	387	31

Exhibit 6-3: Occupations with the largest job growth, 1994–2005 (*in thousands*) (*continued*)

Occupation	Employment Change, 1994–2005			
	1994	Expected by 2005	Numerical	Percent
School teachers, secondary	1,340	1,726	386	29
Marketing and sales-worker supervisors	2,293	2,673	380	17
Teacher aides and educational associates	932	1,296	364	39
Receptionists and information clerks	1,019	1,337	318	31
Truckdrivers, light and heavy	2,565	2,837	271	11
Secretaries, except legal and medical	2,842	3,109	267	9
Clerical supervisors and managers	1,340	1,600	261	19
Childcare workers	757	1,005	248	33
Maintenance repairers, general utility	1,273	1,505	231	18
Teachers, elementary	1,419	1,639	220	16
Personal and home care aides	179	391	212	119
Teachers, special education	388	593	206	53
Licensed practical nurses	702	899	197	28
Food service and lodging managers	579	771	192	33
Food preparation workers	1,109	1,378	187	16
Social workers	557	744	187	34
Lawyers	658	839	183	28

Exhibit 6-3: Occupations with the largest job growth, 1994–2005 (*in thousands*) (*continued*)

Occupation	Employment Change, 1994–2005			
	1994	Expected by 2005	Numerical	Percent
Financial managers	768	950	182	24
Computer engineers	195	372	177	90
Hand packers and packagers	942	1,102	160	17

SOURCE: Bureau of Labor Statistics (BLS). 1995f. *Occupations with the Largest Job Growth, 1994–2005.* Unpublished work. Presented at http://stats.bls.gov/emptab2.htm. Washington, D.C.: U.S. Department of Labor.

Exhibit 6-4: Fastest growing industries (*in thousands*)

Industry	Employment Change, 1994–2005			
	1994	Expected by 2005	Numerical	Annual Rate
Health Services	1,032	1,900	868	5.7
Residential care	602	1,100	498	5.6
Computer and data-processing services	950	1,610	660	4.9
Individual and miscellaneous social services	779	1,314	535	4.9
Miscellaneous business services	1,741	2,932	1,191	4.9
Personnel supply services	2,254	3,564	1,310	4.3
Child daycare services	502	800	298	4.3
Services to buildings	854	1,350	496	4.2

Exhibit 6-4: Fastest growing industries (*in thousands*) (*continued*)

Industry	Employment Change, 1994–2005			
	1994	Expected by 2005	Numerical	Annual Rate
Miscellaneous equipment-rental and leasing	216	325	109	3.8
Management and public relations	716	1,049	333	3.5
Nursing and personal care facilities	1,649	2,400	751	3.5
Amusement and recreation services	1,005	1,434	429	3.3
Job training and related services	298	425	127	3.3
Museums, botanical, zoological gardens	79	112	33	3.2
Water and sanitation	213	300	87	3.2
Automobile parking, repair, and services	796	1,118	322	3.1
Personal services	225	314	89	3.1
Miscellaneous transportation services	195	270	75	3.0
Offices of health practitioners	2,545	3,500	955	2.9
Legal services	927	1,270	343	2.9

SOURCE: Bureau of Labor Statistics (BLS). 1995d. *Fastest Growing Industries (In Thousands).* Unpublished work. Presented at http://stats.bls.gov/emtab-4.htm. Washington, D.C.: U.S. Department of Labor.

As you begin the job search, purchase any of the excellent general guides available on handling the job search, preparing a resumé, and interviewing. Rather than repeat this information, we shall focus our discussion below on concerns unique to WLP.

Your Resumé

The purpose of a resumé is to get an interview—to open the door. Here are a few tips on preparing effective resumés:

1. Keep it short. The readers are busy people. Try to hold it to one page.

2. Always state a general career objective, but try to tailor it to one organization. For example: "A job as instructor at the XYZ Corporation."

3. Provide general information about yourself first, but make it brief. Be sure to include your address and phone number(s). Indicate whether you are willing to relocate. Birthdate, height, weight, or marital status are optional and are often left off the resumé.

4. If you have no work experience directly relevant to WLP, list your education first. Be sure to give the name and address of your school, grade point average (if high), academic major and minor, dates attended, and dates of graduation. List any college or noncredit courses related to WLP competencies (e.g., speech, technical writing, management, computer science).

5. List work experience next. Be sure to provide the name of the employer, your job title, dates of employment, and salary. Furnish a one-sentence description of what you did on the job.

6. List any professional affiliations—particularly if you are a member of such organizations as the ASTD, the Society for Human Resource Management (SHRM), the International Society for Performance Improvement (ISPI), the Society for Applied Learning Technology (SALT), the American Management Association (AMA), or the Society for Technical Communication (STC).

7. List references last.

Once you gain experience, structure your resumé differently. Place experience first, before education. Make sure there are no unexplained gaps in employment, and briefly explain your reasons for leaving jobs if you stayed in them less than two years. Try expressing your experience in terms of the roles, competencies, and work outputs described in *ASTD Models* so the meanings of terms are clearly understandable.

Finding Out About Openings

For a newcomer, learning about job openings in WLP is sometimes a formidable endeavor. Here are some suggestions:

- Inquire about placement with the national headquarters of ASTD (1640 King Street, Box 1443, Alexandria, VA 22313) and ISPI (1126 Sixteenth St., NW, Suite 214, Washington, D. C. 20036). See the ASTD Web site for job items.

- Contact ASTD national headquarters for a list of placement chairpersons or presidents of each U.S. chapter. Query them by letter about job opportunities in their areas.

- If you are in school, enroll in the placement service. Meet recruiters and ask them for the names of the WLP managers in their organizations to whom you can send your resumé. Ask the recruiters about any special training in their organizations so you have clues about what to emphasize in your background.

- Continue reading classified advertisements in local newspapers, as well as those in monthly issues of *Training and Development*, *Training*, and *HRMagazine*.

- Attend national conventions of ASTD, ISPI, and SHRM. Look for the placement service or network with professionals about job openings and career prospects.

- Express your interest in WLP to relatives, friends, and teachers. Find out if any faculty members at your school are members of ASTD. Meet them, and describe the job you are looking for. This is one of the best sources of information for a college student.

- Make inquiries at local job service and employment agencies. Explain your aims carefully, because many agencies unfamiliar with WLP have trouble distinguishing it from personnel management.

- Contact large employers in your area. Most organizations with more than 300 employees will have a WLP department. If nothing else, talk to the Human Resource manager about employers in the area renowned for their employee training efforts.

- Develop a key selling point or skill—something that sets you apart from the crowd of applicants.

- Visit Web sites that list job openings and search for job openings relevant to WLP.

Be willing to try out other ways of finding out about job openings. Above all, do not be shy. Most job openings are hidden and are never advertised anywhere. That is especially true of jobs in WLP! Consequently, the more steps you take in the job hunt, the more likely you are to run across those "hidden jobs."

Conducting the Job Search

Contact organizations in which you want to work. It is helpful to prepare a list of people you want to contact. Establish a goal to reach at least one or two people a day during an intensive job hunt. Keep a log of who you reached and what they said. Make contacts by letter, phone, and personal visit, and follow up later when you receive no response. Above all, do not become discouraged.

Many entry-level WLP jobs are never listed anywhere. Sometimes organizations prefer to promote employees from within or transfer them from other locations to fill these openings when they exist; sometimes advertisements are placed only with specialized employment agencies or national journals. Bear this in mind but also remember that employers will be impressed by determined people with appropriate skills and definite career plans. You may get a chance at a WLP job when you show the desire for one, provided the organization has an opening (or can create one) and hires people for those jobs from the outside.

The Interview

A good job search should result in some interviews. As you prepare for interviews, be sure to dress appropriately. (Dark blue suits with yellow shirt or blouse are good choices for both men and women.) Try to relax as you await the interview, using deep-breathing to calm yourself if you find yourself in a cold sweat. Before you arrive on the day of the interview, prepare for it by doing some research on the organization. Read about it and the industry of which it is part. If you have friends employed in the organization, call them and ask what they know about the organization's WLP program.

During the interview, be ready to show how you can fit in. Sell yourself by relating your knowledge and skills to the job opening. Ask about the job opening first so you have the information you need to relate your abilities to the job. You may also want to ask the interviewers to describe their ideal candidates for an WLP job, including relevant knowledge, skills, and personality traits. That way, you will know what the interviewer is looking for, and you can then relate yourself to those desirable traits.

If possible, show examples of your work during the interview. All WLP professionals should prepare a professional portfolio of work samples for these occasions. That portfolio should include copies of training materials you have developed, articles you have written, or other information relevant to the job. Some WLP professionals go so far as to prepare videotapes of themselves presenting classroom instruction, and (assuming they are good presenters) that practice can be very effective. If you have developed Web-based training, be ready to ask the interviewer to boot up a computer, click on the browser, and have a look-see at what you have done.

During every interview, be prepared to answer tough questions about your career plans, work experience, and education. Be willing to speak honestly about your strengths and weaknesses, rather than just telling interviewers what you think they want to hear. Ask your own questions about the company, the WLP effort, and the job. Remember that the aim is to find a "good fit" between yourself and the job opening—not just to find any job in the WLP field. If asked about salary requirements, talk about ranges—twenties, thirties, or forties, for instance. Another way to deal with the question is to say that your salary requirements are "flexible." At the end of the interview, make a point of asking for the job and explaining sincerely why you want it. After the interview, always send a thank-you note to the interviewer to express appreciation and re-emphasize your interest in the job.

Practicing the interview process can help you prepare for it. Ask a friend to play the role of interviewer and spend an hour or two fielding questions. Think about how you would answer typical interview questions, such as these:

What do you want to do with your life?
Why should we hire you?
What do you know about WLP? This organization?
What are your strengths and weaknesses?

By knowing what you want and why you want it, you will be prepared to interview effectively for a job—provided you *also* have the skills.

CHOOSING YOUR CAREER PATH

After you have gained some experience in WLP, you will want to consider future career paths. There are many to choose from. You can (1) increase the scope of your present job; (2) decrease the scope of your present job; (3) seek promotion from one WLP role to another; (4) move to a larger organization; (5) move to a smaller organization; (6) move from a regional office to corporate headquarters; (7) move from corporate headquarters to a regional office; (8) move from a WLP department in a line division (e.g., marketing) to a central WLP department; (9) move from a central WLP department to one in a line division; (10) move out of a specialized WLP job to one with only some WLP components; (11) become a WLP consultant; (12) move out of WLP and into a different career or occupation; or (13) move out of WLP and into higher-level management jobs. Some career moves have been described at length elsewhere (Chalofsky and Lincoln 1983).

Let's examine this list of 12 career paths in more detail.

Career Path #1: Increasing the Scope of Your Present Job

One potential career move is to expand the range of competencies you use on the job. For example, you may opt for another WLP role or add competencies to what you already do. This choice is useful if you are feeling stale on the job and want to become revitalized. Of course, you may need to seek additional education and training to acquire needed competencies. In most cases, your supervisor must consent to, if not actually encourage, such development.

Career Path #2: Decreasing the Scope of Your Present Job

Another potential career move is to reduce the scope but increase the depth of your present duties. For example, you may give up one or more roles but improve your facility with those you keep. This career choice is appropriate if the department is expanding (more people often means greater specialization) or if you are intensely interested in just one or two roles and their corresponding competencies.

Career Path #3: Seek Promotion in WLP

A traditional career aspiration is to move up the chain of command. Many WLP professionals begin as instructors or instructional designers/writers. In a large WLP department, the next step up is to become a supervisor of instructors in areas like professional, technical, or managerial training, or to become a unit chief responsible for media, instructional design, or evaluation. The final move is to manager of a WLP or training department. Variations in these career paths may depend on the nature of the industry or size of the organization.

Career Path #4: Shift to a Larger Organization

Many WLP professionals begin in relatively small organizations, including smaller banks, hospitals, government agencies, or manufacturing plants. As their competence increases, so do feelings of stagnation. One career move is to remain in the same industry, but shift to a larger organization.

Career Path #5: Shift to a Smaller Organization

Movement up the traditional chain of command is not always easy. People at the top tend to remain in their jobs longer than those at the middle or bottom, thus restricting the upward mobility of qualified people as they gain competence. This problem is expected to worsen in the U. S., because the number of people in age groups customarily associated with middle and upper management jobs will increase as never before. Unfortunately, a corresponding increase in the numbers of middle and upper-level jobs is not likely. In fact, just the reverse is true—organizations are reducing such jobs to improve communication and slash salary and benefit costs.

One alternative to traditional upward career movement is to shift from a larger to a smaller organization. The individual is usually "promoted" in the sense that the change often means a more impressive job title. For example, a technical trainer-instructor with 15 years' experience might be able to move to a smaller organization and be called "Director of Training." In many cases it means changing to the role of a generalist who enacts several roles, rather than being a specialist who concentrates on only one.

Career Path #6: Shift from a Regional Office to Headquarters

In some organizations trainers start out in field offices, where they run their own show and do everything in that location. Corporate-level WLP professionals or trainers, in contrast, may produce training materials and deliver specialized instruction such as executive training. A career move from a regional to a corporate headquarters is thus a possibility if you want increased specialization.

Career Path #7: Shift from Corporate Headquarters to a Regional Office

This is the reverse of the previous career move: a shift from corporate headquarters to a regional office. This change is desirable when you want greater autonomy and wish to become more of a generalist than specialist. It may also be a good idea from the organization's standpoint, because it will create a bridge for communication between corporate and regional offices.

Career Path #8: Shift from a Line Department to a Staff WLP Department

Large organizations sometimes maintain specialized WLP operations in line (operating) departments distinct from a more general but larger staff WLP department. For example, some firms split off training for computer operators and programmers from training that serves the remainder of the organization. One possible career move is from one of these specialized WLP units, where technical skill is usually highly prized, to a central WLP department where broader knowledge of WLP is often more important.

Career Path #9: Shift from a Staff Department to a Line WLP Department

Some WLP professionals begin in a large, central WLP staff department. There they learn how to design, deliver, and evaluate instruction or manage other learning interventions. When they long for career movement and have specialized skills in some area other than WLP (for example, computer programming, marketing, production), they may want to consider moving into an operating department to head up specialized WLP units.

Career Path #10: Become a WLP Consultant

Many people want to become WLP consultants after they have cut their teeth in a WLP Department in an organization. Clearly, the trend toward organizational outsourcing has made this an appealing option. However, do not assume that you can get rich quick as a consultant, especially if your experience is limited (or nonexistent). A good approach is to begin working under the mentorship of another consultant who is more seasoned and has already developed a client base. But if you wish to move into consulting from a full-time WLP job, make sure that you have special expertise that you can sell, that you have a network of professional contacts with whom to market your services, and that you have a sufficient war chest of funds to last you during the dry period that typically accompanies a move into consulting.

Career Path #11: Move out of a WLP Specialization to a Job with WLP Components

Many jobs require competencies linked to WLP work. For example, a field sales manager might devote substantial time to training new sales representatives. For those who see more promise in a career related to (but outside of) WLP, such a career move might be worth considering.

Career Path #12: Move out of WLP Completely

Not everyone wants to make a lifelong career of WLP. In the past, few people even thought of WLP as a profession distinct from others. This view is changing, but it is not accepted by all managers or by all organizations.

Some people might want to try other occupations where they think they can enjoy a competitive advantage due to their unique skills or backgrounds. Some WLP professionals think of moving into an academic institution, for example, but teaching opportunities in higher education require research, writing, and publication in addition to teaching.

The skills of WLP are certainly transferable to other fields. Instructors can become speakers and salespersons. Instructional writers can become technical writers, editors, or even reporters. Media specialists can use their talents in radio, television, or library work. These are just a few examples. Of course, career moves of these kinds might require experience, education, and talents different from the typical skills picked up in WLP work. Additional education might be needed to qualify for such career moves.

Move into Higher Management

In the past, WLP professionals and others rarely moved up the ladder to higher management. Now, however, more of them are aspiring to such jobs.

A job in WLP tends to have high visibility, especially for classroom instructors and those involved in management training. Indeed, many firms rotate their highest potential talent through a tour of duty in the WLP department for just this reason. Although there is a potential for WLP professionals to move up the management ladder, those who want to do so should supplement their credentials and experience with those appropriate to new and more ambitious goals. It is also important that you make friends with people who can help.

CHAPTER 7

Grappling with the Ethical Issues of WLP Work

This Chapter emphasizes the importance of values and ethics in WLP work, defines values and ethics, describes special ethical issues affecting WLP work, and summarizes key ethical dilemmas confronting WLP professionals.

THE IMPORTANCE OF VALUES AND ETHICS

An Ethical Crisis in the U.S.

Ethics is becoming a matter of increasing concern for corporate America and government agencies. During the last several decades, the list of corporations sullied by scandals reads like a *Who's Who* of U.S. industry. The scandals in government are even better known.

The ethical problems of business have not escaped widespread public notice, however. A 1985 survey conducted by the *New York Times* found that 55 percent of Americans viewed corporate executives as inherently dishonest by virtue of their positions (Williams 1985). The results of a 1987 *Time Magazine* poll suggested even stronger sentiment: Americans believed unethical practices in the private sector were contributing to decaying moral values in U.S. society (Bowen 1987).

Public confidence in business leaders has eroded significantly. While fully 70 percent of Americans in 1968 expressed the belief that business leaders were making an honest attempt to strike a balance between shouldering appropriate social responsibility and pursuing profits, only 20 percent felt the same way in 1986 (Hoffman 1986). Along with scandals in government, education, church, and not-for-profit organizations, business scandals have undoubtedly contributed to growing cynicism among Americans about *all* major institutions in their society. That cynicism has, in turn, produced special challenges for those committed to the American system of free enterprise and to the management and motivation of employees.

Ethics and WLP Professionals

Business executives began to question the ethics of their peers as early as 1977 (Brenner and Molander 1977), but today's WLP professionals should be even more keenly aware of ethical and value issues than others. There are several reasons why.

First, WLP professionals are generally responsible for facilitating the socialization of individuals into work settings. *Socialization* is a process by which individuals become enculturated to the work rules and expectations of their employers. As individuals are socialized, they learn to conform to a body of articulated or inarticulated ethical standards and norms of behavior. WLP professionals should study how individuals learn ethics during the socialization process and find ways to improve that learning.

Second, WLP professionals are frequently asked by their employers to prepare and even train others to use and follow the organization's *codes of conduct,* and to implement changes that will bring employee behavior into compliance with legal, regulatory, and other mandated requirements. While there are practical limitations as to how far WLP activities can go in leading employees to comply with legal or other requirements, WLP professionals should be aware of ways to use training and other change interventions to encourage such compliance. (The checklist appearing in Exhibit 7-1 is a helpful resource when planning an ethics audit of an organization.)

Exhibit 7-1: A checklist for an ethics audit

Directions: Review the practices of your organization by comparing them to the criteria on this checklist. For each question appearing in the left column, check *yes* or *no* in the right column. For every "no," consider whether your organization should make a change to install a new procedure.

Ethics Criteria	Yes ( )	No ( )
1. **Does top management have a common understanding of and strong commitment to *ethical values?***	( )	( )
A. Do the organization's goals, responsibilities, and governing principles of conduct stress these values?	( )	( )
B. Are there forums for top managers to discuss the organization's ethical values?	( )	( )
C. Do top managers routinely discuss ethical questions, and work out differences?	( )	( )
D. Are the ethical challenges facing top management clear?	( )	( )

Exhibit 7-1: A checklist for an ethics audit *(continued)*

Ethics Criteria	Yes ( )	No ( )
2. Do management's actions and policies reflect the organization's ethical values?	( )	( )
A. Do individuals chosen for promotion and recognition exemplify those values?	( )	( )
B. Do management's strategic choices reflect those values?	( )	( )
3. Do employees throughout the organization share management's ethical values and commitment?	( )	( )
A. Does management communicate the ethical values that should guide employee conduct?	( )	( )
B. Are these communications clear and effective?	( )	( )
C. Is ethics included in orientation and training programs for new employees?	( )	( )
D. Does management monitor the ethical climate of the firm?	( )	( )
E. Is top management aware of the ethical concerns of employees at all levels?	( )	( )
F. Is top management aware of the barriers to ethical conduct that may exist at various levels of the organization?	( )	( )
4. Does the organization hold seminars, workshops, and discussion groups on ethics?	( )	( )
A. Does the organization periodically revise and update its code of conduct, credo, or ethics statement?	( )	( )
B. Does top management participate in this activity?	( )	( )
C. Do rank-and-file employees participate in this activity?	( )	( )
D. Do employees in various functional areas meet to discuss ethical questions specific to their area?	( )	( )
E. Do managers discuss ethical issues with their subordinates?	( )	( )

Exhibit 7-1: A checklist for an ethics audit *(continued)*

Ethics Criteria	Yes ( )	No ( )
F. Are employees comfortable discussing ethical questions with their bosses?	( )	( )
G. Are ethical matters addressed in formal communications such as newsletters, memoranda, and policy statements?	( )	( )
5. Does management provide employees with ethical guidance when needed?	( )	( )
A. Does management have a method for identifying and clarifying areas where ethical standards are unclear or in conflict with other organizational objectives?	( )	( )
B. Does management monitor and report on ethical problems in the industry that may affect employee ability and willingness to uphold the organization's standards?	( )	( )
C. Do employees have opportunities to raise ethical questions and concerns?	( )	( )
D. Do employees use these opportunities?	( )	( )
E. Does management communicate with employees concerning areas of ethical uncertainty or vulnerability?	( )	( )
F. Do supervisory personnel regard ethical guidance as part of their job?	( )	( )
6. Are ethical considerations included in personnel decisions?	( )	( )
A. Are job candidates informed about ethical expectations and standards?	( )	( )
B. Is commitment to the firm's stated values included among the organization's hiring criteria?	( )	( )
C. Are ethical considerations built into personnel evaluations and promotion decisions?	( )	( )

Exhibit 7-1: A checklist for an ethics audit *(continued)*

Ethics Criteria	Yes ( )	No ( )
7. **Does the firm's system of rewards include ethical accountability?**	( )	( )
A. Does performance reporting include ethical performance?	( )	( )
B. Do employees' goals and objectives include goals related to maintaining a strong ethical climate?	( )	( )
C. Are compensation and bonuses affected by ethical performance?	( )	( )
D. Does the organization identify and recognize individuals who make extraordinary contributions to maintaining the organization's ethical values?	( )	( )
E. Does the compensation system avoid penalizing employees who are unable to achieve financial or other business objectives because of ethical constraints?	( )	( )
F. Is management confident that employees will not be rewarded for financial accomplishments achieved using unethical methods?	( )	( )
8. **Does the organization have a procedure for identifying and dealing with ethical violations?**	( )	( )
A. Does the organization have a hotline, ombudsman, ethics office, or other designated channel for employees to raise ethical questions about the conduct of their immediate supervisor?	( )	( )
B. Are there clear, designated channels for reporting, investigating, and punishing violations?	( )	( )
C. Does the organization have adequate controls to prevent and detect ethical violations?	( )	( )
D. Are reporting relationships directed to promote honest and accurate communication?	( )	( )

Exhibit 7-1: A checklist for an ethics audit *(continued)*

Ethics Criteria	Yes ( )	No ( )
9. Does the organization have someone assigned to monitor and promote an ethical climate?	( )	( )
A. Does the board have a standing ethics committee or other board committee charged with monitoring the ethical climate?	( )	( )
B. Is there an ethics committee or office within the firm to handle day-to-day questions and activities related to ethics (conducting seminars and training programs, carrying on research, providing guidance to employees, investigating ethical violations, reviewing the ethical impact of company policies, etc.)?	( )	( )
10. As a result of all the above, does every employee consider ethical conduct, supervision, and guidance part of the job?	( )	( )

SOURCE: Adapted from Woodstock Theological Center (1990): *Creating and Maintaining an Ethical Corporate Climate.* Washington, D.C.: Georgetown University Press, pp. 16–18. Used by permission of Georgetown University Press.

The third major reason why WLP professionals need to have a good grasp of ethical and values issues is that, like top managers, WLP professionals frequently possess high visibility in their organizations. They should know what their own values and ethical standards are, set positive examples for others, and behave in accordance with appropriate ethical standards. They can scarcely achieve desirable results for their client organizations when they do not act ethically themselves or disagree with what they have been asked to do. In the case of the latter, an individual may be experiencing *cognitive dissonance,* a painful state in which he or she rationalizes or uses other mental defense mechanisms to reconcile disparate beliefs and behaviors.

WLP professionals should study values and ethics related to the field. As in all occupations, ethical dilemmas frequently represent conflicting demands. By studying them, WLP professionals can sensitize themselves to the likely stressors posed by their work, and have workable solutions ready that are consistent with personal and organizational values.

WHAT ARE VALUES, AND WHAT ARE ETHICS?

What Are Values?

Values, in general, are principles freely selected from various alternatives, but theorists differ on more specific meaning. Rokeach, in a classic definition, called them "persistent" beliefs that one way of behaving or one goal is preferable to an opposite way of behaving or another goal (Rokeach 1973). He distinguished between two types: *instrumental values*, which are beliefs about how to achieve goals, and *terminal values*, which are beliefs about the goals themselves.

Regardless of different definitions, most writers would agree with Raths, Harmin, and Simon (1966) that a value is:

Selected:	By choice.
	Among alternatives.
	After consideration.
Cherished:	By virtue of satisfaction.
	By public affirmation.
Used	As a guide for choosing.
	More than once.

These yardsticks can be used to determine whether an individual actually values an idea, an object, a behavior, or some belief.

Clearly, values are not simply abstract concepts of limited practical use. What is valued can guide decision-making among alternatives, dealings between people, and evaluations of ideas, concepts, or people. They are touchstones by which to make judgments.

Individual values are brought to the workplace by each individual employee. They stem from such sources as early programming by parents and peers, educational experiences, religious beliefs and attitudes, and popular culture. As the nineteenth-century English poet William Wordsworth once noted, *the child is the father of the man.* Wordsworth's poetic statement captures the idea that early experiences are internalized into a value system—a set of beliefs about what is good or bad, right or wrong. These beliefs, heavily influenced by historical events or milieu, help individuals *evaluate*—a word that means "the process of valuing"—the world around them.

Organizational values, strong in well-managed firms, stem from three major sources (Peters and Waterman 1982). One source: *the individual values of the chief power brokers and decision-makers.* What top managers have wanted in the past and desire in the future often exerts a powerful influence on decision-making, interpersonal relations, and evaluations of people and ideas. Leadership values are thus crucial in setting the tone for entire organizations. A second source of organizational values: *experiences of the organization.* The results of past actions are retained in an institutional memory and are often manifested in job descriptions, procedure manuals, and other relics of tradition. They demonstrate to a watchful eye where resources are really devoted and what activities are truly valued. A third source of organizational values is *the nature of the business*. Some industries and occupations carry with them an entire value system of their own, arising from the kind of services they deliver. Perhaps one of the strongest value systems is in the healthcare field, where the nature of the industry and the occupations within it lead to a firm belief in the sanctity of human life and the dignity of human beings. Institutionalized and preserved over time, these values are synonymous with an organization's culture.

What Are Ethics?

The word *ethics* comes from the Greek word for *character*. Also known as *moral philosophy*, ethics is perhaps best understood as a system of values about what is "right" and what is "wrong." Ethics are important because they guide and restrict individual behavior.

Value Theory and Ethics

Value theory—essentially the study of ethics—has exerted a profound influence on primary, secondary, and adult education in recent years. Educators now realize that *values clarification*, the process of helping people identify what they value and how it influences their behavior, is central to the development of self-directed individuals. The importance of values clarification and ethics training has recently been emphasized within major corporations, especially in the wake of a spate of major scandals in which the names of prominent people or respected corporations have been sullied by shady activities.

Research in corporate ethics and values, while still in its infancy, has revealed that U.S. managers have distinct value preferences. They most admire responsibility and honesty in themselves and others, for example, but they become less certain of their subordinates' values the higher up in the chain of command they progress. They also believe that effectiveness, the ability to get things done right (linked to *quality*), is the single most important organizational value. Management values in others nations differ from those of U.S. managers (Goodstein 1981). That often creates problems when managers take charge of overseas subsidiaries of U.S. firms, or when U.S.-based WLP consultants are called in to facilitate change in foreign-based organizations.

WHAT ETHICS AND VALUES CHARACTERIZE WLP WORK?

People in the same occupation are likely to share similar values (Flowers et al 1975). This should not be too surprising: In the process of doing similar work, they often acquire similar values, ethics, and even preferences. However, some variation might exist because individuals bring different individual values to their jobs, and organizations gradually develop their own unique "cultures."

Are Similar Values and Ethics Shared by WLP Professionals?

First, we must ask ourselves whether WLP can be considered a profession. There are three general ways to interpret *profession:* the trait, the institutional, and the legal (Lansbury 1978).

For *trait* theorists, a profession has core elements that set it apart from many other occupations. A professional in any field must have a high level of training, specialized knowledge, techniques that can be taught to others, representation by an association of peers, ethical standards, and a sense of purpose.

For *institutional* theorists, professions are identifiable by their stages of development. These stages include: the development of a professional association, a change in name, the acceptance of a code of ethics, gradual recognition by the public, and the advent of special facilities for the training and anticipatory socialization of members.

For *legal* theorists, a profession is simply an occupation requiring State licensure. It may necessitate some specialized certification or an accreditation process to demonstrate competency. Although there has been significant discussion about instituting a certification process for WLP, the field is not yet a profession according to the legal definition.

WLP does meet most of the criteria of a profession listed by trait and institutional theorists, although many continue to debate the common body of knowledge unique to it, or even if there is one.

1. It requires a high level of training.

WLP professionals are increasingly required to have graduate degrees and exercise a wide range of skills in their work.

2. It requires specialized knowledge.

WLP professionals must know how to analyze performance problems, design learning and organizational interventions, select and use delivery methods suitable for meeting a need, evaluate the effectiveness of learning, and gauge the extent of its application on the job.

3. There are techniques that can be taught to others.

WLP professionals can teach others how to analyze performance problems or assess opportunities for improving performance.

4. WLP professionals have self-organization, a major professional society, and several smaller professional societies.

Other societies represent other philosophical views or occupational groups in the WLP field. Small, highly-specialized WLP associations also exist within certain professions, industries, and occupations.

5. WLP has undergone a "name" evolution.

Once solely associated with training and development, it is now understood to include anything that can improve individual and group performance in organizational settings.

6. WLP is gradually being recognized by the public.

Every large news magazine has run articles on the growth of organizational training and related learning events.

7. WLP activities are united by a common sense of purpose.

WLP is a means to the end of improving work performance.

8. WLP has experienced growth in terms of training and networking facilities.

With a computerized database of and for academic programs in the field, it is obvious that more colleges and universities are offering formal degree programs in WLP, even though they are not yet formalized enough to have a common certification process.

9. WLP has its own specialties and subspecialties, schools of thought and theory, and variations in philosophy among its practitioners, just like traditional professions.

There are those who specialize in types of training (e.g., management or clerical), types of delivery (e.g., computer-based or classroom), and specific WLP issues (e.g., brain research or the development of training policy). There are also different schools of thought and theory regarding the nature of human learning and instruction.

10. Variations in philosophy exist among WLP professionals.

No two doctors or lawyers apply their professions in exactly the same way or have exactly the same personal philosophy about their professions, and so it is with those who perform WLP work.

As with any profession, the values, experiences, and personal attributes of the WLP professional will lead to a personal philosophy about WLP and its practice, much as counselors and clinical psychologists develop their own philosophies of practice. This process begins with personal assessment and clarification of values concerning such issues as human nature, the relationship between the individual and organization, the goals of learning experiences, the function and role of the WLP professional in facilitating such experiences, the nature of appropriate trainer-trainee relationships, ways of motivating people to learn, and other issues (see Exhibit 7-2).

The Importance of Articulating Individual Values, Ethics, and Philosophy

When values and ethics have been made explicit, the WLP professional has taken the first step toward developing a personal philosophy of WLP to guide subsequent practice. Though this philosophy is likely to change as the professional gains experience and undergoes socialization in different organizational contexts, it is an important guide to decision-making. Review the issues listed in Exhibit 7-2. On a separate sheet, describe your own beliefs about each issue.

Exhibit 7-2: Components of a WLP philosophy

Issue	*Description of the Issue*	*A Normative Position of WLP*	*What Are Your Personal Assumptions?*
Human Nature	What are the basic characteristics of human beings?	People should be considered self-actualizing.	What do you think about people? Why?
Individual-Organizational Relationship	To what extent are individuals free to exercise initiative in organizations?	The relationship between organization and individual can be mutually beneficial.	What do you think about the relationship between organization and individual?
Goals of Learning	What should learning goals be in an organization?	Ranges from educating the individual to improving job performance to meeting organizational needs. A current view is that workplace learning is key to improving individual performance.	What do you believe learning goals should be? Why?
Function(s) and Role(s) of HRD Practitioners	How do WLP practitioners facilitate learning in organizations?	Described by the competency study, *Models for Excellence* (1983).	To what extent do you see the primary allegiance of the WLP practitioner to the profession? Why?
Nature of Learning in Organizations	How do people learn in an organizational context?	Learning occurs best when it is geared to individual needs, and managers encourage application of training.	How do you believe people learn in an organization?
Trainer-Trainee Relationships	How are people best motivated to learn?	Varies by situation, but WLP generally favors the humanistic, I-thou relationship.	What do you believe should be the relationship between the practitioner and those served?
Means of Motivating Learning	What should be the relationship between WLP practitioners and the group they serve?	People are best motivated to learn through intrinsic rewards, but it may vary by individual.	How do you believe people are best motivated to learn? Why?
Conditions When the Theory Will Not Work	In what kind of organization will one's personal theory not work? For what reasons?	Varies by type of organization. Self-actualization is not easy in authoritarian organizations.	When will your theory not work? Why?
Example of the Theory as It Is Applied	How is the theory applied? What are some guidelines for applications?	Purest expressions by Robert Mager and Tom Gilbert	How can your theory be applied?

WHAT ETHICAL ISSUES CONFRONT WLP PROFESSIONALS?

McLagan's *Models for HRD Practice* (1989) identified some 13 major ethical issues associated with HRD, listed in Exhibit 7-3. Each role description in the book contains a list of relevant ethical issues (see Exhibit 7-4). Subsequent ASTD competency studies also focused on ethical issues. The topic was treated more narrowly than in McLagan's study in both *ASTD Models for Human Performance Improvement* and in *ASTD Models for Learning Technologies*.

But *ASTD Models for Workplace Learning and Performance* (Rothwell, Sanders, and Soper, 1999) revisited the important topic of ethics 10 years after the McLagan study, using a new definition of the field. According to *ASTD Models*, ethical breaches "occur when people fail to live up to their moral principles." *ASTD Models* lists numerous sources of ethical breaches. Of particular importance are those associated with steps in the HPI process model, and those associated with trends affecting WLP.

Exhibit 7-3: Ethical issues for HRD

Maintaining appropriate confidentiality

Saying "no" to inappropriate requests

Showing respect for copyrights, sources, and intellectual property

Ensuring truth in claims, data, and recommendations

Balancing organizational and individual needs and interests

Ensuring customer and user involvement, participation, and ownership

Avoiding conflicts of interest

Managing personal biases

Showing respect for, interest in, and representation of individual and population differences

Making the intervention appropriate to the customer's or user's needs

Being sensitive to the direct and indirect effects of intervention, and acting to address negative consequences

Pricing or costing products or services fairly

Using power appropriately

SOURCE: McLagan, P. (1989). *The Models*. Alexandria, VA: American Society for Training and Development, pp. 40–41. Used by permission of ASTD with all rights reserved. Copyright © 1989 by the American Society for Training and Development.

Exhibit 7-4: Ethical issues by role

Role	Ethical Issues
Researcher	1. Avoiding conflicts of interest 2. Ensuring truth in claims, data, and recommendations 3. Maintaining appropriate confidentiality 4. Managing personal biases 5. Showing respect for copyrights, sources, and intellectual property 6. Showing respect for and representation of individual and population differences
Marketer	1. Avoiding conflicts of interest 2. Ensuring truth in claims, data, and recommendations 3. Maintaining appropriate confidentiality 4. Ensuring customer and user involvement, participation, and ownership (non-manipulation) 5. Showing respect for copyrights, sources, and intellectual property 6. Saying "no" to inappropriate requests 7. Balancing organizational and individual needs and interests
Organization Change Agent	1. Maintaining appropriate confidentiality 2. Ensuring customer and user involvement, participation, and ownership 3. Saying "no" to inappropriate requests 4. Using power appropriately 5. Making the intervention appropriate to the customer's or user's needs 6. Balancing organizational and individual needs and interests.
Needs Analyst	1. Ensuring truth in claims, data, and recommendations 2. Maintaining appropriate confidentiality 3. Managing personal biases 4. Being sensitive to the direct and indirect effects of intervention, and acting to address negative consequences 5. Balancing organizational and individual needs and interests 6. Ensuring customer and user involvement, participation, and ownership

Exhibit 7-4: Ethical issues by role *(continued)*

Role	Ethical Issues
Program Designer	1. Maintaining appropriate confidentiality 2. Being sensitive to direct and indirect effects of an intervention, and acting to address negative consequences 3. Ensuring customer and user involvement, participation, and ownership (non-manipulation) 4. Showing respect for copyrights, sources, and intellectual property 5. Saying "no" to inappropriate requests 6. Making the intervention appropriate to the customer's and user's needs
HRD Materials Developer	1. Ensuring truth in claims, data, and recommendations 2. Showing respect for copyrights, sources, and intellectual property 3. Showing respect for and representation of individual and population differences 4. Saying "no" to inappropriate requests 5. Pricing or costing products and services fairly
Instructor/ Facilitator	1. Maintaining appropriate confidentiality 2. Managing personal biases 3. Showing respect for copyrights, sources, and intellectual property 4. Saying "no" to inappropriate requests 5. Showing respect for and representation of individual and population differences 6. Balancing organizational and individual needs and interests
Individual Career- Development Advisor	1. Avoiding conflicts of interest 2. Maintaining appropriate confidentiality 3. Balancing organizational and individual needs and interests
Administrator	1. Ensuring truth in claims, data, and recommendations 2. Maintaining appropriate confidentiality 3. Showing respect for copyrights, sources, and intellectual property 4. Saying "no" to inappropriate requests 5. Balancing organizational and individual needs and interests

Exhibit 7-4: Ethical issues by role *(continued)*

Role	Ethical Issues
Evaluator	1. Ensuring truth in claims, data, and recommendations 2. Maintaining appropriate confidentiality 3. Managing personal biases 4. Ensuring customer and user involvement, participation, and ownership (non-manipulation) 5. Saying "no" to inappropriate requests 6. Balancing organizational and individual needs and interests
HRD Manager	1. Ensuring truth in claims, data, and recommendations 2. Maintaining appropriate confidentiality 3. Showing respect for copyrights, sources, and intellectual property 4. Saying "no" to inappropriate requests 5. Balancing organizational and individual needs and interests

SOURCE: McLagan, P. (1989). *The Models*. Alexandria, VA: American Society for Training and Development, pp. 50–59. Used by permission of ASTD with all rights reserved. Copyright © 1989 by the American Society for Training and Development.

Ethical Breaches Associated with Steps in the HPI Process Model

Ethical breaches can be committed at each step of the HPI process model—performance analysis, cause analysis, intervention implementation, change management, and evaluation.

According to *ASTD Models*, examples of ethical breaches committed during performance analysis are all of the following:

- Choosing not to conduct a proper performance analysis in order to satisfy the client's request for an immediate intervention
- Conducting performance analysis improperly by bending to undue pressure from executives or other stakeholders, with the result of knowingly misidentifying performance problems
- Not advising clients when the desired level of performance they seek is completely unreasonable, based on industry benchmarks.

During cause analysis, WLP professionals may succumb to such ethical breaches as:

- Deciding not to conduct a cause analysis because the underlying causes seem too ambiguous or complex
- Knowingly attributing a problem to the wrong root causes

- Improperly manipulating data to show the need for a certain intervention when the data do not support that need
- Not acknowledging an awareness of misidentified root causes.

During intervention selection, WLP practitioners can commit such ethical breaches as:

- Knowingly selecting the wrong intervention because the practitioner lacks the ability to implement the appropriate intervention (for example, selecting training when the cause analysis revealed a compensation issue as the root cause of a performance problem)
- Selecting a particular intervention primarily because it best benefits the WLP practitioner
- Selecting an intervention with the primary objective of developing the WLP practitioner's skill level
- Yielding to a desire for unrealistic quick fixes or ineffective quick results
- Consciously building unrealistic expectations among stakeholders about the time and resources needed to implement the appropriate intervention and to reach desired performance objectives.

During intervention implementation, WLP professionals can commit ethical breaches by:

- Failing to monitor the intervention's progress because there are no fees directly associated with this activity
- Intentionally ignoring certain stakeholders because of their opposition to the intervention
- Failing to communicate the intervention's lack of progress
- Giving learners or stakeholders a false impression about their responsibilities in the intervention or the amount of effort required of them.

In change management, WLP practitioners can experience such ethical problems as:

- Allowing the intervention to continue, despite the fact that it is causing an inappropriate level of trauma within the organization
- Knowingly excluding appropriate individuals or groups in the change process
- Not providing employees with the skills and tools they need to effectively adapt to the changes
- Discontinuing communication with the organization because of controversy over the intervention.

During intervention evaluation, WLP practitioners might compromise ethics by:

- Conducting evaluations based on data that is convenient and available, rather than data that is truly indicative of the intervention's impact
- Intentionally developing an evaluation instrument that does not measure the desired outcomes of the intervention (for example, evaluating what facts participants learned in a training experience, when the desired result was to bring about a change in on-the-job behavior)

- Intentionally attributing changes in performance directly to a single intervention, when a number of factors have contributed to the change
- Ignoring evaluation results that do not match the original hypothesis of the analyst
- Failing to admit that an intervention did not produce the desired effect.

The important point to remember, then, is to observe the purpose of each step in the HPI process model and resist taking shortcuts or bending to the pressures of others to take shortcuts.

Ethical Breaches Stemming from Trends Affecting WLP

Bassi, Buchanan, and Cheney (1997) identified 10 key trends affecting WLP. (They will be described at greater length in the next chapter.) Those trends are:

- Skill requirements will continue to increase in response to rapid technological change.
- The American workforce will be significantly more educated and diverse.
- Corporate restructuring will continue to reshape the business environment.
- The size and composition of training departments will change dramatically.
- Advances in technology will revolutionize training delivery.
- Training departments will find new ways to deliver services.
- There will be more focus on performance improvement.
- Integrated high-performance work systems will proliferate.
- Companies will transform themselves into learning organizations.
- Organizational emphasis on human performance management will accelerate.

According to *ASTD Models*, these trends not only drive change but also pose a host of possible ethical dilemmas for WLP professionals. The possible ethical breaches presented by each trend are summarized in Exhibit 7-5.

Exhibit 7-5: Possible ethical breaches stemming from workplace trends

	Trend	*Possible Ethical Breaches*
1	**Skill requirements will continue to increase in response to rapid technological change.**	• Ignoring or understating the costs and effort associated with upgrading the skills of employees who must cope with changing performance expectations resulting from the introduction of new technology • Advocating for a pure technological solution without considering its impact on the workforce • Terminating underskilled employees in lieu of providing sufficient learning opportunities and time for them to adapt to changing skill requirements • Knowingly ignoring the learning requirements, social needs, and human-related factors associated with technological change.

Exhibit 7-5: Possible ethical breaches stemming from workplace trends *(continued)*

	Trend	*Possible Ethical Breaches*
2	**The American workforce will be significantly more educated and diverse.**	• Recommending interventions that make sweeping changes in corporate culture, without fully understanding the impact these changes will produce • Knowingly using interventions that ignore the special needs, talents, or abilities of individuals • Making individual employment decisions based on factors other than the prospective employee's ability to achieve desired performance results or to learn the work • Limiting an employee's access to information in order to hide unethical practices of the organization.
3	**Corporate restructuring will continue to reshape the business environment.**	• Accepting cost reduction as the "right" solution without considering revenue enhancement or productivity improvement alternatives • Knowingly accepting short-term solutions that have a high probability of creating performance problems with immediate and long-term impact • Not taking the risk to explain the full implications of corporate restructuring, in order to preserve a personal relationship with the organization.
4	**The size and composition of training departments will change dramatically.**	• Knowingly recommending or implementing training interventions not linked to organizational strategic objectives or to customers' needs • Knowingly accepting WLP efforts without establishing learner and stakeholder accountability, or without allotting sufficient time or resources.
5	**Advances in technology will revolutionize training delivery.**	• Knowingly recommending or adopting unnecessary technologies (known as "technolust") • Intentionally failing to consider the full costs, time requirements, and importance of learner involvement in applying technology-based delivery methods • Selecting technologies that offer an easier implementation process for the WLP practitioner or a reduced cost for the organization, at the grave expense of the learners • Not equipping line managers with the tools they need to perform on-the-job training and coaching, in order to make formal training appear more effective • Not remaining objective about the effectiveness of alternative forms of training delivery due to a bias toward classroom training.

Exhibit 7-5: Possible ethical breaches stemming from workplace trends *(continued)*

	Trend	*Possible Ethical Breaches*
6	**Training departments will find new ways to deliver services.**	• Someone entering into an outside training contract for personal benefit (payoff, personal agenda, etc.). • Favoring certain providers for undisclosed reasons when the best interests of the organization are to do otherwise.
7	**There will be more focus on performance improvement.**	• Allowing short-term cost reductions or productivity increases to take precedence over long-term customer or employee satisfaction • Viewing performance improvement as the only goal, without regard to balancing individual and organizational needs or considering ethical issues • Allowing performance-improvement interventions to continue, although the level of trauma they are causing to employees is overwhelming • Replacing incumbent workers with new workers in order to avoid training and development costs; incumbent workers deserve a chance to develop the skills necessary to accomplish the desired level of performance.
8	**Integrated high-performance work systems will proliferate.**	• Overemphasizing humanistic or organizational needs at the expense of the other • The intentional misrepresentation to stakeholders that performance can be improved, without due consideration of organizational or humanistic needs • Attempts to apply a solution that is familiar to the WLP practitioner but that is not appropriate to the situation at hand • Honoring a client's request to institute teams in inappropriate situations. Line managers who do not fully understand the true requirements for supporting a team-based structure often prompt requests for teams. In these situations, the manager is simply trying to boost productivity by renaming the "department" a "team." This misunderstanding will probably lead to a botched attempt at teamwork.

Exhibit 7-5: Possible ethical breaches stemming from workplace trends *(continued)*

	Trend	*Possible Ethical Breaches*
9	**Companies will transform themselves into learning organizations.**	• Applying generic and potentially ineffective practices for expedience or ease, rather than defining the learning organization in the context of one corporate culture having unique decision-makers, customers, and stakeholders • Creating the expectation that practitioners can generate conditions characterizing a learning organization quickly, without much work, or with limited resources • "Selling" the idea of learning organizations to stakeholders as a cure-all for performance problems.
10	**Organizational emphasis on human performance management will accelerate.**	• Knowingly capitalizing on the trend by misrepresenting and overplaying the organization's needs in this area and encouraging the creation of programs that fill these "needs."

Adapted from Rothwell, W., Sanders, E., and Soper, J. (1999). *ASTD Models for Workplace Learning and Performance: Roles, Competencies, and Outputs.* Alexandria, VA: The American Society for Training and Development, pp. 99–103. Used by permission of ASTD. All rights reserved.

HOW CAN ETHICAL DILEMMAS BE RESOLVED?

According to *ASTD Models*, WLP professionals encountering an ethical dilemma during the course of their work should pose several important questions. While there is no absolute or infallible guidance, the answers to the following questions posed by the authors should help point the way to the most ethical answer for most situations. The questions are:

- What is just and fair?
- What leads to moderation?
- What results does an action or behavior seek?
- What works best over the long term?
- How would you like to be treated under the same circumstances?

Use these questions to help prompt critical reflection on ethical dilemmas encountered during the practice of WLP.

CHAPTER 8

Gazing into the Crystal Ball: What Changes Will the Future Bring to Workplace Learning and Performance?

WLP is a dynamic field. While the foundation of WLP is helping people and organizations improve performance, the field itself is undergoing dramatic and transformational change as a direct consequence of environmental pressures on organizations, new developments in organizational, group and individual learning theories and methods, and new approaches to achieving organizational results. This Chapter describes 10 trends affecting WLP.

AN OVERVIEW OF THE TRENDS

Ten trends are likely to affect WLP for the foreseeable future, according to Bassi, Buchanan, and Cheney (1997):

- *Trend 1*: Increasing skill requirements in response to rapid technological change
- *Trend 2*: Increasing education and diversity in the U.S. workforce
- *Trend 3*: Continuing corporate restructuring
- *Trend 4*: Changing size and composition of training departments
- *Trend 5*: Revolutionizing training through changes in delivery methods
- *Trend 6*: Finding new ways to deliver services
- *Trend 7*: Increasing focus on performance improvement
- *Trend 8*: Proliferating and integrated high-performance work systems
- *Trend 9*: Transforming into learning organizations
- *Trend 10*: Accelerating organizational emphasis on human performance management

Each trend, which is reported from the Bassi study and elaborated on in *ASTD Models*, presents unique new challenges to WLP professionals, their organizations, and their WLP practices. Like jugglers keeping many balls in the air at one time, WLP professionals are expected to continue helping individuals improve their work performance by learning new ways to do the work, new ways to improve services to customers and other stakeholders, and new ways of dealing with the pressures created by change and by global competition.

Trend 1: Increasing Skill Requirements in Response to Rapid Technological Change

Description and Importance of This Trend

The meaning of this trend should be clear enough. The technology that people use to do work in organizations is changing rapidly. As technology changes with great and increasing rapidity, people must have or be given the knowledge, skills, and attitudes they need to keep pace with these changes. "Without due appreciation for the need to help people use technology, organizations often experience a *productivity paradox* [emphasis added], which means that the level of productivity drops after they install new technology" (Rothwell, Sanders, and Soper 1999). Why does that happen? The answer is simple enough: Investments in gadgetry and gizmos are not enough. People must be shown how to *use* technology in order for productivity improvements to be realized. Unfortunately, it often seems that it takes longer to prepare people than it does to acquire the technology, and that changes in work methods wrought by technology require interventions to help people find new ways to work together.

More than one study has emphasized that changing technology is the most important trend of the future. Few can dispute that, at a time when a personal computer is outdated between the time the order is placed and the box arrives! Similar rapid technological changes are challenging everyone to keep pace. The growing use of e-commerce, which involves conducting business over the World Wide Web, the growing use of Enterprise Resource Planning that taps into the increased efficiency of integrated computer systems, and the increasing availability of desktop videoconferencing are but three of many technological challenges that face managers and workers of the future.

Implications of This Trend for WLP

According to *ASTD Models*, key implications of this trend for WLP include the following:

- "An increased need for continuous training to help people keep pace with changes in computer technology and its applications to tools, equipment, and work processes
- Increased research on informal, real-time learning that enables individuals to keep their skills current with advances in technology
- Increased appreciation for the importance of sociotechnical systems (the integration of technology with human social structures) such as work teams whose members collaborate over groupware
- Increased use of performance support systems, both manual and electronic, to help employees perform within the context of their work settings."

Trend 2: **Increasing Education and Diversity in the U.S. Workforce**

Description and Importance of This Trend

One of the many challenges facing managers of the future is the increase in educational levels and diversity among U.S. workers.

Educational attainment refers to the highest level of education achieved by individuals. This trend was explained by Andrea Adams (1997) of the U.S. Census Bureau and reported in *ASTD Models.* It was succinctly summarized as follows:

"Since the Bureau of the Census first collected data on educational attainment in the 1940 census, educational attainment among the American people has risen substantially. In 1940, one-fourth (24.5 percent) of all persons 25 years old and over had completed high school (or more education), and 1 in 20 (4.6 percent) had completed 4 years of high school or more, and over one-fifth (21.9 percent) had completed 4 or more years of college. The increase in educational attainment over the past half-century is primarily due to the higher educational attainment of young adults, combined with the attrition of older adults who typically had less formal education. For example, the percentage of persons 25 to 29 years old who were high school graduates rose from 38.1 percent in 1940 to 86.7 percent in 1993, while for persons 65 years old and over, it increased from 13.1 to 60.3 percent."

In short, younger people in the U.S. have made dramatic strides in educational attainment, and that can mean dramatic expectations for higher-level responsibilities at an earlier age than for others. That desire for "give it to me now" has only been exacerbated by recent shortages of skilled workers and by increasing cynicism among workers about how much security they can enjoy in the wake of downsizing, smartsizing, and outsourcing.

Diversity simply means differences. "The white population, the largest of the five race/ethnic groups, is projected to be the slowest-growing among the groups" between 1995 and 2025. The Census Bureau (Campbell 1996) also makes the following projections for the same time period:

- Some 24 million immigrants will be added to the U.S. population.
- The Asian population will be the fastest growing segment in all regions of the United States.
- The American Indian population, the least populous group, will grow to be the third fastest-growing population group in all regions of the United States.
- The population of Hispanics will increase rapidly over the 1995 to 2025 projection period, accounting for 44 percent of the growth in the nation's population (32 million Hispanics out of a total of 72 million persons added to the nation's population).
- The elderly population is expected to double in 21 states—age, as well as race and ethnicity, will contribute to an increasingly diverse workforce.

Current and future projections of the U.S. workforce are presented in Exhibit 8-1.

Exhibit 8-1: U.S. civilian labor force, 1982, 1993, and 1994, and projected 2005

Group	*Number (in thousands)*				*Numerical Change*		*Percent Change*	
	1982	1993	1994	2005	1982–1993	1994–2005	1982–1993	1994–2005 (estimated)
Total, 16 years and over	110,204	128,040	131,056	147,106	17,836	16,050	12.2	18.5
Men, 16 years and over	62,540	69,633	70,817	76,842	7,183	6,025	11.5	8.5
Women, 16 years and over	47,755	58,407	60,239	70,263	10,652	10,024	22.3	16.6
16 to 24	24,608	20,383	21,612	23,984	–4,225	2,372	–17.2	11.0
25 to 54	70,506	92,271	93,898	101,017	21,765	7,119	30.9	7.6
55 and over	15.092	15,386	15,547	22,105	294	6,558	1.9	42.2
White, 16 years and over	96,143	109,359	111,082	122,867	13,216	11,785	13.7	10.6
Black, 16 years and over	11,331	13,943	14,502	16,619	2,612	2,116	23.1	14.6
Asian and other, 16 years and over	2,729	4,742	5,474	7,632	2,013	2,158	73.8	39.4
Hispanic, 16 years and over	6,734	10,377	11,975	16,330	3,643	4,355	54.1	36.4
Other than Hispanic, 16 years and over	103,470	117,663	119,081	130,775	14,193	11,694	13.7	9.8
White, non-Hispanic	89,630	99,499	100,462	108,345	9,869	7,883	11.0	7.8

Note: Data for 1994 are not directly comparable with data for 1993 and 1982 because of the introduction of a **major** redesign of the Current Population Survey questionnaire and collection methodology and the introduction of 1990 census-based population controls, adjusted for the estimated undercount.

SOURCE: Bureau of Labor Statistics (BLS). *1994. U.S. Civilian Labor Force, 1982, 1993, and 1994 and Projected 2005. Office of Employment Projections.* Unpublished work. Presented at http://stats.bls.gov/emptab7.htm. Washington, D.C.: U.S. Department of Labor.

Implications of This Trend for WLP

Rothwell, Sanders, and Soper (1999) explored these trends extensively. The possible consequences of this trend include:

- Increased attention devoted to culture-specific, gender-specific, and age-specific interventions that facilitate learning and increase human performance
- Increased recognition of the importance of individual learning styles
- Learning programs customized for each individual that use technology to facilitate and quantify the learning experience
- Continued awareness of, and sensitivity to, individual and group differences during planned learning experiences.
- Individuals with responsibility for WLP will find themselves challenged to customize their services in order to meet diverse preferences and to help organizations learn how to leverage diversity in order to create innovative products and services.
- At the same time, diversity will undoubtedly create some performance problems that will require the problem-solving skills of everyone working in the organization.

Trend 3: **Continuing Corporate Restructuring**

Description and Importance of This Trend

Corporate restructuring, as *ASTD Models* defines it, "refers to the de-layering, business reengineering, and process improvement of organizations." It means that organizational decision-makers will continue to seek ways to work faster, harder, smarter, and leaner. As a direct consequence, efforts will continue to be made to: outsource work that is not related to the core competencies of the organization; use temporary and contingent staffing to cut expensive employee benefit costs and improve communication; and seek technological solutions to problems so as to avoid time-consuming people-oriented improvement strategies. Organizational decision-makers will also continue to pursue cost-containment strategies to reduce all expenses so as to remain globally competitive in labor costs.

Implications of This Trend for WLP

According to *ASTD Models*, the implications of this trend are likely to include all of the following:

- The incorporation of informal learning into work processes as a means of improving work processes without removing employees from the work setting
- The exploration of new organizational structures and designs to save money by de-layering
- A growing use of contingent workers to reduce employee benefit costs
- A continued focus on demonstrating effectiveness and return-on-investment for performance-improvement interventions

- An increased understanding of how greater human learning can improve the financial performance of organizations
- The revival of corporate succession-planning and career-development programs in order to ensure a steady stream of future leaders for an organization
- The increased use of interventions that develop competence and intellectual capital in an organization's workforce
- An increased need to train contingent employees who service the organization's customers.

Trend 4: Changing Size and Composition of Training Departments

Description and Importance of This Trend

ASTD Models explains this trend:

"One result of corporate downsizing has been a reluctance to increase the number of staff members in training departments, despite an increased demand for training services. In fact, the trend has been just the reverse. Many organizations have eliminated traditional training functions or outsourced them to universities, community colleges, vocational schools, consulting firms, and external training organizations. Another strategy is to require line managers or work-team leaders to use their own expertise to train their subordinates."

Despite an increasing demand for training services, then, the available evidence suggests that traditional training departments will continue to shrink. Services will be provided by other providers.

Implications of This Trend for WLP

The likely implications of this trend for WLP will include all of the following:

- Increased integration and sophistication of outsourcing partners—as well as increased expectations of them and increased accountability for results
- A keener awareness among top managers, line managers, and other WLP stakeholders of the practical difficulties in making training, as an isolated strategy, effective in creating or consolidating change efforts
- An increased reliance on alternative training delivery systems, including learning technologies and self-study courses, to train more people using fewer resources.

Trend 5: Revolutionizing Training through Changes in Delivery Methods

Description and Importance of This Trend

As explained in Chapter 2, organizations are seeking more cost-effective ways to deliver training than traditional classrooms. Nor is cost the only driver for making changes in delivery methods. Decision-makers seek to find ways to deliver more instruction at lower cost and to sometimes widely scattered worker populations. At the same time, many younger workers prefer technologically-based instructional delivery methods. As a result, the future holds in store a continuing revolution in ways that learning interventions are delivered.

Implications of This Trend for WLP

The implications of this trend for WLP include the following:

- An increased sophistication among stakeholders (policymakers and managers) and users (learners) about the range of instructional methods (for example, lectures, role play, and simulations), presentation methods (for example, multimedia, video, and electronic performance support systems), and distribution methods (for example, CD-ROM, the Internet, and satellite broadcasts).
- An increased expectation that organizations will apply technology to instruction, often on short notice and in real time.
- An increased willingness by learners to use the new technology and to understand its advantages and disadvantages.
- An increased sensitivity to the need to manage the environment around the users of learning technologies, without assuming that the technology will work effectively to achieve all purposes. This sensitivity will prompt a growing awareness of the importance of creating a total learning environment, which combines technology-based learning systems with social support networks that encourage collaborative learning. Also, it will prompt an increased understanding of how the technology must be transparent to the learner so that they can focus on the content. This transparency requires a deep commitment to masking the distance that inherently exists in "distance learning." The new paradigm must be akin to the "reach out and touch someone" paradigm that currently exists for the telephone.
- An increased willingness to use technology to assess learner progress and evaluate results.
- An increased need for learning professionals who also possess technological competencies such as the ability to use, select, and manage the full array of learning technologies available.

Trend 6: **Finding New Ways to Deliver Services**

Description and Importance of This Trend

WLP professionals will find that advances in technology will permit them to offer their services in new, innovative ways. Some of those are only dreamed of now. Examples of such technologies include Electronic Performance Support Systems, Expert Systems, Virtual Reality, and desktop consulting via desktop videoteleconferencing.

Implications of This Trend for WLP

Implications of this trend may include any or all of the following:

- Group decision technology that captures new knowledge using the Internet or a corporate intranet
- A new value placed on creative solutions that solve performance problems and identify new performance-improvement opportunities
- Real-time delivery methods, including one-on-one training as well as technology-assisted learning.

Trend 7: Increasing Focus on Performance Improvement

Description and Importance of This Trend

Focusing on performance improvement refers to an "awareness of the myriad ways to improve performance in organizational settings" (Rothwell et al 1999). It is necessitated by an increasingly fierce global competitive environment. It means that goals—and ultimate results—should always be at the forefront of attention.

Implications of this Trend for WLP

"An increasing focus on performance results is likely to produce an increased awareness of the full range of solutions applicable to the problems of achieving increased human and financial performance; the potential gains realized by integrating several solutions to achieve positive results in human performance; how changes in one part of an organization can affect other parts; and the organic nature of organizations (that is, the organizational "life cycle" of birth, growth, maturity, regression, and eventually death)" (Rothwell et al 1999).

Trend 8: Proliferating and Integrated High-Performance Work Systems

Description and Importance of This Trend

Since WLP efforts seek to achieve improved performance in organizational settings, it is not surprising that an important goal of WLP is building and sustaining a High Performance Workplace (HPW). A *High Performance Workplace* (HPW) is a work environment in which people can maximize their potential and achieve the highest possible work results. WLP efforts do not occur in isolation. Organizational conditions can help or hinder individual performance. In a HPW, individuals are able to be maximally productive because all barriers to their productivity have been knocked down. Management has thus created an environment inside the organization that promotes, encourages, rewards and maintains high performance.

Implications of This Trend for WLP

According to *ASTD models*, creating and sustaining a high performance workplace requires WLP professionals to:

- Isolate, measure, and maintain effective organizational conditions that are conducive to learning and performance
- Guide managers toward practices that nurture performance and learning
- Link WLP efforts to organizational strategies and core competencies.

Trend 9: Transforming into Learning Organizations

Description and Importance of This Trend

A *learning organization* is one in which people are encouraged to learn and one in which learning leads to performance. Organization decision-makers want to transform their organizations into learning organizations because, according to *ASTD models*, "a 'smarter' organization is a more profitable organization." But, like many terms in WLP, the authorities on the subject do not uniformly agree on the definition or the exact criteria by which to measure a learning organization. Yet, the view is that a learning organization will lead to a High Performance Workplace and thus to competitive success. It is thus likely that decision-makers will focus attention increasingly on finding ways to unleash human creativity so that it can lead to, and promote, competitive success.

Implications of This Trend for WLP

According to *ASTD models*, WLP practitioners will need to do all of the following in order to help their organizations meet the challenges posed by this trend:

- Encourage team learning, because many learning projects and many performance-improvement efforts occur in a group setting
- Establish shared visions so that people see the need for learning
- Build faster communication channels and collaborative communication systems so people can share what they learn
- Maintain a vibrant and efficient infrastructure that nurtures, supports, encourages, and rewards creative thinking that leads to increased performance and competitiveness.

Trend 10: **Accelerating Organizational Emphasis on Human Performance Management**

Description and Importance of This Trend

Performance management, though the term has various definitions, can be understood to mean continuous efforts to help people perform better. Its use is closely associated with the goals of establishing High Performance Workplaces and learning organizations. If individuals receive the right information, tools, and other resources to perform, and understand such things as what they are supposed to do and how to measure it, they can self-correct their own performance-problems and seize their own performance-improvement opportunities. That is the goal of performance management. Expect increasing attention on ways of helping individuals establish, manage, and even assess their own performance in real time.

Implications of This Trend for WLP

According to *ASTD models*, "applying performance-management theory within an organization probably will require WLP practitioners to:

- Establish performance targets and clarify work and performance expectations
- Communicate those expectations to the entire organization on a continuing basis
- Find better ways to provide faster, more specific feedback to performers
- Provide desirable incentives so that people want to perform, and tie meaningful rewards to goals so that people want to achieve the desired results."

PREPARING FOR THE FUTURE

Having reviewed the trends affecting WLP, professionals in the field should do some prognosticating of their own. After all, trends may well affect some industries, organizations, and individuals more than others. Use the Worksheet appearing in Exhibit 8-2 to rank the trends by their importance to your organization and your own job, and describe what you should do to adapt to these changing conditions. Use the Worksheet appearing in Exhibit 8-3 to rank the importance of the trends to the WLP field, and identify how those trends may affect each role of the WLP professional. Use your rankings to help you reflect on what those trends will mean for your organization and your own place in the WLP field.

Exhibit 8-2: A worksheet for assessing the importance of future forces to your organization and job

---

Directions: In Column 3 below, you will find a list of the Future Forces affecting WLP. In Column 1, rank the importance of each Future Force *to your organization*; in Column 2, rank the importance of the Future Force *to your job*. Then, in Column 4, describe what you believe should be done to adapt to (or anticipate) the Future Force as it affects your organization and job.

Column 1 Rank the importance of the future force *to your organization* (1 = Most Important)	Column 2 Rank the importance of the future force *to your job* (1 = Most Important)	Column 3 Future force	Column 4 What should be done to adapt to (or anticipate) the future force as it affects your organization and job?
1.		Increasing skill requirements in response to rapid technological change	
2.		Increasing education and diversity in the U.S. workforce	
3.		Continuing corporate restructuring	
4.		Changing size and composition of training departments	
5.		Revolutionizing training through changes in delivery methods	
6.		Finding new ways to deliver services	
7.		Increasing focus on performance improvement	

Exhibit 8-2: A worksheet for assessing the importance of future forces to your organization and job *(continued)*

Column 1 Rank the importance of the future force *to your organization* (1 = Most Important)	Column 2 Rank the importance of the future force *to your job* (1 = Most Important)	Column 3 Future force	Column 4 What should be done to adapt to (or anticipate) the future force as it affects your organization and job?
8.		Proliferating and integrated high-performance work systems	
9.		Transforming into learning organizations	
10.		Accelerating organizational emphasis on human performance management	

Exhibit 8-3: A worksheet for assessing the importance of future forces to the WLP field

Directions: In column 1 below you will find a list of the roles of WLP professionals. In column 2, you will find a list of future forces affecting the field. In column 3, note what you feel will be the most important future force affecting the role, and what should be done to prepare for it. There are, of course, no "right" or "wrong" answers. Add paper, if necessary.

Column 1 WLP Roles	**Column 2** Future forces affecting the field	**Column 3** What future force will be most important in affecting the role and what should be done to prepare for it?
1. **Manager**	• *Future Force 1*: Increasing skill requirements in response to rapid technological change • *Future Force 2*: Increasing education and diversity in the U.S. workforce • *Future Force 3*: Continuing corporate restructuring • *Future Force 4*: Changing size and composition of training departments • *Future Force 5*: Revolutionizing training through changes in delivery methods • *Future Force 6*: Finding new ways to deliver services • *Future Force 7*: Increasing focus on performance improvement • *Future Force 8*: Proliferating and integrated high-performance work systems • *Future Force 9*: Transforming into learning organizations • *Future Force 10*: Accelerating organizational emphasis on human performance management	
2. **Analyst**	• *Future Force 1*: Increasing skill requirements in response to rapid technological change • *Future Force 2*: Increasing education and diversity in the U.S. Workforce • *Future Force 3*: Continuing corporate restructuring • *Future Force 4*: Changing size and composition of training departments • *Future Force 5*: Revolutionizing training through changes in delivery methods • *Future Force 6*: Finding new ways to deliver services • *Future Force 7*: Increasing focus on performance improvement	

Exhibit 8-3: A worksheet for assessing the importance of future forces to the WLP field *(continued)*

Column 1 WLP Roles	Column 2 Future forces affecting the field	Column 3 What future force will be most important in affecting the role and what should be done to prepare for it?
	• *Future Force 8*: Proliferating and integrated high-performance work systems • *Future Force 9*: Transforming into learning organizations • *Future Force 10*: Accelerating organizational emphasis on human performance management	
3. **Intervention Selector**	• *Future Force 1*: Increasing skill requirements in response to rapid technological change • *Future Force 2*: Increasing education and diversity in the U.S. workforce • *Future Force 3*: Continuing corporate restructuring • *Future Force 4*: Changing size and composition of training departments • *Future Force 5*: Revolutionizing training through changes in delivery methods • *Future Force 6*: Finding new ways to deliver services • *Future Force 7*: Increasing focus on performance improvement • *Future Force 8*: Proliferating and integrated high-performance work systems • *Future Force 9*: Transforming into learning organizations • *Future Force 10*: Accelerating organizational emphasis on human performance management	
4. **Intervention Designer and Developer**	• *Future Force 1*: Increasing skill requirements in response to rapid technological change • *Future Force 2*: Increasing education and diversity in the U.S. workforce • *Future Force 3*: Continuing corporate restructuring • *Future Force 4*: Changing size and composition of training departments • *Future Force 5*: Revolutionizing training through changes in delivery methods • *Future Force 6*: Finding new ways to deliver services	

Exhibit 8-3: A worksheet for assessing the importance of future forces to the WLP field *(continued)*

Column 1 WLP Roles	Column 2 Future forces affecting the field	Column 3 What future force will be most important in affecting the role and what should be done to prepare for it?
	• *Future Force 7*: Increasing focus on performance improvement • *Future Force 8*: Proliferating and integrated high-performance work systems • *Future Force 9*: Transforming into learning organizations • *Future Force 10*: Accelerating organizational emphasis on human performance management	
5. **Intervention Implementor**	• *Future Force 1*: Increasing skill requirements in response to rapid technological change • *Future Force 2*: Increasing education and diversity in the U.S. workforce • *Future Force 3*: Continuing corporate restructuring • *Future Force 4*: Changing size and composition of training departments • *Future Force 5*: Revolutionizing training through changes in delivery methods • *Future Force 6*: Finding new ways to deliver services • *Future Force 7*: Increasing focus on performance improvement • *Future Force 8*: Proliferating and integrated high-performance work systems • *Future Force 9*: Transforming into learning organizations • *Future Force 10*: Accelerating organizational emphasis on human performance management	
6. **Change Leader**	• *Future Force 1*: Increasing skill requirements in response to rapid technological change • *Future Force 2*: Increasing education and diversity in the U.S. workforce • *Future Force 3*: Continuing corporate restructuring • *Future Force 4*: Changing size and composition of training departments • *Future Force 5*: Revolutionizing training through changes in delivery methods	

Exhibit 8-3: A worksheet for assessing the importance of future forces to the WLP field *(continued)*

Column 1 WLP Roles	Column 2 Future forces affecting the field	Column 3 What future force will be most important in affecting the role and what should be done to prepare for it?
	• *Future Force 6*: Finding new ways to deliver services • *Future Force 7*: Increasing focus on performance improvement • *Future Force 8*: Proliferating and integrated high-performance work systems • *Future Force 9*: Transforming into learning organizations • *Future Force 10*: Accelerating organizational emphasis on human performance management	
7. **Evaluator**	• *Future Force 1*: Increasing skill requirements in response to rapid technological change • *Future Force 2*: Increasing education and diversity in the U.S. workforce • *Future Force 3*: Continuing corporate restructuring • *Future Force 4*: Changing size and composition of training departments • *Future Force 5*: Revolutionizing training through changes in delivery methods • *Future Force 6*: Finding new ways to deliver services • *Future Force 7*: Increasing focus on performance improvement • *Future Force 8*: Proliferating and integrated high-performance work systems • *Future Force 9*: Transforming into learning organizations • *Future Force 10*: Accelerating organizational emphasis on human performance management	

3

REVIEWING AND SELECTING PERFORMANCE-IMPROVEMENT STRATEGIES

Part Three comprises Chapters 9 through 16. It summarizes learning interventions and organizational performance-improvement interventions in workplace settings. More specifically, it focuses on these questions:

- What is performance?
- What is a model?
- What model can help conceptualize performance?
- How can the results of human performance analysis be used to select appropriate performance-improvement strategies?
- What is Strategic Planning, and how can WLP help an organization adapt to external environmental change?
- What is Human Resource Planning, and how can WLP help an organization match HR supplies with HR needs?
- What are learning, instructing, and instructional planning, and why are they important for WLP professionals?
- How can WLP develop individuals as instruments of organizational learning, and how can it educate and train them to meet job requirements?

CHAPTER 9

Charting the Big Picture: Analyzing Human Performance in Organizations

WLP is instituted and carried out in organizations to achieve improved performance—improved productivity, profitability, customer service, and quality. It is thus a purposeful effort, directed toward improving human performance by increasing the efficiency and effectiveness of individuals, groups, and organizations through planned change efforts.

But what is performance? Can it be improved through use of a model? And what *is* a model? What comprehensive model can be used to help WLP professionals conceptualize the many dimensions of human performance in organizational settings? How can such a model be applied to select appropriate performance-improvement strategies? This Chapter addresses these important questions.

WHAT IS PERFORMANCE?

Defining Performance

Performance as defined by Nash (1983) means "to do, to accomplish. The act of performing means to carry out a goal or responsibility. Performance is the thing done. At one time the word *perform* meant to discharge one's function, to do one's part. Later, the word *performance* was used to mean the accomplishment, carrying out, or doing of work. It was also used with the connotation of carrying out a command or duty."

Performance now connotes accomplishment, achievement, or results. It should not be confused with *cues to performance*, which are indicators of when people should perform. Nor should it be confused with the *means of achieving results*—observable actions or unobservable mental processes carried out in the process of realizing achievement. Finally, performance should not be confused with *environment*, the setting in which people perform. While cues, means, and environment do affect results and are important, they are not synonymous with performance. (See Exhibit 9-1.)

Exhibit 9-1: Distinguishing between performance, cues, behavior, and environment

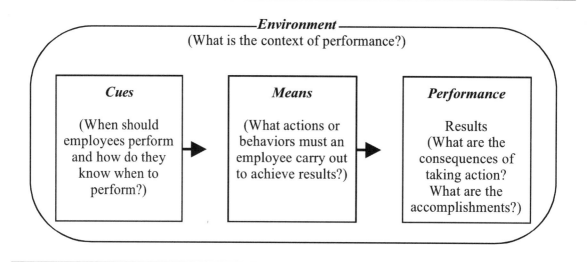

Levels of Performance

Performance occurs on more than one plane of the organizational landscape. In a broad sense, machines, people and capital are all capable of performing. However, WLP professionals usually direct their attention to the human side of the enterprise more than to the organization's financial or market condition.

On the other hand, *human performance* also occurs on more than one level—individual, group, and organizational. Each level is interrelated. Each level may also be appropriately considered the focus of planned change, though the scope and direction of planned change efforts may differ widely. Many variables influence performance at each level.

WLP AND HUMAN PERFORMANCE TECHNOLOGY (HPT)

Many WLP professionals equate WLP closely with Human Performance Technology (HPT) and Human Performance Improvement (HPI). While definitions are not fixed in practice and are thus subject to heated debate, *Human Performance Technology* can be defined as Rosenberg (1990) suggested: "The total performance improvement system is a merger of systematic performance analysis with comprehensive human resource interventions. And the science of linking the total system together is known as human performance technology." In contrast, *Human Performance Improvement* (HPI) has been defined as "the systematic process of discovering and analyzing important human performance gaps, planning for future improvements in human performance, designing and developing cost-effective and ethically justifiable interventions to close performance gaps, implementing the interventions, and evaluating the financial and nonfinancial results" (Rothwell 1996).

Human Performance Technology bears at least eight distinctive characteristics that distinguish it from other fields. They are described below and summarized in Exhibit 9-2.

Exhibit 9-2: A summary of eight distinctive characteristics of human performance technology

---

Characteristic 1

Human Performance Technology distinguishes between human performance and behavior.

Characteristic 2

HPT determines worthy performance as a function of the value of the accomplishment and the costs to achieve it.

Characteristic 3

HPT applies systems approaches to five components of human performance technology systems—the job, the person, responses, consequences, and feedback.

Characteristic 4

HPT focuses on engineering competent human performance.

Characteristic 5

HPT emphasizes analysis of performance problems, needs, and goals.

Characteristic 6

HPT emphasizes the role of exemplary or exceptional performance.

Characteristic 7

HPT focuses on identifying and addressing causes of human performance problems.

Characteristic 8

HPT tends to favor the application of five classes of performance-improvement strategies to problems—training, job performance aids, feedback systems, employee selection, and organizational redesign.

SOURCE: Jacobs, R. (1987). *Human Performance Technology: A Systems-Based Field for the Training and Development Profession.* (Information Series No. 326.) Columbus, OH: ERIC Clearinghouse on Adult, Career, and Vocational Education, The National Center for Research in Vocational Education, p. x. Used by permission.

Characteristic 1: HPT distinguishes between human performance and behavior. Performance is associated with results or achievement; behavior is associated with the process by which results are achieved. The chief thrust of HPT is on improving results (the end sought), and not so much on behaviors (the means to the end).

Characteristic 2: HPT determines worthy performance as a function of the value of the accomplishment and the costs to achieve it. HPT stresses the ratio between high productivity and the costs or investments necessary to realize improvement. No improvement effort or intervention is free, of course. The key question for human performance technologists is this: Will the benefits of an intervention outweigh its costs? In this context, "benefits" is a word loaded with more meanings than just financial value. It can also refer to simpler issues: Did an intervention meet business needs (even when not easily translated into monetary terms)? Did an intervention improve customer service or customer satisfaction? Build or sustain teamwork? Help individuals realize potential? Build market share or shareholder value? All these issues, and more, are related to benefits.

Characteristic 3: HPT applies systems approaches to five components of human performance technology systems—the job, the person, responses, consequences, and feedback. When examining performance problems, human performance technologists look at them against the backdrop of the work, the person doing the work, responses to work-related stimuli or cues, the consequences of the work performed, and feedback received on performance. Separate actions can be taken to improve performance when the underlying cause of a problem is traceable to one or more of these factors. Human performance technologists do not believe that all problems should necessarily be addressed by training, education, or Organization Development; rather, they believe that the solution should be targeted to address the problem. There are many possible solutions or interventions, and they can even be used in isolation or in combination with others.

Characteristic 4: HPT focuses on engineering competent human performance. Organizations exert considerable influence over employee productivity. There are five major strategies for improving productivity. One is to increase production faster than new workers are added. A second is to boost production with the same number of workers. A third is to cut back the number of workers while producing nearly the same outputs. A fourth is to preserve the same level of sales or production with fewer workers. A fifth and final strategy is to reduce the number of workers while increasing sales or production.

Many of today's organizations are striving to become more competitive by reducing staff while maintaining output levels. Innovative staffing solutions, themselves fraught with special challenges for WLP professionals, are also being used to improve employee productivity while cutting labor costs. These strategies include employee leasing, job enrichment and job enlargement, self-directed work teams in which jobs become more enriched and less rigorously-defined, and the growing use of retired, temporary, contingent, or part-time workers.

Characteristic 5: HPT emphasizes analysis of performance problems, needs, and goals. Human performance technologists do not undertake productivity-improvement efforts chiefly for altruistic motives. Instead, they are concerned most about solving identifiable problems, averting possible future problems, meeting organizational and individual needs, and achieving work-related goals. They place less emphasis on WLP efforts geared solely to personal growth and more emphasis on WLP efforts with clearly-identified payoffs to the employer.

Characteristic 6: HPT emphasizes the role of exemplary or exceptional performance. By examining differences between the best and worst performers in a group or organization, performance technologists can often find clues leading to productivity improvement. Performance technologists call the best performers the *exemplars*, meaning "those who excel." By studying exemplars, performance technologists believe it is possible to find innovative ways to do the work and improve performance. One aim is to transform all or most employees into exemplars, or at least to work on narrowing or closing the gap between the best and worst performers.

Characteristic 7: HPT focuses on identifying and addressing causes of human performance problems. Performance technologists believe that the causes of performance problems must be determined before effective solutions can be formulated, identified, and implemented. Some problems stem from knowledge, skill, or attitude deficiencies. These problems may lend themselves to *learning interventions* such as training, education, employee development, career development, or Organization Development. Other problems stem from other causes—such as lack of individual motivation, lack of practice, poor feedback, poor supervision, inadequate incentives, or other causes. These problems lend themselves to *organizational interventions* such as increasing opportunities for individual practice, tackling tough employee discipline issues, improving feedback methods, exploring new approaches to supervision, and introducing innovative employee incentive or reward programs.

Characteristic 8: HPT tends to favor the application of five classes of performance-improvement strategies to problems: training, job performance aids, feedback systems, employee selection, and organizational redesign. Human performance technologists devote their attention primarily, though not exclusively, to five types of interventions to performance problems (Jacobs 1987).

Training is used only when problems are caused by individual deficiencies in knowledge, skill, or attitude. It is the intervention of last resort, not first resort, because rigorous, effective training is expensive to design and deliver. Other solutions are geared to improving workers' real-time access to critical job-related information (such as job performance aids, Electronic Performance Support Systems, or Expert Systems), information that individuals receive before, during, and after they perform (feedback systems), people chosen to perform the work or receive training (employee selection), and the way work duties and tasks are organized and responsibilities are assigned (organizational and job design). Performance technologists are thus concerned about appropriately identifying solutions that are intended to address underlying causes of performance problems.

WHAT MODELS CAN HELP CONCEPTUALIZE PERFORMANCE?

What is a Model?

A *model* is a simplified representation of an otherwise complex phenomenon. A model provides a roadmap to change, allowing WLP professionals to label variables influencing performance. Indeed, it can help in the identification of performance problems and the selection of one or more appropriate solutions.

The process of identifying performance problems using a model is called *performance analysis*, a phrase synonymous with *front-end analysis*. It is the heart of performance technology. After all, performance technologists emphasize analysis of performance problems, needs, and goals (see Characteristic 5 in Exhibit 9-2) and identification of the underlying causes of those problems (see Characteristic 7 in Exhibit 9-2).

Three Kinds of Performance-Analysis Models

There are three kinds of performance-analysis models: *comprehensive, situational,* and *process*. While these distinctions may blur in practice, they can help conceptualize ways of thinking about *performance analysis*, which is (of course) "the process of identifying the organization's performance requirements and comparing them to its objectives and capabilities" (Rothwell 1996).

A Comprehensive Performance-Analysis Model

A comprehensive performance-analysis model focuses on the big picture (macro-level). It is useful for WLP professionals and others who wish to review and analyze many issues affecting human performance economically and quickly in order to highlight potential or existing problems that warrant corrective action. Big picture issues include any of the following: (1) How is the organization adapting to change? (2) How is the organization competing? (3) How are the right people being matched to the right jobs and job assignments at the right times? (4) How is the organization structuring work, establishing guidelines for action, rewarding employee efforts, or matching appropriate leaders to activities? WLP professionals sometimes rely on a comprehensive performance-analysis model to guide their efforts when they are entering an organization for the first time or reviewing the organization's existing status with an eye peeled toward setting long-term improvement priorities.

One of the best-known comprehensive models was devised by Thomas F. Gilbert, who is sometimes regarded as the father of human performance technology. It is described at length in his classic *Human Competence: Engineering Worthy Performance* (1978). The model was originally designed to identify the many important variables that collectively lead to *competence* (meaning "desired performance") in organizational settings

Gilbert's model is based on two key assumptions. First, performance analysis should be carried out through a predictable three-step process. Second, human performance lends itself to analysis from more than one viewpoint. Gilbert believes it is essential to specify that viewpoint at the outset of analysis.

Gilbert's three-step process is fundamentally simple, but analytically powerful. (See Exhibit 9-3). **The first step** is to devise a model of performance. WLP professionals do that by clarifying precisely what is expected or what should be happening. Examples of performance models might include assumptions underlying job descriptions, job performance standards, or measurable performance objectives. The **second** step is to measure existing performance. WLP professionals should collect information about how well individuals, groups, or the organization is presently performing and compare it to the model of performance. The result will indicate the size of the performance gap, the difference between *what is happening* and *what should be happening*. The **third** and final step is to identify appropriate methods of improving performance.

Exhibit 9-3: Three stages of analysis

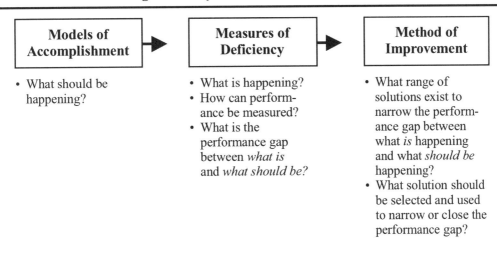

SOURCE: Gilbert, T. (1978). *Human Competence: Engineering Worthy Performance.* New York: McGraw-Hill, p. 124. Used by permission of McGraw-Hill.

Gilbert points out that "we can view human accomplishments at several levels of generality, and the values we assign to these accomplishments at each level will be derived from the level just above them." He proposes six such vantage levels.

Gilbert's three analytical steps and vantage points are combined to form what he calls a *performance matrix* (see Exhibit 9-4). This is useful for identifying human performance problems, measuring deficiencies, and uncovering possible performance-improvement strategies. Training is by no means the only strategy: In the matrix, Gilbert highlights policy (*institutional systems*), strategy (*job systems*), and tactics (*task systems*).

Exhibit 9-4: Gilbert's performance matrix

Stages / Levels	A Accomplishment Models	B Measures of Opportunity	C Methods of Improvement
I Policy (Institutional Systems)	*Organization models* 1. Cultural goal of the organization 2. Major missions 3. Requirements and units 4. Exemplary standards	*Stakes analysis* 1. Performance measures 2. PIPs 3. Stakes 4. Critical roles	*Programs and policies* 1. Environmental programs (data/tools/ incentives) 2. People programs (Knowledge/selection/ recruiting) 3. Management programs (organization/ resources/standards
II Strategy (Job Systems)	*Job models* 1. Mission of job 2. Major responsibilities 3. Requirements and units 4. Exemplary standards	*Job assessment* 1. Performance measures 2. PIPs 3. Critical responsibilities	*Job strategies* 1. Data systems 2. Training designs 3. Incentive schedules 4. Human factors 5. Selection systems 6. Recruitment systems
III Tactics (Task Systems)	*Task models* 1. Responsibilities of tasks 2. Major duties 3. Requirements and units 4. Exemplary standards	*Task analysis* 1. Performance measures or observations 2. PIPs 3. Specific deficiencies 4. Cost of programs	*Tactical instruments* 1. Feedback 2. Guidance 3. Training 4. Reinforcement 5. Etc.

SOURCE: Gilbert, T. (1978). *Human Competence: Engineering Worthy Performance*. New York: McGraw-Hill, p.137. Used by permission of the publisher. Copyright Praxis Corporation, 1976.

Gilbert suggests that attention be focused on nine key questions. The first three questions focus on management issues. WLP professionals should ask these questions: (1) Can performance be improved by changing organizational policies? (2) Can performance be improved by changing the way resources are allocated? or (3) Can it be improved by changing job performance standards? The next three questions focus on environmental issues. WLP professionals should ask: (4) Can performance be improved by changing the information or feedback people receive about their work? (5) Can performance be improved by changing the instruments or tools provided to people to do their work? (6) Can it be improved by changing the incentives or rewards people receive for their work? The last three focus on behavioral issues. WLP professionals should ask: (7) Can performance be improved by changing the knowledge people possess about their work? (8) Can it be improved by changing the people selected to do the work? (9) Can performance be improved by changing the people recruited to do the work?

Gilbert's performance matrix is a powerful aid for troubleshooting performance problems. Other comprehensive models for performance analysis have been proposed. But not all models for analyzing human performance are comprehensive in scope. Some are intended to address specific situations or problems.

A Situational Performance Analysis Model

Unlike a comprehensive performance-analysis model, a situational model focuses on the particulars of one event, situation, problem, or plea for help. It is thus geared to the micro-level. A situational model is useful for in-depth analysis when WLP professionals are approached by operating managers to implement a specific performance-improvement strategy ("My employees need a training course on writing" or "This company needs to conduct an attitude survey"), or when called upon to examine a unique problem affecting one person, work group, or department.

Perhaps the best-known situational model was devised by Robert Mager and Peter Pipe and described in their classic book *Analyzing Performance Problems, or 'You Really Oughta Wanna'* (1970). Study the model carefully (it is shown in Exhibit 9-5). With an existing problem situation clearly in mind, read the model from the top down. The steps in the model suggest a specific sequence of questions for WLP professionals to consider:

1. **What is the problem or performance deficiency?**
2. **Is the problem or deficiency important?**
   - If it is not important, ignore it.
   - If it is important, consider question 3.
3. **Is it a skill deficiency?**
   - If the answer to this question is *yes*, then consider:
     — Are employees used to performing?
       If not, consider formal training.
       If so, consider the next question.
     — Are employees performing the skill often?
       If not, arrange opportunities for them to practice.
       If so, arrange feedback on how well they are performing the skill.

(Text continued on page 207)

Exhibit 9-5: Mager and Pipe's troubleshooting model

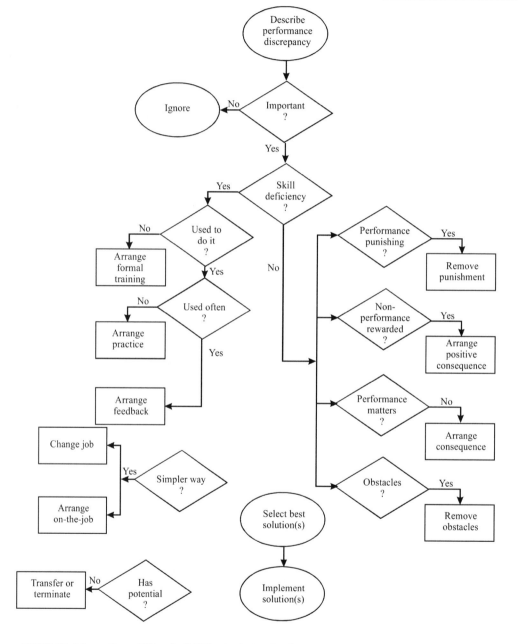

SOURCE: Mager, R. and Pipe, P. (1970). *Analyzing Performance Problems, or 'You Really Oughta Wanna'*. Belmont, CA: David S. Lake Publisher. Used by permission of the publisher.

(Text continued from page 205)

- If the answer to this question is *no*, then consider:
    — Is the performance punishing? Do employees experience some punishment (real or perceived) when doing what they are supposed to do?
        If the performance is punishing, then remove the punishment.
        If the performance is not punishing, then consider the next question.
    — Is the performance unrewarding?
        If so, then arrange rewards.
        If not, consider the next question.
    — Is performance considered important to employees?
        If not, then arrange for employees to see the results or receive information about outcomes of what they do.
        If so, consider the next question.

4. **If there is a skill deficiency, can it be removed by a method simpler than formal training?**
    - If it can, then
        — Change the job through work redesign.
        — Arrange on-the-job training.
    - If it cannot, then design and deliver formal training.

5. **Does the individual have potential for improvement?**
    - If so, offer formal training.
    - If not, transfer or terminate the employee.

6. **Is it clear which solution or solutions will be best-suited to addressing this performance problem?**
    - If not, gather more information.
    - If so, then consider question 7.

7. **Is it clear how to implement solutions?**
    - If not, develop an implementation plan.
    - If so, then:
        — Select content and delivery methods.
        — Select instructors.

This model is a very powerful one, suggesting several performance-improvement strategies as alternatives to planned off-the-job training. The model is usually associated with so-called *front-end analysis*, which involves troubleshooting a performance problem before taking action to correct the deficiency (Harless 1978).

A Process Performance Analysis Model

Unlike a comprehensive performance analysis model that focuses on macro-level issues and a situational model that focuses on micro-level issues, a process performance-analysis model focuses on either one. It is less directed to scope (the size of the change effort) or situation (the events leading to a request for improvement) than it is on the process carried out by WLP practitioners to diagnose the performance problem and find one or more interventions/solutions to address it. A process model is thus useful for guiding WLP practitioners as they go about their work. It can be applied to either or both macro-level or micro-level issues.

Perhaps the best-known process performance analysis model is the HPI process model described in *ASTD Models for Human Performance Improvement* (1996) and in *ASTD Models for Workplace Learning and Performance*. The HPI process model is "a six-step model that describes key steps in conducting human performance improvement work" (Rothwell 1996). Study the model carefully (it is shown in Exhibit 9-6). Like the situational model, the model suggests a specific sequence of questions for WLP professionals to consider:

Step 1: Performance analysis: "At this point, people who do human performance work identify and describe past, present, and future human performance gaps."

Step 2: Cause analysis: "At this point, the root causes of a past, present, or future performance gap are identified. In other words, the question *Why does this performance gap exist?* is answered."

Step 3: Selection of appropriate interventions: "Here people who do human performance-improvement work consider possible ways to close past, present, or possible future performance gaps by addressing their root cause(s)."

Step 4: Implementation: "People who do human performance-improvement work help the organization prepare to install an intervention."

Step 5: Change management: "During this step, people who do human performance-improvement work should monitor the intervention as it is being implemented."

Step 6: Evaluation and measurement: "Those conducting human performance-improvement work take stock of the results achieved by the intervention."

Exhibit 9-6: ASTD human performance improvement (HPI) process model

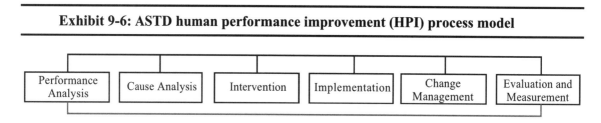

SOURCE: Rothwell, W. (1996). *ASTD Models for Human Performance Improvement: Roles, Competencies, and Outputs*. Alexandria, VA: The American Society for Training and Development, p. 13. Used by permission of ASTD. All rights reserved.

Note that, in this particular model, every stage of the performance-improvement process is covered. Its focus is not on diagnosis or troubleshooting alone: Instead, it emphasizes a systematic process that includes follow-up and follow-through on the intervention selected to narrow or close the performance gap. The HPI process model is an important tool in the toolkit of every WLP professional.

ROTHWELL AND SREDL'S COMPREHENSIVE *PERFORMANCE ANALYSIS MODEL*

The remainder of this Chapter—and this volume—focuses on big picture issues. The comprehensive model described in this section provides a conceptual scheme for thinking about macro-level issues in planning and monitoring organizational performance and selecting appropriate human performance-improvement interventions.

Performance Analysis and Radar

For just a moment, set aside your thoughts about WLP and think about something that may seem totally unrelated to human performance analysis—*radar*. An amazing invention, radar is based on a simple principle: When sound waves are projected from a fixed or moving source, objects entering their path create an echo. The echo bounces back to the source. Through electronic wizardry, the echo is translated into an image on a radar screen. The shape and size of the image roughly correspond to a scaled-down version of the object's shape and size. The object's movement is discernible as new sound waves are projected outward from the source and recurrent echoes return. The center of a radar screen indicates the source of the sound waves; a light beam appearing on the screen indicates the sweep of sound as it is projected outward. As an object approaches the radar source, it moves toward the center of the radar screen.

An Overview of Rothwell and Sredl's Model

Now imagine a powerful series of radar screens that can help an WLP professional review or monitor human performance in organizational settings. (See Exhibit 9-7.) This screen, however, is much more powerful than conventional radar. Comprised of a series of separate but related circles that represent proximity, they allow WLP professionals to identify and trouble-shoot human performance problems and their causes. Moreover, they show that performance issues at each level are affected by conditions at higher levels.

Notice that these radar screens are intended to portray the environment inside and outside the organization. The screens help WLP professionals survey big-picture issues. Unlike traditional radar, any blips appearing on these screens portray images of human performance problems, past, present, or future. Such an overview is needed because in today's frenetically-paced organizations, WLP professionals frequently find themselves facing a quandary as they confront too many performance problems that demand their time, attention, and action. In this respect, WLP professionals are much like overworked air traffic controllers, viewing radar screens jammed with many objects of varying shapes and sizes moving simultaneously in different directions.

Exhibit 9-7: Rothwell and Sredl's comprehensive performance analysis model: An overview

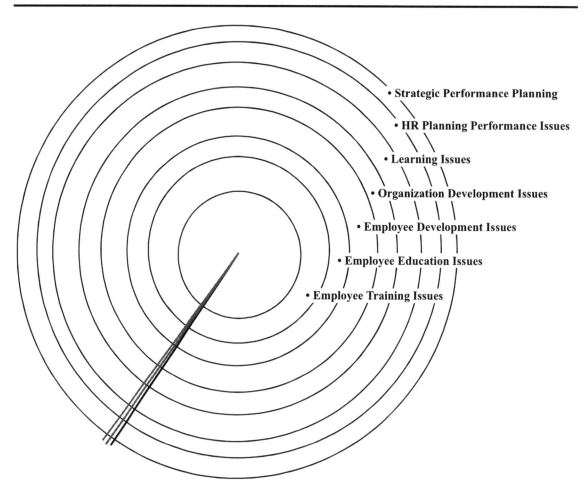

• Strategic Performance Planning

• HR Planning Performance Issues

• Learning Issues

• Organization Development Issues

• Employee Development Issues

• Employee Education Issues

• Employee Training Issues

Appreciating the meaning of each screen is important in its own right; however, reading each screen and assigning priorities for action is more important. Let us now turn to an examination of each successive "screen" in this series of related screens. As you read these descriptions, bear in mind that the assignment of labels to each successive level is somewhat arbitrary. Other, more detailed radar screens can be added for analytical purposes in one organizational setting when necessary.

Strategic-Planning Performance Issues

Begin examining any organization by focusing on how well it is functioning in its external environment and how well it is adapting to and anticipating change. Begin at this level because every organization, like any open system, is absolutely dependent on its external environment for inputs and outputs. After all, organizations obtain raw materials as well as capital and technology for transforming those raw materials into finished goods or services. Once organizational processes have transformed raw materials into finished goods or services, consumers or service recipients in the external environment determine if and how much the organization will profit from its activities. Hence, environmental performance is critical to an organization's continued survival or success.

When examining environmental performance issues, direct attention first to the following questions:

- Is the organization adapting to changes occurring in the external environment?
- Is the organization anticipating external changes before they occur?
- Is the organization itself conducive to performance? (In other words, has management taken steps to create working conditions and a work environment that is conducive to performance by its members?)

If you can answer *yes* to these questions, then consider this radar screen clear. Move on to the next screen.

But if you must answer *no* to one or more questions, then visualize a large blip appearing on the radar screen. You have a performance problem that can impede the organization's continued survival or success. Direct attention to action at this level. See Chapter 10 for more information about Strategic Planning issues and organizational interventions.

HR Planning Performance Issues

In your analysis, turn next to the screen labeled "HR Planning Performance Issues." Human resource issues provide an important context for planning and managing interventions. Performance-improvement strategies can be divided into two major categories: learning interventions and organizational interventions.

When examining HR planning issues, direct attention first to the following questions:

- Is the organization effective in its efforts to match up the number and kinds of people it needs to available supplies?
- Is the organization taking appropriate steps to anticipate and prepare for the number and kinds of people it will need in the future?

If you can answer *yes* to both questions, then consider this radar screen clear. Move on to the next screen.

But if you must answer *no* to one or both questions, then visualize a large blip appearing before you on this screen. You now have a performance problem that can impede the organization's continued survival or success. Direct attention to action at this level. See Chapter 11 for more information about HR planning issues.

Learning Issues

Now turn to the screen labeled *Learning Issues*. WLP has many components, but they share a common base in theories of human learning. WLP's components must be *integrated* if planned learning interventions are to be successful. Devote some time to pondering how well the organization is planning for human learning and instruction.

When examining Learning issues, direct attention to these questions:

- Is the organization effectively planning for human learning?
- Is the organization effectively integrating such activities as Organization Development, Employee Development, Employee Education, and Employee Training?

If you can answer *yes* to both questions, then consider this radar screen clear. Move on to the Organization Development screen.

But if you must answer *no* to one or both questions, then direct attention to action at this level. See Chapter 12 for more information about Learning, Instruction, and Instructional Planning issues.

Organization Development Issues

Turn next to the screen labeled *Organization Development Issues*. At this point, consider how well the organization's *culture* (perhaps best understood as "how we do things here") matches up to environmental and work demands. Successful organizations have cultures contributing to, or leading to, their success. In addition, consider how well people are cooperating and collaborating in solving the problems confronting the organization, its work groups, and its employees.

When examining Organization Development issues, direct attention first to the following questions:

- Does the organization's culture match up to its present demands?
- Will the culture facilitate organizational changes made to anticipate or adapt to external environmental changes?
- Are individuals and work groups cooperating effectively to solve problems and make decisions?

If you can answer *yes* to these questions, regard this radar screen as clear. Devote your attention to the next screen.

But if you must answer *no* to any of these questions, then direct attention to this level. See Chapter 13 for more information about Organization Development.

Employee Development Issues

Organizations are composed of people. To a considerable extent, individuals are the chief instruments by which organizational learning occurs. Hence, to foster organizational learning and human continuity, an organization's leaders frequently sponsor activities intended to search out new ideas from the external environment, give individuals new insights for their own personal growth, and develop them over the long term for more challenging work responsibilities. These are called *Employee Development* efforts.

Having completed analysis of Organization Development issues, focus your attention next on the radar screen labeled *Employee Development Issues*. Ask yourself these questions:

- Is the organization taking steps to develop individuals for positions and work that are critically important to the organization?
- Is the organization taking steps to give individuals new ideas and new insights that may or may not have immediate, practical application?

If you can answer *yes* to these questions, then devote your attention to the next screen. Otherwise, see Chapter 14 for more information on Employee Development.

Employee Education Issues

Few individuals wish to remain static throughout their careers. While some do prefer to forego increasing responsibilities and devote their attention to matters outside the workplace, others are interested in making career progress. To that end, they must take steps to prepare themselves for future jobs or future work responsibilities. When WLP efforts are directed to helping individuals prepare themselves for career advancement, they are called *employee education* efforts. Frequently, these efforts are tied to career planning and career development activities.

When examining employee education issues, pose the following questions:

- Is the organization effectively communicating its present work requirements to employees so they can take steps to prepare themselves for advancement?
- Is the organization effectively communicating its future work requirements to employees so they can keep their skills current?
- Are individuals clarifying their future career goals and taking steps, through planned learning, to realize them?

If you can answer *yes* to these questions, then consider this radar screen clear. Otherwise, direct your attention to Chapter 15 for more information about Employee Education.

Employee Training Issues

Jobs are a key interface between individuals and organizations. Many people find their identity through their jobs. From jobs, individuals take cues about what they are expected to do in the workplace, how well they are expected to perform, to whom they report, and other issues of major importance to their productivity and job satisfaction.

Few individuals enter a job knowing everything they need to know. Few can keep current without needing some training, whether planned or unplanned. When WLP efforts are directed to helping individuals master their job responsibilities or keep current with job requirements, they are called *employee training* efforts. When examining job performance issues from the standpoint of employee training, pose the following questions:

- Is the organization effectively helping individuals learn their job requirements?
- Is the organization effectively helping individuals keep their job skills current and/or prepare for future job changes?

If you can answer *yes* to these questions, then consider this radar screen clear. Devote your attention to other screens.

But if you must answer *no* to one or both questions, then direct your attention to Training. See Chapter 16 for more information about Training issues.

CHAPTER SUMMARY AND A PREVIEW OF FUTURE CHAPTERS

Performance is a complex phenomenon, and it is perhaps best examined through application of a performance-analysis model. This Chapter pointed out distinctions between comprehensive, situational, and process models and introduced a comprehensive model that likens performance analysis to reading a radar screen. This model will be carried further in the Chapters remaining in this volume.

CHAPTER 10

WLP and Strategic Planning Performance Issues

This Chapter describes strategic planning, something WLP professionals should pay close attention to, because the organization's strategic plan can provide direction and focus for their efforts. Whenever there is cause for concern about organizational performance, a good place to begin is with an examination of the strategic plan, or the lack of it. Also, problems calling for management action are often strategic issues, which usually require organizational interventions.

THE NEED FOR STRATEGIC PLANNING

WLP is not an end in itself. Rather, it is a means to the end of "improving individual and organizational performance" (Rothwell et al 1999). Most organizations have a *purpose*, a distinct reason for existing. On a simplistic level, business firms exist to make a profit; government agencies exist to provide a service to the public at the lowest possible cost; nonprofit enterprises exist to provide a service and charge users just enough to recoup the expenses incurred in the process. Beyond such obvious purposes, each organization has its own unique reason for existing that provides a sense of direction to its activities. It also has objectives by which to periodically measure how well that purpose is being achieved. The purpose of the organization and its objectives must influence its WLP plans—the number of learning interventions and organizational interventions that are necessary to meet organizational and human resource needs. At the same time, the number of employees and their respective skills determine the relative ease or difficulty of changing the organization's purpose and objectives.

Organizations do not exist in a static environment. Changes in technology, economic conditions, governmental policies, and other areas can affect an organization's prospects for successfully achieving its purpose. Managers must often reconsider their organization's purpose and the number and type of people they need to achieve that purpose as these environmental changes occur.

The railroad industry's experience serves as a classic example of what can happen to companies that fail to reconsider their purpose as times change. During the 19th century, trains were the fastest mode of transportation. But as automobiles, trucks, and aircraft became more prevalent, railroads lost most of their customers. Rather than take advantage of this trend by, for example, purchasing stock or outright ownership in automobile or plane manufacturers, and thus altering their purpose, railroad companies must now depend on government subsidies for survival (Naisbitt 1983).

The plight of the railroads dramatizes the need for managers to take a long-term view of their organization's purpose and to plan accordingly. This activity is called *strategic planning*. It is the focus of this Chapter because it significantly influences and is, in turn, influenced by workplace learning.

THE STRATEGIC PLANNING PROCESS

Simply defined, strategic planning (SP) is the process by which an organization determines how it will achieve its purpose over the long term, given expected opportunities and problems presented by the outside environment and the strengths and weaknesses of the organization itself. In business and industry, strategic planning refers to how the organization or agency will continue to meet the needs of its constituency or serve its users in light of changing conditions, laws, rules, and regulations.

Strategic planning theorists do not totally agree on steps in the process, or even on the definition of their field. However, most would agree that SP requires members of an organization to:

Formulate:	1.	Organizational goals and objectives (and reformulate those already existing).
Analyze:	2.	The environment in which the organization operates or plans to operate, in order to detect potential threats or possibilities for action.
	3.	The organization's strengths and weaknesses relative to the environment.
Choose:	4.	Among the range of possible strategies for the organization.
	5.	A promising grand strategy that will command the highest priority and integrate all organizational activities over time, but also plan for contingencies in the event of unexpected environmental change.
Implement:	6.	The proposed strategy by selecting appropriate leaders and rewarding them for behavior and results consistent with strategy.
	7.	Policies at all levels and across all function areas that are consistent with strategy.
	8.	An organizational structure consistent with the plan.
Evaluate:	9.	The effectiveness of the plan in the short-term and long-term.

These steps, first described by Guleck and Jauch (1984), are illustrated in Exhibit 10-1.

Exhibit 10-1: The strategic planning process

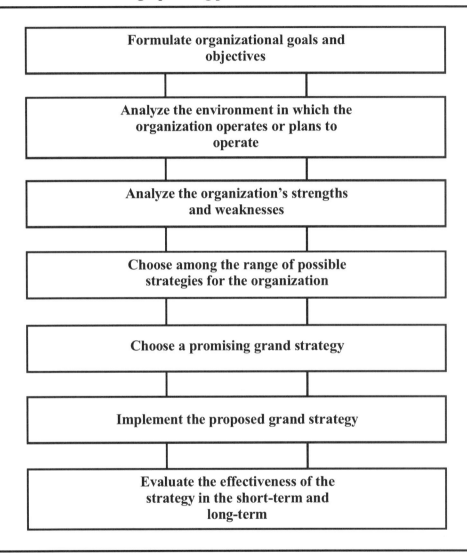

Strategic plans can be classified into two types: (1) *comprehensive plans*, which attempt to integrate all functional activities and corporate subdivisions to achieve organizational objectives, and (2) *market-specific plans*, which identify only markets that the organization should enter or develop in the future.

Methods of conducting the SP process differ. In general, three approaches are used: the *top-down*, *the bottom-up*, and the *negotiated*. In the first approach, corporate grand strategy is formulated at the highest level of management and then communicated to lower levels. In the second approach, grand strategy is a consolidation of independent plans in otherwise autonomous enterprises comprising the corporation. In the third approach, grand strategy is proposed either at the top or the bottom and then negotiated.

Strategic planning deals only with how the organization can achieve its purpose in the long run. It is preceded by two steps: a prophetic vision of the organization's future, and an articulation of organizational purpose.

KEY STEPS IN STRATEGIC PLANNING

Visualizing the Future

To most Americans, imagination is not a trait closely associated with management. Although the pioneering spirit runs deep in American culture, it is tempered by a love of the practical, concrete, and useful. Knowledge and creativity have not traditionally been prized for their own sake, but rather for their potential applications. Americans are generally pragmatic.

The problem is that, without imagination, managers cannot recognize potentially profitable opportunities or predict long-term consequences of their actions. Short-sightedness and complacency are often called the biggest failings of managers in the U. S. since World War II. Organizations reward managers based on short-term goal achievement, not long-term consequences. To make matters worse, the average tenure of top managers in U. S. corporations is just five years, much too short to judge the long-term results of their actions.

Imagination or creativity is actually the essence of entrepreneurial skill. An entrepreneur is one who recognizes an opportunity before others do and takes full advantage of it. No business would exist today except for the initiative of some entrepreneur who recognized the potential for making money and who took considerable financial and personal risks to back an unproven venture.

Joseph Schumpeter, an early critic of capitalism, predicted its ultimate decay as a result of what he believed would be a decline in entrepreneurial skill. As capitalism triumphed and alleviated material needs, Schumpeter argued, fewer people would be willing to take risks. At the same time, big corporations would increasingly be led by professional managers, rather than the founding entrepreneurs. Such professionals would be loathe to risk their jobs or future career prospects by leading their firms into risky but highly profitable activities. The result: economic decline (Schumpeter 1943).

Contemporary observers of American business believe that Schumpeter was at least partially correct in his predictions. Approximately 90 percent of all wealth is concentrated in the hands of 200 large corporations. The remainder is distributed chiefly among remaining businesses in the U. S. Most managers in the largest corporations are indeed professionals, and many are products of business schools that emphasize the accountant's love of prudence, conservatism, and short-term results. However, Schumpeter was wrong about a decline in the number of entrepreneurs: More new, small businesses have been formed in the past ten years than ever before, and they employ more people than their giant counterparts combined.

It is thus in the largest U. S. corporations and government bodies rather than in small business where there is what might be called a *crisis of vision*—or at least a crisis in implementing a vision.

What is vision? It is a clear, concrete picture in the mind of a leader who knows what he or she wants to achieve. In the case of a manager, it is a sense of what the organization should look like and how it should function in the environment. A vision is based on an in-depth knowledge of an industry or an organization; it is focused on continuous improvement and characterized by creative and flexible application. The power of vision is that it is sustained and relatively enduring. It excites enthusiasm and action.

What has contributed to a crisis in vision? There seem to be two main causes: (1) lack of imagination, and (2) lack of sufficient charisma and political power to excite others to act.

Imagination, essential for visualizing the future, has traditionally not been taught in business schools; rather, it is more closely associated with the study of the arts and humanities. It is the ability to re-perceive reality and re-interpret it creatively. In an organizational context, it is the ability to look beyond past traditions and conceive a new future and the organization's place in it. Techniques for creative thinking can be used to stimulate imagination.

Imagination is essential for senior managers whose main function is setting the direction of their respective organizations. However, imagination is not enough by itself. An additional skill is needed: the ability to inspire, enthuse, and even infect others with the vision. All great leaders of the past not only possessed a vision but were successful in getting others to accept it and to work on making it a reality. Some of the best examples of how to integrate vision, inspiration, and enthusiasm have been demonstrated by great religious leaders and statesmen. Napoleon, for example, was able to inspire his countrymen with a vision of a unified Europe; Mohammed inspired his followers with a vision of a world unified in religion. The same skill, though of lesser scope, can be seen in the corporate world: Lee Iacocca was able to inspire Chrysler's employees to work harder and temporarily sacrifice their self-interest for the company's future survival.

Before undertaking strategic planning, it is essential that top corporate managers have some sense of what they think the organization should be like in the future. Only then can they proceed to the next step.

Articulating Organizational Purpose

The articulation of organizational purpose stems from a vision of the future and, to some extent, a sense of present and past. An organization's purpose is sometimes called its *mission*, its reason for existing. A mission is never fully achieved, unless the organization is temporary. It unifies an organization and provides a sense of direction and a rationale for that direction.

As early as 1924, Mary Parker Follett, in her classic book *Creative Experience*, proposed her now-famous Law of the Situation, thus reinforcing the importance of articulating purpose: "When you have made your employees feel that they are in some sense partners in the business, they do not improve the quality of their work, save waste in time and material, because of the Golden Rule, but because their interests are the same as yours." In order to create this "feel," is it essential to know first precisely *what* business the organization is in and *how* it will conduct business.

The question of purpose or mission appears on the surface to be a moot point. A hardware store exists to make a profit by selling hardware; an automobile manufacturer exists to make a profit by selling cars. But there is far more to it than that. Consider: Why should a hardware store exist? If it is simply a matter of profit, more can be made in other businesses or investments. Why hardware? What does that business include or exclude? Discount stores sell hardware and make more money by buying and selling it in volume. Can it be that the old-fashioned hardware store, in which a customer can drop in and pose questions to knowledgeable clerks, is really in the business of providing a service that most discount stores do not?

The better that owners of the hardware store understand the unique purpose of their business, the greater their advantage against competitors. This same principle applies to all other businesses: With a clearly defined purpose, an organization is able to establish a consistent and appropriate business philosophy. In this way, managers and employees alike have defined their organization's "market"—the specific group of consumers they wish to serve. In the case of the hardware store, the market might consist largely of people who need help in making a purchase or, ultimately, in using the merchandise. The owners should consider this and not only hire people who are knowledgeable and who can give good advice, but also think of even more ways to help their customers and, thus, capitalize on their chief market strength and their core competence.

As organizations grow and age, they sometimes lose sight of their purpose. Back to our example of the railroads: Over a hundred years ago, their purpose was transportation. They provided the fastest mode of travel and freight delivery. Then times changed, but railroad owners and managers never looked beyond trains to redefine company purpose. They missed marvelous opportunities to purchase new and eventually more profitable automobile and aircraft manufacturers.

Before beginning any strategic planning process, managers and employees must each have some sense of the organization's purpose. The process of articulating that purpose will be worthwhile in itself, since it will reveal what managers believe their business is.

Determining Organizational Goals and Objectives

An *organizational goal* is a desired end state or condition that an organization attempts to realize. A *goal* is somewhat more general than an *objective*, which is measurable. Goals and objectives stem from a sense of purpose and from a vision of the future shared by those in the organization. Determining goals and objectives is the first step in strategic planning.

Different observers have asserted contrasting theories about the nature of goals. Talcott Parsons believes that organizational goals are derived from what society needs (Parsons 1960). Petro Georgious, on the other hand, believes that goals are essentially distilled from the common wishes of those who are employed by—or have a stake in—the organization (Georgious 1973).

Hall (1977) explains the nature of goals succinctly:

"Organizational goals by definition are creations of individuals, singly or collectively . . . The collectively determined, commonly-based goal seldom remains constant over time. New considerations imposed from without or within deflect the organization from its original goal . . . changing the activities of the organization. . . . The important point is that the goal of any organization is an abstraction distilled from the desires of members and pressures from the environment and internal system."

Although organizations may have only one purpose or a reason for existence, they have several goals (that is, what results are to be achieved). Each part of the organization has a goal that contributes to the continuing achievement of the overall mission; each work group and each job has a goal that also contributes to the mission. This concept is illustrated in Exhibit 10-2.

Exhibit 10-2: The hierarchy of objectives

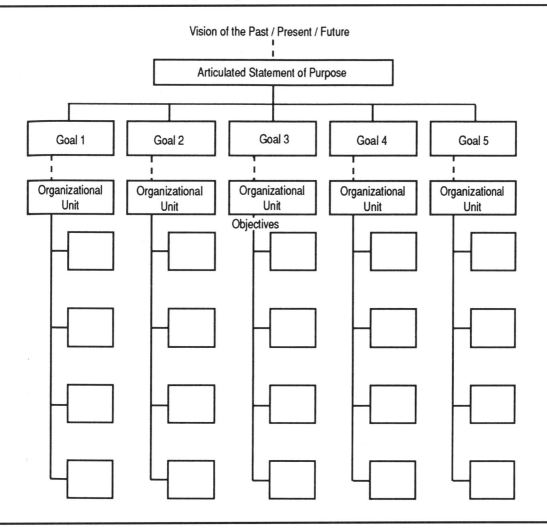

From goals, objectives are derived to measure to what extent the goals were or are to be achieved during a specified time period. They range from broad objectives for the entire organization to more specific objectives for parts of the organization, work groups, and even individuals in their respective jobs. All organizations have objectives, though they are not always clearly articulated or understood. When they are articulated, the result is a well-defined hierarchy of objectives that makes priorities explicit.

How are organizational goals and objectives established and implemented? Management theorists are not in total agreement on the answer. In explaining their disagreement, it is useful to make several distinctions about the nature of organizations and decision-making. On the one hand, classical management theorists such as Frederick Taylor and Henri Fayol assumed that organizations should be structured logically, that tasks should be specialized, and that managers should make decisions solely on the basis of what works the best. They assumed, then, that organizations should be treated rationally—that is, the best solution for any problem should be selected solely for its usefulness. They completely ignored the idea that worker feelings or power struggles between managers or work groups could, in fact, influence the relative ease or difficulty of making and implementing decisions. Human relations theory, however, pointed out that organizations could be treated politically—that the best solution for any problem should be selected solely for the power and personal advantage it would yield to individuals or work groups. Subsequent theorists hypothesized that every organization has two sides: *the formal*, consisting of the allocation of work responsibilities and authority conferred by virtue of position, and the *informal*, consisting in part of worker feelings and expectations about those responsibilities and that authority.

In the context of goal and objective setting, exponents of the formal organization maintain that goals and objectives are purely rational and are intended to maximize profits or to ensure timely, efficient, and effective delivery of service. Exponents of the informal organization assume that goals and objectives are largely political, and are intended to maximize the power of those who control the organization. Still others point to both formal and informal organizations, arguing that the process of developing goals and objectives is political, but the goals and objectives ultimately selected will be rationally related to maximize profits or ensure efficient and effective operations. Most observers would probably agree with this last position.

Only after determining organizational goals and objectives is it possible to proceed to the next step in strategic planning.

Analyzing the Environment

The term *environment* usually refers to the world outside an organization. The organizational environment is that which provides inputs (for example, land, labor, capital, raw materials, and technology), and to which outputs are directed (that is, markets). Every organization is dependent on the environment for its very existence. In fact, all organizations are growing even more dependent as a result of: (1) the increasing rate of technological change, (2) the proliferation of government regulations, and (3) the rise of foreign competition.

As a step in the strategic planning process, environmental analysis identifies characteristics of the environment most critical to the organization and predicts how those characteristics are likely to change in the future. Through environmental analysis, the organization can prepare itself for changes that are often outside its control to influence but are within its control to deal with. The more information managers have about the future, the more likely the organization will be successful in coping with it.

Not all organizations exist in the same environment. Indeed, the most critical characteristics of environment vary by industry and by the size of the organization. For example, what affects General Motors does not necessarily affect Microsoft. They rely on different supplies of raw materials and use different labor skills. A cyclical downturn in the national economy is more likely to affect GM, which sells most of its cars to private individuals in the U.S., than Microsoft, which sells its software globally to individuals and businesses worldwide. On the other hand, the effect of an economic downturn will probably have less influence on GM, the biggest company in the auto industry, than on smaller competitors like Ford or Chrysler. By virtue of size, GM has market power over its smaller competitors.

In general, there are four types of environments—the placid randomized, the placid clustered, the disturbed reactive, and the turbulent field. In the *placid randomized environment*, there is no competition, and resources are available but require some effort to locate. Governmental agencies usually exist in this environment. Success depends on just doing as well as possible under the circumstances. In the *placid clustered environment*, there is no direct competition, but resources are heavily concentrated in certain areas. Charitable organizations and some retailers operate in this environment. Success depends on positioning the organization as closely as possible to resources or consumers. In the *disturbed reactive environment*, several competing organizations jockey for favorable positions. Many businesses in the U. S. face this kind of environment, competing for consumer dollars against counterparts in their own industry. Success depends not only on positioning the organization and its products or services so as to attract the most attention, but also on preventing competitors from attaining a more favorable market position. In the *turbulent field environment*, competing organizations jockey for positions while the environment itself changes. Firms dealing with high technology, such as computers, electronics, and aerospace, face these conditions. Success depends on simultaneously keeping track of changes in the environment, positioning the organization to take advantage (or minimize disadvantages) of environmental change, and preventing competitors from attaining favorable positions (Emory and Trist 1965). Exhibit 10-3 depicts these environmental states in simplified form.

Depending on the type of environment in which they operate, organizations will differ in the importance they attach to such factors as technology, economics, suppliers, distributors, and social trends. Exhibit 10-4 provides a list of environmental factors that could affect organizational success or failure. By analyzing the present and future importance and status of these factors, managers can gain a sense of how their organization will and should fare in the future.

Exhibit 10-3: Four types of environments

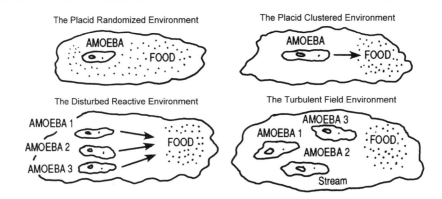

Exhibit 10-4: Environmental factors

Characteristics	Description	How Important is This Characteristic to the Organization	Why?	How Will This Characteristic Change in 5 Years? 10 Years?	Why?
Economic	Includes all factors affecting the state of the business cycles	How much is the organization affected by changes in general business conditions?	Provide the reasons	What will be the likely state of the economy over the long term?	Provide the reasons
Governmental	Includes all factors affecting laws, regulations, policies	How much is the organization affected by regulations?		What factors might influence changes in laws or regulations?	
Market	Includes all factors affecting who can or will purchase or use the organization's products/services	How much is the organization dependent on one kind of market?		What factors might affect the kind of market the organization will serve?	
Technological	Includes all factors affecting the supply of resources needed by the organization and machinery or knowledge affecting work processes	How much is the organization dependent on a few key supplies or on certain types of knowledge or technology?		What factors might affect the future supply of resources and/or the means of making the product or providing the service?	

Exhibit 10-4: Environmental factors *(continued)*

Characteristics	Description	How Important is This Characteristic to the Organization?	Why?	How Will This Characteristic Change in 5 Years? 10 Years?	Why?
Social	Includes public attitudes about the organization and its products or services	How much is the organization dependent on current lifestyles or attitudes?		What factors might alter public attitudes?	
Geographic	Includes all factors affecting the location of key suppliers, distributors, competitors, or consumers	How much is the organization dependent on certain suppliers, etc. in a certain location?		What factors might alter the physical location of suppliers, distributors, consumers, or competitors?	

Environmental analysis typically relies on a variety of forecasting techniques, used to predict changes in relevant aspects of the external environment:

- Economic conditions can be forecast by using leading indicators, consumer sentiments, future markets, per capita income, and other information.
- Technological change can be predicted by expert opinion or by hypothetical scenarios of future events.
- Governmental/legal changes, like technological change, can be forecast by expert opinions through such methods as the Delphi and Nominal Group Technique.
- Market changes can be forecast through changes in population growth, social changes, and analysis of competitors.
- Geographic changes can be forecast by examining census figures, population growth, and movements of important suppliers, manufacturers, and distributors.
- Social changes can be forecast through issue analysis and expert opinions on the sociopolitical environment.

Depending on what is to be analyzed, techniques used will vary in their relative effectiveness. Environmental analysis is far from an exact science; it is usually easier to forecast that environmental change will take place than to forecast the nature or degree of change.

Analyzing Organizational Strengths and Weaknesses

To establish the long-term direction of an organization, managers need more than information about future changes in the environment. They also need good information about the status of the organization: its present standing relative to what managers desire for it or relative to competitors in the same industry. Any organization has internal strengths and weaknesses. A *strength* is what contributes to goal achievement; a *weakness* is that which impedes goal achievement. Both are characteristic of the world inside the organization, its inner workings or *internal environment*. The choice of strategy (that is, how to achieve goals and objectives) is dependent on a comparison of external and internal environments.

The analysis of organizational strengths and weaknesses (sometimes called *internal appraisal*) assesses how well the organization is achieving its purpose at present. Of all steps in strategic planning, internal appraisal is the most difficult.

There are three major problems associated with internal appraisal: objectivity, methods, and criteria. Objectivity requires management to critically assess the performance of all parts of the organization. The problem is that top managers are the ones responsible for their organizations—the principal stakeholders in, and often apologists for, the status quo. They can hardly be objective in their assessments! Managers become so committed to a course of action that, even when it appears to fail, they will persist in the same course. Nor can they rely entirely on information provided to them by subordinates: People often filter their communication to their superiors, and will usually emphasize the positive so as to preserve their chances of being rewarded. Even superiors will conceal their mistakes or perceived shortcomings from those reporting to them.

A second problem concerns methods of conducting internal appraisal. How can strengths and weaknesses be identified? In the U. S., most organizations rely on financial reports. They are published annually by corporations that have stockholders. Managers within the organization receive financial information even more frequently, and use this information (along with figures on production and sales) to detect some potential problems.

Unfortunately, numbers provide information primarily about results of operating problems. They seldom help to pinpoint the exact cause. They may show, for example, that sales are sluggish, but not whether the cause is a general economic downturn, an incompetent sales force, an uncompetitive product, or something else. For this reason, managers often have more trouble identifying the causes of problems than recognizing their symptoms.

A third problem in conducting internal appraisal has to do with the selection and application of criteria—yardsticks for measuring strengths and weaknesses. There is, after all, no such thing as a strength or weakness viewed in isolation. A strength exists only when compared to some criterion, some standard or value indicator of what should be. The same is true of a weakness.

Sources of criteria vary, from the subjective opinions of managers or employees to academic research findings, industry practices, expert opinions, workflow analyses, or governmental regulations or laws. Some theorists have listed organizational attributes that they believe should be considered in an internal appraisal. Others have surveyed managers to determine what they believe should be considered. Exhibit 10-5 depicts some of these attributes.

Exhibit 10-5: Attributes to consider in internal appraisal

Function	*Description*	*What Criteria Can Be Used for Appraisal?*	*How Can Those Criteria Be Used?*
Finance/ Accounting	Raises or invests funds and keeps track of them	• Cost of capital • Good tax conditions • Good systems for budgeting and profit planning	• Compare with industry " "
Marketing	Determines what products or services to offer, what to charge for them, and where and how to sell them	• Market share • A good mix of products or services • Good market research • Good pricing policies • Good distribution • Good promotion strategies	• Compare with competitors " " " " "
Operations/ Production	Produces goods or delivers services	• Low-cost production • Good procedures for designing, scheduling, assessing quality • Use of facilities • Ability to meet the demand	• Compare with competitors " " "
Personnel	Sets policies for recruiting people and maintaining a workforce capable of doing the work	• Good mix of skills and experience of top management • Good integrated policies on recruitment, staffing, training, compensation, etc. • Participative climate and high morale	• Compare with industry " • Compare across many organizations

Several methods are useful for top managers who want to examine organizational strengths and weaknesses. They include portfolio analysis, performance audits, attitude surveys, quality circles, and behavioral science approaches to organizational diagnosis.

Portfolio analysis is a relatively old appraisal method. For business firms, two major approaches to portfolio analysis are prominent: the General Electric (GE) Model and the Boston Consulting Group (BCG) Model.

The GE Model was created to assist decision-makers in that company. Each business in the company is placed on a grid based on its comparative strength and industry attractiveness. Strength is rated good or bad, as is industry attractiveness. If placement on the grid is positive, GE invests more and expands the business; if placement results are mixed, GE exercises restraint and caution; if placement results are negative, GE reduces investments and might try to sell the business.

The BCG Model is similar. Companies that comprise the corporation are placed on a grid based on market share and market growth. The results reveal whether each business can be classified as a *star* showing great promise, a *problem child* showing potential unrealized, a *cash cow* showing continued promise, or a *dog* showing little hope of success.

In the performance audit, an independent analyst (or team of analysts) conducts an examination of an entire organization or its parts. The results are reported to top management for purposes of assessing how well results match intentions or how well resources are used in obtaining results. A performance audit (sometimes called a management audit) can address any issue. It need not focus only on financial matters; it is useful also for identifying and correcting other deficiencies.

Attitude surveys are useful for detecting employee morale problems, assessing training needs, thwarting unionization efforts, and identifying perceived strengths or weaknesses in daily operations. Conducting a survey is not difficult, and standardized questionnaires are available, making it possible to compare results in one organization to results in many others.

Other approaches to diagnosing organizational strengths and weaknesses have been developed by industrial psychologists. Levinson, in a classic treatment, suggested that an organization can be examined by having an outside consultant develop a case history, much like that used in psychoanalysis, which can consist of consultant feelings, documents, information from other organizations, and facts about how the organization is structured (Levinson 1972). Hornstein and Tichy (1973), in a second classic treatment, recommended that managers of an organization work together in a structured setting to develop their own diagnostic model. Nadler and Tushman (1977), in a third classic treatment, suggested a three-step process: (1) Identify what is to be studied, (2) determine what characteristics are most important, and (3) decide how well parts of the organization work together or interact with the environment. Weisbord (1976), in a fourth classic treatment, developed a model useful in assessing how well six aspects of an organization work together: its purposes, rewards, structure, leadership, methods of coordinating technology, and methods of resolving conflict.

When the internal appraisal is completed, top managers are able to consider a range of possible strategies.

Considering Strategic Options

The challenge in any planning activity is to find the best strategy or set of strategies that are most appropriate and that best meet your goals and objectives. An organization must first identify how many ways it might achieve its purpose and objectives successfully over time. This typically involves comparing external trends and internal strengths and weaknesses in order to generate a list of possible directions. How are such comparisons made? Who makes them? What are some of the possibilities that decision-makers can choose?

To compare external trends with internal strengths and weaknesses, all that is necessary is a *means* and a *method*. The *means* is simple enough: set external trends and internal strengths/weaknesses up in a way that allows comparison (see Exhibit 10-6). Selecting a *method* is more difficult. Some common ones include: planning committees, reports generated by strategic planning units or consultants, or judgments of managers at all levels of the organization.

Exhibit 10-6: Comparing external trends with organizational strengths and weaknesses

Environment			Organization		
External Aspect	*How Important Is This Aspect to the Organization?*	*How Will This Aspect Change in 5–10 Years?*	*Internal Attribute*	*What Criteria Can be Used for Appraisal?*	*How Can Those Criteria Be Used?*
Economic			Finance/ Accounting		
Governmental			Legal/ Governmental Relations		
Market			Market		
Technological			Production/ Operations		
Social			Personnel		
Geographic			Location of Facilities		
Others?			Others?		

Top managers—the chief executive and reporting subordinates—bear primary responsibility for generating strategic alternatives. This view is consistent with the notion of *timespan of discretion*: Top-level managers are responsible for creating strategy; their performance can only be judged as a function of how well that strategy works. In contrast, middle managers are responsible for working within the long-term strategy established by superiors, and for creating medium- and short-range plans consistent with that strategy. Field supervisors are responsible for overseeing the work of employees and for daily, weekly, or monthly tactics necessary for implementing medium- and short-range plans (Jaques 1964). Exhibit 10-7 depicts the relationship between management level and plans.

Exhibit 10-7: How planning relates to levels of management

Organizations generally select their grand strategy from six classic and time-tested possibilities. They are: (1) growth; (2) retrenchment; (3) turnabout; (4) integration; (5) diversification, and (6) combination (Glueck and Jauch 1984).

A *growth strategy* simply means that the organization will try to do more of what it is already doing. Resources will be directed to increasing market share, expanding the size of the market served, and perhaps increasing the workforce.

Retrenchment is the opposite of growth: External conditions do not favor the organization, so it will pare down its workforce or its scale of operations in order to cut possible losses and conserve scarce resources. *Downsizing* is another name for retrenchment.

A *turnabout strategy* tries to reverse the decline of a faltering enterprise.

An *integration strategy* calls for acquiring or merging with key suppliers (that is, those firms that provide raw materials or other resources essential to corporate operations), competitors, or distributors (that is, those firms that transport or sell the corporation's finished products or market its services).

A *diversification strategy* involves entering into a new business that appears to offer more promise for the future.

Many mergers, acquisitions, and takeovers in recent years have been geared to an integration or diversification strategy.

A *combination strategy* involves implementing two or more of the above strategies in different parts of the organization at the same time.

Selecting the Strategy

Before the best strategy can be identified, top managers must consider several important factors. Their selection will be, in part, a function of (1) what they value, (2) the (perceived) purpose of the organization, (3) the alternative strategies they recognize and consider, (4) pressures exerted by groups inside or outside the organization, and (5) the size of the organization relative to its industry.

Values are, of course, what managers perceive as desirable or undesirable. They pervade all aspects of strategic planning, and guide decision-making among alternatives. Selecting a strategy frequently involves a trade-off between risk and return. The greater the risk, the greater the potential tradeoff; the smaller the risk, the smaller the potential payoff. The question is: to what extent are top managers willing to accept risk (possible loss of company assets) for return (high profits)?

In most cases, managers tend to be *risk averse*; they accept the prospect of lower returns as long as risk is low. There are exceptions: Venture capitalists, who back fledgling and unproven ventures, will sometimes accept high risk for the prospect of high returns. Entrepreneurs are less risk averse than most professional managers. To select a strategy, managers must assess what they hope to achieve.

To select a strategy, top managers should also consider or even reconsider the purpose of the organization. Are they content to remain in the same business, even if future prospects look bleak? If not, how will a changed sense of purpose affect the organization? Suppose a new business is acquired through diversification: Will the present management team possess the necessary expertise to run the business?

In selecting a strategy, top managers should also be receptive to their options. They must be able to see beyond immediate payoffs, to long-term consequences. Too often, they discount radical alternatives, but they should make a deliberate effort to generate all kinds of alternatives and try out those that appear promising—even the ones that seem outlandish.

Top managers must also be aware of how well various strategies will be accepted by important groups inside and outside the organization, because the reality is that strategy is *not* chosen solely by top managers and then imposed on others. Internal and external coalitions also play an important part in strategic choice. Interestingly enough, the process of selecting strategy reveals more about power and decision-making in the organization than the choice that is ultimately made.

Finally, the size of the organization relative to its industry is an important determinant of appropriate strategy. The reason: Industry leaders frequently have great market power as a result of their size and dominance. If General Motors drops the price of cars, it is national news and might force similar drops by competitors. If a small competitor drops prices, GM will likely survive quite well without following suit.

Implementing the Strategy

Implementation puts the strategic plan into action by adapting the organization to meet expected changes in external conditions. Frequently criticized as the least effectively handled step in strategic planning, implementation requires change in four key areas: the organization's leadership, its rewards, its policies, and its structure.

Changes in strategy frequently call for changes in leadership. Each part of the organization must be led by a person with the right mix of education, experience, motivation, and attitude about implementation. Leaders attuned to one strategy are not always the best ones to engineer dramatic overall change. Leadership changes are particularly important at the highest management levels because strategic direction is guided, if not also formulated, by those at the top. But despite the key importance of leadership in implementing strategic plans, it is quite difficult to identify, let alone find, the *right* person for the *right* job at the *right* time. This is a major problem confronting all U. S. corporations; short-term needs frequently conflict with long-term needs.

Adopting a new strategy frequently requires the organization to reconsider the way it rewards management and employee performance. Most people agree that workers will do what they are rewarded for doing, though theories of motivation and rewards may differ. Nevertheless, it is easy enough to think of instances when desired behavior is not rewarded properly.

In addition to changes in leadership and rewards, a new strategy often requires a review of, or change in, policies. A *policy* is a predetermined and articulated stand on issues relevant to the organization, intended to serve as a guide to action. Policies flow from a sense of the organization's purpose and from a philosophy of what the organization is doing. Suppose, for example, that top managers decide that marketing and advertising specialists will do a more effective job in promoting the organization's products or services than field representatives. The company might then develop a policy prohibiting field representatives from doing any independent, local advertising of company products or services. Another example: Suppose top managers decide that educating employees in electronics will improve the organization's general performance. A policy could then be developed concerning the reimbursement of employee tuition and fees for any college courses in electronics, but not for any other subject.

When a company's grand strategy changes, all existing policies should be reviewed to make certain that they are consistent with the change. Back to our examples: If a firm decides to adopt a combination strategy, such as growth in the existing business as well as diversification into a new business, it might be necessary to rethink policies concerning field representatives arranging for their own advertising and on employee tuition reimbursement. After all, local advertising may stimulate growth, and tuition reimbursement for courses other than electronics might help equip employees with the skills they need to function effectively in a new business.

In rethinking policy, managers can draw on techniques from a specialized field of study called *policy analysis,* which uses a variety of methods to examine the likely future impact on organizational performance if a particular policy is changed. Policy analysis is closely related to another specialized field, called *evaluation research*, which examines results of policy changes on overall organization performance.

A new strategy often calls for a corresponding change in the allocation of work duties and responsibilities—the structure of the organization. Chandler, the first strategic planning theorist, hypothesized that structure is always an outgrowth of strategy (Chandler 1962). But the structure that exists at the time a new strategy is contemplated—entrepreneurial, functional, divisional, project, or matrix—can also influence what strategy is chosen, partly because the structure often determines who the strategists are. The entrepreneurial is the simplest structural form; matrix is the most complicated (see Exhibit 10-8).

Exhibit 10-8: Types of organizational structure

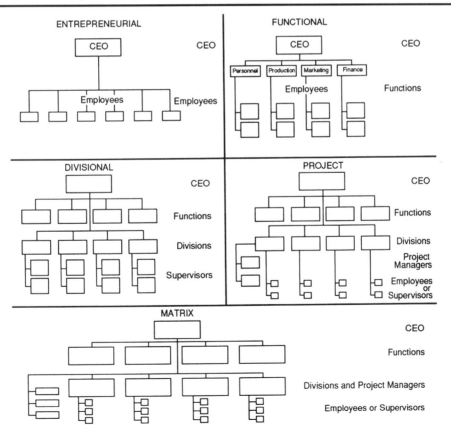

In an *entrepreneurial structure*, all employees answer to one manager. In the *functional structure*, managers are inserted between the top manager and employees. These managers oversee such traditional functions as personnel, finance, marketing, and operations. In the *divisional structure*, managers are added below functions to concentrate on some unique division of work, such as product or service types, geographical regions, or (in a multiservice or multiproduct corporation) the industry. In the *project* structure, a layer of management is added below divisions to oversee every work project from beginning to end. In *matrix management*, the structure is the same as in the project type, though there is one important difference: project managers are equal, not subordinate, to divisional managers. There is no universally correct structure, but some are more appropriate than others for dealing with different environments or for implementing different strategies. Dynamic environments call for a flexible structure such as project or matrix; more stable environments call for more traditional structures.

Evaluating the Strategy

Evaluation, the final step in strategic planning, is used to compare strategic results or outcomes with organizational goals and objectives. To be successful, strategic evaluation requires people who want to evaluate results, some method by which to measure results, a means of collecting information relevant to the desired results, and a willingness to take corrective action to bring results in line with strategy and vice versa. Much research has been devoted to evaluation of strategic planning. Several writers have shown that a dizzying array of different performance measures can be used to gauge success in the evaluation process.

HOW WLP FITS INTO STRATEGIC PLANNING

Top managers usually indicate that they want WLP efforts to meet business needs and help bring about an improvement in performance. There is good reason why: Productivity leaders across industries tend to handle their human resources strategically. WLP practitioners need to pay heed: their career success may depend increasingly on their ability to think strategically and adopt the long-term perspective of top managers. The growing importance of intellectual capital to competitiveness highlights the role workplace learning needs to play in every organization.

Obstacles to Linking Strategic Planning With WLP Initiatives

In recent years, much attention has been devoted to long-range and strategic planning for WLP. However, there is one unfortunate side effect: paying attention to WLP planning and ignoring other areas too often implies that management of organizational learning is the prerogative of that department. Yet every WLP professional knows that this is utterly untrue. The learning process so permeates what happens in organizations; managing it is a key—if not *the* key—to strategic success. Everyone shares some responsibility for the learning process, including line managers, prospective learners, and, of course, WLP professionals. WLP department plans should be an outgrowth of learning plans for the entire organization; they will be successful only if and when they are integrated with such other activities as recruitment, compensation, and individual career planning.

What has research revealed about the major impediments to linking organizational strategic plans and long-term instructional/learning initiatives? To summarize them briefly, these impediments include: simple ignorance of the potential value of WLP efforts; the experiential nature of planning; the short-term focus of most training departments; the past-centered orientation of traditional methods of instructional planning; the possibility that instructional efforts might have a longer-term impact than organizational strategy; and the low status of WLP professionals in the management hierarchy.

Clearly, no attempt will be made to link organizational and instructional plans if decision-makers are ignorant or unconvinced of the potential benefits. Nor is such awareness likely to come from formal management education, which too often emphasizes the value of short-term results. The typical graduate business school curriculum, crucial for its role in anticipatory socialization to professional management practice, does well if it offers one or two class periods on WLP in a course on human resources management. Such scant attention being paid to describing these important tools for organizational learning is unlikely to raise awareness of this issue.

Despite the wide coverage given in WLP literature to linkages between organizational and instructional plans, many managers still have never heard of the idea. Until it is widely understood, the necessary integration will not happen. After all, when decision-makers lack knowledge of this or any other issue or lack the motivation to deal with it, progress is unlikely.

Organizational strategic planning is not entirely different from learning and instruction: they are both inherently experiential and learning-oriented. Strategy-making does begin with organizational goals and objectives, but they remain tentative and subject to revision as a result of unexpected external change or increased experience gained through implementation. Indeed, the process of implementation is much like that of experiential learning, because the very act of grappling with problems prompts discoveries that were unforeseen at the time of strategy formulation.

Linking organizational and instructional initiatives will not be easy, but present and future WLP practitioners must overcome these and other impediments.

Overcoming the Obstacles

Future decision-makers will not likely enjoy more stable external environments. Indeed, just the opposite is true: As the basis of the economy moves away from manufacturing and toward information processing, a central problem will be how to increase the speed and effectiveness with which technological and informational advances can be introduced and integrated into the workplace. Overcoming traditional resistance to change is likely to emerge as a key problem of this decade. A possible solution lies in future-oriented instruction, planned over the long term and intended to deal simultaneously with needs and their implications for job transfer. Along the way, WLP practitioners *and* line managers will have to rethink what they are doing.

First, WLP people will have to take the lead in educating and informing others of potential roles in strategic planning that can be played by training, employee education, and development. They can do so by circulating professional literature to raise consciousness, by gaining visibility through seminars on strategic planning and WLP, by successfully facilitating the start-up of strategic planning in organizations that have formally practiced it, and by setting an example so that others can see the differences between short-term, medium-term, and long-term employee improvement efforts.

It is true that WLP practitioners cannot do everything themselves. *But they can do what they presumably do best:* serve as change agents, performance engineers, and learning facilitators. To overcome simple ignorance of the value of WLP as a strategic tool, they need to raise the issue and provide information. To overcome lack of motivation, they need to use the best available evaluative data to point out benefits of adopting a long-range view of human development and organizational learning.

Second, the experiential nature of strategic planning is less an impediment than an opportunity to link it to WLP. Assume that adult identity stems from experience, and that organizations change what they do based on experience. Further assume that John Dewey was right when he said: "We always live at the time we live and not at some other time, and only by extracting at each present time the full meaning of each present experience are we prepared for doing the same thing in the future." Is it not possible to simulate in the present any likely future external conditions that will be encountered by the organization, work groups, individuals, and job incumbents? If experience, which is inherently past-oriented, is one key to learning, then why not simulate likely conditions of the future to produce artificial experience?

The benefits of this approach should be apparent. If people define their learning needs based on experience, then will they not do a better job of it when they have experienced future possibilities first-hand? Experiential exercises can be developed for this purpose. They may, of course, include simulations, games, case studies, critical incidents, and roleplays. While there is always danger that forecasts of the future will be mistaken, there is an equal and perhaps greater danger in encouraging the unspoken assumption that the future will be the same as the more certain present or past.

Third, the notorious myopia of training departments is not an uncorrectable condition. Some WLP professionals are short-sighted because they are rewarded for it by those who have never thought of an alternative. As experts on human performance, WLP practitioners should take the lead of pointing out the implications of reward systems within which they function and suggesting alternatives more likely to produce favorable long-term outcomes.

Fourth, the past-centered orientation of instructional planning is an impediment that can be overcome by placing traditional needs assessment information in a larger context. Popular approaches, such as performance and competency analysis, can serve to identify present organizational strengths and weaknesses. The traditional results of instructional needs assessment information should be paired with what is expected in the future so that activities become adaptive-oriented and thus capable of facilitating organizational learning. Quite apart from identifying learning needs, such analysis is a basis for examining how well the strategic planning process itself is being implemented. In this sense, WLP practitioners are able to function as strategy analysts and engineers.

Fifth, it is probably true that organizational learning has a life span longer than that of strategic plans. After all, individuals can work in organizations for 30 years or more without significantly altering what they have learned through cultural immersion during those years. Yet there is a common link between organizational learning and planning: both are influenced by life cycles. Just as learning interests for individuals are influenced by their central life concerns and crises in each developmental stage, so learning interests for organizations are influenced by their stage of development. What we need is more information about what kinds of long-term learning strategies work best in different organizational stages.

Finally, it is also probably true that WLP professionals rarely enjoy direct participation in formulating organizational strategy. As a result, the element of human potential is often missing in long-term plans. While participation might be a goal for which WLP professionals should strive, it is not essential for linking organizational and instructional initiatives. In fact, WLP planning can be conducted apart from strategic planning. WLP professionals need only show that strategic plans imply the need for knowledge, skills, and abilities that must be acquired over time. When decision-makers understand that, they will begin to see the advantage of establishing long-term learning plans.

No longer can WLP professionals remain complacent, assuming that methods used in the past will serve them in the future. No longer can they assume that their efforts are only quick fixes for removing immediate skill or knowledge deficiencies. They must, instead, master strategic thinking and begin to focus on facilitating organizational as much as individual learning. As they do so, the value of their efforts will become increasingly obvious.

SELECTING, IMPLEMENTING, AND USING ORGANIZATIONAL INTERVENTIONS

Recall from Chapter 9 that not all problems can be solved by learning interventions. Indeed, as much as 90% of all performance problems stem from the work environment in which people perform. Such performance problems require management action called *organizational interventions*. We choose to treat these interventions in this Chapter because they are often strategic in their scope and nature, requiring active management participation and action.

Consider, for a moment, all the factors that can influence human performance. If you subtract factors that have an element of learning to them, you will find that they include many strategic issues affecting organizations. How much and how well, for example, does the organization:

- Recruit people? (If the answer is "not as well as desired," then consider an organizational intervention to improve recruitment practices for the organization or for targeted job categories.)

How well does the organization:

- Select people? (If the answer is "not as well as desired," then consider an organizational intervention to improve selection practices for the organization or for targeted job categories.)
- Place people in their jobs? (If the answer is "not as well as desired," then consider an organizational intervention to improve placement practices for the organization or for targeted job categories.)
- Define and communicate work responsibilities? (If the answer is "not as well as desired," then consider an organizational intervention to improve the definition and/or clarification of work duties, responsibilities, or competencies equated with work success.)
- Define and communicate performance expectations? (If the answer is "not as well as desired," then consider an organizational intervention to improve the definition and communication of performance objectives, expectations, work standards, or other performance management issues.)
- Provide incentives for people to perform? (If the answer is "not as well as desired," then consider an organizational intervention to improve incentives for performance so as to encourage people to perform and to see what's in it for them.)
- Reward people for performance after they take action? (If the answer is "not as well as desired," then consider an organizational intervention to improve reward systems, including both financial and nonfinancial rewards.)
- Provide feedback on how well they perform? (If the answer is "not as well as desired," then consider an organizational intervention to improve feedback systems on how well people perform.)
- Provide a work environment where information about organizational policies, procedures, and past successful actions are readily available? (If the answer is "not as well as desired," then consider an organizational intervention to improve the nature, quality, specificity, and flow of information about organizational policies, procedures, and past successful actions. This might include the creation of an Electronic Performance Support System, a manual [not electronic] performance support system, an Expert System, or other approach to conveying information in real time.)
- Provide the right tools and equipment to perform and make them available as they are needed? (If the answer is "not as well as desired," then consider an organizational intervention to improve the nature, type, and quality of tools and equipment provided to performers.)
- Provide disciplinary action when people willfully misbehave or transgress previously-stated and well-communicated organizational policies, procedures, or work rules? (If the answer is "not as well as desired," then consider an organizational intervention to ensure the consistent application of discipline as it is needed.)

How well does the organization:

- Ensure that tools and equipment are user-friendly and fitted to individual needs or disabilities, as necessary? (If the answer is "not as well as desired," then consider an organizational intervention to improve the ergonomic design and nature of the tools and equipment that people use.)
- Ensure that organizational plans, policies, procedures, and goals are well-articulated and communicated? (If the answer is "not as well as desired," then consider an organizational intervention to improve the consistent and articulated formulation and application of organizational plans, policies, procedures, and goals.)

The answer to each question and many others can help pinpoint the causes of organizational and individual performance problems, and can provide clues to WLP professionals about what organizational interventions to formulate, implement, and evaluate.

As we have said before, *WLP professionals cannot be all things to all people.* Nor can they possess expert knowledge of all organizational and learning interventions. But they should at least be able to recognize the need for organizational interventions as a result of performance analysis, and should be able to clarify what results (outcomes) will surely close performance gaps between what is (actual conditions) and what should be (criteria or desired conditions). For additional information on organizational interventions, see references associated with them, such as Langdon (1999) and Stolovitch and Keeps (1992).

CHAPTER 11

WLP and HR Planning Issues

This Chapter describes Human Resources Planning (HRP) as it relates to strategic planning and WLP. A strategic plan serves as a guide for the long-term direction of an organization. Implementing this plan requires the organization to marshal and deploy its resources, both human and financial. HRP is intended to ensure that the right people with the right skills are on hand at the right time to facilitate implementation of strategy. WLP practitioners should pay close attention to systematic HR plans when they exist. Even though HRP is not a developmentally-oriented activity, it resembles strategic planning in that HR plans can influence—and be influenced by—WLP. HRP is sometimes referred to as "staff planning," or "workforce planning," "performance management," or even the old-style term "manpower planning." No matter what it is called, HRP is critical in helping an organization plan for, invest in, and manage its intellectual capital and knowledge assets.

THE NEED FOR HUMAN RESOURCE PLANNING

Human resource planning is an integration of all HR activities with overall strategic plans. HRP also involves the coordination of hiring, promotion, training, and other diverse activities. Much has been written about it. However, a majority of the country's largest corporations do not seem to be systematically and comprehensively planning for the long-term use of their human or their knowledge assets, much less the small ones.

WHAT IS "HUMAN RESOURCE PLANNING"?

Human resource planning has been a hot topic for the past several years and the subject of several books and countless academic and professional articles. What accounts for such intense interest in HRP? Here are a few reasons why it is capturing so much attention:

1. *HRP is critically important.* An organization's long-term success depends largely on its collective human skills, talents, and performance. Leadership is particularly important.

2. *It is complicated.* Planning for the long-term use and development of people is not as easy as planning for production, finance, or marketing. Individuals affect plans made about them and, indeed, must participate in the planning process if they are expected to commit to realizing the goals and objectives of the plan.

3. *HRP is pervasive.* Unlike plans for other business functions, HRP pervades an entire organization. It is not the sole responsibility of the HR department. Instead, everyone shares a role in establishing future HR goals and helping implement them.

Despite obvious interest in the subject, the existence of a professional society, and journals devoted exclusively to HRP, professionals do not agree on a single definition of HRP. In this respect, HRP is like WLP: Both have been treated in so many different ways that simple definitions have become elusive.

Generally speaking, HRP consists of translating organizational plans at various levels into HR plans that guide the long-term acquisition, use, and development of intellectual capital and knowledge assets. HRP can also suggest a range of performance-improvement strategies to address specialized HR problems. Some believe that Human Resource Planning is one of the most important challenges currently facing organizations.

HRP is necessary in order to:

• *Integrate HR initiatives and organizational plans.* Implementing a strategic plan requires the right kinds of people. Unless organizational and HR plans are integrated, HR initiatives might retard or block some of the organization's planning efforts.

• *Integrate HR initiatives horizontally.* There is strong interdependency among such HR activities as recruitment, selection, training, development, education, compensation, benefits, labor relations, and employee appraisal. Without integrating these initiatives, one HR activity can retard, impede, or utterly block others.

A Model for Human Resource Planning

There are many models for HRP. Most require the following:

1. The integration of HRP and strategic planning.
2. Analysis of future HR demands.
3. Analysis of HR supplies.
4. Analysis of environmental trends and conditions likely to affect the availability of HR supplies.
5. Comparisons of HR demands and anticipated supplies.
6. Action to match HR demands and supplies.
7. Evaluation of plans and results.

This process is depicted in Exhibit 11-1.

Exhibit 11-1: A model for human resource planning

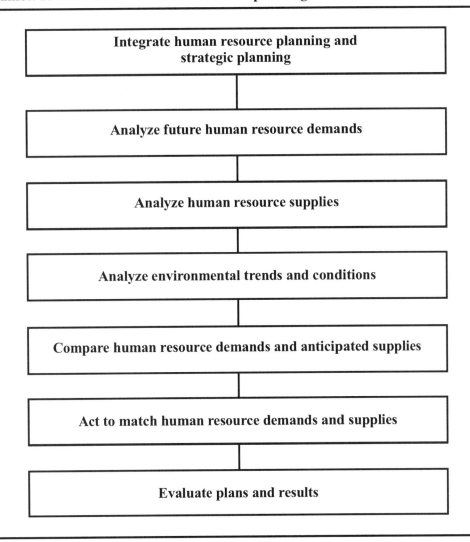

There are other ways to conceptualize HRP. For example, it is possible to distinguish between long-term and short-term HR plans. A *long-term* (or *strategic*) *HRP* focuses on relating the organization's environment to personnel policies. A *short-term* (or *operational*) *HRP* focuses instead on such daily concerns as who to promote into what job or who to transfer. An alternative is to distinguish between technical and management plans. A *technical plan* compares HR supplies and demands; a *management plan* identifies ways to coordinate organizational activities in order to close the gap between supplies and demands.

HR planning methods differ in much the same ways as strategic planning methods. A *top-down approach* ignores individuals and work groups, concentrating instead on the collective HR needs of an entire organization over time. A *bottom-up approach* analyzes individual and work group needs to derive HR objectives for the organization. A *negotiated approach* synthesizes specific needs of individuals and work groups with the collective HR needs of the organization.

KEY STEPS IN HUMAN RESOURCE PLANNING

Integrating HRP and Strategic Planning

The first step in HRP is to integrate it with strategic planning. Despite its importance, this step is sometimes neglected in actual practice. Relatively few organizations establish HR plans before or at the same time as business plans. Unfortunately, some managers think that integrating strategic and HR planning efforts is unnecessary because talented people are always available externally.

Much of what has been written on integration consists of exhorting HR professionals to make the attempt. It is considered one way to upgrade the status of the Human Resources function. Some contend that a key difference between successful and unsuccessful firms is the ability to deal with human resource issues strategically, rather than focus exclusively on short-term issues of individual selection, training, promotion, appraisal, and job design. Numerous case studies describe attempts by various firms to integrate HRP and strategic planning.

Unfortunately, there is little agreement on how to go about such integration. A method that works in one organization may not work in another, largely because most strategic decisions are made and implemented informally. Differences in organizational cultures and management-values require tailor-made approaches in each setting.

Despite these complications, there are effective ways to approach plan integration:

1. *Examine the purpose of the organization.* In what ways can the HR function contribute to this purpose? Is HR mentioned in any formal purpose statement of the organization?
2. *Include HR issues in the strategic planning process.* During organizational planning, have guidelines been established for recruitment, training, performance appraisals, and other HR functions?
3. *Consider strategic plans in HR initiatives.* Before taking action, do HR management professionals check what they propose to do against strategic objectives?
4. *Build communication links between organizational and HR planning functions.* Do corporate and HR planners talk to each other? How can their interaction be improved?

Predicting Future Human Resource Demands

The second step in HRP is to forecast the numbers and kinds of people who will probably be needed by the organization in the future. This issue has attracted more attention than any other in HRP. Indeed, some have suggested that forecasting is the key component of HRP.

There are two major considerations associated with this step: identifying a predictor of HR demands, and conducting the forecasting process itself.

To analyze future HR demands, planners need some way to correlate numbers of employees and amounts of work load or work outputs. Several variables have been used or suggested:

- *Historic variables.* Planners know how many people the organization has and what production levels they have achieved. If production must be increased by 50 percent, for example, they know that staffing should be increased by that same amount.
- *Intuitive variables.* Planners survey managers, who estimate intuitively how many people they will need to produce at a given level.
- *Productivity variables.* Using historical data, planners forecast future productivity per worker, and then divide output by a productivity index.
- *Time-series variables.* Historical staffing levels are adjusted to take seasonal and cyclical trends into account.

Unfortunately, not one of these methods is totally satisfactory. Historic variables do not consider the potential of existing staff to improve their productivity. Intuitive variables are just guesses prone to overestimation or underestimation. Productivity variables do not necessarily include limits on growth. Time-series variables are prone to miscalculation. Even worse, all these variables concentrate attention on *numbers* of people rather than on their *skills* and *talent,* and on the *past* rather than on prospects for the *future.*

Methods of conducting the forecasting process are quite advanced, in theory. They include *regression analysis,* where planners use statistical techniques to correlate numbers of employees and quantities of work; *judgmental approaches,* where planners can use delphi analysis, curve fitting, and other social science approaches to supplement statistical methods with expert opinions; and *linear programming,* where planners use specialized mathematical techniques to determine the optimal solution to a complex problem. In linear programming, the focus is on HR changes that must be made to achieve certain objectives, given identified constraints. This is a powerful approach, though not commonly used. Its focus also tends to be more short-term than long-term.

Rarely is an attempt made to identify skills or knowledge needed by people to deal with future conditions that might be quite different from current conditions.

Analyzing Human Resource Supplies

The third step in HRP is to analyze the organization's current work force. At this point, planners should consider how well future demands can be met with people already in the organization. There are two approaches: static models and flow models.

A *static model* is comparable to an accountant's balance sheet. It represents current human resources at one point in time. There are two types: succession charts, and skill inventories.

Succession charts depict the readiness of employees for promotion. Such charts are most commonly used for the highest management levels, but they can be developed for all but entry-level jobs in an organization.

Skill inventories list the known abilities of every employee. Hundreds of items can be cross-referenced, including prior work experience, education, training, knowledge of foreign languages, publications, hobbies or interests, and career aspirations.

Though static models were once quite popular, they have not been as successful as one might expect.

A *flow model* is much like an accountant's income statement. It represents expected changes or human resource movements over time. There are, after all, only six possible changes that an individual can make: in, out, up, down, across, or grow in an existing job by improved performance, behavior, knowledge, or skills. Markov or semi-Markov analysis is used in flow modeling. The basic idea of Markov analysis is to estimate the probability that specific employees will remain in their present positions or move to new positions. Historical data can provide some guidance in estimating these probabilities, but accuracy can be improved by using expert opinion to supplement historical data.

Substantial progress has been made in analyzing expected future HR supplies. Sophisticated computer simulations can even be used to assess the potential impact of changes in personnel policies. Such simulations still remain out of reach for all but large organizations. In time, however, microcomputers and HRP software will probably make such simulations more affordable and, thus, commonplace in even small firms.

Analyzing Environmental Trends

The fourth step in HRP is to analyze external environmental trends likely to affect the future availability of HR supplies. At this point, planners should consider how well future HR demands can be met by the external labor market. This step has particular importance when there is a significant discrepancy between available internal supplies and expected future demands.

Few firms have the resources to effectively track all the variables affecting the U. S. labor market. The Bureau of Labor Statistics (BLS) publishes an *Occupational Outlook Quarterly* and other publications that some consider useful. Unfortunately, Bureau assumptions may not bear up for the needs of one firm in one area and would not, in any case, help multinational corporations doing business across national boundaries.

The external supply of labor depends on such variables as business fluctuations, social and demographic trends, and attitudes.

Fluctuations in the business cycle. When the U. S. enters a recession, unemployment increases; the external supply of labor, viewed in the aggregate, is relatively plentiful. As the nation enters recovery, unemployment decreases and the external supply of labor grows more scarce. The problem is that increases in unemployment are not uniform: white-collar workers, for example, are less prone to layoff than skilled or unskilled production labor. Even in the depths of a recession, spot labor shortages in special occupations remain acute.

Social trends and attitudes. Depending on the mood of the nation, people can be more or less inclined to work in certain occupations or for certain companies. During the Vietnam war, many talented college students avoided majoring in business because leading corporations were associated with the unpopular war effort. During the 1980s, college students favored relatively high-paid fields such as business, accounting, engineering, or computer science over low-paid but socially desirable occupations like social work or schoolteaching. In the late 1990s, it became clear that college students were becoming more selective in choosing among prospective employers because demand clearly outstripped supply for talent.

Demographic trends. The availability of labor is obviously influenced by birth rates. Between 1946 and 1964, one-third of the present U. S. population was born. It was the largest generation in history, and its age cohorts are already in the labor market. Employers in the U.S. have grown accustomed to expecting a relatively plentiful supply of college-educated labor; that has changed in recent years, however, creating a labor shortage (See Exhibit 11-2.) At the same time, birth rates declined after 1964. The result: growth in the labor force has been slowing. (See Exhibit 11-3.) Other variables influencing availability of labor include geographical movements of business, technological innovations, and employee satisfaction levels that affect turnover.

Exhibit 11-2: Workforce availability to remain a serious problem for years to come

---

A few quick facts about why the labor shortage will get worse rather than better.

Conditions in the job market have made it increasingly difficult to recruit qualified workers. In fact, there is a looming crisis in workforce availability in the United States that will affect organizations for decades to come.

Everywhere you turn, there are warning signals:

1. The nation's unemployment rate is the lowest it's been since 1970, making it difficult for employers to find qualified workers. At 4.4% in February of 1999, the national unemployment rate was well below the roughly 5% that economists have long considered "full employment."
2. Time magazine noted in its May 10th, 1999 issue that the birth rate per 1,000 Americans was at its lowest level since the government began keeping records in 1909. This virtually guarantees a tight job market for decades to come.

Exhibit 11-2: Workforce availability to remain a serious problem for years to come
(continued)

3. The March 11, 1999 issue of Electronic Recruiting News stated that for the 15 years beginning in 2000, the number of available 25 to 44 year olds in the economy will be lower than this year's peak. The decline will be as steep as 15% fewer workers in this age group than we have today.

4. The July 15, 1999 issue of Electronic Recruiting News estimates that "the ratio of jobs to workers will hit 1.1 : 1.0 (10% more jobs than workers) sometime in 2002. It will happen even if the bottom falls out of the economy."

5. According to a survey by Wirthlin Worldwide, American business executives are more concerned about a shortage of skilled labor than global competition or a downturn in the economy.

Clearly, forward-thinking employers who prepare themselves now will be in the best position to succeed in the years to come: It's *not* getting any easier.

SOURCE: "Workforce Availability to Remain a Serious Problem for Years to Come" (No date). *Nation's Jobs.* Used with permission from http://www.nationjob.com/headlines/laborshortage.html

---

Exhibit 11-3: Expected growth in the U.S. labor force

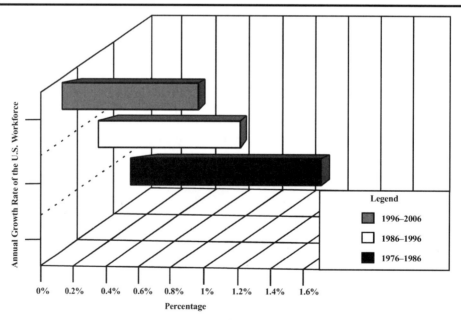

SOURCE: Adapted from data found in Fullerton, H. (1997, November). Labor Force 2006: Slowing Down and Changing Composition. *Monthly Labor Review*, p. 25.

Comparing HR Demands and Supplies

The fifth step in HRP is to compare HR demands and supplies. At this point, planners determine how well present HR inventories match up to what will be needed in the future. From this comparison they can then begin to weigh alternative methods—initiatives of the Human Resource department and other departments—to meet HR demands.

Despite the obvious importance of this step, little guidance is available from published sources about how to make the comparison. What evidence exists suggests that mostly large organizations use a comprehensive approach to establish separate yet coordinated objectives for different HR activities. As a result, the vertical and horizontal integration of such different functions as recruitment, selection, training, and appraisal does not exist (Rothwell and Kazanas 1994).

Acting to Match HR Supplies with Demands

The sixth step in HRP is to take action to match HR supplies and demands. It is to HRP what implementation is to strategic planning. Yet it is obvious that, without being preceded by a systematic and comprehensive comparison of HR supplies and demands, this crucial step is unlikely to be successful.

The range of possible HR actions is staggering to contemplate. (Look at Exhibit 11-4, which represents areas included in the HR function.) Consider:

- Changes in organizational or work group structure or job design can alter HR supplies and demands by reallocating work duties, thus meeting some old HR demands while creating new ones.
- Changes in HRP itself can alter how the organization assesses its HR supplies and demands. The result: new definitions and thus new ways of looking at old issues.
- Changes in selection practices can affect how the organization meets its HR needs, by changing the basis on which people are hired, promoted, demoted, or transferred.
- Changes in HR research and information systems can affect amounts and kinds of data that managers use to identify and cope with problems of HR supplies and demands.
- Changes in compensation and benefits can affect employee turnover, retention, and behavior, thus affecting HR supplies and demands.
- Changes in employee assistance programs can affect individual performance and, through it, organizational performance. The result can be changes in HR supplies and demands through changes in individual productivity.
- Changes in union/labor relations practices can affect how well the organization functions. Labor contracts can influence HR supplies and demands by limiting management prerogatives on employee selection, retention, promotion, transfer, and compensation.

Exhibit 11-4: The human resource wheel

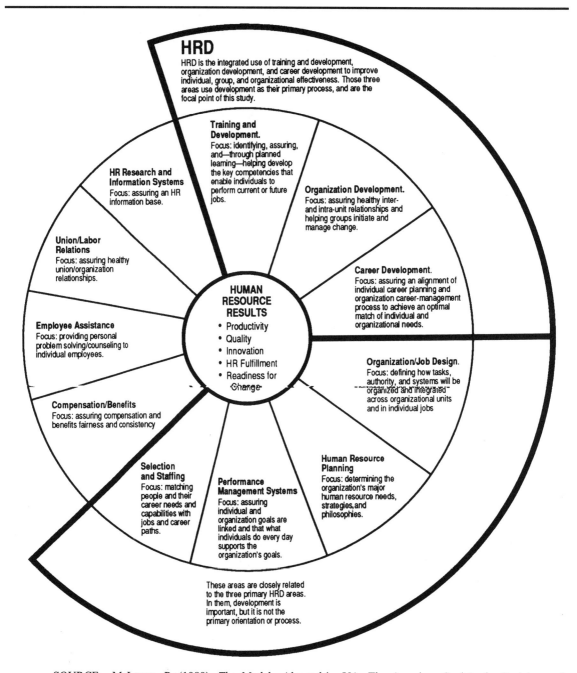

HRD

HRD is the integrated use of training and development, organization development, and career development to improve individual, group, and organizational effectiveness. Those three areas use development as their primary process, and are the focal point of this study.

Training and Development.
Focus: identifying, assuring, and—through planned learning—helping develop the key competencies that enable individuals to perform current or future jobs.

HR Research and Information Systems
Focus: assuring an HR information base.

Organization Development.
Focus: assuring healthy inter- and intra-unit relationships and helping groups initiate and manage change.

Union/Labor Relations
Focus: assuring healthy union/organization relationships.

Career Development.
Focus: assuring an alignment of individual career planning and organization career-management process to achieve an optimal match of individual and organizational needs.

HUMAN RESOURCE RESULTS
• Productivity
• Quality
• Innovation
• HR Fulfillment
• Readiness for Change

Employee Assistance
Focus: providing personal problem solving/counseling to individual employees.

Organization/Job Design.
Focus: defining how tasks, authority, and systems will be organized and integrated across organizational units and in individual jobs

Compensation/Benefits
Focus: assuring compensation and benefits fairness and consistency

Selection and Staffing
Focus: matching people and their career needs and capabilities with jobs and career paths.

Performance Management Systems
Focus: assuring individual and organization goals are linked and that what individuals do every day supports the organization's goals.

Human Resource Planning
Focus: determining the organization's major human resource needs, strategies, and philosophies.

These areas are closely related to the three primary HRD areas. In them, development is important, but it is not the primary orientation or process.

SOURCE: McLagan, P. (1989). *The Models.* Alexandria, VA: The American Society for Training and Development, p. 6. Used by permission.

- Changes in training, education, and development can affect individual productivity on a present job or in preparation for a future one. The result: possible changes in HR supplies and demand.
- The introduction of Organization Development programs can affect how people in the organization adapt to pressures inside and outside and how well work groups interact. The result: possible changes in HR supplies and demand.

Any of these areas can furnish tools for altering existing HR supplies or for meeting HR demands. In a sense, each represents possible performance-improvement strategies. However, none of these actions taken individually can solve *all* supply and demand problems. For example, changing compensation and reward practices will work only if employees value the rewards, have the skills to perform well enough to achieve them, and believe that there is a reasonable chance they can actually attain what they want.

Matters are complicated further in two respects: Changes in any area of the HR wheel will affect all other areas to some extent, and the scope and time frames of change efforts can vary.

The activities of the HR wheel are interdependent. Suppose that the structure of an entire organization is changed. The effect will much like tugging on one strand of a spider web—the entire web will vibrate. For instance:

- A reorganization will change reporting relationships, tasks, roles, work groups, and even individual jobs. There will be a major shift in how the work is allocated, with a corresponding change in the distribution of human resources. New work demands will be created while old ones are given up.
- A reorganization will change HR planning methods. Historical data on staffing levels wiii become useiess under new conditions, without precedent.
- A reorganization will affect selection and staffing because the nature of jobs, work groups, reporting relationships, and other matters will change. New managers, created by the reallocation of duties, may not have the same values and expectations as their predecessors.
- The introduction of self-directed work teams or some other innovative approach to staffing and managing the work will affect *all* areas on the HR Wheel, so the likely impact of such a change should be considered before it is made.

As these changes are felt, they will create others. The initial effects of a reorganization will produce many side effects. These can include a fundamental shift in perceptions about quality of work life, levels of productivity and employee satisfaction, appropriate employee development activities, and degrees of readiness for change. The result: a dramatic alteration in HR supplies and demands under radically new conditions.

The scope and time frame of change efforts also can differ, which will in turn influence the extent of changes in HR supplies and demands. Look at Exhibit 11-5, which depicts the hierarchy of plans. Consider:

- Changes in organizational strategic plans will affect long-term, intermediate-term, and short-term HR initiatives. When a new strategy is adopted, new HR demands are created and the value of existing supplies is changed.
- Changes in coordinative plans will affect HRP at all levels. When a middle manager adopts a new approach in interactions with others, the effects are subtle but still affect the entire organization.
- Changes in operational plans will affect HRP at all levels, but primarily at the operational level. How a field supervisor approaches tasks and deals with employees will have an effect, but it will be very subtle and its impact primarily short-term.

Exhibit 11-5: The hierarchy of plans

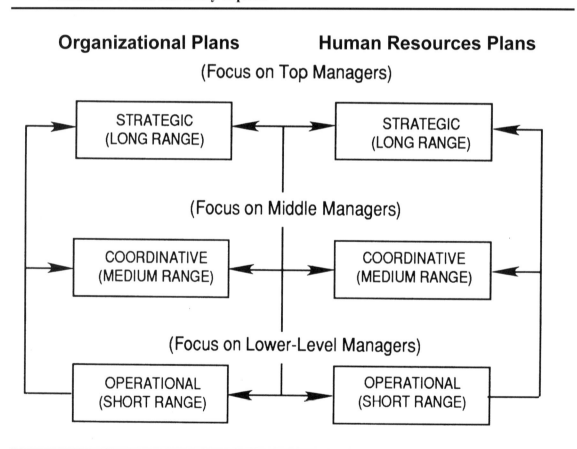

The range of potential HR actions that can be taken to match supplies and demands is thus quite broad. Because one change can affect conditions in all HR areas, coordination of efforts is vital. However, there is little evidence that such coordination is either achieved or attempted in most organizations.

Evaluating HR Plans and Results

The seventh and final step in HRP is to evaluate HR plans and results. At this point, planners take stock of how well plans have been or are being implemented. As might be expected, evaluation can scarcely be successful if nobody has considered alternatives, established objectives for each area of the HR wheel, or taken action to coordinate and integrate HR activities.

There are two approaches to evaluating HRP: by dollar value, or by managerial judgment.

The dollar-value approach places a so-called "bottom-line figure" on HR initiatives: It compares the cost of taking action (an HR initiative) to solve a problem with the cost of *not* taking action. If the difference results in a net savings, the HR action is or was justified; if the difference results in a net loss, the HR action is or was unjustified. This method can be used to weigh alternative change efforts before action or convince hard-nosed managers that past actions were not just expensive boondoggles. Various methods for utilizing the dollar-value approach have been suggested.

Managerial judgment, on the other hand, compares results with intentions. Of course, it can only be used when: (1) desired outcomes have been specified in advance; (2) there is some way to assess outcomes; (3) managers will value results; and (4) results are linked to what managers value (strategic plans or individual intentions, for example). Relatively little has been written about the managerial approach to evaluating HRP, probably because HR professionals are more worried about demonstrating the bottom-line value of their efforts than they are about whether the results matched up to intentions.

HOW HRP RELATES TO WLP

Human resources planning is best understood as a process in which an organization's present HR supplies are compared with its expected future needs and actions are taken over time to narrow any gaps. HRP is thus quite broad, encompassing any and all activities on the HR wheel (Exhibit 11-4). WLP is similar to HRP. Any WLP activity can change existing HR supply-and-demand relationships by furnishing groups or individuals with new skills, knowledge, behaviors, and insights that they can use to improve work performance and thus work output (see Exhibit 11-6).

Exhibit 11-6: The WLP wheel

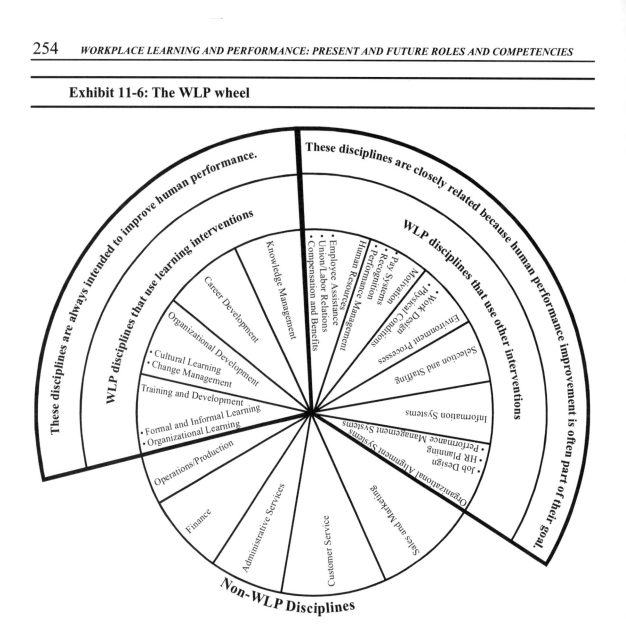

Rothwell, W., Sanders, E., and Soper, J. (1999). *ASTD Models for Workplace Learning and Performance.* Alexandria, VA: American Society for Training and Development.

Any HRP action can affect WLP efforts; any WLP action can affect HR supplies and demands and, through them, HRP. To elaborate:

1. A change in organizational, work group, or job design will create learning needs. When the allocation of job duties change, individuals must acquire a new repertoire of skills to do the work and interact with other people in new social groupings. Training may be needed.

2. A change in selection and staffing practices will also create learning needs. The skills, knowledge, and abilities of people entering or advancing in the organization will affect what they need in their present training and future education and development.

3. A change in HR research and information systems will probably produce new learning needs as well. The quality and quantity of data collected about human performance and satisfaction will affect identification of areas in which new skills, knowledge, or behaviors are needed.

4. A change in compensation and benefit practices will influence employee motivation and, through it, learning needs. Such a change will affect the motivation of people to perform and learn how to improve their performance.

5. A change in employee assistance programs will influence learning needs by changing individual perceptions of self and others. As a result, individuals will need to approach job tasks and interpersonal relations in new ways. This may require training.

6. Changes in union/labor relations practices will influence the work setting and, through it, change conditions in which learning occurs as well as the job tasks and interpersonal relations of individual employees. The result can be new learning needs.

7. Changes in training, education, and development practices will alter individual knowledge, skills, attitudes, and (potentially) job performance. The result: new learning needs for supervisors and even co-workers who deal with individuals who have developed a new awareness of self, others, and job tasks. There may also be new HR supplies and demands for the organization.

8. Changes in Organization Development practices will create the need for new interpersonal skills in dealing with self, members of an individual's work group, and members of other work groups. Training, education, and development are tools for furnishing such skills and reinforcing large- and small-scale OD interventions.

While this is a rather simplistic summary, it demonstrates that WLP efforts can play an important role in reinforcing HRP initiatives. At the same time, planned learning experiences will change an organization's HR supply and demand relationships in the present and future.

CHAPTER 12

Planning for Learning and Instructing

WLP is one way to implement Strategic and HR plans. It brings about change and improved human performance through integrated learning and organizational interventions. To be successful, WLP professionals must have a firm grasp of learning, instructing, and instructional planning. Gaining that grasp is not as simple as it sounds, because there are many theories of learning and instruction. This Chapter summarizes those theories, describes unique characteristics of adult learners, and discusses key methods of planning long-term instructional plans called *curricula*.

WHAT ARE THEORIES OF LEARNING?

What is a Theory?

A *theory* is a plausible principle or a group of principles offered to predict and explain facts, observations, or events. A theory is abstract because it seeks to explain reality through such media as language or symbols. Theories are explanatory in that they assert underlying causes that affect or give rise to a phenomenon. Finally, theories are predictive because they imply that manipulating variables or conditions will result in different but foreseeable outcomes. Theory development ranges on a continuum, from empirically-based to intuitively-based methods. Typically, theory development begins with exploration, and then advances through concept development, hypothesis generation, and hypothesis testing. This process of cycling and recycling between theory development and testing is how disciplines progress through scientific (sometimes called *positivistic*) methods.

What Is Learning, and What Is Instructing?

Learning refers to a change in knowledge, skill, or attitude; *instructing* means guiding a learner through change. Instruction is often associated with what an instructor does to guide or facilitate learning, but instruction need not be planned for people to learn. And even though it is intended to promote learning, instruction is also capable of stifling it.

FOUR THEORIES OF LEARNING

Although some would disagree, theories of learning are not as advanced nor as detailed as theories in disciplines such as physics or biology. In many cases they represent merely philosophical beliefs about the nature of learning, supported by some research. Writers in this area have proposed different means of classifying such theories. First, learning can be viewed as a process of giving or receiving information. Sometimes called *pedagogy*, this theory is focused more on instructing than on learning. Second, learning can be viewed as an association of a series of stimuli and accompanying responses, a theory called *behaviorism*. Third, learning can be viewed as a serendipitous result of insight and perception. This theory is called *cognitivism*. Finally, learning can be viewed as a means of meeting human needs, a theory called *developmentalism*. Each theory makes key assumptions about human nature, learning, the trainee's role, and the role of instructor. They serve as foundations for different applications of WLP.

Learning Theory 1: Pedagogy

Pedagogy is not really a formal theory of learning at all. It is, instead, an informal philosophy about teaching that can be traced to the instructional practices of medieval universities (Knowles 1980). However, it has had a profound impact on modern educational practice. Based on assumptions about human learning, it is pervasive enough to deserve treatment as a formal theory of learning.

Advocates of pedagogy assume that learning occurs by exposing people to subject matter. In a university, the pedagogical environment is the student's college major, the sequence of subjects within a discipline through which learners must progress to graduate. Learning, to pedagogues, consists of mastering increasingly sophisticated bodies of knowledge. The purpose of learning is to absorb information. The learner is, on the one hand, a passive receiver. The instructor is, on the other hand, an active sender of information. In pedagogy, learning is a linear, one-way process of communication and change. To foster learning, the instructor places greatest emphasis on organizing information in logical sequence.

Learning Theory 2: Behaviorism

Behavioral theory has had a lasting impact on learning theory and training practice. The word *behaviorism* was coined in 1913 by John B. Watson. Advocates use rigorous psychological research to derive principles that explain and predict relationships between stimuli (the means to induce behavior), behavior (observable actions that are presumably in response to stimuli), and consequent conditions (rewards or punishments for action). Sometimes called "Second Wave psychology," *behaviorism*—synonymous with behavioralism—stresses the importance of external, environmental influences on specific, observable, and measurable human behavior. To behaviorists, thinking and feeling have relatively little to do with learning because they are internalized and are thus unobservable and only indirectly measurable.

As a school of psychology, behaviorism encompasses a range of viewpoints. However, advocates do share three primary assumptions. First, they focus attention on present behavior, not on past determinants of it. Second, they believe that only external and observable phenomena are important. Finally, the desired results of instruction should be specified prior to instruction and should be expressed in measurable terms.

Behaviorists have been sharply attacked for fostering a mechanistic, manipulative view of learning. Under the force of such attacks, some have modified their view that humans are mere products (or puppets) of the environment and shaped by its myriad stimuli. Indeed, some have gone so far as to argue that behavioral change can arise from internal forces within learners, as well as from external forces.

Early behavioralistic learning theorists included Ivan Pavlov (1849–1936), John D. Watson (1878–1958), Edwin Guthrie (1886–1959), and Edward Thorndike (1874–1849). Pavlov is generally credited as the grandfather of behaviorism. His experiments demonstrated that when dogs received food after a buzzer was sounded, they came to associate the buzzer with food. Food is an *unconditioned stimulus*; salivation in anticipation of food is an *unconditioned response*. When the buzzer is sounded just before feeding, it becomes a *conditioned stimulus* that will lead to salivation, a *conditioned response*. This is called *signal learning*, since a conditioned stimulus (the buzzer) literally signals an unconditioned stimulus (food).

As the father of behaviorism, Watson built his work on Pavlov's. He argued that all differences between human beings result from learning. To demonstrate his belief, Watson used an 11-month-old boy in a series of experiments. Pairing a loud noise and a white rat, Watson taught the boy to fear the rat through association.

Edwin Guthrie, another contributor to learning theory, rejected Watson's assertion that learning is improved through practice. Instead, he contended that a connection between stimulus and response is formed when they are first paired. No amount of practice improves performance. Instead, when a stimulus is repeated, the learner tends to repeat the same response.

To change a conditioned response, Guthrie suggested three techniques: (1) tiring the learner by repeatedly presenting the stimulus; (2) replacing the response by varying the degree to which the stimulus is presented; and (3) presenting the stimulus under conditions in which the response cannot take place (Guthrie 1935). Simple examples should illustrate these three techniques. To break the habit of smoking, a smoker can: (1) be forced to smoke too much; (2) be given tobacco that is increasingly weaker; or (3) be given access to tobacco only in strictly enforced "no smoking" areas. (All of these techniques have been used in smoking-cessation programs, incidentally.)

Edward Thorndike has had a profound influence on learning theory. Founder of *connectionism*, he believed that learning occurs through formation of a bond between stimulus and response. Unlike his predecessors, he accepted the notion that learning, synonymous with bonding, is improved through practice. He further believed that bonding between a stimulus and a response is improved through vigor (that is, a strong response and a strong stimulus and frequency of occurrence).

Thorndike codified seven laws of learning. *The law of effect* suggested that a response is strengthened when followed by satisfaction, but weakened when followed by annoyance. *The law of readiness* suggested that a response is satisfying when the learner is predisposed to act; an inability to respond is annoying when a learner is predisposed to act; and a forced response is annoying when a learner is not predisposed to act. *The law of exercise* suggested that the bond between stimulus and response is strengthened when used, but weakened when unused. *The law of multiple response* suggested that when a response to a stimulus does not lead to satisfaction, the learner will try other responses. *The law of prepotency* suggested that a learner will selectively perceive the stimulus to which a response will be made. *The law of analogy* suggested that an agent will respond to a new stimulus based on analogy with responses to similar but known stimuli. *The law of associative shifting* suggested that an agent can be taught to make a connection between a stimulus and response, even when the stimulus is not presented. From a given connection, the researcher gradually withdraws the stimulus, but the agent still makes the association in the new situation. Many educators believe that Thorndike's major influence on modern learning theory is his Law of Effect.

Subsequent behaviorists have built on the foundations constructed by their predecessors. They include Clark Hull, Kenneth Spence, and B. F. Skinner. Each contributed to the gradual development of learning theory.

Hull was a true behaviorist in the tradition of positivism (Hull 1952). Not content with vague theorizing, he stated over 100 hypotheses about learning and then set out to verify them systematically through a long series of tightly-controlled laboratory experiments. Like his forerunners, he believed all learning was essentially the result of a stimulus-response connection. Inspired by systems theory, he called the stimulus by a new name: the *input*. The response he called *output*. Hull postulated the existence of a third set of variables—*intervening* ones, which are the effects of an environmental stimulus on an individual.

Although Hull's theory is quite complex, it can be summarized in one statement: the response potential of a given stimulus is the result of multiplying such intervening variables as *habit strength* (the number of previous and reinforced pairings of a stimulus and a response), *drive* (the need to meet certain requirements of the body), *stimulus dynamism* (the strength of a stimulus), and *incentive*—the strength of a reward that will meet body requirements (Lefrancois 1982).

A simple example should serve to clarify the theory. A rat will learn to master a maze provided that: previous efforts to do so have been reinforced (rewarded), the reinforcement met the rats' needs, the rat recognized the relationship between the maze and the reward resulting from mastering it, and the reward was sufficiently worthwhile to induce effort.

Kenneth Spence built on Hull's work and modified it (Spence 1960). Contrary to Hull, Spence concluded that habit strength is solely a function of pairing stimulus and response. He also re-examined the basic relationship between habit strength, drive, stimulus dynamism, and incentive. Spence defined their relationship as additive, not multiplicative.

B. F. Skinner challenged mainstream behaviorism and substituted his own thinking (Skinner 1953). In doing so, he left a major imprint on learning theory. Earlier theorists believed that responses are always elicited by a stimulus, a view called *classical conditioning*. But Skinner believed that some responses are made without reference to a specific stimulus. If such responses are reinforced, they are more likely to be repeated. This view is called *operant conditioning*. While Skinner did not utterly reject classical conditioning, he did assert that its value was limited in explaining human learning. Instead, he emphasized the importance of reinforcement. Primary reinforcers satisfy basic needs, such as those for food, water, and sex; secondary reinforcers are learned through association with primary reinforcers. There are two basic reinforcers: positive and negative. A *positive reinforcer* will increase the likelihood of a response when provided; a *negative reinforcer* will increase the likelihood of a response when removed. Punishment differs from a negative reinforcer because it does not provide an indication of what behavior should be.

As conceptualized by mainstream behavioristic learning theorists, human nature is primarily reactive. People respond to stimuli. Hence, observable and measurable behavior is the means by which learning occurs. A change in external behavior produces changes in internal attitudes, beliefs, and values. Human beings are shaped by their surroundings.

By extension, the role of learners is dependent. They are products of environmental stimuli contrived by instructors and other people. Reinforcement through various rewards is used to shape desired behavior. Learning itself is largely external; it begins with behavior.

Social learning theory bridges behaviorism and another major tradition—cognitivism. The term "social learning" is linked closely with "socialization"—adaptation to a cultural environment. Appropriate behaviors vary across cultures, depending on norms regulating interaction whenever the individual is introduced to a new role or environment.

For advocates of social learning, most learning results from *observation* and *imitation*. The individual observes behaviors of others and the resulting outcomes, later imitating what was rewarded. The stimulus may be vicarious in that an observer can form an association between a response and a reward or reinforcer. The response might also be a means of meeting primary or secondary needs. Repeated observations of a model or representations of behavior may have the same effect as repeated performance of a behavior by learners themselves. Behavioral change occurs when learners perceive some benefit from imitating acts performed or even suggested by others.

Social learning theorists believe that human nature is highly imitative and shaped by behaviors appropriate to the unspoken norms of a culture. The role of learner thus consists of imitating behaviors demonstrated by others; the role of the instructor is to provide a model to be imitated. Learning occurs when behavior is demonstrated and reinforced.

Learning Theory 3: Cognitivism

Unlike behavioralism, cognitive learning theory is concerned with insight and understanding. Its focus is on the internal and the personal, not the external and impersonal influences of stimuli and responses. For the most part, cognitivists firmly reject the behavioralistic assumption that people are products of their environment; rather, they see people as major influences on the environment. Although the Gestalt school of psychology contributed most to the development of cognitive learning theory, Edward Tolman (1886–1959) and Kurt Lewin (1890–1947) can also be viewed as major exponents.

Cognitive theory began with the work of Gestalt psychologists at about the same time as behaviorism. While Pavlov's early experiments laid the foundations of behaviorism, Wolfgang Kohler's observations of apes laid the foundations of cognitivism. Stranded on a tropical island at the beginning of World War I, Kohler occupied his time with experimentation. He placed a bunch of bananas just out of reach of some caged apes. He noticed they were cunning enough to move boxes and even place one box on top of others to reach the food. In another experiment they used a stick to knock down the bananas. He concluded that learning is a result of *insight*, a sudden flash of recognition indicating that relationships exist between the parts of a larger problem.

Kohler was a Gestalt theorist. As used in psychology, the German word *Gestalt* refers to a system or pattern of phenomena. Gestalt theorists attack behaviorism for reducing elements of learning to such separate parts as stimuli and responses, while ignoring the larger pattern of relationships between them. The pattern, not the parts, is important. Indeed, the whole (the pattern) is greater than the sum of its parts (specific stimuli and responses). Gestalt theorists emphasize the uniquely personal side of learning, since they see it as essentially a process of discovering relationships. Individual change results from acute awareness; hence, Gestalt theorists emphasize *perception* as fundamental to learning.

Gestalt psychology has proposed six principles about the nature of perception.

The first is the *principle of direction*: Stimuli that appear to be meaningful and that form a pattern will stand out against a neutral background. Observers will perceive the pattern.

The second is the *principle of contiguity*: Stimuli that are close together tend to be perceived as grouped together.

The third is the *principle of embeddedness*: A large figure with a great number of stimuli will stand out from small figures with lesser numbers of stimuli.

The fourth is the *principle of likeness*: Similar objects will tend to be perceived together.

The fifth is the *principle of joint destiny*: Objects that move together tend to be perceived together.

The sixth is the *principle of closure*: The mind will tend to perceive as complete otherwise incomplete experiences or patterns.

These general principles are essentially an outgrowth of the Gestalt belief that every psychological event (every experience) tends to be perceived as meaningful and complete.

Edward Tolman is considered another major adherent of cognitive learning theory. Although sharing many views with behaviorists, he differed from them in his belief that behavior is directed toward achieving some purpose. Since behavior is goal-directed, expectations (the *cognitive*) play a crucial role in learning.

Tolman's theory of learning was based, like so many others, on experimentation with rats. He released rats in a maze, giving them more than one way to the exit and sufficient opportunity to unlock the secrets of the maze. He then blocked several routes. He hypothesized that the rats, finding the shortest route blocked, would try the second shortest. Results of the experiment confirmed his expectations, leading to *sign theory*. A sign is a stimulus.

Tolman found that learning occurs through development of *cognitive maps*, meaning internalized associations between a goal, a behavior (or series of behaviors), and an awareness of the environment in which the goal is located. Learning occurs when expectations are aroused in connection with some behavior. Aroused expectations are called *significates* and are associated with a sign.

Unlike behaviorists, Tolman did not view learning as a result of many stimuli-response relationships. Instead, he viewed learning as composed of large units of behavior unified in their perceived relationship to a purpose or goal. To him, cognition is an expectation of good performance within a unique environmental context.

Kurt Lewin's theory of learning shares important features with the ideas of Tolman and the Gestalt theorists. His work has had a major impact on WLP. He was influenced by *phenomenology*, the belief that people interpret experience and that their interpretations are central to existence. For Lewin, individuals exist in a life space consisting of everything that affects their behavior. At the center of the life space is the individual as perceiver of environment. The environment itself has no inherent meaning; rather, the way each individual perceives it is crucial to understanding behavior (Lewin 1951).

The life space can be considered in terms of *valence*, a word Lewin used to mean the relative attractiveness of a goal to the individual. A *barrier* is a perceived difficulty or drawback in achieving a goal. Life space varies as individual goals change.

Like Tolman, Lewin believed that human behavior is essentially purposive and oriented toward goals with strong valence in a given life space. Unlike Tolman, however, he did not emphasize cognitive mapping. Lewin's work is important as the foundation of experiential learning: the act or transfer of learning through personal experience. In addition, his work is also the basis of action research, an important foundation of mainstream Organization Development that has historically suggested that group learning occurs through the unfreezing of old beliefs, the restructuring of those beliefs, and then refreezing (acceptance of new beliefs).

Jerome Bruner is classified as a cognitive theorist because he emphasized the internalized nature of learning (Bruner 1961). For him, human learning is not a function of stimulus-response as it is for behaviorists. Instead, human development corresponds to the evolution of the species: The child progresses through periods in which the focus is on the amplification of motor abilities, sensory abilities, and intellectual facility in the same way that the human race evolved from enhancements to motor abilities (for example, tool and weapon making), sensory abilities (for example, the telescope and microscope), and finally intellectual facility (for example, the computer).

Human learning occurs through *categorization*, the classification of similar objects or ideas. Categories are based on *attributes*, qualities that objects must have to be classified as stimuli. A *coding system* is a hierarchy of categories in which the most general category (for example, humans) is more generic than those below it (for example, men and women). To learn is to form or attain an inference between categories (or concepts) within the coding system. *Concept formation* involves an inference that two objects belong in the same category; *concept attainment* is a discovery of attributes that are useful in helping to distinguish between objects that do or do not belong in the same category.

According to Bruner, the ability to create a coding system depends on such individual qualities as set, need, species, and diversity. *Set* is a readiness to perceive. *Need* is a motivation to learn based on drives. A *species* suggests that the more a learner already knows about objects in a possible generic coding system, the easier it will be to create a coding system. *Diversity* suggests that the more widely an object or event is experienced, the easier it will be to relate it to other objects or events.

Concept attainment resembles the creation of categories. Bruner suggests four general approaches to concept attainment: (1) *Complete scanning:* attempting to generate all possible relationships between categories; (2) *Partial scanning:* developing a hypothesis and testing it to see if it holds true; (3) *Conservative scanning:* accepting the first attribute observed between two categories; and (4) *Gambling:* changing attributes to see if categories still appear similar.

Based on his experimentation, Bruner concluded that people do adopt such learning strategies in the process of concept attainment.

To cognitive learning theorists, human nature is more complex than it is to behaviorists. They see human beings as highly adaptive to their environment but capable of changing it. The role of learner is active, since all learning is uniquely personal and experiential. The instructor's role is to create an environment that will lead to learning, a quintessentially individualized matter.

Learning Theory 4: Developmentalism

Developmental learning theory is a descriptive term encompassing the work of such modern writers as Jean Piaget, Carl Rogers, and Malcolm Knowles. Influenced by cognitive theory, their ideas represent a rejection of behaviorist assumptions about the nature of human beings. They prefer an emphasis on human freedom, rather than on determinism. They share a deep faith in the human capacity to act on the environment rather than merely react to it.

Jean Piaget (1896–1980) devised a theory of learning based on stages of a child's development. He did not consider the stages of individual development as a reflection of human evolution. In fact, his view of childhood development is somewhat similar to that of Sigmund Freud.

Piaget has been widely influential in U.S. and European education (Piaget 1972). He started out with two simple questions: (1) How are children able to adapt to their environment? and (2) How can stages of childhood development be conceptualized? In answering the first question, he concluded that children play, they imitate, and they combine play and imitation. Play is a means of using objects for activities that have already been learned. It is a process of reinforcing the known. Imitation is a means of modifying behavior to that which was previously unknown. Through imitation, children internalize the world and develop cognitively.

In answering the second question, Piaget concluded that children develop through four stages. In the first (birth to age 2), they master language, come to understand objects, and discern cause-and-effect relationships. In the second (ages 2 to 7), they learn to solve problems through intuition. In the third (ages 7 to 11), they learn that it is possible for objects to retain the same bulk or space despite optical illusions. In the fourth stage (ages 11 to 15), they learn to compare actual conditions to hypothetical conditions.

Based on Piaget's work and the countless research studies it has spawned, teachers have attempted to gear instruction to the child's stage of development. More important for WLP professionals, Piaget's work has directed attention to the efforts of Erik Erikson and others to show developmental stages beyond childhood (Havighurst 1970). Even Piaget believed that adults adapt to their environment through the same two basic techniques as children: *assimilation* (repetition of activities already learned) and *accommodation* (change in behavior resulting from environmental pressure).

Carl Rogers is seldom classified as a learning theorist, since his vocation was clinical psychology. But his writings have had a profound and revolutionary impact on teachers, trainers, and learning theorists. Beginning with the assumption that psychological counseling is essentially a learning experience, he proposed four hypotheses. First, learning is entirely internal. For this reason, teaching is impossible because only the learner governs what is learned. Second, people will learn only what they perceive to be worthwhile. Third, people resist learning experiences they perceive as threatening to their self-concept. Fourth, self-concept becomes more rigid when threatened. Hence, significant learning is fostered only in a supportive climate. For Rogers, people learn to satisfy their needs. They are inclined to seek greater freedom and strive to become what they are capable of becoming. An exponent of Maslow's theoretical hierarchy of needs, Rogers revolutionized psychology and ushered in a new era in learning theory (Rogers 1969).

Malcolm Knowles argues that adults learn in ways different from children, so instruction geared to adults must take their special needs into account. As a leading exponent of the adult education movement, he distilled the theory of androgogy into four key points. First, learning is a result of self-direction. People have a need to function with greater autonomy as they grow older. Second, learning is intimately influenced by individual experience. Adults have a deep need to participate actively in learning rather than become passive sponges of information. Third, learning is influenced by the timing of the experiences. Adults are most willing to learn when faced with specific life problems, called *teachable moments*, to which they seek answers. Fourth, learning is problem-oriented. Adults learn solely to meet needs (Knowles 1984).

For Knowles, as for Rogers, human beings have a drive to become more of what they are capable of becoming. Learning is strictly internal, influenced by human developmental stages. Instructors only facilitate learning. Individuals are self-actualizing learners.

To sum up, developmental learning theorists are often more cognitive than behavioral in their orientation to learning. For them, learning is internal. The instructor's role is to help learners. The learner's role is crucial; learning is natural, and human nature is essentially growth-oriented. Exhibit 12-1 summarizes information about the four primary theories of learning.

Exhibit 12-1: Summary of major learning theories

	Pedagogy	Behavioral	Cognitive	Developmental
Theorists	None	John B. Watson Ivan Pavlov Edwin Guthrie Edward Thorndike Clark Hull Kenneth Spence B. F. Skinner Albert Bandura	Wolfgang Kohler Edward Tolman Kurt Lewin Jerome Bruner	Jean Piaget Carl Rogers Malcolm Knowles
Definition of Learning	General awareness of knowledge: information received	Conditioning	Development of internal classification schemes	Problem-solving: influenced by stages of development
Human Nature	Passive, reluctant learners	Influenced by the environment	Influenced by individual interpretations of external events	Active, eager learners
Role of Instructor	Crucial	Model	Provides environment suitable to learning	Facilitator
Role of Learner	Unimportant	Shaped by environment	Crucial	Crucial

THE FOUR THEORIES OF INSTRUCTION

Logically, theories of instruction are based on theories of learning. There are four general theories of instruction, just as there are four theories of learning. The first theory of instruction is the *subject-centered*. It focuses on what will be taught. The second theory is *objectives-centered*. Based on behaviorism, it focuses on the results or outcomes of instruction. The third theory is the *experience-centered*. Based on cognitivism, it focuses on what learners experience during instruction. The fourth theory is the *opportunity-centered*. Based on developmentalism, it focuses on matching individual needs to appropriate instructional experiences. These theories are not mutually exclusive.

Theory of Instruction 1: Subject-Centered Instruction

What general principles are useful for instruction based on a subject-centered approach?

Although there is no one spokesperson for the theory, Malcolm Knowles has summarized it while describing his own developmental theory. Advocates believe instructors should plan instruction carefully, sequencing information by the logic of the material. They should ignore learners' experiences. They should assume learners will understand that what they learn will have future uses not readily apparent to them during instruction. And they should assume that the learner is dependent on the instructor for guidance. Pedagogues believe that they have every right to use strong discipline to force learning when students lack motivation. They also believe that, as instructors, they should be expert in the subject matter rather than in instructional design. Pedagogues often reach these conclusions based on their own experiences.

Theory of Instruction 2: Objectives-Centered Instruction

What general principles are useful for instruction based on an objectives-centered approach? How would learning theorists of the behavioral school deal with instruction?

For Pavlov and Watson, instructors should pair a neutral object or subject (what is to be learned) with another already viewed positively (wealth, beauty, prestige). Based on Thorndike's views about learning, instructors should reward learners for correct performance and correct them promptly for incorrect performance. Further, instructors should encourage repetition of acts performed correctly, give frequent examinations to gather feedback on learning progress, and emphasize ways to elicit numerous correct responses from learners.

Based on Guthrie's views, however, instructors ought to state objectives clearly in advance, because the instructor should know what responses should be elicited from what stimuli. Further, instructors should provide many different variations of the same stimuli, because each stimulus-response bond is unique.

Based on the views of Hull, instructors should produce anxiety among learners so they have an incentive to learn. In addition, instructors should vary subjects so that learners do not become fatigued, and arrange subjects in disjointed order to increase learner attention span. To Hull, learning will only occur when the learner wants something or must do something, and when the learner sees learning as a way of achieving that which he or she wants. Spence would largely agree with these views.

Based on the views of Skinner, instructors should rely on secondary reinforcers (such as praise, grades, and challenging assignments) to encourage learning and define behaviorally what learners will be able to do after instruction. Instructors should also:

- Reinforce learner behavior 100 percent of the time after the first few responses, but then gradually switch to partial reinforcement.
- Make learning experiences as individualized as possible (for example, utilize programmed instruction instead of lectures).
- Avoid punishment (rather, simply ignore or fail to reinforce inappropriate behaviors).

For Bandura, however, instructors should model the behaviors they teach. They should also establish clearly-defined objectives for behavioral change, gain learner commitment to change, devise ways to record or measure the extent of behavioral change, and allow learners to establish their own reward systems for successful achievement of objectives. Generally, instructors using a behavioristic learning orientation should:

- Keep learners active, since repetition of appropriate responses is generally important to behaviorists.
- Reinforce appropriate responses.
- Encourage practice.
- Motivate learners by making explicit the link between learning and achieving goals.

Objectives-centered instruction has had a lasting impact on WLP practices because it stresses the measurement of learning that is so important in justifying expenditures on human performance-improvement interventions. This approach, though requiring specialized expertise in instructional design, is still widely applied in many organizations.

Theory of Instruction 3: Experience-Centered Instruction

What general principles are useful for instruction based on an experience-centered approach? How would learning theorists of the cognitive school deal with instruction?

Based on Gestalt theory, WLP professionals can glean valuable clues to instructing others. For instance, gestaltists would generally agree that instructors should:

- Emphasize learner understanding more than behavioral change.
- Present a step-by-step model of an entire process first, and then relate parts to the whole.
- Help learners solve problems, because unsolved problems create uncomfortable ambiguity for learners.

Based on Tolman's views of learning, instructors should provide learners with opportunities to test hypotheses and solutions to problems, serve as consultants to learners engaged in problem-solving activities, and expose learners to a variety of interpretations so that these views can be tested in the relative safety of the learning environment.

Based on Lewin's views about learning, instructors should encourage the "unfreezing" of learners' stereotypes, as well as the restructuring of views so that learners are more open to new experiences. Instructors should also encourage learners to refreeze what was learned through the restructuring process.

Based on Bruner's views about learning, instructors should encourage the human predisposition to learn, structure information so learners can readily assimilate it, sequence instruction in concept hierarchies, and provide reinforcement for student learning.

Generally, the instructor who accepts a cognitive orientation to learning should:

- Structure learning problems, so learners perceive the most important features first.
- Emphasize the meaningfulness of the learning event and its importance in achieving desired goals.
- Provide frequent feedback to learners in order to confirm appropriate responses or correct inappropriate ones.
- Allow learners to establish or participate in establishing instructional goals.
- Encourage creative thought.

This approach has had a substantial influence on Organization Development.

Theory of Instruction 4: Opportunity-Centered Instruction

What general principles are useful for instruction, based on an opportunity-centered approach? How would learning theorists of the developmental school deal with instruction?

Based on the views of Piaget, instructors can glean the following guidance:

- Be aware of the learner's stage of development and cultural background.
- Provide challenging learning experiences that will allow both assimilation and accommodation.
- Individualize instruction, tailoring it to learners' special needs.

Based on the views of Carl Rogers, instructors should create a supportive climate for individuals and/or groups, help learners clarify their own needs, and encourage learners to think for themselves through diligent but reflective questioning. Rogers' views are compatible with those of Malcolm Knowles, who believes that instructors should encourage learner self-direction and autonomy, provide groups of learners with every opportunity to pool individual experiences and insights, and assess individual readiness to learn by analyzing problems that the learners are facing in their present career or work. Further, they should pose instruction in the form of challenging real-life problems, rather than boring and seemingly irrelevant facts or theories.

Like the objectives-centered and experience-centered approaches, this approach to instruction claims many adherents among WLP professionals. It has prompted greater attention to individual life and career planning, since life and career stages provide a cluster of needs to which instruction can be geared.

To conclude, each major theory of instruction is based on a theory of learning. What instructors do should be guided by *how they believe students learn.* Each theory of instruction makes certain assumptions about the nature of learning, the role of instructor, the role of learner, and human nature. The key points of these theories of instruction are summarized in Exhibit 12-2.

Exhibit 12-2: Key points of major theories of instruction

Theory	Key Points
Subject-Centered Instruction	*Instructors should:* — Plan instruction carefully and sequence it by the logic of the material. — Ignore learners' experiences. — Assume that learners will understand that what they learn will have future uses not readily apparent to them. — Assume that the learner is dependent on the instructor for guidance. — Use strong discipline to force learners to be motivated. — Be experts on the subject matter, not so much on instructional design.
Objectives-Centered Instruction	*Instructors should:* — Reward learners for correct performance and correct them promptly when performance is incorrect. — Encourage repetition of acts performed correctly. — Give frequent examinations to gather feedback on learning progress. — Emphasize ways to elicit numerous correct responses from learners. — State objectives clearly in advance. — Provide many different variations of the same stimuli, because each stimulus-response bond is unique. — Create an atmosphere of anxiety for learners in order to provide an incentive to learn. — Vary subjects so learners do not become fatigued. — Arrange subjects in disjointed order to increase learner attention span. — Rely on secondary reinforcers (praise, grades, challenging assignments) to encourage learning. — Reinforce learner behavior 100 percent of the time after the first few responses, but gradually switch to partial reinforcement. — Make learning experiences as individualized as possible. — Avoid punishment. — Illustrate (model) what they teach. — Establish clearly-defined behavioral objectives. — Gain learner commitment to change. — Measure behavioral change. — Allow learners to reward themselves and their accomplishments.

Exhibit 12-2: Key points of major theories of instruction *(continued)*

Theory	Key Points
Experience-Centered Instruction	*Instructors should:* — Emphasize learner understanding more than behavioral change. — Present a step-by-step model of an entire process first, and then relate parts to the whole. — Help learners solve problems. — Provide learners with opportunities to test hypotheses and solutions to problems. — Serve as consultants to learners engaged in problem-solving. — Expose learners to various interpretations and viewpoints. — Encourage "unfreezing" of learner stereotypes. — Encourage restructuring of views so that learners are more open to new experiences. — Encourage "refreezing" of what was learned through the restructuring process. — Encourage the human predisposition to learn. — Structure information so that learners can readily assimilate it. — Sequence instruction in concept hierarchies. — Provide reinforcement for student learning.
Opportunity-Centered Instruction	*Instructors should:* — Be aware of the learner's stage of development and cultural background. — Provide challenging learning experiences. — Individualize instruction. — Create a supportive climate for individuals and/or groups. — Help learners clarify their own needs. — Encourage students to think for themselves through diligent but reflective questioning. — Encourage learner self-direction and autonomy. — Provide groups of learners with every opportunity to pool individual experiences and insights. — Assess individual readiness to learn by analyzing problems that the learners are facing in their careers or work at present. — Pose instruction in the form of problems rather than facts.

HOW THEORIES OF LEARNING AND INSTRUCTION APPLY TO ADULT LEARNERS

Before 1950, many educators assumed that theories of learning and instruction were as applicable to adults as to children. Since formal education in the United States has been focused largely on those between ages 6 and 21, most research studies before the mid–1960s centered on people in those age groups. Despite the best efforts of scholars, pedagogy has largely remained the dominant philosophical orientation of teachers in primary, secondary, and higher education. At the same time, behaviorism still dominates WLP practices in organizations, though the influence of pedagogy, especially through unspoken expectations of operating managers about desirable WLP practices, is often apparent in this context as well.

However, Knowles has pointed out that teachers of adults began to question the validity of pedagogical assumptions in the early 1960s. Cyril Houle's classic 1961 study, *The Inquiring Mind,* propelled the movement forward. Examining just 22 people, Houle found that adult learners can be classified into three groups: (1) *the goal-centered,* who use learning experiences as means to the learners' own ends; (2) *the activity-centered,* who participate in learning for purposes having little to do with its objectives or outcomes; and (3) *the learning-centered,* who are interested in learning and knowledge for their own sake.

Houle's student Allen Tough continued the work of his teacher. From his research, he found that adults initiate an average of eight personal learning projects each year, and almost always consult at least one other person in the course of such projects. Teachers, Tough learned through his research, tend to interfere with adult learning by imposing a pedagogical structure on an otherwise natural, freewheeling, and discovery-oriented problem-solving process (Tough 1971). Few learning projects are associated with formal schools or WLP departments.

There remains only a limited body of knowledge applicable to teaching adults, even though much has been written about it. Indeed, what is known can be summarized in a few major points. According to various writers, adults initiate their own learning projects in response to significant life events—such as marriage, divorce, parenthood, promotion, or job transfer (Zemke and Zemke 1981). Their motivation to learn increases as the number of significant events in their lives increases. Adults tend to pursue learning experiences directly related to these significant events. Generally, they are especially open to learning before, during, and after a significant life event.

Adults also prefer knowledge or skill that can be applied immediately. They are motivated to preserve their self-esteem, prefer to focus on one major concept at a time, and are inclined to take fewer risks than children when they learn. They integrate new learning with what they already know and are slow in accepting new information that conflicts head-on with their experience or their values. They prefer self-directed to instructor-guided learning, and they learn best through open-ended instruction in which a group of learners share experiences. Finally, they prefer a learning climate that is both physically and psychologically comfortable, posing no threat to self-esteem.

The nature of the learning task and the needs of the learners will provide clues to which learning or instructional theory will probably work best. The subject-centered approach usually works best when learners have no prior knowledge of a subject; the behavioral approach works best when learners are faced with acquiring a measurable or observable skill; the cognitive approach works best when the aim is to stimulate creativity and examination of attitudes; and the developmental approach works best when the focus is on personal growth or career planning. In short, learners differ in "readiness" for self-directedness, and the instructor's approach should match up to it.

In general, what is known about *instructing* adults seems consistent with what is known about *managing* them. The teachers of adults, like managers, should clarify their own expectations, since expectations will have a major impact on the perceived success of experiences. Teachers should also assess individual needs and developmental stages for use in motivation and in instructional design, rely on influence and modeling, and match instructional approaches to the situation just as effective leaders match their styles of supervision to the situation. While the instructor's role varies in learning experiences, adults should usually be allowed considerable participation in all aspects of the design, delivery, and evaluation of instruction.

CURRICULUM DESIGN FOR WLP

The planning process for WLP requires the professional to: (1) manage all learning experiences sponsored or coordinated by the WLP department; and (2) manage the function or department. The first task will be covered in this Chapter; the second will be discussed in Chapter 17.

What Is a Curriculum?

Although many definitions have been suggested, *curriculum* usually means a plan for instruction or learning. The time span of a curriculum can range from a few minutes to several years, or even over the entire lifetime of an individual or institution. Curriculum issues include: (1) goals and objectives of instruction; (2) the values underlying the goals and objectives; (3) methods of selecting, organizing, and delivering content; (4) processes to facilitate learning; (5) methods of evaluating intentions, methods, outcomes, and the curriculum itself; (6) instructor selection; (7) identification of learners; and (8) management of the setting in which the curriculum is implemented. *Curriculum design* involves careful planning of the curriculum before taking action; *curriculum development* includes the gradual evolution of a plan from initial conception through implementation.

Components of an Organizational Curriculum

The term *program* is frequently used synonymously with curriculum. However, in this book *curriculum* refers to a long-term, strategic instructional plan for all formal learning events sponsored by the WLP department. In contrast, *program* means a single course or other planned learning experience with a definite beginning and end. A program *offering* is a single presentation of a program that is given many times. To cite a simple example: A one-shot workshop on supervision is an *offering* or *program offering*; a workshop on supervision with similar subject matter given repeatedly to different people is a *program*; a series of related programs on supervision in which the whole is greater than its parts (programs) is a rudimentary *curriculum*.

We will limit the term *organizational curriculum* to mean all formal, planned learning activities of the WLP department or those coordinated by the department. It includes all programs offered in the classroom, planned job rotations, external seminars, college courses, professional accreditations, individualized study materials, industry-sponsored educational programs, and other delivery methods integrated into a coherent whole greater than the sum of their respective parts.

The organizational curriculum serves to guide the long-term direction of developmental, educational, and training activities. Planning an organization's curriculum is akin to strategically planning to meet the long-term learning needs of the organization. With this curriculum, decision-makers help an organization adapt to changing external conditions and/or maintain efficient and effective internal work methods. It is a policy tool with which managers can guide learning, as well as a vehicle for helping individuals cope with existing roles and prepare for others.

A *limited-scope curriculum* is part of the total organizational curriculum. It is geared to job classes and helps organize the sequence and subject matter of instruction. For example, the nursing curriculum is only part of a hospital's organizational curriculum. Other parts are geared to other job classes. Each limited-scope curriculum is, in turn, comprised of a series of planned learning experiences. Each program is comparable to operational plans of first-line supervisors, while each limited-scope curriculum is comparable to intermediate plans of middle managers.

Key Steps in Designing an Organizational Curriculum

Designing an organizational curriculum can be thought of as an eight-step process:

1. *Establishing purpose and goals.* What is the purpose of the curriculum? (Keep in mind that meeting long-term learning needs should be emphasized.)
2. *Determining a means of organization.* How will the curriculum be organized?
3. *Categorizing the organization.* How will the curriculum be subdivided into limited-scope curricula? Will the curriculum be designed to gear training to each job class, or will some other categorizing method be used?
4. *Assessing needs.* What should be included in the limited-scope curricula? (Again, emphasize long-term needs.)
5. *Determining delivery methods.* How will needs be met? What kind of programs will be included?

6. *Determining sequence.* In what order should programs be delivered? For what groups of learners?
7. *Implementing the curriculum.* What kind of structure, policies, and instructional leadership will be needed?
8. *Evaluating the curriculum over time.* Emphasize the curriculum as a whole, not discrete programs.

These steps are illustrated in Exhibit 12-3.

Exhibit 12-3: A model of organizational curriculum design

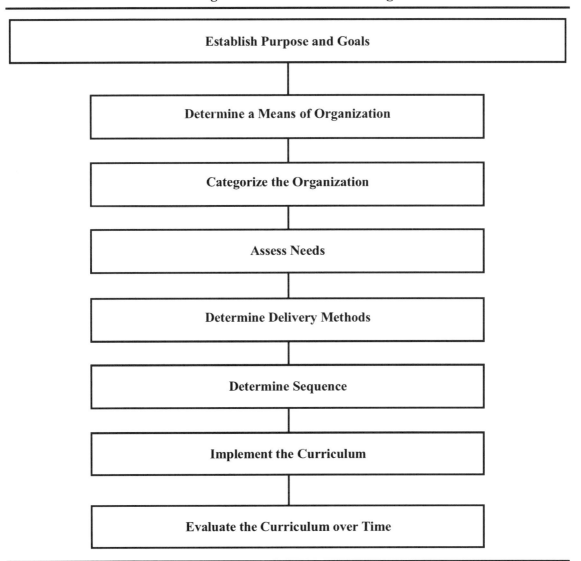

Establishing purpose and goals is handled in much the same way as it is in long-term planning for the department. WLP professionals, working with key decision-makers, address four questions: (1) Why does an organizational curriculum exist? (2) What should it include? Exclude? (3) What is the relationship between formal learning activities and organizational plans? HR plans? WLP department plans? Plans of other departments? (4) What learners will be served? Over what time span? To what general and specific ends? By answering these questions, decision-makers will determine how to engineer or encourage long-term Organization Development through organized learning activities. The way the questions are answered will reflect the values of decision-makers by showing what they consider important.

Determining the means of organization is the second step in the design process. This involves deciding on what basis instruction will be planned and structured. For example, a curriculum can be geared to individuals, work groups, job classes, departments or divisions, strategic issues (quality, customer service), geographical locations (job sites), projects, or any combination of them.

A curriculum organized by individual will use learning contracts for each person. If organized by work group, courses and other experiences will be separately established for many small groups across the organization. A curriculum structured by job class or job progression ladder will match programs to position titles, and a structure by department or location will match programs to the organization chart. A project structure will organize learning experiences by project type, needs, and duration. A team structure will organize learning experiences by intact work groups/self-directed work teams.

The third step, categorizing the organization, is merely a continuation of the second. At this point decision-makers sketch out the types of limited-scope curricula. For example, what will be the size of the management-training component? What will be the other components? Some typical ones might include: sales training, professional training, technical training, and skilled-worker training. Employees are placed in the appropriate category and a curriculum is designed for each group.

The fourth step, assessing needs, begins to address the kinds of programs that will be included in each limited-scope curriculum. At this point, it is worthwhile to consider the organization's strategic plan and any known individual career plans. In this step, general titles can be assigned to programs.

The focus of this step should be on long-term needs, such as orienting new employees, preparing employees for promotion or more advanced work in their fields, or updating employee skills. These needs should be considered long-term because everyone has them to some extent. Curriculum needs assessment is thus centered around predictable needs stemming primarily from job entry or future job movement. In contrast, program needs are more specific, being geared to the present and to a specific group.

In the fifth step, decision-makers determine delivery methods. What approaches will be used to meet needs? Examples include planned individual job rotations, classroom courses, self-study experiences, external seminars, external college courses, correspondence study, web-based instruction, industry-oriented educational programs, or planned on-the-job learning experiences. Each has its own advantages and disadvantages, which should be carefully examined during the curriculum-design process.

The sixth step addresses the question: In what sequence should experiences be offered? Depending on the learners, some experiences are prerequisites to others. They should be identified and scheduled accordingly, within limited-scope curricula.

In sequencing programs for a limited-scope curriculum, three categories of programs should be considered. First are those related to topic areas. Some examples: management, computer science, and engineering. Second are those related to job class. Employees in lower-level job classes on a job progression ladder take specific programs appropriate to that level; other programs are specified for higher levels. Third are those related to individual progress. Programs are geared to maintenance (what are the policies and procedures of the organization?), job (what are the duties?), and promotion (what skills are needed for the next higher job?). These categories overlap and are not mutually exclusive.

Four major designs can be used to sequence programs in a limited-scope curriculum: the *horizontal,* the *vertical*, the *diagonal*, and the *spiral*. The vertical design is perhaps most familiar (see Exhibit 12-4). A newcomer begins with basic programs and gradually moves up. Programs may be described as basic, intermediate, and advanced.

Exhibit 12-4: The vertical design

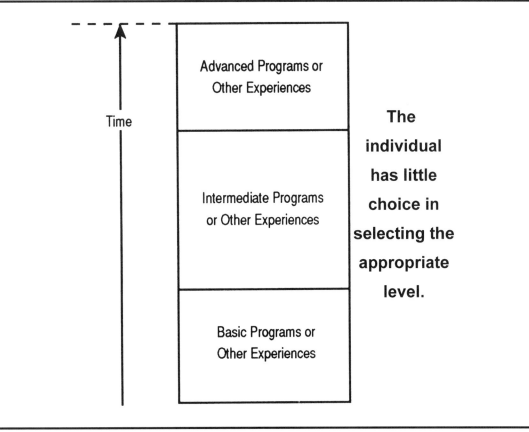

The horizontal design is somewhat different. (See Exhibit 12-5). The learner simultaneously receives or has the opportunity to receive exposure to all three levels. For example, a basic program on general management can be followed by an advanced treatment of some specialized topic. Another example: a maintenance-geared program such as employee orientation is followed by a promotion-geared program such as one on the principles of supervision. The individual has some discretion in choosing programs, but little discretion in choosing the content of the program.

Exhibit 12-5: The horizontal design

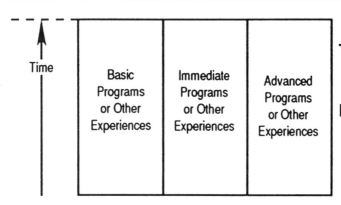

The diagonal design is a compromise between horizontal and vertical (see Exhibit 12-6.) The learner can choose some but not all programs or experiences. For example, orientation (maintenance-geared) is required, but the individual can choose an elective that is job-geared or promotion-geared.

Finally, the spiral design is organized on the principle of repetition. (See Exhibit 12-7.) Individuals are exposed over time to the same concepts, topics, or ideas but in increasingly sophisticated forms. For example, a group of learners may take a series of interrelated programs, such as Principles of Supervision I, II, III, and IV.

In the seventh step, the organizational curriculum is implemented through programs and limited-scope curricula. These experiences can be specifically tailored to the unique individual and work-related requirements of the learners. Decision-makers assess needs before each program offering, select appropriate instructors, and establish rewards and policies to support the curriculum purpose and goals.

Exhibit 12-6: The diagonal design

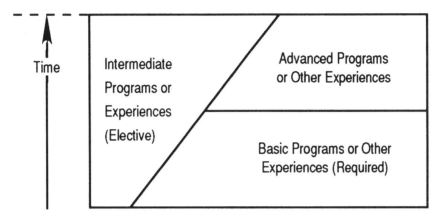

Exhibit 12-7: The spiral design

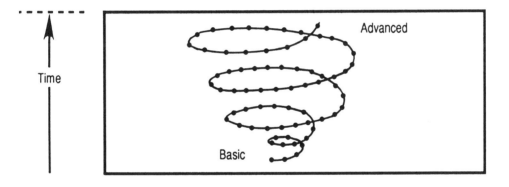

Evaluation is sometimes thought of as the final stage, although in reality it is a continuous process. Evaluation takes place during and after each program offering. Information is then fed upward to help improve limited-scope curricula. Periodically the organizational and limited-scope curricula are reviewed in their entirety for their aggregate long-term impact. This evaluation focuses on the overall results of the curriculum, rather than on individuals, programs, or offerings.

Though the model implies that an organizational curriculum is designed from the top down, there are alternatives. For instance, instructional plans can begin as short blocks of instruction that are gradually put together to form programs first, then limited-scope curricula, and finally an organizational curriculum. With this approach, curriculum design proceeds from bottom (lesson or unit) up. Alternatively, the organizational curriculum is established but is considered apart from required experiences for individuals or work groups. The curriculum stands alone while learners pick and choose programs like people selecting food in a cafeteria. If this approach is used, curriculum design is continuous and can be negotiated between learner and organization.

WLP professionals should look beyond individual programs to the broader limited-scope and organizational curricula. It is not enough to do the short-term planning that program or course-level thinking implies; rather, professionals should consider the intermediate and long-term impact of all WLP activities on the development of the organization through its employees. In this way, OD, employee development, employee education, and training can become long-term change efforts.

BASING THE ORGANIZATIONAL CURRICULUM ON MAJOR LEARNING THEORIES

An organizational curriculum can be based on any one or all of the four major theories of learning and instructing. This means that it can be subject-centered, objectives-centered, experience-centered, and/or opportunity-centered, and so can the limited-scope curricula and the programs. To further complicate the process, within each major approach several distinct methods can be used. Choice of approach and method depends on the purpose and goal of the curriculum, values of decision-makers, and the needs of learners.

The subject-centered curriculum grows out of assumptions of pedagogy. Planning is simple: instructors, not learners, make decisions about subject matter. Programs are classified as required or elective; they are typically organized in logical sequence from basic to advanced. Instructors actively control the flow of information from themselves to learners. Learners master increasingly complicated treatments of an idea or discipline. Learners are passive sponges of information whose experiences prior to instruction are considered largely unimportant or irrelevant. On the other hand, the objectives-centered curriculum is based on the learning and instructional assumptions of behaviorism. Planning focuses on observable, measurable behavior, and the arrangement of instructional experiences is devised from careful analysis of job tasks. Instructors serve as behavior engineers who orchestrate effective job performance through learning experiences and other work improvement methods. Learners are actively involved because they must demonstrate through behavior that they can apply skills in conformance with predetermined standards in circumstances similar to those encountered on the job.

The experience-centered curriculum is based on the assumptions of cognitivism. Planning focuses on identifying patterns larger than single tasks, such as cognitive maps or models of an entire process. Instruction proceeds from whole to part so that learners see interrelationships and configurations connecting them.

This type of curriculum is based on *phenomenology*, the belief that reality exists only as perceived and interpreted through the mind of the observer. For this reason it is possible to define the curriculum variously as what is:

- Approved by decision-makers, or set forth in formal policies and manuals.
- Perceived by instructors.
- Observed by those watching instruction as it is delivered.
- Experienced by participants.
- Applied by trainees on the job.
- Perceived by supervisors of trainees on the job.

The opportunity-centered curriculum is based on the assumptions of developmentalism. Instructional planning gives learners the responsibility of identifying their own needs. Experiences are best designed to coincide with significant events in the lives of learners, including stages of socialization in the organization. The learning process stresses mutual sharing, and instructors facilitate learning rather than direct it.

In this section, we will point out the major advantages and disadvantages of each of these four approaches to curriculum design, and discuss ways to use each approach.

The Subject-Centered Approach

Historically, the subject-centered approach has been the preferred one; despite the best efforts of educational and WLP writers to promote other approaches. High school and college students naturally associate curriculum with a series of courses that must be taken to graduate. Predictably, managers carry over this notion into organizational settings and associate planned learning with courses needed by an employee to satisfy either probationary requirements or, in some professions, mandatory continuing education requirements.

Developing a subject-centered curriculum is relatively simple. The WLP professional asks line managers what topics should be offered to each level of employee by job class or by the individual's stage in the socialization process, arranges the program in some logical fashion (usually from basic to intermediate and advanced), and offers the programs on a regular basis. These steps are illustrated in Exhibit 12-8.

Exhibit 12-8: Steps in designing a subject-centered curriculum

Ask line managers for topics
Arrange topics in logical order
Offer programs on each topic or subject

Asking managers about what should be taught is called *needs assessment*. In a small organization, it might be done in meetings; in larger organizations, a survey of employees and managers might be needed. As an alternative, the WLP practitioner can examine job descriptions and develop a series of program titles to correspond to each major job activity area. A separate, more specific needs assessment should be conducted before any program is offered, because specific individuals and groups will vary in their learning needs.

The subject-centered approach has three major advantages: it is easy, it is inexpensive, and it is fast. Offsetting these advantages are some serious disadvantages. First, the curriculum only appears to match instructional offerings to learner needs. Specific individual needs can differ sharply, but this is not taken into account by the subject-centered approach, which considers only general needs by job class or group. Second, planning focuses on topics or subjects, rather than on the ability to apply skills on the job. Third, learners and managers outside the WLP department do not always participate in selecting subjects or setting priorities, and may not accept a curriculum thrust on them. The second disadvantage is perhaps the most serious, because the instructional offerings might not correspond to the needs of the job.

The Objectives-Centered Approach

Developing an objectives-centered curriculum is a complex process. There are two kinds: the *decision-based* curriculum and the *competency-based* curriculum. The first focuses on correcting performance problems, while the second focuses on making the most of opportunities for performance improvement. The distinction can be sharper than it might appear. Decision-based curricula attempt to discover barriers or impediments to performance; competency-based curricula attempt to define good performance and then facilitate or improve it.

The Decision-Based Curriculum

To design a decision-based curriculum or program, WLP professionals should follow several clearly-identifiable steps, outlined in Exhibit 12-9.

The first step—to conduct a performance audit—is more comprehensive than many forms of training needs assessment. Based on a model of human performance, it analyzes such factors as job context (do people know when to perform?), employee skills (do people possess the abilities needed to perform?), behavior (do people know what they are to perform, and do they possess necessary tools and/or resources?), results (are people rewarded appropriately for good performance? Do rewards matter to them?), and feedback (are people informed about whether performance was adequate?).

Selecting an appropriate performance-improvement approach depends on the nature of a deficiency. Since training is one of the most expensive approaches, it is warranted only when its costs are outweighed by potential benefits.

Exhibit 12-9: Steps in designing a decision-based curriculum

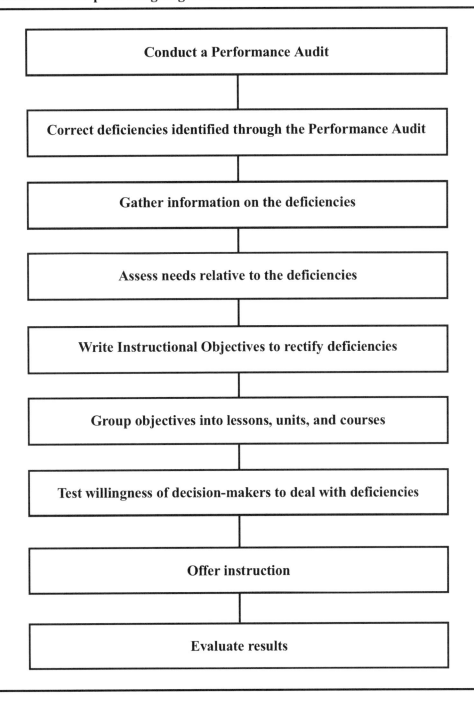

Major advantages of the decision-based curriculum are four-fold. First, it emphasizes analysis to uncover the underlying causes of problems. Improvement efforts then focus on these causes, rather than on mere symptoms. Second, it emphasizes a range of improvement efforts. The WLP professional becomes more than a snake oil merchant peddling training for every ill. Alternative improvement strategies are considered. Third, it emphasizes cost-benefit analysis. The WLP professional selects the improvement strategy that will do the best job at the least expensive cost. Fourth, it emphasizes pressing problems. WLP professionals focus on getting results where they are most needed in terms of impact on individual and organizational performance. Since adults are problem-centered in their approaches to learning, decision-based interventions usually gain strong support from those most concerned about, or affected by, a problem.

Of course, there are also disadvantages to this curriculum. Analysis can be costly and time-consuming. Some people might not recognize that the role of WLP professional encompasses more than just standing at the front of a classroom and playing schoolteacher. Operating managers may have formed their own notions about the cause(s) of performance problems and resent what they perceive as the meddling of WLP professionals who know less than operating managers do about detailed technical aspects of the work. Finally, correcting deficiencies is usually past-oriented, not future-oriented. As job conditions change, performance is altered, and so are deficiencies. For this reason, some thought should be given to likely future job conditions. Even with the disadvantages of the decision-based method, though, it is clearly superior to a subject-centered approach because it focuses on improving performance, not just the transmission of information.

Competency-Based Curriculum

There are three types of competency-based curricula: *instructional systems design* (ISD), *behavioral skills-outputs* (BSO), and the *DACUM method*. (These categories are rather arbitrary distinctions.)

Instructional Systems Design lends itself to all jobs, though it is probably more associated with technical training than with so-called "soft skills" instruction (such as communications or most management training). ISD is a thoroughly integrated method. The steps in one ISD model are shown in Exhibit 12-10. There are also many other models.

The major advantage of Instructional Systems Design is its comprehensiveness. It focuses systematically on every step of instructional design and delivery. It is useful for planning instructional projects regardless of size or scope. Another advantage is that instruction is evaluated before, during, and after widespread use. Materials are improved before learners are exposed to them, so that results can be reasonably predicted. Wasted time and effort are minimized, though testing itself can be time-consuming and expensive. Finally, ISD emphasizes appropriate behavior or performance. Instead of focusing on what is wrong, ISD concentrates on gearing performance to norms based on job, task, or content analysis.

Exhibit 12-10: Steps in designing a curriculum using ISD

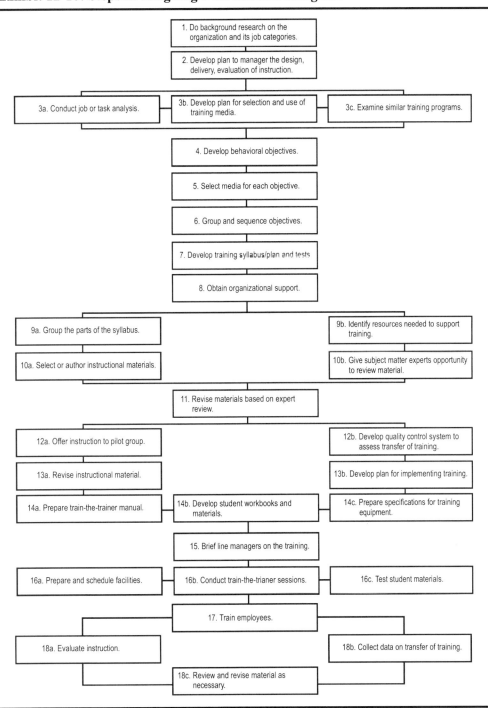

But there are disadvantages to Instructional Systems Design. (It is almost heresy to suggest that!) First, and most important, ISD is time-consuming and costly, but instructing people improperly can be even more costly. Second, ISD tends to emphasize present performance. Third, and finally, ISD places its primary emphasis on work-related behaviors, without regard to how changes in a work group or department will affect the way people interact.

BSO (behavioral skills-outputs) is another type of competency-based curriculum. The steps in applying BSO are illustrated in Exhibit 12-11. Alternative models of BSO are described in other sources.

Exhibit 12-11: Steps in designing a curriculum using behavioral skills-outputs

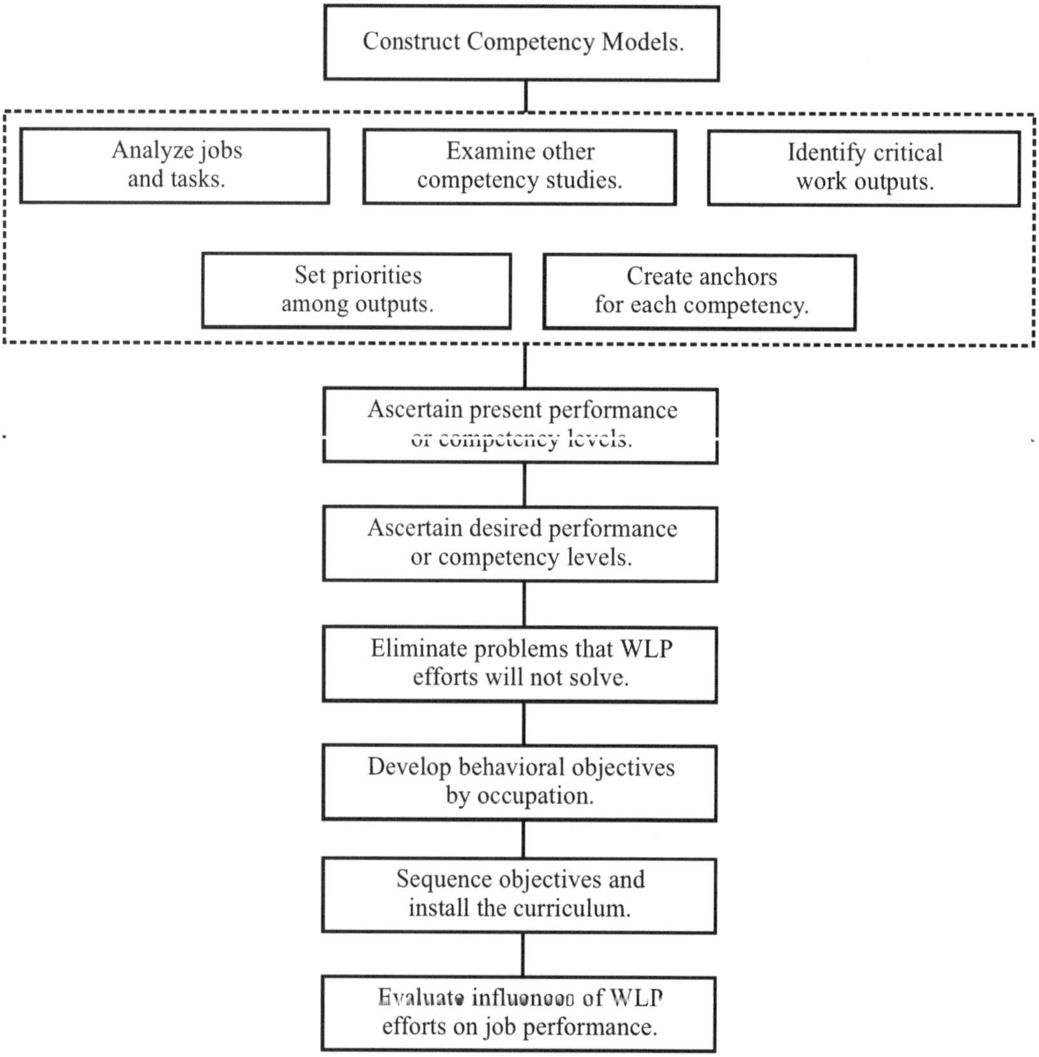

Behavioral skills-outputs has two chief advantages. First, it emphasizes work outputs. Since professional and managerial jobs often involve unobservable mental activity, this BSO feature makes it uniquely suited for dealing with these jobs. Second, it focuses specifically on desired performance.

The disadvantages of BSO include its typical emphasis on the present, its high cost, and the specialized skills needed to design a BSO curriculum. While BSO does not have to emphasize the present, it is usually based on information about the present performance of exemplary performers. It does not necessarily consider how performance will have to change to cope with future and perhaps unknown job conditions (although this can be taken into account.) Finally, developing a competency model is not simple and may require help from an external vendor.

Despite these drawbacks, the BSO method is growing more popular. It also lends itself to instruments for employee selection, job analysis, and employee performance appraisal. Indeed, its wide applicability makes it extremely useful for identifying career paths and corresponding needs for training, education, and employee development.

The DACUM Curriculum

Another competency-based approach is the DACUM method. DACUM stands for **D**eveloping **a Cu**rriculum. It is a powerful approach to occupational analysis that has been proven to be immensely useful in preparing job training. DACUM, operated through the sponsorship of the National Center for Vocational Education, has been widely used by community colleges to prepare their curricula and design their training for business and industrial organizations.

DACUM is based on three chief assumptions. (1) Expert or experienced workers are the most competent to describe their own jobs. (2) Any job can be analyzed by the tasks performed in it. (3) Each task has direct implications for occupational training. The steps in developing a DACUM chart are shown in Exhibit 12-12. The result of a DACUM analysis is a chart indicating tasks performed in a job. From these tasks, instructional objectives can be inferred. A sample DACUM chart appears in Exhibit 12-13.

DACUM is advantageous because it is a cost-effective method to prepare off-the-job or on-the-job training. Its chief disadvantage is that DACUM is sponsored by a governmental body.

The Experience-Centered Approach

Developing an experience-centered curriculum is relatively easy when compared with the complexities of objectives-centered methods. There are three types of experience-centered curricula: (1) the *creativity-based*, (2) the *action-based*, and (3) the *concept-based*. The first two overlap somewhat with the opportunity-centered approach.

Exhibit 12-12: Steps in using the DACUM method

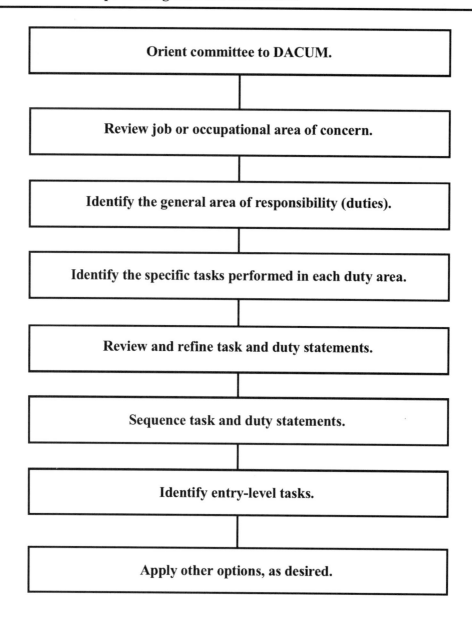

Orient committee to DACUM.

Review job or occupational area of concern.

Identify the general area of responsibility (duties).

Identify the specific tasks performed in each duty area.

Review and refine task and duty statements.

Sequence task and duty statements.

Identify entry-level tasks.

Apply other options, as desired.

SOURCE: Norton, R. (1985). *DACUM Handbook*. Columbus, OH: The National Center for Research in Vocational Education, The Ohio State University, 1960 Kenny Road, Columbus, Ohio 43210, pp. 1–2. Used by permission

Exhibit 12-13: A sample DACUM chart

Hierarchy of Competencies for Continuing Education Professionals

Facilitator: William J. Rothwell, Ph.D., Dept. of Adult Education, Instructional Systems and Workforce Education and Development, College of Education, 305C Keller Building, University Park, PA 16802—Phone: 814-863-2581 (C and DE Subcommittee: Mary Kay Cote, Connie Caverno, Walt Fullam, Elaina McReynolds and Terry Riley)

Categories			Activities							
Level of Competency	Category	Row/ Column Number	A	B	C	D	E	F	G	H
Basic	Office Management and Personal Organization	1	Manage time and priorities and meet deadlines	Schedule and prepare for meetings	Establish and maintain basic files/ recordkeeping/ follow-up systems	Use appropriate office technologies and software				
	Communication Skills	2	Write/ dictate letters, reports and memos	Give presentations	Facilitate meetings, seminars and ceremonies	Actively listen to others	Use e-mail for communication			
	Internal Relations	3	Develop knowledge about the C & DE function at Penn State	Participate in campus meetings	Develop knowledge about the campus/ culture/values	Identify and establish working relationships with appropriate campus/ university units	Develop knowledge about the university/ culture/values	Develop familiarity with/linkages to academic departments	Market continuing education internally to the university community	Participate on university committees
	Program Support	4	Pick up and deliver supplies and materials	Schedule and maintain facilities	Handle arrangements with food service/ caterer	Handle arrangements with hotel/ conference facilities	Order instructional materials	Arrange/ coordinate audiovisual assistance and support	Provide logistical support	Coordinate travel arrangements with faculty
		5	Arrange/ coordinate registration of students and collection of fees	Confirm registration and logistics to participants	Arrange/ coordinate selling of textbooks and supplies	Maintain program records and statistics	Assess participant reaction to programs			
Intermediate	Financial Management and Budgeting	6	Monitor existing individual program budgets	Analyze and adjust existing program budgets	Prepare new individual program budgets	Evaluate profitability of individual programs	Initiate and approve purchases for program materials and support	Identify potential funding sources	Cultivate relationships with potential funding sources	Spell out components of Memoranda of Agreement
		7	Work with faculty, contract, and grants office to write grants	Administer contracts and grants	Secure scholarships	Identify and negotiate with vendors	Make purchasing decisions for officewide equipment, services, etc.	Utilize IBIS for financial decision- making	Develop and monitor budget for total CE office	Evaluate CE office profitability
	Student Relations and Service	8	Understand/ communicate University requirements to students	Recruit students	Facilitate adult reentry to higher education	Arrange/ coordinate registration of CE students	Arrange/ coordinate counseling for CE students	Develop student tracking system and track student progress	Recognize student achievement	Mediate conflicts among students and faculty

Exhibit 12-13: A sample DACUM chart *(continued)*

Categories			Activities							
Level of Competency	Category	Row/ Column Number	A	B	C	D	E	F	G	H
		9	Provide access/ referrals to student services (financial aid, career development, etc.)	Conduct student surveys						
	Faculty Relations	10	Recruit and hire adjunct faculty, working with DAA as appropriate	Orient part-time faculty	Give directions and information to faculty members	Assist faculty with curriculum development	Monitor and follow-up faculty evaluations	Work to foster positive relationships with faculty		
	Client Management	11	Identify possible clients	Gather information about clients	Understand competitors	Respond to client requests	Build relationships with clients	Assess client needs	Make initial calls on potential clients	Source best ways to meet client needs
		12	Maintain contact with clients	Build project teams with clients	Negotiate contracts/ agreements with clients					
	Training and Organization Development	13	Choose appropriate methods to assess training needs	Separate training from non-training (management) needs	Identify gaps that can be corrected by training	Prioritize training needs, aligning with organizational goals	Develop training strategies	Establish instructional goals	Deliver and evaluate training	
	External and Community Relations	14	Articulate goals/mission of the CE unit to the community and community organizations	Join with and participate in community organizations, professional associations, community meetings, and boards, including work with alumni	Identify and meet with potential partners in the community	Consult with community resource people about community needs and programs	Develop alliances and articulation agreements with other institutions	Interface with local, state, and federal politicians	Interface internationally as opportunities may arise	
	Marketing and Promotion	15	Read newspapers and other publications in the service area to identify prospective clients	Develop understanding of marketing and demographic resources in the service area	Acquire indepth familiarity with products and services of competitors	Identify, purchase, organize, and supervise mailing lists	Form partnerships to market programs	Assess current market needs formally (survey) or informally (discussion)	Prepare marketing plans and strategies	Write advertising copy
		16	Develop newsletters, program brochures, and catalogs	Write press releases	Conduct open houses	Conduct telemarketing campaigns	Write proposals for training programs	Develop program pricing strategies to accomplish marketing goals	Position the institution properly as a supplier of education/ training	

Exhibit 12-13: A sample DACUM chart *(continued)*

Level of Competency	Category	Row/Column Number	A	B	C	D	E	F	G	H
Categories			**Activities**							
	Programming	17	Identify and analyze needs	Understand CE requirements of professional groups and other groups	Identify program topics and outcomes based on needs	Select appropriate media for program delivery	Set programming objectives	Obtain necessary college approvals	Work with faculty to develop curriculum and materials	Negotiate program locations and schedules
		18	Learn/meet accreditation requirements for PSU to serve as provider of accredited CE by accrediting agencies	Implement programs	Monitor ongoing programs	Establish and utilize program evaluation procedures	Use evaluation results to improve programs	Use NCRR program management screens	Understand program approval process for PSU CE requirements	Conduct environmental scanning to identify future program needs
		19	Understand CE requirements of various groups as they affect marketing impact							
Advanced	Recruitment, Hiring, and Orientation	20	Identify staffing requirements	Recruit prospective staff	Interview prospective staff	Select staff members from among multiple possibilities	Orient and train staff			
	Supervision	21	Supervise staff on a daily basis	Mentor staff	Establish and communicate staff accountability	Delegate work as necessary	Support staff members in achieving their goals	Provide feedback and counseling to staff on performance on a continuing basis	Evaluate staff performance	Provide staff members with professional development and growth opportunities
		22	Promote staff	Lay off or terminate staff as necessary						
	Management	23	Manage office workflow	Make decisions promptly and effectively	Identify/manage priorities on a daily basis	Juggle multiple/conflicting priorities	Utilize database management systems			
	Leadership	24	Serve as an exemplary role model	Motivate/encourage department and staff	Remain aware of public issues	Tolerate ambiguity with the organization and community	Appreciate and actively support diversity in thought and deed	Lead strategic planning for the unit	Develop/articulate a vision for the CE unit	Articulate values and guiding principles for the CE unit
		25	Build enthusiasm for the unit's mission inside and outside	Set policy for the CE unit	Arbitrate disputes and conflicts	Form coalitions with others in the University and community	Lead the continuous quality improvement efforts of the unit	Develop and maintain "content expert" status		

Exhibit 12-13: A sample DACUM chart *(continued)*

Categories			Activities							
Level of Competency	Category	Row/Column Number	A	B	C	D	E	F	G	H
Continuous	Personal and Professional Development	26	Establish personal and professional goals	Read broadly, remaining aware of events affecting personal and professional goals	Attend conferences and training programs relevant to personal and professional goals	Participate in professional societies and associations relevant to personal and professional goals	Pursue advanced degrees and professional certification/ licensure	Conduct research on issues relevant to personal and professional goals	Make presentations relevant to personal/ professional goals	Publish on issues relevant to personal/ professional goals
		27	Mentor others whose personal/ professional goals coincide							

© Copyright 1996 by William J. Rothwell, Ph.D.

The Creativity-Based Curriculum

This method focuses on evoking new ideas rather than on building specific skills or transferring specific information. Most organizations are more familiar with *convergent thought*, which is characterized by a search for one solution based on marshalling facts. *Divergent or creative thought* is characterized by such activities as generating new ideas, thinking about multiple ideas simultaneously, generating unusual ideas, shifting the context of ideas so as to explore comparisons, and seeing beyond obvious solutions to possible long-term outcomes and consequences of action taken to address problems. Divergent thinking offers perhaps the greatest potential for working smarter, not harder.

To develop a creativity-based curriculum, the WLP professional should carry out a series of identifiable steps. This model is illustrated in Exhibit 12-14.

A creativity-based curriculum is focused less on individual and more on organizational performance. Advantages of this method include its heavy emphasis on problem-solving and creativity. The disadvantages of the method include the high cost of group problem-solving, the often inordinate length of time between generation of ideas and their subsequent exploration, and the possibility that participants in the process may not have sufficient information to make meaningful contributions on specific problems.

The Action-Based Method

This method of curriculum development is very similar to the creativity-based. (The steps for carrying out this method are illustrated in Exhibit 12-15.) It is an Organization Development approach to curriculum development, based heavily on the action research model of Lewin.

Exhibit 12-14: Steps in designing a creativity-based curriculum

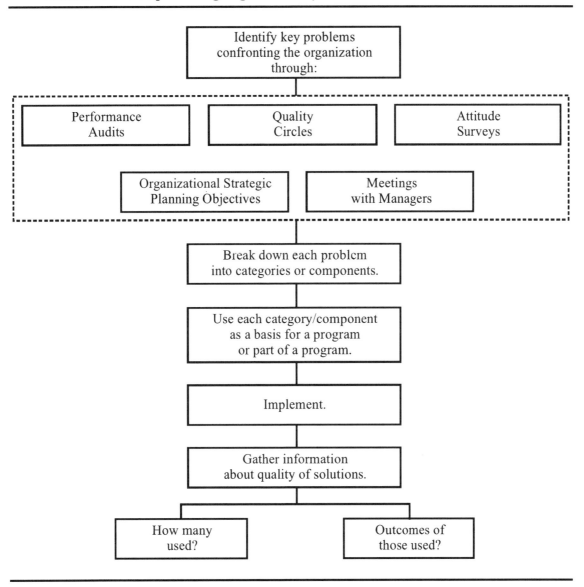

Exhibit 12-15: Steps in designing an action-based curriculum

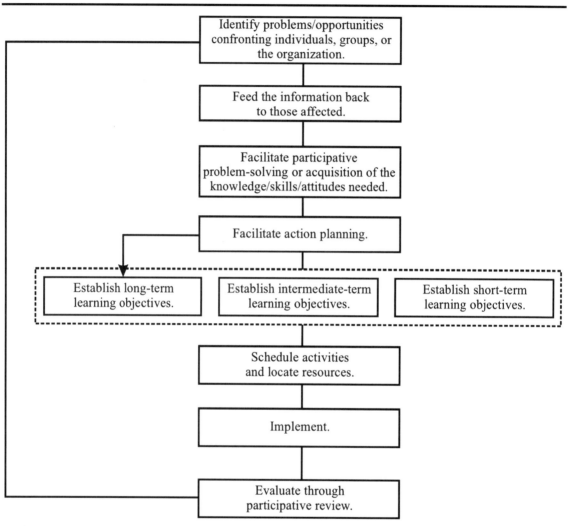

The advantages of the action-based approach are similar to those for the creativity-based. An additional advantage is that this method places more emphasis on participative decision-making in the selection of problems and methods of dealing with them. Disadvantages include the high cost and the significant length of time needed to identify and act on those problems.

The Concept-Based Method

This method is quite different from the two others treated in this section. Based on the thinking of Jerome Bruner (1961), a *concept* is defined as a category by which an individual organizes and interprets experience. A concept has a name, a definition, and identifiable characteristics, and can be readily linked to examples.

To develop a concept-based curriculum, WLP professionals should begin by identifying key or critical concepts associated with successful job performance by talking to job incumbents or supervisors, or observing successful and unsuccessful performers. Then they then rank concepts according to priority, establish a "learning hierarchy" so that basic concepts are introduced before complicated ones, and then group parts of the hierarchy into programs, lessons, and units. They make sure that each lesson and unit contains a rule (definition), a definition of the concept's characteristics, and examples. Finally, they implement the curriculum and evaluate it periodically. (See Exhibit 12-16.)

Exhibit 12-16: Steps in designing a concept-based curriculum

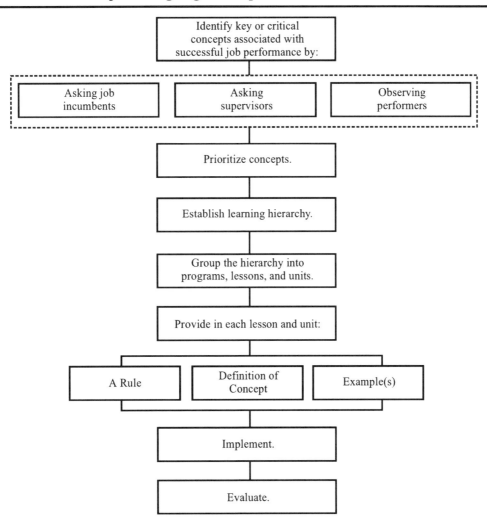

One of the advantages of this approach is that it emphasizes work concepts and the most important facets of a task, job, or role. Focusing on key areas of the work to the exclusion of less important areas makes maximum payoff more likely. Disadvantages include the time needed to translate critical activities into concepts and the typical past orientation (rather than future orientation) of the approach.

The Opportunity-Centered Approach

There are essentially four methods of developing an opportunity-centered curriculum: (1) the *individualized-informal*; (2) the *individualized-contractual*; (3) the *group-oriented*; and (4) *action learning*. All are based on the assumptions of developmentalism, though they vary in how those assumptions are applied to instructional planning.

In the first two methods, individuals make their own decisions about learning needs and priorities. They identify their own goals, objectives, and desired learning initiatives, perhaps linked to career aspirations. Next, they identify methods for achieving their own goals and objectives, develop an individualized curriculum of learning projects, meet their needs through formal and informal learning events, and evaluate outcomes based on personal goals and objectives. (These steps are illustrated in Exhibit 12-17.)

If the curriculum is individualized-informal, people establish their own goals without necessarily consulting others. Learning plans are not usually formalized in writing. If the curriculum is individualized-contractual, people negotiate goals, objectives, and corresponding activities with superiors, counselors, and/or WLP practitioners. Learning plans are formalized in writing. Sometimes they are geared explicitly to career plans and forwarded to the WLP department so it can use them (1) in identifying and scheduling instructional offerings, and (2) for information about the collective aspirations of employees generally.

The advantages of these methods include emphasis on individuals and their career needs. Since individual differences vary widely, it is important to take them into account. This method does best in this respect. The method also allows individuals to select their learning activities according to their significant life concerns and career objectives, and the result is usually high motivation to achieve.

On the other hand, there is a major disadvantage: People might be encouraged to meet their personal needs to the possible exclusion of, or even at the expense of, organizational needs. By helping people advance in their careers, the organization will risk higher turnover and loss of investment in human potential.

To develop a group-oriented curriculum, the WLP practitioner needs to: formulate broad, general questions pertinent to job incumbents at each level and in each job class of the organization; establish programs to address each broad question; formulate more specific questions for each program or component of a program; offer each program, organize each program for maximum participant interaction; and evaluate each program in terms of individual perceptions. This model is illustrated in Exhibit 12-18.

Exhibit 12-17: Steps in designing an individualized curriculum

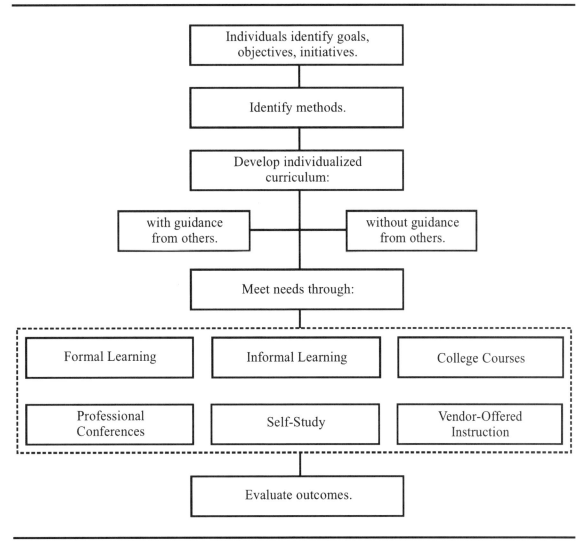

This method is based on the Socratic approach of asking questions. Instructors serve as facilitators; learners share insights. Learning occurs through discovery, group interaction, and experience-sharing. Indeed, the emphasis is on group interaction, team building, and creative thought. Individuals learn to draw on and reflect on their own insights.

The major disadvantage of this method is that it is difficult to plan precise outcomes. The value of the group experience depends entirely on the experience level of participants and their willingness to interact.

Exhibit 12-18: Steps in designing a group-oriented curriculum

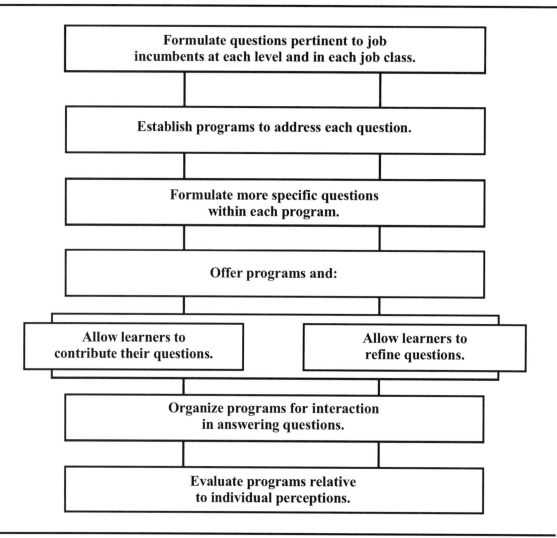

Action learning is the fourth and final curriculum approach. Its versatility is attracting widespread attention. In its traditional form, action learning was used for executive development. Teams of learners are formed to solve a business problem. Typically, learners are selected based on their need for individual development *and* for their expertise in being able to attack a business problem. However, action learning can also be applied to instructional design, with a team of Subject Matter Experts (SMEs) paired with one or more instructional designer experts (IDEs) for the purpose of designing instruction to meet a business need (Rothwell 1999).

A key advantage of action learning is that it involves learners and can also serve as a means by which to transfer the technology of instructional design from WLP professionals to line managers or other relevant stakeholders. A key disadvantage of action learning is that it requires time away from the job for busy workers at a time when organizations are trying to operate with leaner staffs. However, action learning can be a powerful tool for developing individuals while also building the competence of line managers or other stakeholders in learning interventions.

HOW TO SELECT A CURRICULUM APPROACH

What approach to use? The answer to this question depends on curriculum purpose and goals, values of decision-makers, and learner needs.

Any curriculum can be effective for at least one purpose. If the emphasis is on disseminating information, then a subject-centered approach is usually appropriate. If the emphasis is on building measurable skills, then an objectives-centered approach is appropriate. If the emphasis is on generating new ideas, then the experience-centered approach is appropriate. Finally, if the emphasis is on providing individuals with a means by which to match their needs to available learning experiences, then an opportunity-centered approach is appropriate. There is no right or wrong approach in an absolute sense. However, there can be inappropriate approaches or methods for a particular purpose.

The values of decision-makers are of crucial importance for sustaining any long-term instructional effort. If they back a venture because it suits their real or perceived needs, adequate resources will or should be forthcoming. If they do not see the value of a venture, it will not receive support and will very likely fail for that reason alone. While WLP professionals do have a responsibility to educate decision-makers on options available, they will have to ask:

- What key groups of decision-makers are or will be affected by a program or the curriculum?
- What results does each group hope to gain? Over what time span?
- What, if anything, might each group fear about the instructional effort?
- What curriculum approach is each group likely to prefer? Why?

By addressing these questions, WLP professionals can gain important clues for choosing an appropriate curriculum approach, identifying needs, establishing initial and continuing support for the WLP effort, and ensuring effective transfer of learning back to the job. Top management, middle and lower management, and trainees may all have their own individual goals, and these goals may conflict. Whose goals should take priority under the circumstances?

Finally, any instructional effort is sure to fail if it does not address learner needs. The basic questions are: *What needs? What learners?* And *in whose view?* Since individuals undoubtedly differ in their needs, their perceptions should be considered in assessing needs and choosing the appropriate curriculum.

CHAPTER 13

WLP and Organization Development

Adapting to and anticipating change is a major challenge confronting individuals and their organizations as they seek to improve performance. Organization Development (OD) has important applications to that end. But what is OD? And when is OD appropriate for addressing existing or possible future performance problems? What is organizational culture? How can organizational culture be changed? Why does OD lend itself particularly well to initiating and implementing change to culture? How should OD be planned and implemented? This Chapter addresses these important questions and thereby provides an introduction to OD.

WHAT IS ORGANIZATION DEVELOPMENT (OD)?

Definition of OD

In a classic definition of OD, French and Bell describe it as "a top-management-supported, long-range effort to improve an organization's problem-solving and renewal processes, particularly through a more effective and collaborative diagnosis and management of organizational culture—with special emphasis on formal work team, temporary team, and intergroup culture—with the assistance of a consultant-facilitator and the use of the theory and technology of applied behavioral science, including action research" (French and Bell 1984).

Each part of this definition deserves elaboration.

OD is supported by top-management. Top managers have historically commanded the key resources and rewards of their organizations. While their power may be gradually diminishing as front-line employees are given more latitude in decision-making and as technology equips them with tools to process and analyze information, top managers still remain responsible for committing their organizations to large expenditures. Moreover, top managers make the final decisions about their organization's long-term strategic direction and the employees who will be promoted to or removed from top and middle management positions. While an OD effort can be successfully initiated and carried out without overt top-management participation, the long-term success of any change effort depends on the support of the chief power-holders and powerbrokers of the organization. If top managers actively oppose a change effort, it is most likely doomed to eventual failure. For this reason, OD should be carried out with at least passive support, but preferably the active involvement, of top managers. At the same time, as front-line employees gain more power through active participation and involvement in decisions affecting them, their support of OD change efforts is growing increasingly important.

OD is a long-range effort. Unlike employee training, which is a short-range effort designed to produce immediate behavioral change, OD is a long-range effort. It is decidedly not a quick fix. The reason: it takes time to produce real changes to culture because organizations, as organized groups, simply take longer to change than one person.

OD focuses on improving an organization's problem-solving and renewal processes. OD is directed to identifying and solving problems affecting an organization, groups within it, or individuals employed by it. As part of this process, the organization is led to a renewal or rebirth as its members re-examine time-honored and tradition-bound norms governing group interaction and group problem-solving.

OD facilitates more effective and collaborative diagnosis and management of organizational culture. WLP professionals working in OD should resist the temptation, sometimes fostered by members of an organization, to "play expert." Instead, they should encourage problem-solving by the organization's members. The distinction is an important one. The traditional consultant's role resembles a medical doctor, who diagnoses diseases and prescribes treatment (Schein 1969).

But OD consultants should function differently. They should resist playing experts. They should be more interested in helping members of an organization undertake their own diagnosis to identify underlying problems and reach agreement on corrective action. Above all, they emphasize *participation* in problem-solving and decision-making because they believe that increased participation by employees leads to increased employee productivity, commitment, loyalty, and job satisfaction. In recent years, the literature on employee participation has grown rapidly, and much of it tends to support the assumptions and beliefs long associated with OD.

OD emphasizes team culture. OD focuses on team or group culture. It helps teams, intact work groups, and other groups address conflict and improve interpersonal and intrapersonal interaction. While OD does not rule out interventions other than those emphasizing feelings and interpersonal relationships, it is particularly effective for addressing dysfunctional interpersonal conflict.

OD makes uses of the assistance of a consultant-facilitator. While every manager must initiate, implement, and assess productive and progressive change, many changes can be managed better when a third-party consultant-facilitator is imported from outside the organization or group to foster and support the change process. Third-party consultant-facilitators are useful because they bring a fresh perspective to bear on organizational problems. Moreover, they are free to focus their attention on *how effectively people interact*—that is, on work process—as well as on *what they are doing*. The way groups and individuals interact has a greater influence on employee and group performance than most managers recognize or plan for.

OD makes use of the theory and technology of applied behavioral science, including action research. Basic behavioral science consists of such fields as Psychology, Sociology, Anthropology, and Archeology. Each focuses, in its own unique way, on how people behave;

each is a respectable academic discipline; and each has a body of knowledge and research unique to it. In contrast, *applied behavioral science* is derived by distilling the key principles and research findings from these different academic disciplines. Directed toward applying what is known about human behavior to group and organizational life, it is inherently practical.

Action research is an approach to identifying and solving problems. While the word *research* may conjure up images of impractical academic theories and the pursuit of useless knowledge, *action research* means *investigation* or *analysis*. It is the basis of all OD interventions. The steps in one model of action research will be described in detail later in this Chapter.

A Primer of OD Terminology

Some terms are unique to OD. To learn about OD, WLP professionals should prepare to master a new nomenclature. The following terms are of special note: (1) *change agent*; (2) *client;* and (3) *intervention.*

Change agent has a special meaning in OD. It is synonymous with *consultant* or *third-party consultant-facilitator.* A *change agent* initiates, facilitates, and coordinates organizational change efforts. Some authorities in the field argue that a change agent should usually be imported from outside the organization or group. These external change agents, it is argued, can be more effective because they are not bound by organizational conventions or reporting relationships that restrict the actions of an internal change agent. However, OD professionals can (and do) function successfully as internal change agents.

The *client* is the organization, group, or individual whose interests are served by the change agent. Though it is often said that change agents facilitate change rather than manage or direct it, they do function under an explicit (or implicit) contract with a person or group for that purpose. However, the individual or group who pays the consultant's fees is not necessarily the client. The client is that group or person whose purposes and needs the change agent serves and represents. The client can change, even within one OD intervention. Often the most nagging question to answer before and during an OD effort is the identification of the client.

The word *intervention* simply means a planned change effort, a performance-improvement intervention. If an intervention does not occur, existing conditions will usually remain unchanged. The term "intervention" can be applied to one change activity or to a sequence of such activities, a family of related change activities, or the plan for an entire change program.

WHEN IS ORGANIZATION DEVELOPMENT APPROPRIATE FOR ADDRESSING PERFORMANCE PROBLEMS?

OD has broad applications. It may be applied to existing or expected problems confronting organizations, groups, pairs, or individuals. It may also be used to improve operations of otherwise smoothly-functioning operations or address otherwise unexpected, emergent future problems. In short, it is a long-term strategy for solving group or organizational performance problems and implementing or coping with change.

As an aid to identifying when OD is or is not an appropriate performance-improvement strategy, consider the questions appearing in Exhibit 13-1. Generally speaking, OD can be usefully applied to any situation in which the answer to any or all these questions is *yes*. OD can still be applied, though perhaps not as usefully, to any situation in which the answer to any or all these questions is *no*.

Exhibit 13-1: Identifying appropriate and inappropriate uses of organization development

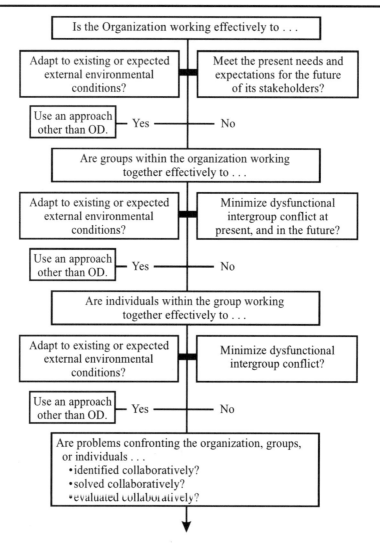

Exhibit 13-1: Identifying appropriate and inappropriate uses of organization development *(continued)*

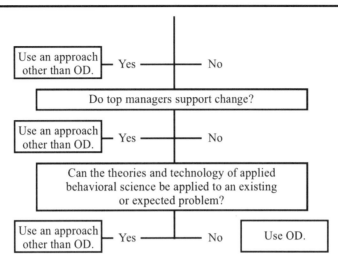

WHAT IS ORGANIZATIONAL CULTURE?

Few topics in the past 20 years have fired up the imaginations of CEOs and WLP professionals quite like the subject of organizational culture. While culture has long been a topic discussed in Anthropology and in OD circles, popular business interest in it was aroused with the publication of two major books in 1982—*In Search of Excellence* (Peters and Waterman 1982) and *Corporate Cultures* (Deal and Kennedy 1982). Both books revealed the linkage between successful corporations and the unique, shared values and beliefs among their employees. Of all performance-improvement strategies based on planned learning, OD is best suited to changing organizational culture.

Definition of Culture

Culture has been defined in different ways. Most authorities on the subject, however, would agree that culture "consists of the behavioral patterns, concepts, values, ceremonies, and rituals that take place in the organization. . . . Cultural values provide employees with a sense of what they ought to be doing, and how they should behave to be consistent with organizational goals. Culture represents the feeling, emotional, intangible part of the organization" (Daft 1983).

Culture at Multiple Levels

Culture exists on more than one layer or level. Superficially, culture manifests itself through an organization's logos and slogans, office layout and furnishings, and employee behavior around top managers. On a second and deeper level, it encompasses the organization's prevailing values and beliefs. Experienced employees can usually describe those values and beliefs when prompted. (See the sentence stems in Exhibit 13-2.) The common patterns of employee responses to these items can provide clues to the second, deeper layer of organizational culture.

Exhibit 13-2: Identifying prevailing values and beliefs in an organization's culture

---

Ask one or more experienced (long-service) employees to complete the following sentences:

1. To me, this organization *most* values _____.

2. To me, this organization *least* values _____.

3. Not everything that is taken for granted in this organization is good. Perhaps the most damaging belief here is that_____.

4. If I had to point out *one idea or belief* in this organization that everyone pretty much takes for granted, I guess it would be that _____.

5. If someone asked me to describe my feelings about this organization in a single word, I suppose that word would be _____.

6. Around here, it is obvious that managers think of employees as _____.

At the third and deepest layer, culture is reflected by rites, stories, and language. To gain perspective on them, consider: What social activities (*rites*) regularly occur in the organization? What do they signify? What descriptions of past events (*stories*) do employees tell about top managers, their immediate supervisors, promotions, demotions, firings, and other emotionally-charged issues? (See Exhibit 13-3.)

WLP professionals who wish to make a systematic examination of the culture of their organizations can conduct a *culture audit*. It is an in-depth review of the existing and desired culture. Although a culture audit can rely on many different techniques for data collection and analysis, typical questions usually focus on existing or desired norms regarding communication, decision-making, problem-solving, interpersonal relationships, individual job satisfaction, group morale, customer service, product quality, and service quality.

Exhibit 13-3: Organizational rituals and stories

Pose the following questions to several experienced (long-service) employees:

1. What social activities are scheduled for the organization each year? Make a list. Be sure to include common ones such as Christmas parties, retirement dinners, and sales banquets, and ones that are less common and perhaps unique to your organization. Then explain the significance or meaning of each activity.

2. What kind of person was the founder of your organization? Tell me a story about the founder.

3. How are firings handled in this organization? Tell me a story to describe how one such incident was handled.

4. How are decisions made in this organization? Could you tell me a story to describe how they are made?

5. Tell me a story that you feel gives the best description about what this organization is like. When you finish, explain why you think the story does such a good job of describing what it feels like to work for this organization.

6. What are top managers *really like* in this organization? Tell me a story to give me a sense of what they are really like.

HOW CAN ORGANIZATIONAL CULTURE BE CHANGED?

Three Ways of Changing Culture

According to a classic theory of OD, changes to organizational culture generally occur in only three ways. One way is that members of the culture may be forced to change under threat of punishment. This is called *coercive change*. While effective in the short run, it produces such nasty side effects as turnover, absenteeism, and even sabotage. A second way to change culture is to persuade members of the organization to change because it is in their best selfish interests to do so. This is called *persuasive* or *rational change*. It is based on the view that people will act when they recognize "what's in it for them." A third way to change culture is to furnish members of the organization with new ways to approach problems or address issues confronting them. This is called *normative re-educative change*. It stems from a belief that people will change when they acquire, through learning, new ways of approaching problems and interacting with others (Chin and Benne 1969).

OD is usually considered a *normative re-educative* approach to change (French and Bell 1984). It encourages people affected by problems to help identify and solve them. It is uniquely appropriate for addressing culture change because it is long-term, is focused on addressing feelings as well as facts, and is aimed at addressing the group norms comprising culture.

Organizational culture is especially resistant to quick fixes and slick sales slogans. Indeed, the difficulty and time it takes to change culture should not be underestimated, as it often is, by managers who want to introduce and consolidate changes quickly. People do not like to shake off their assumptions, and an organizational culture comprises an entire view of how the world does and should work.

How Culture is Maintained

Culture is maintained through individual socialization, group norms, and organizational leadership. To change culture, these issues should be examined and addressed.

Socialization

The process by which individuals are gradually initiated into an organization, learn the ropes, and are accepted by others is called *socialization*. Socialization, which is of vital importance to WLP professionals, affects employee turnover and performance. It involves the rites of passage for newcomers in organizations (or groups) where individuals gradually master the explicit work rules and implicit group norms. A *work rule* is an articulated code of conduct or behavior, such as this example: "Employees caught stealing company property will be terminated immediately."

Group Norms

Not always articulated but usually understood by experienced group members, *group norms* are unwritten rules of individual interaction within groups. After listening to experienced employees for a week, a WLP professional might conclude that a group norm in one organization might be expressed as follows: "Seasoned veterans of this organization will complain bitterly about their boss, the company, and the quality of products manufactured by the company." Group norms are formed as groups develop and regulate interpersonal relationships. Once established, they are relatively enduring. However, they can change when:

- Membership within the group changes dramatically
- A respected group member questions the norms
- New assumptions are borne out by organizational learning and experience

Leadership

Individuals who exert influence over the behavior of others are known as *leaders*. Though leadership is difficult to reduce to a simple formula, it can decidedly affect organizational culture. Leaders establish and enforce work rules and/or norms. Individuals chosen as leaders are often reflections or indications of what the culture is. They embody characteristics prized by the culture. The first step in changing culture is often to change leaders and bring into the organization potential leaders who have not been socialized into "the way things are done around here."

HOW SHOULD ORGANIZATION DEVELOPMENT BE PLANNED AND IMPLEMENTED?

While OD focuses on different problems and uses varying intervention modes, it often relies on one of several common models for problem-solving and change to guide its efforts. One such model is called *action research*, a term coined by John Collier (French and Bell 1984). It was first used in a change effort by Kurt Lewin (Marrow 1969). Sometimes referred to as one schematic underlying OD, it consists of a clearly identifiable sequence of activities that are directed toward continuous improvement by means of a cycle in which information about problems is collected, fed back to people affected, used to stimulate action, and evaluated. While there is more than one way to think about action research (Brown 1972), the steps in one model are illustrated in Exhibit 13-4. Each step appearing in that model deserves some elaboration because it clarifies possible phases in an OD intervention.

The Action Research Model, Step-by-Step

Entry

The first step in the action research model is *entry*. Before and during this step, decision-makers must conclude that a change of some kind is needed; that OD is an appropriate approach for planning and implementing the change; and that a change agent is needed to facilitate the effort. During this stage, an initial meeting with the change agent is also held. WLP professionals might find themselves looking at this stage from one of two perspectives: (1) *as client*, someone who needs the help of an external change agent or who helps others in the organization recruit, select, or work with one; or (2) *as change agent*. The following discussion describes issues for consideration from both perspectives.

Exhibit 13-4: Steps in action research: A model

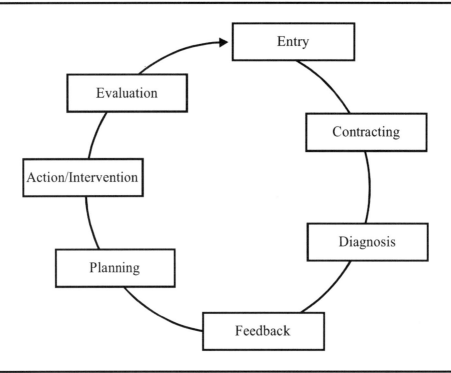

Before any attempt can be made to begin an OD intervention, someone has to recognize a need for it. Often such recognition stems from a major or minor crisis affecting the organization, though it can also result from visionary leadership. Examples of major crises might include loss of a major market to a competitor, a sales disaster, or a merger. Minor crises may also stimulate a desire for change, though perhaps the desire is not as strongly felt or as widely shared by the organization's key decision-makers. Examples of minor crises might include increasing turnover rates among the sales force or among production workers, loss of a difficult-to-replace executive, evidence of employee sabotage, or personality conflicts between the leaders or employees of different work groups. Crisis, whether major or minor, stimulates interest in change and sensitizes decision-makers to the need for fresh ideas and new approaches.

An impetus for change can also result from visionary leadership, a new image in the mind of a charismatic or influential leader about what should be happening in the organization. Such a vision excites others and influences their thinking. It also builds their enthusiasm to such a point that they want to make that vision a reality.

Beyond recognizing that change is needed, managers must also select Organization Development as the appropriate approach to planning and implementing change. That is all the more difficult, because not all managers are familiar with OD. Some associate it with such controversial training methods as sensitivity training or New Age training. Better-informed managers know that OD is, instead, an embodiment of participative management and clearly consistent with the attempts made by many organizations to empower employees (and thus increase the autonomy they exercise over decisions affecting them) and tap what they know to improve quality and productivity. In short, OD represents a real alternative to change that is initiated or managed autocratically or coercively.

WLP professionals might have to educate managers about OD before it can receive a fair hearing as a possible performance-improvement strategy. To that end, some WLP professionals can circulate articles about OD among managers, discuss its benefits during in-house training seminars, or invite outside speakers to speak to management groups about it. External WLP consultants can educate others about OD by describing appropriate applications through direct-mail or direct-phone campaigns.

Once decision-makers have concluded that OD is an appropriate approach for initiating and implementing desired organizational change, they should recruit and select a third-party change agent. Decision-makers may decide to recruit and select one or more external third-party change agents from outside the organization, internal third-party change agents from inside the organization, or a team composed of a combination of the two. To recruit and select an internal change agent, decision-makers can turn to other organizational units, such as the corporate WLP department, corporate HR department, or an operating department. To recruit and select an external change agent, decision-makers should turn to such useful sources of information as their own networks of professional or industry contacts and to professional associations like ASTD or the OD Network.

WLP professionals who find themselves helping managers recruit and select an external change agent for an OD intervention should be sure to consider just how much top managers are committed to the change effort and to the use of a change agent to facilitate it. Three good acid tests are these:

- How willing are the decision-makers to commit funds for contracting with an external change agent?
- How much time are the decision-makers willing to commit to the effort?
- How realistic is their assessment of the time it will take to introduce, implement, and consolidate a change effort?

If funding for an external change agent is not available, WLP professionals should find out why. Does that signal limited top-management support, lack of resources, distrust of "outsiders," or some other issue? If it signals limited support, then the change effort will be difficult for anyone to facilitate successfully. Additional effort might be needed to build an impetus for change among the organization's management group, perhaps by finding an "idea champion" or other standard-bearer within the organization. If lack of funding is traceable to a simple lack of resources, then consider postponing the effort until appropriate resources are available. If lack of funding signals distrust of outsiders, then determine whether that problem can be addressed or whether it means that an internal change agent *must* be used if the change effort is to be successful.

If funding is not available, then there is little point to exert effort recruiting an external consultant. Choose someone from inside the organization to spearhead the change effort. If necessary, consult skill inventories or ask around the organization. Look for someone who knows what OD is and who has had some experience with it. Often this responsibility will fall to WLP professionals. Of course, it goes without saying that the person chosen should have had some training on OD.

Once a change agent has been selected, an initial meeting should be arranged with the client. Before that meeting, external change agents should receive a brief orientation to the organization in which the organization's history, structure, industry standing, financial status, and other key issues are described. If internal change agents are selected, they should be briefed on the problem that has led to the request for the OD intervention. WLP professionals who are assisting the client should prepare an agenda for the first meeting with the change agent; if they are serving as the "change agents," they should prepare a list of key questions for that initial meeting that focus around what is happening, what led up to the problem or issue at hand, what efforts have already been made to address the problem or issue, who is involved in the problem or issue, and other such matters. Ultimately, after one or more meetings, OD consultants should provide a proposal for solving the problem by an OD intervention.

Contracting

The second step in the action research model and in most OD interventions is *contracting*. Whether WLP professionals function as external or internal change agents, they will probably be involved in contracting. Before offering their services or allowing others to do so, they should be sure that they have a signed, written agreement that spells out specifically who will do what, what is to be done, when each phase of the change effort will be reached and concluded, where the change effort will occur, why the change effort is being conducted, and how it will be conducted. While the agreement can be modified during the change effort, it is important to make clear to all concerned what will and will not happen. In all likelihood, the contracting step will move quickly, assuming the organization's key decision-makers are committed to change and that the steps in the change process have already been discussed.

Diagnosis

The third step in the action research model and in most OD interventions is *diagnosis*. It is necessary first to explore the problem (or problems) to be addressed or identify an improvement that is necessary. It is coordinated by the change agent but is focused on meeting the client's needs.

Think of diagnosis as comprising two steps: (1) clarifying preliminary questions and issues; and (2) preparing a plan to guide the diagnosis.

Clarify preliminary questions and issues by spending time with the client to find out as much as possible about the issue to be investigated. Be sure to pose the following questions to the client:

1. Who is noticing the problem or issue?
2. Who is especially concerned about it?
3. What exactly is the problem or issue?
4. When did it first become noticeable or attract attention?
5. Where is the problem most acute, or where is the issue most important?

6. Why does the problem exist, or why is the issue worth addressing?

7. What will happen in the future if no action is taken?

Then spend some time researching the problem or issue. Network with professional colleagues to find out whether other organizations have faced similar problems, and what they have been doing about them. Benchmark best practices. Visit an academic library or surf the Web and research what has been written about the topic.

Use the results of this first diagnostic step to prepare a plan that is more detailed than was tentatively established during contracting. Identify specifically what issues will be investigated, who will investigate them, and how they will be investigated. Treat it much like a research plan. As part of the plan, be sure to cover how information will be collected and analyzed. Such typical social science research methods as interviews, questionnaires, observation, and secondary data can be used to diagnose the problem. The appropriate choice of a method to analyze the results depends on the information collected. If it is quantitative, then various statistical methods can be applied to analyzing the results; if it is qualitative, then various qualitative methods can be applied.

Approaches to diagnosis differ by organization. Management support is often crucial in most public and private sector organizations. However, management support can have less influence in organizational settings such as universities or professional societies, where authority is nebulous. As a consequence, change agents working in these settings should pay special attention to identifying individuals or groups whose support for the OD intervention is crucial. These individuals and groups should be approached early in the intervention so that their support for the effort can be cultivated.

Feedback

The fourth step is *feedback*. It is at this point that information collected during diagnosis is fed back to the client so the client can draw conclusions about the problem's cause, identify appropriate solutions, and establish a plan of corrective action. Feedback is crucial if a problem is to be properly identified and appropriate solutions are to be identified.

The results of diagnosis, provided through feedback, can lead a client to one of several typical reactions to a problem or issue: (1) utter rejection; (2) complete acceptance; or (3) partial acceptance. Rejection is a defensive reaction, intended consciously or unconsciously to shield the client from taking responsibility for the existence of a problem to which the client might have contributed. It is no easy matter overcoming rejection of the results: that can doom a change effort from the outset.

The change agent can facilitate the client's acceptance of results from diagnosis by presenting them as simply as possible, perhaps with a narrative summary distributed in advance. The tone of the problem-solving meeting is vital if change is to be initiated, and the change agent must establish a positive, problem-oriented meeting climate. Great care should be taken to avoid scapegoating or allowing others to find scapegoats.

If the client rejects the results or accepts them only partially, the change agent may need to exert extra effort to prompt corrective action. It is sometimes common for the client to request more information, a follow-up, or confirmation of the initial findings. There is no harm in doing that, as long as it is not a delaying tactic designed to draw attention away from corrective action.

Planning

The fifth step in the action research model is *planning*. During this step, the focus of attention should shift from problem identification to solution identification. The client should establish concrete objectives and a specific plan of action for addressing the problem or issue.

The change agent's role should be to help the client discover an appropriate agenda for addressing the problem that has been identified. While responsibility for the objectives and the agenda must remain the client's, change agents should resist efforts to play "expert" and end up recommending a solution that is not acceptable to the client. Change agents can share with the client their own insights about the problem and perceptions about the organization, and they can also provide resource materials that can help the client explore solutions, develop fresh insights, and think through the possible negative consequences of any proposed solutions. They can also conduct small-scale pilot tests of proposed solutions so that the results can be judged without committing an entire organization or work unit to an untried solution. It is vital that the change agent help the *client* find a solution. The goal of the OD consultant is facilitation.

Action

The sixth step is *action*. At this point, the change objectives and agenda are actively pursued. The change agent's role is to help the client stay on course, maintaining the momentum of continuous improvement.

Evaluation

The seventh step is *evaluation*. This step should coincide with the action step, since the aim is to produce continuous improvement through participative problem-solving. The results of action should thus be regularly compared to plan objectives, problems, or issues. When differences are noted, the change agent can facilitate the client's review and diagnosis of this gap between what *is* and what *should be*.

Early writers on Organization Development equated evaluation with termination, the end of an intervention. The idea that interventions can be started and ended suggests that organizational change is a linear process. The aim is thus to move the client's organization from a static state to another static state.

However, more recent writers on OD equate change with dynamic improvement: Evaluation is appropriately viewed as part of a continuous improvement cycle of entry, contracting, diagnosis, feedback, planning, action/intervention, and evaluation. OD itself is thus capable of becoming a long-term and, indeed, never ending process of continuous improvement.

WHAT OD INTERVENTIONS ARE AVAILABLE?

We recommend that change agents be familiar with the range of OD interventions, because understanding that range helps to clarify what issues are the appropriate focus of OD and provides an indication of what methods can be used to effect organizational change. For the sake of simplicity, several common OD interventions are briefly summarized in Exhibit 13-5.

Exhibit 13-5: Summary descriptions of common OD interventions

Target Group	Intervention	Brief Description
Total System or Organization	**Strategic Planning**	Strategic Planning is introduced in an organization in which it has never before been used. The Action Research Model is used as the basis for introducing this change.
	Succession Planning	Succession Planning is introduced in an organization where the Action Research Model is used as the basis for introducing this change.
	Sociotechnical Systems	Organizations have two primary components: people and technology. Change one, and the other will also be changed. The Action Research Model is used as the basis for introducing and implementing change.
	Survey Feedback	An attitude survey is conducted in the organization and is then used as the basis for participative improvement planning.
	Grid OD	Managers and/or employees are trained on the managerial grid and use it as the basis for planning increased participation by placing equal emphasis on people and tasks.
Intergroup Relations	**Organizational Mirroring**	Impressions about one group/department are collected from other groups/departments and fed back to the client. These impressions become the basis for self-reflection and action planning.

Exhibit 13-5: Summary descriptions of common OD interventions *(continued)*

Target Group	Intervention	Brief Description
	Confrontation Meetings	Two or more groups with members whose views are quite different are brought together to plan improved relations.
	Process Consultation	Members of two or more groups are brought together to discuss and improve how they interact with each other.
Teams or Groups	**Team Building**	OD methods, relying on the Action Research Model, are used to analyze and increase the cooperation and cohesiveness of work group members.
	Role Analysis	OD methods, relying on the Action Research Model, are used to analyze the roles of members in a group/team and to clarify/change those roles.
Pairs/Triads	**Gestalt OD**	The theories and techniques of Gestalt psychotherapy and counseling are applied to OD interventions. Gestalt approaches focus on the present, rather than on past or future. They also emphasize individual responsibility and accountability, and discourage efforts to place blame on others.
	Third-Party Peacemaking	The change agent functions as peacemaker with two or more people (sometimes leaders of different groups) who are experiencing dysfunctional interpersonal conflict that complicates their work relationships.
Individuals	**Life and Career Planning**	OD methods, using the Action Research Model, are applied to introduce life and/or career planning in an organization.
	Coaching and Counseling	OD methods, using the Action Research Model, are applied to introduce coaching and/or individualized counseling to an organization.

CHAPTER 14

WLP and Employee Development

In the last Chapter, we described Organization Development as a long-term strategy for improving organizational, group, or individual problem-solving and decision-making. In this Chapter, we turn to long-term individual development. Our focus will be on Employee Development.

WLP professionals and operating managers alike now understand that individuals play a large role in the strategic success of their competitive organizations. Individual learning and development has an impact on organizational learning, and it is key to the intellectual capital of an organization (Senge 1990). Individual development also plays a part in achieving strategic business objectives, implementing Human Resource plans, realizing WLP plans, and successfully introducing and consolidating organizational change.

Employee Development need not be limited to planned learning activities that are intended to help individuals achieve their career goals, as Employee Education is. Nor does ED have to be tied directly to work requirements, like Employee Training is. However, ED can encompass those activities. It is long-term and less definable in outcomes than training, and encompasses a broad range of planned and unplanned on-the-job, near-the-job, and off-the-job learning activities. Because it can be difficult to plan and distinguish from the work itself, it is tough to justify to the green-eyeshade pennypinchers and bean counters. But that does not lessen its importance as a tool for individual growth and organizational learning.

But what is Employee Development (ED)? When is it appropriate? How should it be planned, implemented, and monitored? How can it be encouraged when left unplanned? We will introduce Employee Development by answering these questions.

WHAT IS EMPLOYEE DEVELOPMENT (ED)?

Definition of Development

Development comprises any long-term learning intervention that is intended to evoke individual insight and/or build creativity. As individuals are exposed to new ideas or experiences, they begin to build a foundation for culture change: they do it by challenging taken-for-granted assumptions about what works and how an organization approaches its goals and objectives.

Employee Development and Other Forms of Stakeholder Development

Employees are not the only group that can be developed by an organization. Indeed, some organizations deliberately encourage other kinds of development activities directed toward other stakeholders. Among these activities are:

- *Supplier Development,* which is intended to make suppliers' employees more sensitive to the unique requirements of the organizations they serve.
- *Distributor Development,* which is intended to make distributors' employees more capable of reaching the right consumers by understanding the products they distribute.
- *Customer Development,* which is intended to make customers more aware of when and how to use a product or service, and what need that product or service is intended to meet.
- *Stockholder Development,* which is intended to increase the stockholders' participation and sense of ownership in an organization.
- *Union Development,* which is intended to sensitize union officials to unique competitive conditions facing an organization.
- *Family Development,* which is intended to sensitize employees' family members to the working conditions and issues faced by the organization and its employees.
- *Community Development,* which is intended to contribute to the economic, social, and other conditions of the community (or communities) of which an organization is part.

We will focus on Employee Development throughout this Chapter, but it is important to understand that many of the same approaches can also be applied to developing and cultivating other key stakeholder groups.

Definition of Employee Development

Definitions of ED reflect philosophical differences among those who have written about it; some professionals advocate informal, unplanned or "loose" ED, while others advocate more formal, planned, or "tight" ED.

Those advocating loose development structures believe that ED should not emphasize performance-related issues at all. *Loose development,* in that sense, focuses on individual improvement: The aim should be to foster personal growth, pure and simple, perhaps taking advantage of continuing and growing interest in the complete gamut of self-help issues that range from weight control and smoking cessation to improving one's quality of life. Balancing work and personal life, for instance, is an important issue in loose development.

Tight development, on the other hand, focuses on the individual as a tool for organizational improvement. Those advocating tight development believe that ED should be tied to HR Planning, Succession Planning, and diversity efforts. They believe it ought to be a way for the organization to manage individual preparation for meeting long-term organizational needs, usually from the top-down. The top-down orientation of ED contrasts with the traditional bottom-up orientation of Employee Education, which is tied to the realization of an individual's career goals.

WHEN IS EMPLOYEE DEVELOPMENT APPROPRIATE?

Since ED is a long-term effort and any payoffs are not immediately apparent, it is not appropriate as a quick-fix for crisis situations. That would be akin to pouring molasses on fire: By the time the languid liquid hits the flames, they've already spread beyond control! However, we should not minimize the importance of creativity as a tool for finding better, faster, and easier ways to meet or exceed customer expectations, find new business opportunities, or expand market share.

Supporters of "loose" Employment Development believe that it should energize and help people "grow." It should help them shake off complacency, stagnation, and burnout, and equip them with new ideas and approaches first for life and then for work. It is also a means of meeting the deep human need for growth and of realizing individual potential. Critics of loose ED question how often organizations sponsor such activities and how effective these funded but non-job-related activities are at fostering improvement.

Supporters of tight ED believe that it should be used to plan and carry out long-term learning activities that are of practical long-term value to the employer. Not all learning of practical value lends itself to on-the-job training, short classroom experiences, electronically-dependent approaches, or off-the-job educational ventures. ED activities, broadly encompassing more informal and incidental approaches to learning on- and off-site, may work for nearly everything else. They make the individual a vehicle for organizational learning, creating a potential for culture change by adding to the *institutional memory* (the collective memory of an organization's management and employees) and *cultural relics* (such as written directives, job descriptions, and procedure manuals). They are also a means by which organizations can implement HR Plans or Succession Plans.

For those advocating the tight approach, ED is appropriate to use when an organization must "grow" their present employees over long timespans, rather than "buy" (recruit) new workers or "outsource" (use vendors and consultants). "Growing" staff is especially important when some (or many) employees functioning in highly technical jobs cannot be easily replaced because what they do is unique to the organization or industry. These people hold the jobs that make decision-makers shake their heads, wondering if trained replacements can be recruited externally anywhere on the planet.

Critics of the tight approach question whether it is necessary (or even desirable) to tie all human learning to employer needs (Gardner 1963). They take it on faith that what is good for individual development can be, and usually is, best for the employer. This is why they believe organizations have a responsibility to meet human learning needs that are not necessarily tied to company, industry, career, or work requirements.

Of course, the loose and tight approaches to Employee Development are *not* mutually exclusive. It is possible to strike a balance by planning and structuring some long-term ED activities and simultaneously encouraging other, less-structured individual growth efforts.

HOW SHOULD EMPLOYEE DEVELOPMENT BE PLANNED, IMPLEMENTED, AND MONITORED?

In many respects, it is easier to describe the "tight" approach to ED, because planned activities necessarily require some kind of structure and oversight. That is typically absent from the loose approach.

Employee Development and Succession Planning

One way to plan, implement, and monitor ED is to tie it to a Succession Planning or a Replacement Planning effort. As we will define it, *succession planning* is a top-down effort made by leaders of an organization to identify individuals or groups of people to prepare for key positions over time. A succession plan is, of course, the product of a planning process. The results are sometimes presented graphically, in the form of one or more organization charts. These charts depict key positions in the organization, as well as individuals who might be suitable replacements for job incumbents, permanently or temporarily, as a result of predictable changes (such as retirements or dismissals) or unpredictable changes (such as sudden accidents, disabilities, or deaths). A simplified succession chart appears in Exhibit 14-1. Similar charts can be prepared for each component of an organization.

Succession planning is widely practiced, though limited in scope. Unlike HR plans, which may be extended all the way to the bottom of an organization's chain of command, succession plans are usually limited to the top positions only. Individuals in these positions, of course, exert major influence over the lives of everyone in the organization.

Most succession planning systems include several key elements: (1) an evaluation of individual skills; (2) an evaluation of individual experiences; (3) individual development plans; (4) an assessment of individual characteristics; (5) a current job analysis; and (6) a strategic analysis of future needs (Rothwell 1994).

Exhibit 14-1: Organization succession planning chart

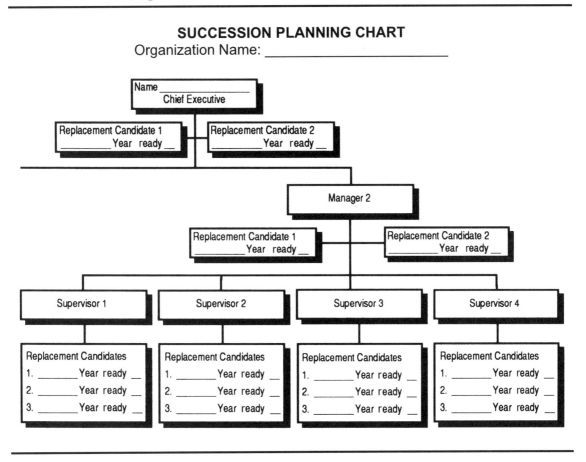

STEPS IN SUCCESSION PLANNING

Let's spend a moment describing steps in a simple model of Succession Planning, presented in Exhibit 14-2. WLP professionals who are presently or expect to be involved in coordinating preparation of succession plans, individual profiles, and individual development action plans will find it particularly helpful. The WLP professional:

1. Meets with the Chief Executive, Chief Operating Officer, or other top-level executives to clarify the steps in the process.
2. Participates in, or leads, one or more group meetings of top managers to brief them on the Succession Planning process, elicit their support, and clarify instructions.

3. Meets with top-level managers individually to offer advice, support, or encouragement in completing forms or conceptualizing succession or development issues.
4. Receives and arranges Succession Planning charts and forms.
5. Presents the results or a summary of results to the highest-level managers, and clarifies next steps.
6. Follows up on questions or issues identified in the process, such as ways to develop individuals.
7. Coordinates meetings between top-level managers and the CEO, COO, or others.
8. Provides guidance for follow-up meetings, evaluation of the process, and other issues.

Exhibit 14-2: Steps in a model of succession planning

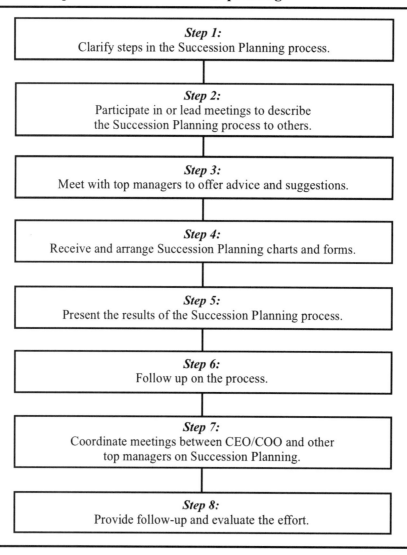

Step 1:
Clarify steps in the Succession Planning process.

Step 2:
Participate in or lead meetings to describe
the Succession Planning process to others.

Step 3:
Meet with top managers to offer advice and suggestions.

Step 4:
Receive and arrange Succession Planning charts and forms.

Step 5:
Present the results of the Succession Planning process.

Step 6:
Follow up on the process.

Step 7:
Coordinate meetings between CEO/COO and other
top managers on Succession Planning.

Step 8:
Provide follow-up and evaluate the effort.

Now let's discuss each step.

Step One: Clarify Steps in the Succession Planning Process

Begin the Succession Planning process by clarifying precisely what results the CEO hopes to achieve from it. (If top management support is lacking, then it will be difficult to succeed with this assignment!) Be sure to clarify at the outset what "products" or "deliverables" are to result from the effort, such as succession charts for the organization and/or parts of the organization, forms, and other information that top managers desire to see. In addition, be sure to clarify timetables (when is the information to be made available, and to whom?), surface the issues on which the forms are to be based (how will information be collected?), determine how much top managers will personally participate in the process, and plan an agenda for introductory and follow-up meetings. Take nothing for granted.

Most succession plans include charts for each component of the organization, identification of "replacement candidates" and the "year when the individual will be ready" to assume the duties of each higher-level position. Most succession plans will also include forms to be completed by the top manager in charge of each major division and/or component of the organization. These forms can include any or all of the following:

- *An Individual/Work Profile* — This form addresses such questions as:
  — What are the duties of each position to be "replaced"?
  — What are the qualifications of the incumbent?
  — What are the qualifications of designated successors for each position?
  — What changes, if any, are expected to be made in the duties, activities, and responsibilities of the position in the future? (These should be tied to, or at least compatible with, the organization's Strategic Business Plan and its HR Plan.)
- . *An Evaluation of Individual Skills and Experience* — This form identifies how well a designated successor for a key position presently matches up to its requirements. (Think of it as a performance appraisal of the individual for the job he or she is to be groomed for, *not* the present job he or she is performing.) Most individual skill evaluations focus on so-called *success factors*, understood as characteristics the individual must possess to advance in this organization.
- *An Individual Development Plan* — This form is an Action Plan intended to equip identified successors with the knowledge, skills, and experience they need to perform competently. It is essentially an Employee Development Plan that extends from one year to many years.

Examples of these forms appear in Exhibits 14-3, 14-4, and 14-5. The important point to understand, however, is that the unique requirements of an organization might mean significantly modifying one or all of these forms.

Exhibit 14-3: Sample individual/work profile

Directions: Please fill in the blanks below, updating or changing information as necessary. Otherwise, please verify the information that already appears on this form. Add sheets if necessary. Thank you for your cooperation.

Biographical Information

Name: Birthdate:

Position Title: Job Code:

Company: Pay Grade:

Division: Date Hired:

Date Appointed to Present Position: Supervisor:

Today's Date:

Education:

Date	Degree	Academic Major	School	City/State
	1			
	2			
	3			
	4			
	5			

Exhibit 14-3: Sample individual/work profile *(continued)*

Other Credentials (List licenses/accreditations/degrees pending):

Date Received	Credential		Sponsor
	1		
	2		
	3		
	4		

Work Experience (Present Employer):

Title	Department/Division	Dates	
		Started	Ended
1			
2			
3			
4			

Work Experience (Previous Employers):
(List most recent positions first.)

Title	Organization(s)	Dates	
		Started	Ended
1			
2			
3			
4			

Exhibit 14-3: Sample individual/work profile *(continued)*

Internal Successors:
(List from most ready to least ready. If none, write "outside candidate.")

	Name	Date Ready	Why most qualified?	
1				
2				
3				
4				

Work Duties (Key Position):
(List most important duties first.)

	Duties	Percentage of Time Devoted to the Duty
1		
2		
3		
4		
5		
6		
7		

Exhibit 14-3: Sample individual/work profile *(continued)*

Desirable Characteristics (Key Position):
(List most important personality characteristics/attitudes first.)

Characteristics	Explain briefly
1	
2	
3	
4	
5	

Expected Change:
(List changes in duties/characteristics of the key position over the next 5 years)

What will change?	Why will the change occur?
1	
2	
3	

Exhibit 14-4: Sample individual skill/experience evaluation

Directions: Please assess the individual using the issues identified as strategically important for the organization. (These are called *success factors*.) Remember that they may change from year to year. This year, we have chosen criteria linked to the U. S. Department of Commerce's Malcolm Baldridge National Quality Award. For each Success Factor listed and described in the left column, circle the individual's present status in the center column and the individual's desired future status to be a serious "successor" candidate for the key position indicated. Thank you for your cooperation.

Name   **Present Title**

Successor Candidate for (position title):

Success Factors	Present Status			Desired Status		
	Below Requirements	**Meets Requirements**	**Exceeds Requirements**	**Below Requirements**	**Meets Requirements**	**Exceeds Requirements**
1 LEADERSHIP The individual is personally involved in and visibly participates in developing and maintaining an environment for quality excellence in the organization.	1 2	3	4 5	1 2	3	4 5
2 QUALITY VALUES The individual expresses quality values and visibly supports the organization's quality values.	1 2	3	4 5	1 2	3	4 5
3 MANAGEMENT FOR QUALITY The individual integrates quality values into day-to-day leadership, management, and supervision.	1 2	3	4 5	1 2	3	4 5

Exhibit 14-4: Sample individual skill/experience evaluation *(continued)*

Success Factors	Present Status						Desired Status					
	Below Requirements		Meets Requirements		Exceeds Requirements		Below Requirements		Meets Requirements		Exceeds Requirements	
4 PUBLIC RESPONSIBILITY The individual works to extend the organization's quality leadership to the community.	1	2	3	4	5		1	2	3	4	5	
5 SCOPE AND MANAGEMENT OF QUALITY DATA AND INFORMATION The individual selects, processes, and maintains quality information for planning and day-to-day management.	1	2	3	4	5		1	2	3	4	5	
6 COMPETITIVE COMPARISONS AND BENCHMARKS The individual selects and applies quality-related competitive comparisons for quality planning, evaluation, and improvement	1	2	3	4	5		1	2	3	4	5	
7 ANALYSIS OF QUALITY DATA AND INFORMATION The individual collects, analyzes, and uses data to support the organization's quality objectives.	1	2	3	4	5		1	2	3	4	5	

Exhibit 14-5: Sample individual development plan (confidential)

Name:

Present Title:

Successor Candidate for (title):

Ready to Assume Position (year):

Directions: Please prepare a plan to help close the gap between the individual's present knowledge, skills, and experience and those that he or she will need to be "ready" to assume the position for which he/she has been designated as a successor candidate (above). This plan can have a lengthy duration, but it should be updated at least annually. Use additional sheets, if necessary.

Objectives
(Briefly describe the knowledge, skills, and experience the "successor" candidate needs.)

To be suited to assume the position, the candidate needs to:

1

2

3

4

5

To rectify areas needing improvement in the present position, this candidate needs to:

1

2

3

4

5

Exhibit 14-5: Sample individual development plan (confidential) *(continued)*

Development Experiences
(Describe below how the "Successor" will be prepared to assume the new position:)

New Assignments/Positions:	Dates	
	Started	**Ended**
1		
2		

Other Planned Development Experiences:	Dates	
	Started	**Ended**
1		
2		
3		
4		

Evaluation
(Describe below how the relative success of developmental experiences will be evaluated.)

Approval

Signed by:

Position Title: **Date:**

Step Two: Participate in or Lead Meetings About the Succession Planning Process

As the next step, WLP professionals will usually find it necessary to brief those involved in the process about what outcomes to expect from it, how to complete charts or forms, and what special issues to consider as they go about their planning. On some occasions, WLP professionals will actually conduct the briefings with groups of top managers; on other occasions, they might participate in a meeting introduced by the CEO or COO. The direct participation of the CEO and COO in this effort is highly desirable. Consult the sample agenda appearing in Exhibit 14-6 and modify it to meet the special requirements of your organization.

Exhibit 14-6: Sample agenda for a briefing on succession planning

Agenda

Section	Topic	Speaker
I.	**Opening Remarks**	**CEO:**
	<ul><li>Why do we do Succession Planning?</li><li>What is Succession Planning?</li><li>Why does Development play an important part in the process?</li></ul>	
II.	**The Process**	**HRD Executive:**
	<ul><li>Overview of Process</li><li>Forms and Methods</li><li>Timelines</li><li>Arranging Assistance</li><li>Questions and Answers</li></ul>	
III.	**Closing Remarks**	**COO:**
	<ul><li>What will we do with the results?</li><li>How does this process link to our Strategic Business Plans?</li></ul>	

Step Three: Meet with Top Managers to Offer Advice and Suggestions

As top managers think about Succession Planning and their own areas of responsibility, they will have questions. Some will prefer to meet with you individually in order to structure the steps they need to take. Prepare an agenda for this meeting, even if it is only you and one other person, so the meeting is well-structured and an efficient use of everyone's time. Rest assured, advance preparation is appreciated and is usually impressive.

In these meetings, you will probably be asked for advice or suggestions. Examples of typical questions might include these:

- Why is succession planning necessary at all? Is it not possible to handle replacement needs by reorganizing parts of an organization and shifting responsibilities to others? Is it not possible to take action other than promoting from within to meet replacement needs?
- What advice do you have about how I generally handle people who are not performing effectively in their present positions?
- How do I find out about high performers in other parts of the organization who might flourish under the developmental experiences my area could provide?
- When do I know that the person is developed adequately?
- How do I plan for development when the responsibilities of a key position are changing and it is not yet apparent what knowledge or skills will ultimately be required?
- How do I develop people over the long term? What methods should I use, especially if the person is too valuable or important to "move around" in order to expose him or her to other parts of the organization or division?

These and other questions are difficult to field on the spur of the moment, but they are somewhat predictable, since they tie into the purposes and goals of succession planning. Consult Exhibit 14-7 for suggestions about how to field these common questions.

Exhibit 14-7: Possible answers to predictable questions about succession planning

Questions	Possible Answers
Why is succession planning necessary at all? Is it not possible to handle replacement needs by reorganizing parts of an organization and shifting responsibilities to others when an unexpected vacancy arises? Is it not possible to take action other than promoting from within to meet replacement needs?	Yes, it is possible to meet replacement needs other than by promoting from within or transferring people in from other parts of the organization. Sometimes it is necessary to recruit from outside the organization. Sometimes it is necessary to re-think how the work is performed and/or how the responsibilities for the work are distributed. However, succession planning is necessary so as to encourage employee development and identify legitimate "needs" for talent in the organization.

Exhibit 14-7: Possible answers to predictable questions about succession planning *(continued)*

Questions	Possible Answers
What advice do you have about how I handle people who are not performing effectively in their present positions?	Tell me first what you have done to help the person perform. Have you provided coaching? Have you made the duties clear? Have you provided feedback and given appraisals? Have you shown, through salary actions taken in the past, that performance is inadequate? Have you trained him or her? If you *have* done all these, then have you also taken steps to discipline the person progressively, document those actions, and counsel the individual that his or her continued employment is in jeopardy?
How do I find out about high performers in other parts of the organization who might flourish under the developmental experience my area could provide?	As part of this process, we are preparing a list of "high potential" people to receive special developmental attention. You will hear more about that as we proceed with this project.
When do I know that the person is developed adequately?	Compare the person's knowledge, skills, and experience to the requirements of the position.
How do I plan for development when the responsibilities of a key position are changing and it is not yet known what competencies will ultimately be required for success in the position?	You will never be able to develop people if you do not know what they need to know or do. Clarify these issues as soon as possible, and update as needed.
How do I develop people over the long term? What methods should I use, especially if the person is too valuable to "move around" in order to expose him or her to other parts of the organization or division?	If the position will remain unchanged, then ask the incumbent how he or she was "developed." There are other steps you can take. Look at the job description and, for each duty or activity listed on it, consider what can be done to develop the likely "successor."

The biggest danger WLP professionals are likely to encounter in these meetings is that some managers will be inclined to argue that they should "leave people where they are and keep them doing what they've always been doing" to develop them. But that is not always an appropriate way to develop people. To be developed, people must be presented with new challenges and learning opportunities. Nor do they *necessarily* need to leave their jobs for other full-time or part-time assignments to do that. Indeed, there are many ways to develop people. Some of them are listed and described in Exhibit 14-8.

Exhibit 14-8: Methods for employee development

Method	Brief Description
Short Work Assignments	While the employee remains in his or her present job, the immediate supervisor gives him/her assignments intended to provide exposure to and experience with new areas of the organization and/or new work duties.
Task Force Assignments	While the employee remains in his or her present job, the immediate supervisor sees that the employee is assigned to a task force composed of people from other areas of the organization, division, or department.
Job Rotations	The employee is moved to other areas of the organization or division and is given a new job, temporarily or indefinitely. The employee can be assigned various rotations, such as "startups" (getting something off the ground), "turnabouts" (turning around failing activities), "shutdowns" (stopping an activity), or "combinations" (taking on more than one major challenge simultaneously). Job rotations also expose the employee to new leadership/management styles, since he or she usually has a new "boss" who may be especially skilled in areas the employee needs to develop and who can serve as a suitable "role model."
Formal Mentoring	While the employee remains in his or her present job, he or she is assigned to a mentor for formalized coaching and discussions about development. The mentor can be the organizational superior of the employee's immediate supervisor or can be from another part of the organization.
Off-the-Job Development	The employee remains in his or her present job, but uses time off the job to build knowledge, skills, and experience through involvement in community, church, professional, or charitable organizations. These activities are supported by the employee's immediate supervisor.

Step Four: Receive and Arrange Succession Planning Charts and Forms

Once top managers or others involved in the succession planning process have completed their succession planning charts and forms, they will send them to you. Be prepared for that by thinking ahead about how you will organize this information, store it, and ensure proper security. Some WLP professionals will find that their organizations have mainframe-based or microcomputer-based Human Resource Information Systems that lend themselves to entering, storing, and maintaining succession planning information. Others will find that they have to establish their own record-keeping and retrieval systems.

If possible, use Individual Profiles to prepare a Skill Inventory of management talent for the organization. Annual updates will help keep it current. If users require more current information, establish the means to update more often than annually.

Step Five: Present the Results

The presentation of information about succession plans is critical to its acceptance by the highest-level decision-makers. Prepare a short summary of results, noting any special questions raised by the participants and issues identified in the process. In addition, make notes about future action steps, recommending what steps should be taken and who should take them. Provide succession planning charts if they are requested. Do not provide detailed information about individuals, since that will usually be too voluminous and might raise confidentiality issues. Prepare an agenda before a meeting with the highest-level officials. Be sure to have at least a list of questions about next steps, and recommendations for each step.

Step Six: Follow Up on Questions or Issues Identified in the Process

Be sure to follow up on any unanswered questions or issues left unresolved during the succession planning process. If, for example, top managers have requested information about developmental opportunities, do the research and provide the feedback as an aid to their decision-making.

Step Seven: Coordinate Meetings between the Highest Officials and Others

Many organizations follow up the succession planning process with meetings between the CEO or COO and top managers. The purpose of these meetings is to review and discuss the succession plan for each component of the organization and, in some cases, the individual development plans for "high potential" individuals. Meetings can also be opportunities to resolve conflicting "claims" on individuals as successors for more than one position.

The term *high potential employee* is open to interpretation and debate. It usually refers to an individual capable of benefiting from development. WLP professionals have defined the term differently, depending on the needs and cultures of the organizations in which the term is used.

Some link the term directly to succession plans and think of high potentials as individuals identified as "successors" to key spots. Others use the term to refer to employees who show great promise for the future and who can benefit from special attention and/or planned or unplanned learning experiences. Still others refer to high potentials as individuals capable of promotion or capable of "leaping" several organizational layers. Finally, some use the term "high potential" to mean employees who should be given special treatment because they are members of protected labor groups that have historically been underrepresented in the internal labor market of the organization. Before, during, or after meetings, make a list of high potential employees. If the organization supports special programs to develop high potentials—and many do, often calling them leadership development programs—then design and implement those programs using such methods as planned short-term work assignments and job rotations.

Step Eight: Provide Follow-Up and Evaluate the Effort

The final step is the Achilles heel of succession planning and Employee Development in many otherwise well-respected corporations: WLP professionals should establish a means by which to make certain that Employee Development activities are actually carried out. They should also make a diligent effort to evaluate how well the succession planning process is working.

There is no "right" method for providing follow-up. One approach is to make random site visits to top managers who have committed to developing their employees. Another approach is to hire an outside consultant to follow-up with managers who are committed to developing their employees. A faculty member of a nearby college might be appropriate, since he or she will have credibility, can be trained quickly, can be sworn to secrecy, and is not likely to charge a huge fee.

Evaluate the succession planning process over time by following up to see how many people are actually placed in positions for which they were identified as potential replacements. Do not expect a perfect placement rate.

HOW CAN EMPLOYEE DEVELOPMENT BE ENCOURAGED, IF IT HAS NOT YET BEEN PLANNED?

Employee Development does not have to be tied to succession planning, as supporters of the so-called loose approach point out. Indeed, it can be encouraged in ways that are largely unplanned and unstructured. The primary burden of responsibility for such efforts, while sometimes funded by employers, often falls to employees themselves. Let's spend a moment describing what a manager can do to encourage Employee Development without formally planning it. We will present these suggestions within the framework of a simple model (shown in Exhibit 14-9). Managers can encourage ED by:

1. Asking employees how enthusiastic they are about their work.
2. Probing how much enthusiasm and creativity employees believe they should have. (The aim is to assess whether employees feel complacent or burned out with their work.)
3. Exploring work assignments and nonwork-related learning activities that employees can pursue, with their supervisor's support, to grow personally or professionally.
4. Periodically following up with employees to assess the extent to which they are pursuing developmental activities.

Exhibit 14-9: Steps in a model for encouraging employee development

---

Managers should:

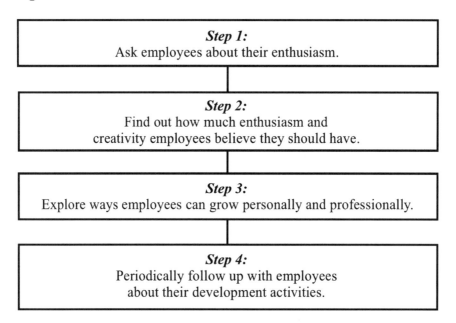

Step 1:
Ask employees about their enthusiasm.

Step 2:
Find out how much enthusiasm and
creativity employees believe they should have.

Step 3:
Explore ways employees can grow personally and professionally.

Step 4:
Periodically follow up with employees
about their development activities.

Let's discuss each step briefly below.

Step One: Ask Employees About Their Enthusiasm

Most managers are accustomed to carrying out annual performance appraisals, but many are not accustomed to conducting "personal growth discussions" with their employees. (Some managers do not even know how to open such a discussion, even if they are willing!)

WLP professionals must build support for such developmental discussions, because there is evidence that many people yearn for them. Employers have a responsibility to encourage their employees to become more creative, insightful, and energetic. Likewise, it is important for employers to help their people avoid burnout, which can lead to negative or cavalier attitudes about customer service or product or service quality issues.

Developmental discussions that are followed up with developmental activities (initiated by employees and supported by employers) help to do that. They do not need to be carried out in formal meetings like performance appraisals, though they can be handled that way. Instead, managers can casually ask employees how they are feeling about their work. (This question must be posed with more seriousness than the casual "How are you doing?") Employees needing a developmental discussion will usually make it a point to snap at this kind of opening, and that is a sign that a longer meeting is appropriate.

WLP professionals who set out to encourage developmental discussions between managers and employees do, however, run into roadblocks. Some managers, often those priding themselves most on their authority, will not be in favor of holding such discussions. They will cite such reasons as these:

- "People should be thankful they have jobs, and not worry about their personal growth or feelings. They should be happy they are getting a paycheck."
- "I don't think employers should be in the business of counseling people about their future growth, because it might build unrealistic expectations. It could lay us open to litigation, too, if what we promise cannot be delivered."
- "If I held talks like you are suggesting, people who are doing fine now would suddenly start wondering how they are doing. I would have been guilty of putting a thought in their heads that was not there before. I might cause myself problems later, since they might decide to look elsewhere for a job. Then I would have to waste time training a replacement."
- "I won't do anything that undermines my authority. Appraisals are a necessary evil to document poor performers and give a slap on the back to good performers. But developmental sessions are not as important. I do not have time for such frivolity."

Be prepared to answer these and similar objections. In some cases, it works best to begin modestly, with one or more managers who are champions of human development. Encourage them to take the lead, monitor the results, and later cite their lead when advocating broader use of developmental discussions in the organization.

Step Two: Probe How Much Enthusiasm and Creativity Employees Believe They Should Have

Sometimes the employees most in need of developmental discussions are least inclined to participate in them. If they feel trapped in an occupation, job, or company, they might be reluctant to open up and discuss their feelings. Moreover, some will not see that there is any way for them to experience a rebirth of wonder or get a new perspective on what they do and who they are.

Managers are usually aware of such people in their departments. Sometimes these people make caustic remarks to others, reflecting negative attitudes and their own sense of frustration. That is a sure signal that a developmental discussion is in order, especially when the individual feels that he or she was "passed over" for promotion or a choice work assignment. (If a developmental discussion does not address the root of the negative attitude and the employee continues to undermine the performance of the organization by making negative remarks to other employees or customers, a later step might be to institute progressive discipline.)

Managers should set aside time and minimize interruptions when carrying out a developmental discussion of this kind. They should start out the conversation positively, emphasizing what the employee is doing right and doing well. Above all, managers should avoid mentioning the employee's negative attitudes as demonstrated through specific situations or behaviors. (If the employee is confronted directly at this point, the developmental discussion will be ruined.)

Managers should use these meetings to do some in-depth probing. After making very clear that employee performance is *not* being evaluated, the managers should ask questions like these:

- How are you feeling about your job?
- What problems have you been encountering lately?
- What can I do to help you improve the energy and positive attitude you should bring to your job?
- What do you think would really help you grow and develop as a person and employee? Tell me about this.

Managers should then use the answers to these questions to suggest other questions. The aim of the discussion is to build trust, encourage the employee to undertake personal growth activities, and show managerial support for those activities. An added benefit: the employee's "bad attitude" might diminish when he or she sees that the manager really cares.

Step Three: Explore Ways Employees Can Grow Personally and Professionally

Whenever employees and managers sit down for developmental discussions, one issue that frequently comes up is this: What methods or strategies are available for the employee to develop himself or herself?

Managers should be careful not to promise what they cannot deliver, such as opportunities for development or promotion. Instead, they should emphasize that the chief responsibility for personal development rests with the employee. They most certainly ought to provide information on how employees can develop themselves on and off the job, however.

Step Four: Periodically Follow up with Employees About Their Development Activities

Managers who raise the topic of Employee Development should not just talk about it once and then forget it; rather, they should periodically follow up with their employees to assess their feelings by asking them about developmental activities in which they are engaged (and then, encouraging such efforts), and re-emphasizing the importance of development to the individual and the organization. These follow-ups should be done at least annually, and preferably months before the employee's scheduled performance appraisal.

CHAPTER 15

WLP and Employee Education

More than a few WLP professionals find themselves deeply immersed in Employee Education (EE) because they serve as administrators of employee educational assistance programs, industry education programs, or professional accreditation programs. Many are also asked to establish career ladders, identifying educational and experience requirements along the rungs of those ladders. Others find themselves counseling employees about steps they should take to qualify for advancement or in order to remain employable in uncertain times. Still others sponsor on-site college courses for employees after hours, or oversee internship and school-to-work programs for students enrolled in educational institutions. EE encompasses all of these activities—and more.

But what is Employee Education? When is EE appropriate? How should it be planned, implemented, and monitored? This Chapter provides background information about Employee Education for WLP professionals administering, overseeing, or operating such programs.

WHAT IS EMPLOYEE EDUCATION (EE)?

Definition of Employee Education

Employee Education focuses on identifying, assuring, and helping develop, through planned learning, the key competencies that enable individuals to prepare for career advancement. EE differs from other efforts designed to improve performance through planned or unplanned workplace learning. Unlike Organization Development, EE is geared more to individual than to group change. Unlike Employee Development, EE is often—but not always—linked to formal education programs sponsored by colleges, secondary schools, vocational schools, professional associations, or industry groups. Unlike employee training, it is rarely tied to the unique work or performance requirements of one organization or one occupation.

Scope and Spending on Employee Education Programs

Most major corporations and many smaller or medium-sized firms already sponsor employee educational assistance programs. By way of editorializing, however, we hasten to add that we do not share the view of some federal bureaucrats or corporate employee benefits professionals, who classify educational assistance as a "fringe benefit" and argue that it should be subject to taxation. We do not believe that it should be peripheral to employment (as the term "fringe benefit" seems to imply) at a time when increasing education and investing in intellectual capital is rapidly becoming essential for individual and organizational competitiveness in a global economy.

FORMS OF EMPLOYEE EDUCATION IN ORGANIZATIONS

Employee Education takes three different but related forms: *remedial*, *qualifying*, and *continuing education*. While they overlap conceptually, the distinctions between them help crystallize key purposes to be achieved by Employee Education programs. (See Exhibit 15-1 for a visual representation of the differences between remedial, qualifying, and continuing education. Study the Exhibit carefully.)

Exhibit 15-1: Three types of employee education

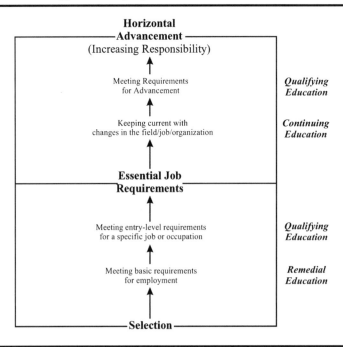

Remedial Education

This form of Employee Education is directed toward improving the basic skills essential for employment. It closes the performance gaps between what people must know or do to meet any employer's needs and what they actually know or can do. In recent years, U. S. workers have been found seriously wanting in such basic skills as reading, writing, speaking, and computing. Remedial education is a tool to help people become employable and participate successfully in qualifying education.

Organizations sponsor remedial education by: (1) encouraging employees to complete a G. E. D. (General Education Diploma, the equivalent of a high school diploma); (2) offering in-house instruction on reading, writing, computing, and other basic skills; (3) using tuition reimbursement programs to fund efforts to send workers to local educational institutions (during or after work) to improve their basic skills; and (4) offering English-as-a-second-language to the growing number of workers in the U. S. whose native language is not English.

Employers have been forced to invest in remedial education because deficiencies in basic skills create barriers to the introduction of labor-saving technology and individual advancement. However, remedial education is just one performance-improvement intervention for addressing basic skills deficiencies. Employers can also use any number of performance-improvement interventions to deal with the problem. For example, employers can address basic skill deficiencies by:

- Toughening selection standards to screen out applicants with basic skill deficiencies
- Automating work in order to reduce dependence on human skills
- Creating job aids to help employees perform tasks they could perform if they possessed adequate basic skills
- Simplifying job requirements/tasks so they can be performed by workers who are deficient in some basic skills
- Bringing educators in as consultants, to design or deliver basic skills training
- Sending employees to off-site educational programs in order to correct deficiencies
- Bringing training vendors in to design basic skills programs and/or provide training
- Redesigning work systems so that tasks or activities requiring competence in basic skills are assigned to only a relatively small number of workers
- Laying off or terminating employees who are deficient in basic skills

The short-term steps that employers are taking to address basic skill deficiencies within present workers are matched by long-term steps to head off similar deficiencies with future workers—students still enrolled in educational institutions. The long-term steps they are taking have, in part, prompted cries for educational reform in many states, and have helped forge closer ties between employers and educational institutions. Employers can contribute to long-term work force improvements by providing students with internships, furnishing schools with badly-needed resources, participating in school-to-work programs, and helping displaced workers master the skills they need to find and keep new jobs. This is a daunting national challenge that threatens the competitiveness of U. S. businesses at home and abroad.

Qualifying Education

People who meet the basic skill requirements essential for finding and keeping any kind of employment must still meet the requirements for entering a special line of work or occupation. There was a time when all you had to do was hire "a warm body" for almost any job. Employers today find that is no longer true: Many jobs or occupations now require extensive pre-entry education. For this reason, people must have "qualifying" education that equips them with the specialized skills necessary to meet entry-level occupational requirements, to progress in that occupation, or to make a career transition out of it. Examples of qualifying education are easy to point out. For instance, a college degree in accounting is often considered necessary for those wishing to enter an accounting career. (It is hard to imagine enrolling in accounting courses for entertainment!) A college degree in accounting might also be a ticket out of another occupation and into accounting. Qualifying education is also necessary to help people advance professionally: College-educated engineers often return to school for Master of Business Administration degrees in preparation for management positions in engineering departments or firms.

Organizations sponsor qualifying education in many ways. One way is to offer tuition reimbursement for after-hours instruction at local educational institutions, so people can earn educational qualifications necessary for advancement. A second way is to sponsor professional accreditation in occupational specialties such as accounting, data processing, engineering, and human resources. A third way is to sponsor industry-oriented education, such as manufacturing or insurance courses. There are a burgeoning number of industry education programs, many co-sponsored by educational institutions or specialized educational groups within different industries.

Continuing Education

The term *continuing education* is used to refer to two different educational paths. The ambiguity of the term is often a source of confusion. In one sense, continuing education refers to efforts made by individuals to stay abreast of changes in their occupations. Mandatory continuing education has been added to statutory professional licensing requirements in many states for such fields as medicine, law, accounting, real estate, insurance, and teaching, to name but a few. Continuing education requirements are usually expressed as a minimum number of classroom hours (40, 60 or 80) to be met by each professional during a specific time period, such as one year.

Mandatory continuing education is now being required for more than just the renewal of some state certifications or licenses. Some college administrators, recognizing the rapid and sweeping changes occurring in many fields, have discussed imposing continuing education requirements on college graduates. In effect, that would lead to yearly-renewable college degrees. Some companies, too, are mandating continuing education, making it a condition for continued employment.

There are two problems with all these mandates. First, they can differ widely and often unnecessarily among sponsors or licensure authorities. As a result, employee "students" and WLP professionals must familiarize themselves with a dizzying array of requirements, many of which might easily be standardized within or between occupations. This issue is an especially important one in large organizations, where WLP professionals must offer advice about continuing education to employees in widely diverse occupational specialties. The second problem is that stating mandates in terms of activities, such as a specific number of hours of participation, does little to emphasize the importance of outcomes, results, and contributions of continuing education to improved work performance or future advancement.

In another sense, however, continuing education can refer to a means by which individuals can advance horizontally in their careers by gaining increasing technical knowledge, skill, and experience, rather than advance vertically in their organizations by gaining increasing supervisory responsibility. When career advancement is linked to increasing technical proficiency rather than management responsibility, it is called a *technical career ladder* in order to distinguish it from a *functional or management career ladder*. In a so-called *dual career ladder* with technical and functional or management tracks, promotion on the functional/management track is tied to increasing responsibility. By way of contrast, promotion on the technical career ladder occurs through horizontal advancement in professional competence. In the wake of dramatic corporate downsizing, mergers, reductions in middle management, and promotion logjams created by so many baby boomers at roughly the same point in their careers, some observers of the contemporary business scene believe that technical career ladders will continue to play an increasingly important role as a way of satisfying increasing employee frustration about insufficient opportunities to advance up the traditional functional/management career ladder.

WHEN IS EMPLOYEE EDUCATION APPROPRIATE?

Employee Education is usually considered an intermediate-term change effort used to: help individuals overcome deficiencies that hamper their employability; qualify for entry to a job or occupation; upgrade skills in light of dynamically shifting organizational, professional, and technological requirements; prepare for career advancement (horizontally or vertically); or prepare for career transitions from one occupation to another.

On the other hand, Employee Education *is not appropriate* for:

- Addressing performance problems rooted in issues outside the boundaries of individual control;
- Planning and managing group change, learning, or development;
- Fostering skill development across or within groups;
- Applying informal learning practices to individual preparation for advancement;
- Providing job-specific or organization-specific instruction; or
- Improving group interaction.

Since relatively long time spans are necessary for individuals to change or acquire their repertoire of knowledge or skills, Employee Education is also inappropriate as a quick fix for crisis situations or as a trendy solution to deal with pressing problems.

HOW SHOULD EMPLOYEE EDUCATION BE PLANNED, IMPLEMENTED, AND MONITORED?

A Model for Planning an Employee Education Program

Most employers already sponsor various forms of Employee Education, even those without in-house training programs or employee development efforts. For this reason, WLP professionals often find themselves needing to bring unity and purpose to programs otherwise lacking them. One way to do that is to apply an approach called *functional analysis*, widely used in planning corporate employee benefits programs. To apply this approach to Employee Educational Policies and Programs, even if they are not employee benefits, G. Hallman (1988) believes that WLP professionals should:

- Identify key strategic needs affecting the organization, and career needs affecting employee groups.
- Classify needs into logical, functional categories.
- Classify employees into categories linked to needs.
- Set priorities.
- Prepare recommendations for an employee educational policy, a revised policy, or a series of related policies.
- Estimate costs of implementing a new educational assistance policy or changing the organization's existing educational assistance policy.
- Evaluate alternative methods of funding the policy.
- Make final determinations about the employee educational assistance policy.
- Implement the policy through planned educational programs.
- Communicate the policy and programs to employees and their supervisors.
- Counsel individuals, as needed, on their educational needs and the value of education as a vehicle to help achieve personal career goals and organizational goals.
- Periodically review the employee educational assistance policy and programs in light of changing organizational and employee needs.

These steps are illustrated in Exhibit 15-2. The same steps, of course, can also be applied to other WLP initiatives—such as existing OD, ED, or employee training programs.

Exhibit 15-2: A model for planning employee educational programs

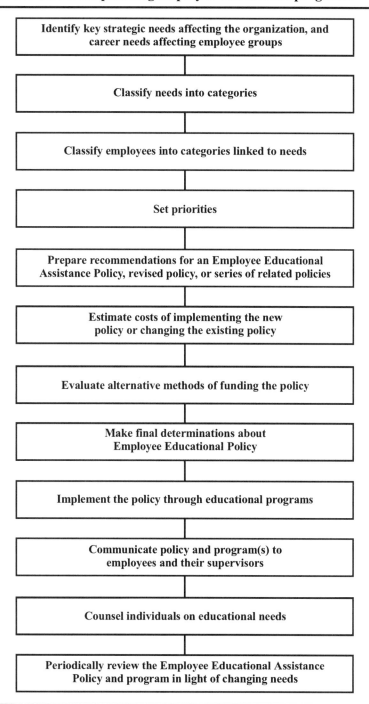

Identify key strategic needs affecting the organization, and career needs affecting employee groups

Classify needs into categories

Classify employees into categories linked to needs

Set priorities

Prepare recommendations for an Employee Educational Assistance Policy, revised policy, or series of related policies

Estimate costs of implementing the new policy or changing the existing policy

Evaluate alternative methods of funding the policy

Make final determinations about Employee Educational Policy

Implement the policy through educational programs

Communicate policy and program(s) to employees and their supervisors

Counsel individuals on educational needs

Periodically review the Employee Educational Assistance Policy and program in light of changing needs

Step One: Identify Key Strategic Needs Affecting the Organization, and Career Needs Affecting Employee Groups

In many organizations, the strategic planning process identifies or underscores key driving issues to serve as focal points for long-term corporate initiatives. Top managers might, for instance, indicate that the organization ought to improve customer service, address product quality, or enhance global competitiveness through the ISO process or through other means. To be useful at the operating level, such ill-defined goals must be translated into clearly-stated, measurable objectives for each function. In one sense, the vagueness of strategic goals can also be viewed as corporate expressions of need for a good employee educational-assistance policy.

WLP professionals must take the lead, and translate these often-vaguely-worded corporate strategic objectives into educational objectives. To that end, it might be enough to merely list strategic objectives and ask several key decision-makers to identify education initiatives they believe will contribute most toward meeting the organization's objectives. This process can be carried out through focus groups, education surveys, interviews, or education committees.

The thrust of such questions should be three-fold:

1. What is the organization already doing to meet its objectives through remedial education? What should the organization be doing?
2. What is the organization doing to meet its objectives through qualifying education? What should it be doing?
3. What is the organization doing to meet its objectives through continuing education? What should it be doing?

The aim of these questions is to frame new educational initiatives based on the organization's key strategic issues and objectives. That clearly links education to business needs as expressed in strategic issues and objectives.

Another set of issues and needs arises from the employees themselves. These needs are linked to employee career goals. Among them:

1. What is the organization already doing to help individuals identify and address their own basic skills deficiencies? What should the organization be doing?
2. What help is already being given to individuals to help them identify and meet the education and experience requirements for career advancement? What help should be given?
3. What assistance is given to employees to keep their occupational skills current amid changing conditions in the organization and in their respective fields? What assistance should be given?

By answering these questions, WLP professionals can begin to formulate clear goals and objectives to guide Employee Education policy and programs in an organization. (A *policy* provides direction; a *program* is an area of activity intended to activate policy.) But if these questions are ignored, the payoffs of EE to the organization will be difficult to quantify. Nevertheless, EE will remain a real morale booster for the few employees who take advantage of it.

Step Two: Classify Needs into Categories

As a next step, WLP professionals should classify needs (identified in Step 1) into logical, functional categories. One way to do that is to construct a *needs/program matrix* that indicates educational needs and matches them to existing programs. Needs may be linked directly to corporate strategic issues and employee career issues, or to remedial, qualifying, and continuing education. The resulting list might resemble this one:

Exhibit 15-3: Needs/program matrix

Need	*Program Area*
Remedial Education	• Basic employability skills seminars for employees
	• Adult basic education sponsored by educational institutions
	• Job-search skills for employees who are being outplaced
	• Programs sponsored by educational institutions for students, job applicants, and the disadvantaged
	• Programs co-sponsored with educational institutions ("adopt-a-school" efforts, pre-entry programs for job applicants, and team teaching efforts in which employees and educators share instructional responsibilities)
Qualifying Education	• Career seminars sponsored by groups outside the organization or by the organization
	• Programs sponsored by educational institutions off-the-job (such as college courses, correspondence courses, and Executive MBA programs)
	• Programs sponsored by educational institutions on the work site during working hours (some on-site courses, various apprenticeship or internship programs, and other cooperative educational ventures)

Exhibit 15-3: Needs/program matrix *(continued)*

Need	*Program Area*
	• Programs sponsored by educational institutions on the work site before or after work (on-site courses, vestibule instruction)
	• Programs sponsored by vendors or other groups (short or long seminars)
	• Programs sponsored by industry-education groups (e.g., the Life Office Management Association in the insurance industry)
Continuing Education	• Programs sponsored by or for professional or occupational groups (e.g., licensure, accreditation, or certification programs for real estate, insurance, accounting, or data processing, or courses intended to help people retain state licenses).
	• Non-degree-related college-sponsored programs
	• Industry or professional conferences
	• Short vendor-offered public seminars
Programs not Otherwise Classified	• Educational assistance or scholarship programs for employees' family members
	• Educational assistance to community or charitable groups (the United Negro College Fund, the Urban League)
	• Educational assistance to suppliers, distributors, franchisees, or other organizational stakeholders
	• Educational grants to local schools, community colleges, or universities

This list is by no means intended to be complete. Many things can be added to it, including specialized needs stemming from the organization's strategy or employees' career goals.

Step Three: Classify Employees into Categories Linked To Needs and Programs

If the aim of planning EE is to weight program objectives according to the organization's strategic objectives and employee career objectives, it will eventually become clear that needs vary in importance. So, too, do the employee groups whose needs are to be met by educational assistance policies and programs. After all, some groups and individuals have unique needs that require special attention. Indeed, some groups might even require different educational policies and programs.

For these and other reasons, it is essential to link employee categories to educational needs and programs. This process of targeting educational programs is a form of *market segmentation*. As in marketing, it is a process of linking up identifiable consumer groups to products or services for them.

There are various ways by which to classify employee groups, of course. For instance, employees can be classified by occupational groups (managers, accountants, engineers, salespersons, secretaries), organizational parts (division, department, work unit), length of service, age, sex, protected/nonprotected labor status, or exempt and nonexempt.

Many WLP professionals find it helpful to select a scheme for classifying employees that is compatible with other methods already in use by the organization. More specifically, employee categories can be linked to salary structures or qualifications for determining employee benefits, or to employee training requirements by job category.

After identifying employee groups, WLP professionals should then link up needs, educational assistance policies, and programs to each group. Care should be taken to express remedial, qualifying, and continuing education needs in terms suited to each group. As part of this step, a detailed audit should be conducted to assess exactly how the organization's employee education policies and programs contribute to meeting corporate strategic objectives and employee career objectives. At this level, the focus should be on actions taken for *each* employee group.

Several key questions should be posed at the outset of the audit. For example: Does the organization have one (or more) written policies on employee educational assistance? If no written policy exists, does the organization reimburse employees for tuition and/or does it participate in activities sponsored by educational institutions? If a written policy does exist, how long has it been since it was last revised? When and for what reasons was it revised? Why was the policy prepared in the first place? What educational programs does it cover? What programs are not described in it, and why are they not described?

WLP professionals should then pose questions about desired educational policies and programs for each employee group. For instance, operating managers could be asked these questions: If you could have any wish come true about employee educational assistance, what would you wish for? How would realization of those wishes support the organization's strategic business plans or help employees achieve their individual career objectives? What special programs, unique to your part of the organization or the occupations of employees in your areas, would be most desirable? What off-the-job education would you like your employees to participate in? What employee educational programs would be most useful in helping your work unit or department meet its goals?

WLP professionals should then examine the responses, summarizing existing and desired needs/programs by employee group. A similar process can be used to gather information for establishing or revising education policies and programs focused on the organization's involvement with such stakeholder groups as local educational institutions, employees' family members, job applicants, and charitable or community agencies.

Step Four: Set Priorities

No organization can satisfy every educational need, because no organization has the time or resources to do that. For this reason, policy and program priorities must be established.

One way to do that is to examine each employee group and prioritize EE assistance policies and programs in isolation. Ideally, top and middle managers, supervisors, employees, and union officials should be asked to identify their priorities, which can then be cross-checked with information about the organization's key strategic objectives/issues, to ensure that EE priorities match the organization's strategic priorities.

Step Five: Prepare Recommendations for an Employee Educational Assistance Policy, Revised Policy, or Series of Related Policies

Based on the priorities identified and the results of previous steps, WLP professionals should prepare tentative recommendations for an employee educational assistance policy. At this stage, these recommendations can simply be listed in priority order for each employee group and for the organization's entire EE program. This list will provide essential details about writing or revising such a policy and any program descriptions.

Step Six: Estimate Costs of Implementing or Changing the Educational Assistance Policy

Before finalizing education policy and making final recommendations, WLP professionals should first estimate costs. If few changes will be made to existing education policy, that should be easy. WLP professionals need only consider historical participation rates in organization-sponsored educational programs and then extrapolate into the future. How much, for instance, has the organization traditionally spent each year on employee tuition reimbursement, internships, adopt-a-school efforts, or similar programs? Those preferring a different approach might find it useful to create a classification scheme for remedial, qualifying, and continuing education expenses, and lump together all spending estimates for each classification so that it is possible to see what the organization is spending on each one.

If many changes are to be made to education policy, however, it might be difficult to estimate costs. Clearly, historical evidence will not be helpful when there is no history upon which to rely! In these cases, WLP professionals must make assumptions about the expenses that will be incurred or allowed by the organization, and then select a representative random sample from the employee groups targeted for the new policy/program. These people should then be contacted by written or phone survey. The survey results can become the basis for estimating the costs of implementing a new or revamped policy or program.

Step Seven: Evaluate Alternative Methods of Funding the Policy

In this step, direct attention to the many details of decision-making and the funding impact of each decision. First, consider alternative policy and program assumptions that affect funding. Among them:

- Who is eligible to participate? Can restrictions be placed on what groups are able to qualify? Should such restrictions be placed on any or all programs?
- How is eligibility determined? By whom? How is authorization to participate in the program granted? By whom?
- What expenses will be allowed? What kinds of educational expenses will the organization permit? Not permit? Why?
- Should restrictions be placed on participation? Should there be a spending maximum per employee per year? Should that be a total dollar amount for all programs, or should different amounts be allocated to different programs?
- What incentives, if any, should be given to employees for participating? (For example, should the organization award a bonus for successful completion of high school or college courses/degrees? If so, how much?)

Second, consider sources of funding. Do not assume that the organization must pick up the tab for the entire Employee Education effort. Sources of funding include government, the organization, and employees themselves. Explore the preferences of top managers about the relative burden to be borne by each group. Would they be willing for the organization to shoulder all the expenses, or would they be willing to shift costs wherever possible? If so, what percentage of the costs would they prefer to shift? What do they believe the organization should fund, and what expenses do they believe other groups should bear?

Third, monitor tax issues. The U. S. Congress has been redefining which employee educational assistance reimbursements are to be tax exempt to employees. If necessary, request help from accounting professionals to track this important issue, and assess its potential impact on the organization's Employee Educational Assistance programs.

WLP professionals should be creative enough to explore many policy and program funding alternatives, since many variations are possible. The decisions made on these issues can, of course, have a major impact on the ultimate costs of implementing and operating educational programs. They can clearly influence how much employees are willing to participate.

Step Eight: Finalize the Details of the Employee Educational Assistance Policy

In this step, WLP professionals should finalize details concerning any employee educational assistance policy and programs. A good way to start this process is to draft a written policy and circulate it for comment among such key stakeholders as top managers, middle managers, and employees. WLP professionals might also want to do some benchmarking to see what similar Employee Education policies or programs have been adopted by industry competitors or other organizations in the same locale.

Step Nine: Implement the Program

At this point, it should be possible to unveil the revised employee educational assistance policy and base programs on it. If WLP professionals have reason to doubt how successfully the policy will actually work, they can delay implementation and take steps to avert problems. Here are a few strategies for doing that:

- Ask a group of managers to examine the policy and note any issues that they feel might cause problems or raise questions upon implementation. Do they notice anything that might be questioned or that might create otherwise unanticipated problems?
- Ask professional peers in organizations having similar policies or programs to describe any problems they have experienced. What did they do about them?
- Try out the policy and programs in a geographically or organizationally isolated area, such as one field office, one occupation group, or one department. Take note of any implementation problems, and revamp the policy/programs before unveiling them across the organization.

WLP professionals should worry not only about the policy and program, but also about the costs. They should estimate spending on a monthly or quarterly basis, and then compare actual to projected expenses. Most importantly, they should identify any unexpected expenses incurred and their causes. Costly budget variations should be addressed as soon as possible.

Step Ten: Communicate the Program To Employees and Their Supervisors

Employee educational assistance policy and programs are only effective when they are properly communicated. For this reason, it is important to plan and carry out a deliberate campaign to explain the purpose of employee educational assistance policies and procedures to those targeted for participation. Common methods of communicating include all of the following methods: (1) sending memoranda directly to all employees; (2) posting descriptions on the organization's bulletin boards; (3) displaying posters; (4) publishing articles in the organization's in-house newsletters; (5) giving informal talks to employee groups during lunch hours; (6) describing the organization's employee educational assistance policy and programs during new-employee orientations or other in-house training efforts; (7) sponsoring award dinners or recognition banquets for employees who participate; (8) establishing a "speaker's bureau" of department managers to extol the virtues of education; (9) sponsoring in-house career and education fairs; (10) preparing special brochures to describe the organization's policies and programs, leaving them out in areas frequented by employees; (11) inviting representatives of local schools to set up tables in the employee cafeteria during lunch hours; (12) sending e-mails to all workers; or (13) stuffing paychecks with informative brochures. There are many ways to encourage participating; indeed, approaches to communicating about EE are limited only by the imagination!

Step Eleven: Counsel Individuals

Many WLP professionals find themselves providing individualized advice and counseling to employees who participate in organization-sponsored EE activities. While some employees will want career advice, others are interested only in finding out about reimbursement procedures or learning about the requirements for a degree or professional designation.

To be successful in counseling individuals for EE, WLP professionals must be good listeners. Quite often, that alone will satisfy many people. WLP professionals must also learn the organization's procedures for educational reimbursement and familiarize themselves with the most frequently-pursued industry education programs and professional designations. In these ways, they can be most helpful to employees.

Although not all organizations are large enough to sponsor full-time employee career or education counselors, even smaller organizations can encourage employees to bring their questions and concerns to the assigned employee-education representative. If nothing else, WLP professionals can set up tables themselves in the employee cafeteria to offer on-the-spot, convenient counseling or to encourage employees to visit them with questions they may have.

Step Twelve: Periodically Review the Employee Educational Assistance Policy

As a final step in planning, implementing, and monitoring employee education, WLP professionals must be willing to strive for continuous improvement. To do that, they should establish some regular routine for reviewing employee educational assistance policies and programs to make certain that they remain responsive to organizational and employee needs. In some respects, EE is a product like any other, with an identifiable life cycle. To make sure that the product keeps its interest for the "consumers," WLP professionals should take steps to introduce periodic improvements so that it is always "new and improved."

Refer to the Checklist appearing in Exhibit 15-4 to assess the educational programs presently sponsored by your organization.

Exhibit 15-4: A checklist for assessing employee education programs

Directions:	Use this checklist to assess the employee educational programs sponsored by your organization.

	Yes	**No**

1. Are employees in the organization willing to participate in formal programs of learning intended to help them qualify for their occupations, preserve their knowledge and skills, and prepare for advancement?

2. Is it clear that is the responsibility of each employee to comply with the organization's standards for continuing education?

3. Is the organization committed to complying with the highest standards for developing, presenting, measuring, and recording continuing education?

4. Do all programs state learning objectives?

5. Do all programs identify the level of knowledge that participants should bring to the program?

6. Are all program developers qualified in the subject matter?

7. Are all program developers qualified in instructional design?

8. Are program materials technically accurate, current, and sufficient to meet the program's learning objectives?

Exhibit 15-4: A checklist for assessing employee education programs *(continued)*

	Yes	No

9. Are program materials reviewed by a qualified person (or persons) before they are used, to ensure program quality?

10. Are participants always notified in advance about the educational program's objectives, prerequisites, content, advance preparation required, teaching method(s), and recommended credit (if any)?

11. Are efforts made to admit only those people who have met the program's prerequisites?

12. Are instructors selected for their qualifications in subject-matter expertise <u>and</u> their demonstrated presentation skills?

13. Are efforts made to ensure that the number of people who can participate in an educational program is appropriate for the subject matter?

14. Are efforts made to ensure that the physical facilities for an educational program are appropriate for the subject and delivery methods?

15. Are effective means used to evaluate the quality of educational programs?

16. Does the organization document the participation of employees in formal educational programs, noting the . . .

    a.   Sponsor?

    b.   Content?

Exhibit 15-4: A checklist for assessing employee education programs *(continued)*

	Yes	No

c. Date(s) of participation?

d. Location?

e. Number of hours?

f. Who participated?

g. Materials used?

h. Program evaluations?

CHAPTER 16

WLP and Employee Training

WLP has in recent years been linked closely to employee training, but it is unfortunate that the two terms are generally considered interchangable. Many WLP professionals regard themselves as "trainers," devoting entire careers to employee training and rarely venturing into the uncharted territories (for them) of Organization Development, employee development, and employee education—let alone other interventions.

Training is increasingly recognized now for what it is: just one way to change people and bring about performance improvement. WLP is a broader term than training, encompassing integrated and synergistic efforts to improve performance and get results.

This chapter introduces employee training as a tool for improving performance. It addresses three simple questions: What is training? When is it appropriate? How should it be systematically planned and implemented?

WHAT IS EMPLOYEE TRAINING?

Definition of Employee Training

Training is generally understood to mean a short-term intervention designed to change individuals by equipping them with the necessary and sufficient knowledge, skills, and attitudes they need to meet or exceed customer requirements and achieve results. It is intended to help people perform what they must perform to meet these expectations.

The Difference between Employee Training and Other Components of WLP

As noted above, training differs from other efforts to initiate change. Unlike organizational interventions, training does not change the work environment in which people perform. Unlike Organization Development, employee training is not so much geared to group change and interpersonal relations as it is to helping individuals meet their present job requirements. Unlike employee development, training is usually oriented to short-term change that lends itself to immediate application on the job. Unlike employee education, employee training is not usually linked to formal education programs or degree requirements of colleges, secondary schools, vocational schools, professional associations, or industry groups. It more often refers to applying knowledge, skills, and attitudes in the unique cultural context of one organization.

The Importance of Employee Training

All forms of WLP are important, of course. Each component contributes in its own way to improving organizational competitiveness, supporting product/service quality, fostering effective customer service, enriching the quality of work life enjoyed by individuals, and helping individuals achieve their career goals. But the importance of employee training has been the focus of special attention. It has been widely (and increasingly) recognized as essential to successful work performance. It is also necessary to help organizations promote worker safety, avert lawsuits stemming from employee negligence, comply with government mandates, prepare for the introduction of future technology, promote social equity, and encourage the celebration of diversity.

A Primer on Employee Training Terminology

To learn about employee training, WLP professionals should start by mastering its special terminology. Among special terms they should learn are these: (1) *off-the-job training;* (2) *vestibule training;* (3) *on-the-job training;* (4) *cross-training;* and (5) *planned and unplanned training.*

Off-the-job training is conducted at a location away from the employee's day-to-day job site. The term is somewhat vague because it is phrased in terms of where training is *not* held, rather than where it *is* held. Off-the-job training can be conducted in such varied locations as a classroom on the employer's premises, in a classroom at a local college, in a classroom at a distant college, in a trailer positioned just outside of an industrial plant, or even in a recreational vehicle parked outside the front entrance of an employer's office building! It can also be individualized, computer or WorldWideWeb-based, or delivered by means of videoconference, CD-ROM, interactive video, or correspondence. The key point: off-the-job training is held away from the job site. It is usually, but not always, carefully planned to economize employees' time away from the job.

Vestibule training is near-the-job training. (A *vestibule* refers to an entrance or a lobby.) Popular early in the century when factory owners established training schools close by their industrial plants, the term has gradually been falling into disuse. However, the approach (if not the term) is still widely used. Factories continue to train workers in quiet areas that resemble in minute detail the work environment in which they will eventually carry out their jobs. Even expensive machinery is simulated or made available. Banks use the same approach to train tellers: a bank "window," removed from the job site but precise in all details, is used as the setting for training. Insurance companies also use the approach, on occasion, to train agents: the entire interior of an insurance office is replicated so that salespeople will have opportunities to practice in a setting quite similar to the one in which they will eventually apply their training. The aim of vestibule training is to provide a "quiet place" for training away from the hustle and bustle of daily work but similar enough to the actual job site to make it easy for trainees to transfer back to their jobs what they learn in training.

On-the-job training (OJT) is the counterpart of off-the-job training. Carried out at the employee's workstation, OJT can be conducted before the trainee is expected to produce, or during the work itself. Until World War I, OJT was not typically planned or organized. Workers were not systematically trained on the job site by their supervisors or by more experienced co-workers. A shortage of shipbuilders in World War I led to the introduction of the first organized approach to planned OJT.

Charles R. "Skipper" Allen devised the approach from the work of the nineteenth-century German psychologist Johann Friedrich Herbart. Allen suggested that after conducting a thorough job breakdown, supervisors should carry out OJT in four distinct steps:

1. *Preparation*. Supervisors should place workers in proper position.
2. *Presentation*. Supervisors should tell workers about the work tasks they are to perform.
3. *Application*. Supervisors should allow learners to do the work.
4. *Inspection*. Supervisors should follow-up with the learners, making sure that they know what to do and how to perform.

In World War II, the model was refined and transformed into seven key steps as part of the war effort's Job Instruction Training Program. Supervisors were trained to:

- Show workers how to perform the task.
- Explain key points.
- Let the worker watch the instructor/supervisor perform the task again.
- Let the worker perform simple parts of the job.
- Help the worker perform the whole job.
- Let the worker perform the whole job, but watch him or her.
- Put the worker on his or her own.

Many organizations sponsor in-house training for OJT. Supervisors and workers receive training on the following topics:

- Showing learners how to perform the work task
- Having learners perform the task with the trainer observing
- Putting learners at ease
- Providing feedback to learners on how well they are performing a task or procedure
- Demonstrating all steps of effective OJT
- Emphasizing key points for learners to remember
- Analyzing work tasks or procedures
- Motivating workers to learn
- Telling learners how to perform a task
- Questioning learners on the key points of what they are learning
- Clarifying the learners' performance standards
- Placing learners in the correct work setting to learn the task
- Showing learners how to correct errors they make
- Finding out what learners already know about the task
- Documenting training progress
- Modifying OJT methods, based on individual learning styles
- Modifying OJT methods to deal with learning disabilities

Cross-training is carried out to ensure continuity in operations. No matter how well individual employees perform, they are rarely able to sustain perfect attendance. On occasion, they must be absent from work due to vacations or sick time. Yet important work tasks must be carried out without delay, even when individuals are absent. The purpose of cross-training, then, is to make certain that there is always a "backup" worker, suitably trained, to carry out essential activities competently.

Cross-training has the additional advantage of providing each worker with knowledge about more than one job. This knowledge can be motivating and energizing to employees who might otherwise become bored with the same tedious day-to-day routine. In today's downsized and rightsized firms, cross-training also provides employers with flexibility about who they can assign to do certain tasks and even how many such tasks they can assign to each employee. A key tool in creating self-directed workteams, it is sometimes associated with teams and worker *multi-skilling*.

Relatively little has been written about the intricacies of planning and carrying out cross-training. But cross-training is not difficult to do. Once workers have received OJT for their current jobs and are performing competently, supervisors, team members, or experienced co-workers should:

1. Make a list of all jobs in the intact work group.
2. Identify individuals to serve as "backups" for *each* job in the work group.
3. Prepare a breakdown for each job, using current job descriptions and/or more specific task analysis information.
4. Prepare a training plan, such as an outline of job tasks or work duties, on which to cross-train each designated "back-up" worker.
5. Prepare a training schedule so that the cross-training effort proceeds in a deliberate way.
6. Train workers on OJT so that they can cross-train their co-workers.
7. Apply the steps of OJT to cross-training.
8. Ask workers for their feedback on the cross-training they receive to ensure that it was effective.
9. Periodically update cross-training as jobs (or the duties of the work group) change.

Planned training is organized instruction, whether it is set off-the-job, near-the-job, or on-the-job. Someone structures the training before delivery, often using an outline or lesson plan based on job requirements or duties. Training is planned in order to increase its *efficiency* ("doing it right") and *effectiveness* ("doing the right thing"). Planned training, intended to be more results-oriented than unplanned training, is geared to achieving predictable outcomes in a pre-determined timeframe. It is organized logically so that trainees can learn new information or skills as quickly and easily as possible, becoming fully productive in a shorter time than would otherwise be possible with unplanned training.

Managers sometimes object to planned training because they feel it is time-consuming. They also object to the seemingly significant expense necessary to prepare it, deliver it, and keep it current. Some managers are not capable of planning training, however, even when time, money, and staff are abundantly available. Managers usually expert in the subject matter or the work itself find it difficult to logically structure information from the most simple terms and concepts to the most complex procedures. Their tendency is to lapse into jargon as shorthand, a practice that only confuses new employees who are struggling to learn.

Unplanned training is unstructured. Nobody plans the outcomes in advance, and the progress of a trainee is difficult to track. There are several kinds; among them are *sink or swim training* and *learning by osmosis*.

Sink or swim training is carried out while inexperienced employees, not sure what they are doing, fumble through the work without prior instruction or guidance. Learning occurs through trial-and-error and casual observation of others. "Sink or swim training" is not really training at all, though many operating managers will argue that it is.

Learning by osmosis, on the other hand, refers to a principle in biology by which single-cell animals absorb food from their environment by placing themselves in close proximity to it. Trainees are expected to learn what to do by sitting with more experienced workers (or following them around) and simply observing them as they go about their daily tasks. Trainees might receive explanations about *what* the more experienced workers are doing, *why* they are doing it, *where* the work goes when finished, *who* cares about that work, *when* tasks should be performed, and *how* (in what order) tasks should be performed.

However, unplanned training is not organized completely at random (though some employees may feel that it is). The guiding organization scheme is the same as the order of problems occurring on a daily basis, or the tasks that must be performed due to daily work cycles. Since problems rarely arise in a logical sequence and daily work tasks usually vary, workers trained through unplanned methods are frequently confused and are rarely consistently prepared. They are exposed to some problems, but not others. The employees struggle to make sense of what seems chaotic, guessing what they are expected to do on their jobs and how their performance will be judged, as well as why it is at all important to anyone. Unplanned training can require a lengthy time period, perhaps several years, before supervisors are confident that employees really know what to do.

While some managers will complain about the time and expense required to conduct training, they will rarely complain with the same vehemence about the wasted time, high expense, and poor customer service associated with ignorance! While it is difficult to pinpoint the reasons for lost sales, poor quality, and shabby customer service, it is clear that these are side effects of poor or inadequate employee training. Nor is it unusual to hear employees complain bitterly about the anxiety they felt as they were treated to unplanned training, particularly when they are likely to have been exposed to more systematic, planned training. For many of today's employees, unplanned training is perceived as an indication that their employer is poorly-managed, inefficient, and ineffective—or worse, that the employer does not care how well employees perform!

WHEN IS TRAINING APPROPRIATE?

Employee training is usually considered a *short-term* change effort. It can help individuals qualify for a specific line of work, meet essential entry-level job requirements in *one* organization, or preserve their job-related knowledge and skills. It should be used for these purposes.

But it should *not* be used when other, less expensive methods are also suitable for solving performance problems or are more clearly targeted to address the cause of a performance problem.

More specifically, WLP professionals should not use training to address problems stemming from deficiencies in employee motivation (*workers don't want to perform*), memory (*workers don't remember how to perform, because they do so rarely*), rewards (*workers are punished for performing, rewarded for not performing, or experience no consequences from performing*), feedback (*workers are not informed when they perform poorly, or given corrective guidance so they can improve*), or ability (*they are physically or mentally incapable of performing*). Nor should training be used to:

- Address performance problems rooted in issues outside the boundaries of individual control;
- Plan and manage group change, learning, or development;
- Foster skill development across or within groups;
- Apply informal learning practices to individual preparation for advancement;
- Improve group interaction.

Since employee training lends itself to solving immediate, practical, work-oriented problems, WLP professionals occasionally find themselves pressured by operating managers to use it inappropriately as a quick fix for complex problems.

HOW SHOULD TRAINING BE SYSTEMATICALLY PLANNED?

A Model for Systematically Planning and Implementing Training

When training is the appropriate solution to a performance problem, WLP professionals should plan and implement it systematically. Many models have been conceptualized to guide training design and delivery. One approach is to base training design on a series of questions:

1. What methods are used by the organization to identify, develop, or test new information and translate that information into implications for improved performance?
2. What is the role of the WLP department in linking WLP programs to business needs?
3. What are the training needs?
4. Who are the prospective trainees?
5. What changes should result from the training?
6. How should training be integrated with career development and OD efforts?
7. What specific training objectives, training content, and activities should be used?
8. What instructional materials should be used to meet the training objectives?
9. How should training be administered?
10. How should training be presented or facilitated?
11. How should training be evaluated?

This model is illustrated in Exhibit 16-1. By applying it, WLP professionals are relying on a systematic approach to training design. Each step in the model deserves brief review.

Exhibit 16-1: A model for systematically designing and delivering training

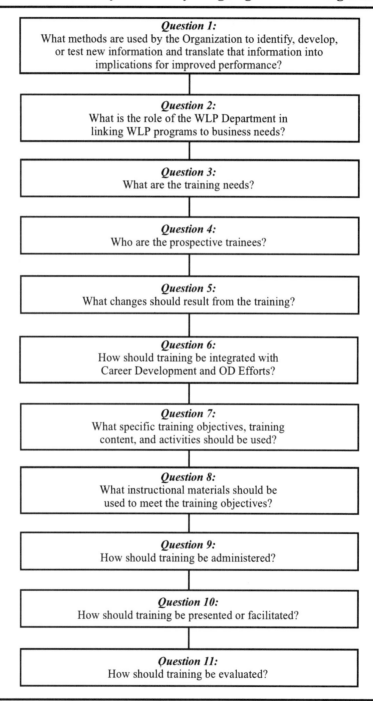

Question 1:
What methods are used by the Organization to identify, develop, or test new information and translate that information into implications for improved performance?

Question 2:
What is the role of the WLP Department in linking WLP programs to business needs?

Question 3:
What are the training needs?

Question 4:
Who are the prospective trainees?

Question 5:
What changes should result from the training?

Question 6:
How should training be integrated with Career Development and OD Efforts?

Question 7:
What specific training objectives, training content, and activities should be used?

Question 8:
What instructional materials should be used to meet the training objectives?

Question 9:
How should training be administered?

Question 10:
How should training be presented or facilitated?

Question 11:
How should training be evaluated?

Identifying, Developing, or Testing Ways to Improve Performance

Say the word *research* and most managers, as well as most WLP professionals, conjure up a vague image of the useless or impractical. While that may be the unfortunate connotation that the word has acquired from its association with overzealous academicians, the word in its purest sense means simply *deliberate study*. Quite often, WLP professionals are called on to come up with new ideas or approaches and then to implement them to realize improved performance and productivity.

Linking WLP Programs to Business Needs

WLP departments can adopt different roles in meeting the business needs of the organizations that they serve. There is more than one way to link WLP or training programs to business needs. Determining that role is an essential part of the WLP manager's job.

Identifying Training Needs

It is one thing to identify business needs and it is another to pinpoint what people need to know or do. When WLP professionals sense that training is needed to meet business needs, they then enact the role of *analyst*. Often the identification of training needs begins with work- or task-analysis that is carried out to clarify precisely what people must know or do to carry out their jobs competently. Alternatively, the need for training might become apparent when WLP professionals, operating managers, or even customers experience a bad situation or feel that all is not right, that something is "broken" and should be "fixed."

But it does little good to identify problems without coming up with corresponding solutions. For this reason, WLP professionals who focus on training should compare

- what people should know, do, or feel to perform their jobs competently, *and*
- what people already know, do, or feel.

The result of this comparison is a *performance gap*, a discrepancy between *what is* and *what should be*, that must be closed by training.

In recent years, WLP professionals have begun to move away from a static approach to analyzing training needs. In addition to *present* performance gaps, they have also begun to direct attention to *future* performance gaps that underscore differences between

- what people should know, do, or feel *in the future* to perform their jobs competently, *and*
- what people *presently* know, do, or feel.

One way to identify future performance gaps is to prepare job descriptions as they might exist at a future time and compare them to present job descriptions, thereby underscoring the difference between *present* and *future* job duties and training needs.

Identifying Prospective Trainees

This step of training design means identifying who should be trained. In another sense, it also means gaining necessary support from top managers and other key stakeholders to create an impetus for change. Training is but one tool for implementing change, of course. Among others: litigation (suing for change), leadership switches (installing new leaders who favor change), and policy shifts (issuing new guidelines for action).

Clarifying the Changes Desired from Training

Influencing is a major part of the WLP professional's job. Part of that influence should be directed toward progressive (useful) change. More often than not, this influence should be directed toward line (operating) managers who have authority over groups of people and major responsibility for getting the organization's work out.

Integrating Training with Career Development and OD Efforts

While the impact of training on individual career planning and Organization Development issues is not usually considered in training situations, it should be. The reasons: Training can raise expectations about individual career prospects and can influence the success or failure of organizational change efforts. It is essential to clarify what benefits can be realistically expected by trainees who are successful in mastering training.

Identifying Training Objectives, Content, and Activities

This step is very important, because the preparation of training requires WLP professionals to transform training needs (expressions of problems) into specific training objectives, content, and activities (expressions of necessary solutions). As an interim step between needs and objectives, WLP professionals usually begin by examining ways that work *should* be performed, a procedure called *task analysis*. Each activity is broken down into subcomponents called *tasks*. Then efficient and effective ways of performing each task are clarified.

The results of needs assessment and task analyses provide WLP professionals with the information they need to formulate rigorous instructional objectives. An *instructional objective* expresses what trainees should know, do, or feel upon completion of training. The purpose of instructional objectives is to satisfy needs and close present (or future) performance gaps.

Once this step has been completed and the desired results of training are clear, WLP professionals can then turn their attention to choosing an instructional strategy. An *instructional strategy* answers the simple question "How will the objectives be achieved?" It is the fundamental approach that will be used to close the performance gap.

Instructional strategies include off-the-job training, near-the-job training, on-the-job training, or some combination of all these. WLP professionals should try not to take this step for granted, because the decision made at this point will greatly affect training costs. Indeed, each strategy should be compared for its relative costs and benefits before the next step is taken.

Preparing, Selecting, or Modifying Training Materials

The next step in the model is to develop training materials to achieve the instructional objectives and carry out instructional strategy. Instructional materials can be produced in-house, purchased from outside sources, or purchased and tailored to meet organizational needs. This choice is essentially the same as a "make or buy" decision in purchasing.

Administering Training

To deliver training, WLP professionals must provide logistical support for it. *Logistics* is associated with efforts intended to support the training effort. This step in the training design model includes such things as arranging facilities, organizing equipment, and finding instructors for classroom training.

Presenting or Facilitating the Training

Once instructional materials are prepared and facilities have been chosen, training must be delivered to the learners. Of course, training can be delivered to one person at a time (as in most OJT or computer-based training), to small groups, or to large groups. Its purpose can be to inform, to evoke insight, or to improve interpersonal relations.

Evaluating Training

All training and all WLP efforts should be evaluated and incorporated into training design and delivery to create a means for continuous improvement of the training effort.

REFERENCES

REFERENCES

Abernathy, D. J. (1999). Leading-edge learning: Two views. *Training and Development*, *53*(3), 40–42.

Adams, A. (1997). Educational attainment. *Current Population Reports*, Series P20-476, U.S. Bureau of the Census. [From the Web site of the U.S. Bureau of the Census.]

Adams, A. (1997). Educational attainment. Current Population Reports, Series P20-476. Washington, D.C.: U.S. Bureau of the Census, p. 17. [For the complete report, see the U.S. Bureau of the Census Web site.]

Alkhafaji, A. (1995). *Competitive global management: Principles and strategies*. Delray Beach, Fla.: St. Lucie Press.

Allen, P. (1984). Human resource management develops a new role. *Savings Institutions, 106*(8), 62–69.

Allerton, H. (1996). Hot! New job titles for trainers (and others). *Training and Development, 50*(7), 20–23.

American Association of Retired Persons. (1989). *Business and older workers*. Washington, D.C.: American Association of Retired Persons.

American Society for Training and Development. (1983). *Career planning for HRD professionals: A leader's guide and materials*. Washington, D.C.: The American Society for Training and Development.

American Society for Training and Development. (1983). *Careers in training and development*. Washington, D.C.: The American Society for Training and Development.

American Society for Training and Development. (1983). *Finding the right job in training: A leader's guide*. Washington, D.C.: The American Society for Training and Development.

American Society for Training and Development. (1985). *Your career in HRD: A guide to information and decision-making*. Alexandria, Va.: The American Society for Training and Development.

American Society for Training and Development. (1994). *The best of performance support in the workplace*. Alexandria, Va.: The American Society for Training and Development.

American work force: 1992–2005. (1994). Washington, D.C.: U.S. Department of Education.

Anderson, C. A. (1992). Curing what ails U.S. health care. *Quality Progress*, *25*(4), 35–38.

Andrews, D. H., Dineen, T., and Bell, H. (1999). The use of constructive modeling and virtual simulation in large-scale team training: A military case study. *Educational Technology*, *39*(1), 24–28.

Andrews, K. (1989). Ethics in practice. *Harvard Business Review*, *67*(5), 99–104.

Anfuso, D. (1995). Colgate's global HR unites under one strategy. *Personnel Journal*, 74(10), 44–54.

Appelbaum, D., and Lawton, S. (1990). *Ethics and the professions.* Englewood Cliffs, N.J.: Prentice-Hall.

Apprenticeship: Past and present. (1987). Washington, D.C.: U. S. Department of Labor, Employment and Training Administration, Bureau of Apprenticeship and Training, p. 2.

Argyris, C. (1994). The future of workplace learning and performance. *Training and Development, 48*(5), S36.

Argyris, C. (1994). The future of workplace learning and performance. *Training and Development, 48*(5), S36–S47.

Ashkenas, R., Ulrich, D., Jick, T, and Kerr, S. (1995). *The boundaryless organization: Breaking the chains of organizational structure.* San Francisco: Jossey-Bass.

Atwater, D. and Niehaus, R. (1993). Diversity implications for an occupation human resource forecast for the year 2000. *Human Resource Planning, 16*(4), 29–50.

Austin, J., and Garnier, L. (1998). The virtual office: A behavior engineering model (BEM) perspective. *Performance Improvement Quarterly, 11*(4), 7–21.

Avery, M. (1997). Rising salaries reflect HR's new role. *HR Magazine, 42*(11), 87–92.

Axel, H. (1996). Competing as an employer of choice. *HR Executive Review*, 3, 2–11, 14, 17.

Baker, N. (1997). Heightened interest in ethics education reflects employer, employee concerns. *Corporate University Review, 5*(3), 6–9.

Baker, N. (1999). Giving teams a winning edge. *Corporate University Review, 7*(1), 29–33, 70.

Baldwin, T. T., Danielson, C., and Wiggenhorn, W. (1997). The evolution of learning strategies in organizations: From employee development to business redefinition. *Academy of Management Executives, 11*(4), 47–58.

Bantel, K. (1994). Strategic planning openness: The role of top team demography. *Group and Organization Management, 19*(4), 406–424.

Bantel, K. A. (1993). Top team, environment, and performance effects on strategic planning formality. *Group and Organization Management 18*(4), 436–458.

Barner, R. (1996). The new millennium workplace: Seven changes that will challenge managers and workers. *Futurist, 30*(2), 14–18.

Barrier, M. (1998). Develop workers—and your business. *Nation's Business, 86*(12), 25–27.

Barrier, M. (1998). Doing the right thing. *Nation's Business, 86*(3), 32–38.

Barron, T. (1999). Whither skill standards? *Technical Training, 10*(2), 18–23.

Barry, B. (1998). A beginner's guide to strategic planning. *Futurist, 32*(3), 33–36.

Barry, T. (1994). *Excellence is a habit: How to avoid quality burnout.* Milwaukee, Wis.: American Society for Quality Control.

Bartholomew, D., Forbes, A., and McClean, S. (1991). *Statistical techniques for manpower planning.* Chichester, England: John Wiley & Sons.

Bartlett, C., and Ghosal, S. (1998). Beyond strategic planning to organization learning: Lifeblood of the individualized corporation. *Strategy and Leadership, 26*(1), 34–39.

Bartz, D., Schwandt, D. and Hillman, L. (1989). Differences between "T" and "D." *Personnel Administrator, 34*(6), 168.

Bassi, L., and Van Buren, M. (1999) *The 1999 ASTD state of the industry report.* [A supplement to *Training and Development*]. Alexandria, Va.: The American Society for Training and Development.

Bassi, L., Buchanan, L., and Cheney, S. (1997). *Trends that affect learning and performance improvement: A report on the members of the ASTD benchmarking forum.* Alexandria, Va.: The American Society for Training and Development.

Bassi, L., Buchanan, L., and Cheney, S. (1997). *Trends that affect learning and performance improvement: A report on the members of the ASTD benchmarking forum.* Alexandria, Va.: The American Society for Training and Development.

Bassi, L., Cheney, S., and Lewis. E. (1998). Trends in workplace learning: Supply and demand in interesting times. *Training and Development, 52*(11), 51–75.

Bassi, L., Cheney, S., and Van Buren, M. (1997). Training industry trends. *Training and Development, 51*(11), 46–59.

Bassi, L., Gallagher, A., and Schroer, E. (1996). *The ASTD training data book.* Alexandria, Va.: The American Society for Training and Development.

Bates, S. (1998). Building better workers. *Nation's Business, 86*(6), 18–27.

Bazigos, M. N., and Burke, W. W. (1997). Theory orientations of organization development (OD) practitioners. *Group and Organization Management, 22*(3), 384–408.

Beckhard, R. (1969). *Organization development: Strategies and models.* Reading, Mass.: Addison-Wesley, p. 9.

Benchmarking code of conduct, The. (1998). *Journal for Quality and Participation, 21*(2), 56–58.

Bengtson, B. *An analysis of CEO perceptions concerning trainer roles in selected central Pennsylvania manufacturing firms.* Unpublished Doctoral Dissertation. University Park: Pennsylvania State University, 1994.

Bennis, W. (1969). *Organization development: Its nature, origin, and prospects.* Reading, Mass.: Addison-Wesley, p. 2.

Berenbeim, R. (1987). *Corporate ethics.* New York, N.Y.: Conference Board.

Berenbeim, R. (1988). An outbreak of ethics. *Across the Board, 25*(5), 14–19.

Berenbeim, R. (1992). *Corporate ethics practices.* Report No. 986. New York: The Conference Board.

Berriman, C. D. (1999). A view of networked distance learning from Cisco. *Multimedia and Internet Training, 6*(1–2), 14–21.

Berrol, B. J. (1999). Corporate universities can suit small companies, as the Pacific Exchange's experience shows. *Corporate University Review, 7*(1), 50–53.

Bishop, T., and King, A. (1991). Functional requisites of HR: Personnel professionals' and line managers' criteria for effectiveness. *Public Personnel Management, 20*(3), 285–298.

Blackiston, G. (1996). Juran Institute: A barometer of trends in quality management. *National Productivity Review, 16*(1), 15–23.

Blancero, D. (1996). Key competencies for a transformed human resource organization: Results of a field study. *Human Resource Management, 35*(3), 383–403.

Blumfield, M. (1997). Sorry, no vacancy. *Training, 34*(7), 5–7.

Bogan, C. E. and English, M. J. (1994). Benchmarking for best practices: Winning through innovative adaptation. New York, N.Y.: McGraw-Hill.

Bohren, J. (1992). Reinforcing ethics at work. *Human Resources Professional, 4*(2), 55–58.

Bolles, R. (1999). *Job-hunting on the Internet* (2nd ed.). Berkeley, Calif.: Ten Speed Press.

Bolles, R. (1999). *The 1999 what color is your parachute? A practical manual for job-hunters and career-changers.* Berkeley, Calif.: Ten Speed Press.

Bonczek, S. (1992). Ethical decision making: Challenge of the 1990's—A practical approach for local governments. *Public Personnel Management, 21*(1), 75–88.

Bontio, N. (1996, Summer). There's a price on your head: Managing intellectual capital strategically. *Business Quarterly*, pp. 43–44.

Bordwin, M. (1998). The three R's of ethics. *Management Review, 87*(6), 59–61.

Boudreau, J., and Ramstad, P. (1997). Measuring intellectual capital: Learning from financial history. *Human Resource Management, 36*(3), 343–356.

Bowen, E. (1987, May 25). Ethics: Looking to its roots. *Time*, pp. 26–29.

Bowie, N., and Duska, R. (1990). *Business ethics.* Englewood Cliffs, N.J.: Prentice-Hall.

Boxwell, R. J., Jr. (1994). *Benchmarking for competitive advantage.* New York, N.Y.: McGraw-Hill.

Boyd, S. (1999). Breathing life into dull safety training sessions. *Technical Training, 10*(2), 37.

Branch, S. (1999, January 11). The 100 best companies to work for in America. *Fortune*, 139, pp. 118–144.

Brenner, S. and Molander, E. (1977). Is the ethics of business changing? *Harvard Business Review, 55*(1), 57–71.

Brethower, D. (1995). Specifying the human performance technology knowledge base. *Performance Improvement Quarterly, 8(*2), 17–39.

Brewster, J. (1972). *A study of an emerging occupational group: State directors of law enforcement training: Their backgrounds and perceptions of their role.* Unpublished doctoral dissertation. Washington: George Washington University.

Broad, M. (1997). Overview of transfer of training: From learning to performance. *Performance Improvement Quarterly, 10*(2), 7–21.

Brooking, A. (1996). *Intellectual capital*. London: International Thomson Business Press, p. 10.

Brothers, T. (1991). *Corporate ethics: Developing new standards of accountability*. New York, N.Y.: Conference Board.

Brown, A. (1987). Is ethics good business? *Personnel Administrator, 32*(2), 71–74.

Brown, L. (1972). Research action: Organizational feedback, understanding, and change. *Journal of Applied Behavioral Science, 8*, 697–711.

Brown, M. (1990). *Working ethics: Strategies for decision making and organizational responsibility*. San Francisco, Calif.: Jossey-Bass.

Brown, M. (1998). Improving your organization's vision. *Journal for Quality and Participation, 21*(5), 18–20.

Brown, T. (1997). My fair HR professional. *HR Focus, 74*(6), 4–5.

Brown, W. (1996). In search of a successful ethics seminar. *HR Magazine, 41*(12), 115–119.

Brumback, G. (1991). Institutionalizing ethics in government. *Public Personnel Management, 20*(3),353–364.

Bruner, J. (1961). The act of discovery. *Harvard Education Review, 31*, 21–32.

Bruner, J. (1966). *Towards a theory of instruction*. Cambridge, Mass.: Harvard University Press.

Bryson, J. (1995). *Strategic planning for public and nonprofit organizations: A guide to strengthening and sustaining organizational achievement*. San Francisco, Calif.: Jossey-Bass Publishers.

Burke, W. W. (1997). The new agenda for organization development. *Organizational Dynamics, 26*(1), 6–20.

Bushnell, D. S., and Halus, M. B. (1992). TQM in the public sector: Strategies for quality service. *National Productivity Review, 11*(3), 355–370.

Busse, C. (1992). Ethics emerging as a growing, but not pressing, priority. *Training Directors Forum Newsletter, 8*(5), 1–3.

Buyer's guide. 1999. *Inside Technology Training*, 1–80.

Byrne, B. S. (1999). Distance learning in Kenya, and the African Virtual University. *Technical Training, 10* (1), p. 40.

Byrne, J. (1988). Corporate integrity. *Business Week, 3038,* 56–57.

Byrne, J. (1996). Strategic planning. *Business Week, 3490*, 46–52.

Caiazza, K. (1999). The big splash: Training for a new product rollout. *Technical Training, 10*(2), 29–31.

Callahan, M. (1997). *From training to performance consulting*. INFO-LINE. Alexandria, Va.: The American Society for Training and Development.

Cameron, W. (1988). *Training competencies of human resource development specialists in Tennessee*. (Summary Report, Research Series No. 1). Knoxville, Tennessee: University of Tennessee.

Camillus, J. (1996). Reinventing strategic planning. *Strategy and Leadership, 20*(3), 6–12.

Camillus, J., Sessions, R., and Webb, R. (1998). Visionary action: Strategic processes in fast-cycle environments. *Strategy and Leadership, 26*(1), 20–24.

Camp, R., and Blanchard, P. (1986). How to apply strategic planning to the training program. *Trainer's Workshop, 1*(2), 59–64.

Campbell, A., and Alexander, M. (1997). What's wrong with strategy? *Harvard Business Review, 75*(6), 42–51.

Campbell, P. (1996). *Population projections for states by age, sex, race, and Hispanic origin: 1995 to 2025*. PPL-47. Washington, D.C.: U.S. Bureau of the Census.

Cantelon, John E. (1995). The evolution and advantages of distance education. *New Directions for Adult and Continuing Education, 64*, 3–10.

Carey, A. and Varney, G. (1983). Which skills spell success in OD? *Training and Development Journal, 37*(4), 38–40.

Carnevale, A. (1982). *Human capital: A high yield corporate investment*. Washington, D.C.: American Society for Training and Development.

Carnevale, A. (1986). The learning enterprise. *Training and Development Journal, 40*(1), 18–26.

Carnevale, A., Gainer, L and Villet, J. (1990). *Training in America: The organization and strategic role of training*. San Francisco: Jossey-Bass, p. 24.

Carnevale, E. (1990). Motorola sets the benchmark for training. *Technical and Skills Training, 1*(3), 28–33; Wiggenhorn, W. (1990). Motorola U: When training becomes an education. *Harvard Business Review, 90*(4), 71–83.

Carr, A. A. (1997). User-design in the creation of human learning systems. *Educational Technology Research and Development, 45*(3), 5–22.

Caruth, D., and Handlogten, G. (1997). *Staffing the contemporary organization: A guide to planning, recruiting, and selecting for human resource professionals*. Westport, Conn.: Praeger.

Cathcart, J. (1986). How to conduct a strategic planning retreat. *Training and Development Journal, 40*(5), 63–65.

Cava, A. (1990). Teaching ethics: A moral model. *Business and Economic Review, 36*(3), 10–13.

Chakravarthy, B. (1996). Flexible commitment: A key to strategic success. *Strategy and Leadership, 24*(3), 14–20.

Chalofsky, N. (1992). A unifying definition for the human resource development profession. *Human Resource Development Quarterly, 3*(2), 175–182.

Chalofsky, N. and Lincoln, C. (1983). *Up the HRD ladder: A guide for professional growth*. Reading, Mass.: Addison-Wesley.

Chandler, A. (1962). *Strategy and structure: Chapters in the history of American industrial enterprise*. Cambridge, Mass.: Massachusetts Institute of Technology.

Chang, R. (1990). *Introduction to human resource development careers*. Alexandria, Va.: The American Society for Training and Development.

Chen, L. (1990–1991). Interactive video in education: Past, present, and future. *Journal of Educational Technology Systems, 19*(1), 5–19.

Chin, R., and Benne, K. (1969). General strategies for effecting changes in human systems. In W. Bennis, K. Benne, and R. Chin (eds.), *The planning of change* (2nd ed.). New York: Holt, Rinehart and Winston.

Christensen, C. (1997). Making strategy: Learning by doing. *Harvard Business Review, 75*(6), 141–156.

Church, A. H., Burke, W. W., and Van Eynde, D. F. (1994). Values, motives, and interventions of organization development practitioners. *Group and Organization Management, 19*(1), 5–50.

Clark, J., and Koonce, R. (1995). Meetings go high-tech. *Training and Development, 49*(11), 32–38.

Clements, P. (1988). Ethics and business conduct training. *Performance and Instruction, 27*(7), 6–10.

Colletti, J. (1998). Harnessing the power of visual strategic deployment. *National Productivity Review, 17* (3), 67–73.

Condodina, J. (1997). Echoes from the line: HR lacks strategic initiative. *HR Focus, 74*(7), 2.

Condodina, J. (1997). Echoes from the line: HR lacks strategic initiative. *HR Focus, 74*(7), 2.

Connelly, R., and Light, K. (1991). An interdisciplinary code of ethics for adult education. *Adult Education Quarterly, 41*(4), 233–240.

Connor, J., and Ulrich, D. (1996). Human resource roles: Creating value, not rhetoric. *The Journal of the Human Resource Planning Society, 19*(3), 16–17.

Cooley, M. (1997). HR in Russia: Training for long-term success. *HR Magazine, 42*(12), 98–106.

Corey, S. (1953). *Action research to improve school practices*. New York: Bureau of Publications, Teachers College, Columbia University.

Corporate Support Programs. (1995). Technology for adult education and job training. Atlanta, Ga.: IBM.

Cosier, R. A. and Dalton, D. R. (1993). Management training and development in a nonprofit organization. *Public Personnel Management, 22*(1), 37–42.

Cottrell, D. (1991). Performance analysis: Holding up the bottom line. *Technical and Skills Training, 2*(8), 16–21.

Crowe, M., and Bodine, R. (1996). Integrating electronic learning and performance support tools. *CBT Solutions, May/June,* 14–19.

CU soon? But is it a critical strategy link or a waste of training resources? 1999. *Training Directors' Forum Newsletter, 15*(1), 1–3.

Cummings, L. and Schwab, D. (1973). *Performance in organizations: Determinants and appraisal*. Glenview, Ill.: Scott Foresman.

Cunningham, P. (1992). *Adult and continuing education does not need a code of ethics*. San Francisco: Jossey-Bass/Pfeiffer.

Cyr, D. (1995). *The human resource challenge on international joint ventures*. Westport, Conn.: Quorum Books.

Daft, R. (1983). *Organization theory and design.* St. Paul, Minn.: West Publishing, p. 482.

Dalke, D., and Ankerstar, S. (1995). *Balancing personal and professional ethics.* Amherst, Mass.: HRD Press.

Darraugh, B. (1990). *Negotiation skills for salespeople.* INFO-LINE, Alexandria, Va.: The American Society for Training and Development.

Darraugh, B. (1991). *Ethics for business.* INFO-LINE. Alexandria, Va.: The American Society for Training and Development.

Davis, M. (1988). Working with your company's code of ethics. *Management Solutions, 33*(6), 4–10.

Davis, B. (1999). Profits from principle: Five forces redefining business. *Futurist, 33*(3), 28–33.

Deal, T. and Kennedy, A. (1982). *Corporate culture.* Reading, Mass.: Addison-Wesley.

Dean, P. (1992). Making codes of ethics "real." *Journal of Business Ethics, 11*(4), 285–290.

DeBaylo, P. W. (1999). Ten reasons why the Baldrige model works. *Journal for Quality and Participation, 22*(1), 24–28.

Delaney, J., and Sockell, D. (1990). Ethics in the trenches, Part 1. *Across the Board, 27*(10), 15–26.

Delaney, J., and Sockell, D. (1990). Ethics in the trenches, Part 2. *Across the Board, 27*(10), 31–39.

Delaney, J., and Sockell, D. (1992). Do company ethics training programs make a difference? An empirical analysis. *Journal of Business Ethics, 11*(9), 719–727.

Denison, E. (1985). *Trends in American economic growth, 1929–1982.* Washington, D.C.: The Brookings Institute as cited in Carnevale, A. and Gainer, L. (1989). *The learning enterprise.* Alexandria, Va.: The American Society for Training and Development and The U. S. Department of Labor, Employment and Training Administration, p. 3.

Densford, L. (1999). Motorola University: The next 20 years. *Corporate University Review, 7*(1), 15–23.

Devine, I., and Dimock, H. (1996). OD in voluntary organizations: A training program for national health organizations. *Organization Development Journal, 14*(3), 62–70.

Dew, J. (1998). *Managing in a team environment.* Westport, Conn.: Quorum Books.

Dick, W. (1995). Response to Gordon Rowland on "Instructional Design and Creativity." *Educational Technology, 35*(5), 23–24.

Digh, P. (1997). Shades of gray in the global marketplace. *HR Magazine, 42*(4), 90–98.

Dixon, V.; Conway, K.; Ashley, K.; and Stewart, N. (1995). *Training competency architecture,* and *Training competency architecture toolkit.* Toronto, Ontario: Ontario Society for Training and Development.

Do the right thing: Ethics training gains ground. 1990. *Conference Board Briefing, 3*(7–8), p. 4.

Dockery, K. L., and Sahl, R. J. (1998). Team mentoring boosts employee development. *Workforce, 77*(8), 31–36.

Donaldson, T. (1996). Values in tension: Ethics away from home. *Harvard Business Review, 74*(5), 48–62.

Downes, L., and Mui, C. (1998). The end of strategy. *Strategy and Leadership, 26*(5), 4–9.

Drucker, P. (1998). The future that has already happened. *Futurist, 32*(8), 16–18.

Duane, M. (1996). *Customized human resource planning: Different practices for different organizations.* Westport, Conn.: Quorum Books.

Dubois, D., and Rothwell, W. (1996). *Developing the high performance workplace: Organizational assessment instrument.* Amherst, Mass.: Human Resource Development Press.

Dyer, W. (1983). *Contemporary issues in management and organization development.* Reading, Mass.: Addison-Wesley.

Eaves, T. (1985). *Trainer competencies: An examination of existing research.* Paper presented at the National Adult Education Conference of the American Association for Adult and Continuing Education, Milwaukee, Wis.

Edwards, G., and Bennett, K., (1987). Ethics and HR: Standards in practice. *Personnel Administrator, 32*(12), 62–66.

Elliott, P. (1996). Power-charging people's performance. *Training and Development, 50*(12), 46–49.

Ellson, S. (1992). Managerial ethics training: Critical for managerial success. *Journal of Healthcare Education and Training, 6*(3), 2–7.

E-mail training. 1999. *Workforce Strategies, 17*(3), WS13–WS16.

Embracing the witch doctors. (1997). *Training, 34*(7), 41–45.

Emery, F. and Trist, E. (1965). The causal texture of organizational environments. *Human Relations, 18,* 21–32.

Epstein, J. (1972). *Line managers' perceptions and expectations of the operation function of an employee development specialist in a federal government research and development organization.* Unpublished doctoral dissertation. Washington, D.C.: George Washington University.

Estes, R. (1996). *Tyranny of the bottom line.* San Francisco: Berrett-Koehler Publishers.

Ettorre, B. (1992). Ethics Inc.: The buck better stop here. *HR Focus, 69*(6), 11.

Ettorre, B. (1996). 2020: What's the world coming to? *Management Review, 85*(9), 33–37.

Ettorre, B., and Capowski, G. (1997). Value-added HR: People, performance, and the bottom line. *HR Focus, 74*(7), 9–11.

Eubanks, J., Marshall, J., and O'Driscoll, M. (1990). A competency model for OD practitioners. *Training and Development Journal, 44*(11), 85–90.

Filipczak, B. (1998). How to put clout in your training career. *Training, 35*(6), 29–35.

Fisher, D. C. (1994). *Measuring up to the Baldrige: A quick and easy self-assessment guide for organizations of all sizes.* New York, N.Y.: American Management Association.

Fister, S. (1999). Tech trends. *Training, 36*(3), 24, 26.

Flowers, V., Hughes, C., Myers, M. and Myers, S. (1975). *Managerial values for working*. New York: AMACOM.

Flynn, G. (1995). HR's year in review. *Personnel Journal, 74*(12), 63–76.

Flynn, G. (1995). Make employee ethics your business. *Personnel Journal, 74*(6), 30–41.

Flynn, G. (1998). Texas Instruments engineers a holistic HR. *Workforce, 77*(2), 30–35.

Fogg, C. D. (1994). *Team-based strategic planning: A complete guide to structuring, facilitating, and implementing the process.* New York, N.Y.: AMACOM

Follett, M. (1924). *Creative experience.* London: Longman, Green and Co.

Ford, R. (1999). Traditional vs. real-time training: A difference in design logic. *Performance Improvement, 38*(1), 25–29.

Ford, R., and Bean, W. (1995). *Strategic planning technology workbook for small businesses.* Amherst, Mass.: Human Resource Development Press.

Foshay, W., Silber, K. and Westgaard, O. (1986). *Instructional design competencies: The standards.* Iowa City, Iowa: The International Board of Standards for Training, Performance, and Instruction, p. i.

Foshay, W., Silber, K. and Westgaard, O. (1988). *Instructor competencies volume I: The standards.* Iowa City, Iowa: The International Board of Standards for Training, Performance, and Instruction.

Foshay, W., Silber, K. and Westgaard, O. (1990). *Training manager competencies: The standards.* Iowa City, Iowa: International Board of Standards for Training, Performance, and Instruction.

Frank, E. (1988). An attempt at a definition of HRD. *Journal of European Industrial Training, 12*(5), 4–5.

Frank, E. (1988). HRD in the United States—a short history. *Journal of European Industrial Training, 12(*5), 6–17.

Frazis, H. et al. (1998). Results from the 1995 survey of employer-provided training. *Monthly Labor Review, 121*(6), pp. 3–13.

Frederick, C., and Atkinson, C. (1997). *Women, ethics, and the workplace.* Westport, Conn.: Praeger.

Freeman, E., and Gilbert, D., Jr. (1988). *Corporate strategy and the search for ethics.* Englewood Cliffs, N.J.: Prentice-Hall.

French, W. (1969). Organization development: Objectives, assumptions, and strategies. *California Management Review, 12*, 23–34.

French, W. and Bell, C., Jr. (1984). *Organization development: Behavioral science interventions for organization improvement* (3rd ed.). Englewood Cliffs, N.J.: Prentice-Hall, 1984.

Frohman, M., Sashkin, M. and Kavanagh, M. (1976). Action research as applied to Organization Development. *Organization and Administrative Sciences, 7*, 129–161.

Fulkert, R. (1997). *Competencies required to be a trainer: A Delphi study.* Unpublished doctoral dissertation. Toledo: University of Toledo.

Fuller, J. (1998). Planning is dead, long live planning. *Across the Board, 35*(3), 35–38.

Fuller, M. (1996). Strategic planning in an era of total competition. *Strategy and Leadership, 24*(3), 22–27.

Fulmer, R. M., and Wagner, S. (1999). Leadership: Lessons from the best. *Training and Development, 53*(3), 28–32.

Galagan, P. (1989). IBM gets its arm around education. *Training and Development Journal, 43*(1), 35–41.

Galagan, P. (1997). Go with the cash flow. *Training and Development, 51*(11), 18–23.

Galagan, P. (1997). Strategic planning is back. *Training and Development, 51*(4), 32–37.

Galagan, P., and Carnevale, E. (1994). The coming of age of workplace learning: A time line. *Training and Development, 48*(5), S4–S21.

Galagan, P., and Carnevale, E. (1994). Trends that will influence workplace learning and performance in the next five years. *Training and Development, 48*(5), S29–S35.

Ganzel, R. (1999). What price online learning? *Training, 36*(2), 50–54.

Gardenswartz, L., and Rowe, A. (1998). Why diversity matters. *HR Focus, 75*(7), S1–S3.

Gardner, J. (1963). *Self-renewal: The individual and the innovative society.* New York: Harper Colophon Books.

Gardner, J., Rachlin, R., and Sweeny, H. (1986). *Handbook of strategic planning.* New York, N.Y.: John Wiley & Sons.

Garone, S. (Ed.). (1994). *Business ethics: Generating trust in the 1990s and beyond.* Report no. 1057-94-CH. New York: The Conference Board.

Garvin, D. A. (1993). Manufacturing strategic planning. *California Management Review, 35*(4), 85–106.

Gaspar, R., and Thompson, T. (1995). Current trends in distance education. *Journal of Interactive Instruction Development, 8*(2) 21–27.

Gayeski, D. (1991). Futures for performance technologists—Part 1: What we can learn from our past mistakes. *Performance and Instruction, 30*(1), 1–4.

Gayeski, D. (1995). Changing roles and professional challenges for human performance technology. *Performance Improvement Quarterly, 8*(2), 6–16.

Gayeski, D. (1997). Rewiring your organization's learning and communication system. *Performance Improvement, 36*(3), 36–39.

Geber, B. (1995). The right and wrong of ethics offices. *Training, 32*(10), 102–109.

Gellerman, S. (1989). Managing ethics from the top down. *Sloan Management Review, 30*(2), 73–79.

Gellermann, W., Frankel, M., and Ladenson, R. (1990). *Values and ethics in organization and human systems development: Responding to dilemmas in professional life.* San Francisco, Calif.: Jossey-Bass.

Genfan, H. (1987). Formalizing business ethics. *Training and Development Journal, 41*(11), 35–37.

Georgious, P. (1973). The goal paradigm and notes toward a counter paradigm. *Administrative Science Quarterly, 18*(3), 291–310.

Gerity, P. (1999). *A study to identify community college workforce training and development professionals' perceived competencies and their perceived professional development needs.* Unpublished Ph.D. dissertation. University Park: Pennsylvania State University.

Gibson, J., Ivancevich, J., and Donnelly, Jr. (1985). *Organizations: Behavior, structure, processes* (5th ed.). Plano, Tex.: Business Publications.

Gilbert, T. (1978). *Human competence: Engineering worthy performance.* New York: McGraw-Hill, p. 137.

Gilbreath, R. (1987). Business ethics. *New Management, 4*(4), 23–55.

Gilley, J. (1998). *Strategic planning for human resource development.* INFO-LINE. Alexandria, Va.: The American Society for Training and Development.

Gilley, J. and Eggland, S. (1989). *Principles of human resource development.* Reading, Mass. and Menlo Park, Calif.: Addison Wesley and University Associates, p. 311.

Gilley, J. W. (1992). *Strategic planning for human resource development.* INFO-LINE. Alexandria, Va.: American Society for Training and Development.

Gilley, J., and Coffern, A. (1994). *Internal consulting for HRD professionals: Tools, techniques, and strategies for improving organizational performance.* Burr Ridge, Ill.: Irwin Professional Publishing.

Ginkel, K., Mulder, M., and Nijhof, W. (1994). Role profiles of HRD professionals in the Netherlands. Paper presented at the conference "Education and Training for Work." Twente: University of Twente.

Ginzberg, E. (1958). *Human resources: The wealth of a nation.* New York: Simon and Schuster.

Glaser, M. (1991). Tailoring performance measurement to fit the organization: From generic to germane. *Public Productivity and Management Review, 14*(3), 303–319.

Glueck, W. and Jauch, L. (1984). *Business policy and strategic management* (4th ed.). New York: McGraw-Hill.

Goad, T. (1988). *The HRD practitioner: A person of many roles.* New York: Nichols Publishing.

Godfrey, J. (1988). Ethics as an intrapreneurial venture. *New Management, 5*(4), 58–59.

Golembiewski, R. (1990). *Ironies in organizational development.* New Brunswick, N.J.: Transaction Publishers.

Golembiewski, R. T. (1992). Enhancing world-wide strategic planning: Part 1: An OD design and its theoretic rationale. *Organization Development Journal, 10*(1), 31–54.

Goodstein, L. (1981). American business values and cultural imperialism. *Organizational Dynamics, 10*(1), 42–63.

Goodstein, L. D., and Butz, H. E. (1998). Customer value: The linchpin of organizational change. *Organizational Dynamics, 27*(1), 21–33.

Goodstein, L. D., Nolan, T. M., and Pfeiffer, J. W. (1992). *Applied strategic planning: A comprehensive guide.* San Diego, Calif.: Pfeiffer & Company.

Gordon, E., and Baumhart, J. (1997). Ethics for training and development. *Info-Line,* No. 9515. Alexandria, Va.: The American Society for Training and Development.

Gordon, E., Petrini, C., and Campagna, A. (1997). *Opportunities in training and development careers.* Lincolnwood, Ill.: VGM Career Horizons.

Gossage, L. (1967). *Qualifications and education needs of industrial training directors.* Unpublished doctoral dissertation. Los Angeles: University of California, Los Angeles.

Grant, L. (1998, January 12). Happy workers, high returns. *Fortune, 137*(1), p. 81.

Greengard, S. (1997). 50% of your employees are lying, cheating, and stealing. *Workforce, 76*(10), 44–53.

Greengard, S. (1998). Economic forces are squeezing growth potential: But HR can unlock a prosperous future. *Workforce, 77*(3), 44–54.

Grefe, E., and Linsky, M. (1995*). The new corporate activism: Harnessing the power of grassroots tactics for your organization.* New York, N.Y.: McGraw-Hill.

Grover, H. (1974). *The federal training community: An exploratory study of role perception and job performance ratings.* Unpublished doctoral dissertation. Washington: George Washington University.

Guillen, M. (1994). The age of eclecticism: Current organizational trends and the evolution of managerial models. *Sloan Management Review, 36*(1), 75–86.

Gundling, E. (1991). Ethics and working with the Japanese: The entrepreneur and the "elite course." *California Management Review, 33*(3), 25–39.

Gunn, R., and Burroughs, M. (1996). Work spaces that work: Designing high performance offices. *Futurist, 30*(2), 19–24.

Gustafson, K., and Branch, R. (1997). Revisioning models of instructional development. *Educational Technology Research and Development, 45*(3), 73–89.

Guthrie, E. (1935). *The psychology of learning.* New York: Harper & Row.

Haas, H., and Tamarkin, B. (1992). *The leader within: An empowering path of self-discovery.* New York: HarperBusiness.

Hacker, M., and Akinyele, A. (1998). Focusing on visible management at a USPS distribution center. *National Productivity Review, 17* (4), 45–52.

Hackos, J. (1997). Integrating training and documentation. *Performance Improvement, 36*(3), 23–29.

Haines, S., and McCoy, K. (1995). *Sustaining high performance: The strategic transformation to a customer-focused learning organization.* Delray Beach, Fla.: St. Lucie Press.

Haire, M. (1968). Approach to an integrated personnel policy. *Industrial Relations*, pp. 107–117.

Hall, R. (1977). *Organizations: Structure and process* (2nd ed.). Englewood Cliffs, N.J.: Prentice-Hall.

Hall, W. (1993). Making the right decision: Ethics for managers. New York: John Wiley & Sons.

Hallman, G. (1988). Functional approach to employee benefits. In J. Rosenbloom (ed.), *The handbook of employee benefits: Design, funding, and administration* (2nd ed.). Homewood, Ill.: Business One, Irwin, p. 17.

Hanabury, E. (1998). A catalyst for change. *Human Resource Executive, 12*(14), A17–A19.

Harbison, F. (1973). *Human resources as the wealth of nations.* New York: Oxford University Press.

Harlan, M. (1996). Corporate distance learning systems for employee education. *Journal of Instructional Delivery Systems, 10*(1), 14–16.

Harless, J. (1978). *An ounce of analysis is worth a pound of objectives.* Newnan, Ga.: Harless Performance Guild.

Harless, J. (1997). *Analyzing human performance: Tools for achieving business results.* Alexandria, Va.: The American Society for Training and Development.

Harrington, S. (1991). What corporate America is teaching about ethics. *Academy of Management Executives, 5*(1), 21–30.

Harrison, R. (1995). *Consultant's journey: A dance of work and spirit.* San Francisco, Calif.: Jossey-Bass.

Harsha, B. (1999). Online training "Sprints" ahead. *Technical Training, 10*(1), 27–31.

Hartnett, J. (1999). The best laid plans of WBT. *Inside Technology Training, 3*(1), 38–40.

Hatcher, T. (1997). Improving corporate social performance: A strategic planning approach. *Performance Improvement, 36*(9), 23–27.

Havighurst, R. (1970). *Developmental tasks and education* (2nd ed.). New York: McKay.

Head, T. C., Murphy, L. P., and Sorensen, P. F. (1992). Current trends in organization development: 1990. *Organization Development Journal, 10*(3), 77–89.

Hemmelgarn, A. et al. (1995). Trends in research design and data analytic strategies in organizational research. *Journal of Management, 21*(1), 141–157.

Hequet, M. (1995). The new trainer. *Training, 32*(12), 23–29.

Hienes, J. (1998). Learning from the past. *Multimedia and Internet Training Newsletter, 5*(9), 6–7.

Hitt, W. (1990). *Ethics and leadership: Putting theory into practice.* Columbus, Ohio: Battelle Press.

Hoffman, W. (1986). Developing the ethical corporation. *Business Insights, 2*(2), 10.

Hornstein, H. and Tichy, N. (1973). *Organizational diagnosis and improvement strategies.* New York: Behavioral Science Associates.

Houle, C. (1961). *The inquiring mind.* Madison, Wis.: University of Wisconsin Press.

Houle, C. (1972). *The design of education.* San Francisco: Jossey-Bass.

How one training leader is turning his staff into '21st century trainers'. 1996. *Training Directors' Forum Newsletter. 12*(11), 1–3.

How to create training fast for IT apps. (1999). *Multimedia and Internet Training, 6*(3), 4–5.

HR plays a central role in ethics programs. (1998). *Workforce, 77*(4), 121–123.

Hull, C. (1952). *A behavior system.* New Haven, Conn.: Yale University Press.

Hunt, D. (1999). *A practitioner-identified list of competencies needed to design web-based training.* Unpublished Ph.D. dissertation. University Park: The Pennsylvania State University.

Hunt, E. (1979). *The history of economic thought: A critical perspective.* Belmont, Calif.: Wadsworth, 1979.

Hunt, J. (1991). Ethics and experiential education as professional practice. *Journal of Experiential Education, 14*(2), 14–18.

Hunter, G. (1995). A historical background of the Carl D. Perkins vocational and applied technology education act. *Journal of Studies in Technical Careers, 15*(3), 141–145.

Huselid, M. (1993). The impact of environmental volatility on human resource planning and strategic human resource management. *Human Resource Planning, 16*(3), 35–51.

Huselid, M. (1994). Documenting HR's effect on company performance. *HR Magazine, 39*(1), 79–85.

Hutchison, C. (1989). An instructional technologist's guide to job hunting. *Performance and Instruction, 28*(8), 25–27.

Hutchison, C.; Stein, F.; and Shepherd, J. (1988). *Instructor competencies volume I: The standards.* Batavia, N.Y.: The International Board of Standards for Training, Performance, and Instruction.

Imel, S. (1988). *Trends and issues in adult education 1988.* Columbus, Ohio: ERIC Clearinghouse on ACVE.

Industry report 1997. (1997). *Training, 34*(10), 33–34, 36–37.

Inman, P., and Vernon, S. (1997). Assessing workplace learning: New trends and possibilities. *New Directions for Adult and Continuing Education, 75*, 75–85.

Ireland, K. (1991). The ethics game. *Personnel Journal, 70*(3), 72–75.

Is there a learning curve in the business? (1999). *Training, 36*(2), 28–39.

Jackson, C. N., and Manning, M. R., eds. (1992). *Organization development annual, Volume IV: Intervening in client organizations.* Alexandria, Va.: American Society for Training and Development.

Jackson, C. N., and Manning, M. R., eds. (1994). *Organization development annual, Volume V: Evaluating organization development interventions.* Alexandria, Va.: American Society for Training and Development.

Jacobs, R. (1987). *Human performance technology: A systems-based field for the training and development profession.* (Information Series No. 326.) Columbus, Ohio: ERIC Clearinghouse on Adult, Career, and Vocational Education, The National Center for Research in Vocational Education, p. x.

James, B. (1994). Narrative and organizational control: Corporate visionaries, ethics, and power. *International Journal of Human Resource Management, 5*(4), 927–951.

Jaques, E. (1964). *Timespan handbook.* London: Heimann.

Johnson, J. A., and Boss, R. W. (1992). Organization development interventions in health services: Looking back and moving forward. *Organization Development Journal, 10*(1), 73–78.

Johnson, P. (1996, March/April). The future of multimedia in training. *CBT Solutions,* 36–43.

Johnson, R. (1993). Strategic issues top trainers' benchmarking wish list. *Training Directors' Forum Newsletter, 9*(1), 1–3.

Jonassen, D. (1989). Performance analysis. *Performance and Instruction, 28*(4), 15–23.

Jones, D. (1982). *Doing ethics in business.* Cambridge, Mass.: Oelgeschlager, Gunn, and Hain.

Jopson, J., and Smith, H. (1997). A job by any other name. *Training and Development, 51*(6), 28–30.

Kahn, W. (1990). Toward an agenda for business ethics research. *Academy of Management Review, 15*(2), 311–328.

Kapp, K. (1999). Moving training to the strategic level with learning requirements planning. *National Productivity Review, 18*(2), 15–21.

Karp, H., and Abramms, B. (1992). Doing the right thing. *Training and Development, 46*(8), 37–41.

Katz, D. and Kahn, R. (1978). *The social psychology of organizations* (2nd ed.). New York: Wiley.

Katz, J. H., and Marshak, R. J. (1996). Reinventing organization development theory and practice. *Organization Development Journal, 14*(1), 40–47.

Kaufman, R. (1995). Mega planning: The changed realities—Part I. *Performance and Instruction, 34*(10). 8–15.

Kaufman, R. (1996). Mega planning: The changed realities—Part II. *Performance and Instruction, 35*(1), 4–5.

Kaufman, R. (1996). Mega planning: The changed realities—Part III. *Performance and Instruction, 35*(2), 4–7.

Kaufman, R., and Kaufman, J. (1992). What should high-risk operations evaluate relative to safety and safety training? *Performance Improvement Quarterly, 5*(3), 16–25.

Keen, C. (1994). Tips for effective strategic planning. *HR Magazine, 39* (8), 84–87.

Kelley, C. (1987). The interrelationship of ethics and power in today's organizations. *Organizational Dynamics, 16*(1), 4–18.

Kelly, C. (1988). *The destructive achiever.* Reading, Mass.: Addison-Wesley.

Kendrick, J. (1976). *The formation and stocks of total capital.* New York: National Bureau of Economic Research.

Kenny, J. (1982). Competency analysis for trainers: A model for professionalism. *Training and Development Journal, 36*(5), 142–148.

Kenyon, H. (1999). Leaders in learning technology share success strategies. *Corporate University Review, 7*(1), 39–42, 65.

Kimmerling, G. (1995). Surveying the suppliers' market. *Training and Development, 49*(10), 34–39.

King, A., and Bishop, T. (1994). Human resource experience: Survey and analysis. *Public Personnel Management, 23*(1), 165–180.

King, M. (1998). *The relationship between community college education professionals' education and work experience and their professional development needs.* Unpublished Ph.D. dissertation. University Park: Pennsylvania State University.

King, M., King, S., and Rothwell, W. (2000, in press). Competency-based instructional delivery. [tentative title]. New York: AMACOM.

King, S. (1998). *A practitioner verification of the human performance improvement analyst competencies and outputs among members of the International Society for Performance Improvement.* Unpublished Ph.D. dissertation. University Park: Pennsylvania State University.

Kirk, J. (1991). Exploring how HRD managers differ from other managers. *Human Resource Development Quarterly, 2*(4), 373–386.

Kirrane, D. (1990). Managing values: A systematic approach to business ethics. *Training and Development Journal, 44*(11), 53–56.

Kiser, K. (1999). Working on world time. *Training, 36*(3), 28–34.

Kizilos, P. (1991). Fixing fatal flaws. *Training, 28*(9), 66–70.

Knowles, M. (1980). *The modern practice of adult education* (rev. ed.). Chicago: Follett.

Knowles, M. (1984). *The adult learner: A neglected species* (3rd ed.). Houston: Gulf Publishing.

Kochanski, J. (1996). Introduction to special issues on human resource competencies. *Human Resource Management, 35*(1), 3–6.

Koonce, R. (1997). How to find the right organizational fit. *Training and Development, 51*(4), 15.

Koonce, R. (1998). Plan on a career that bobs and weaves. *Training and Development, 52*(4), 14.

Koonce, R. (1999). Stand-up trainer to stand-out facilitator: How to make the transition. *Technical Training, 10* (1), p8.

Kossoff, L. (1998). Tying quality to strategy to insure the success of both. *National Productivity Review, 18* (1), 29–36.

Krohe, J. (1997). The big business of business ethics. *Across the Board, 34*(5), 23–29.

Kuhn, T. (1962). *The structure of scientific revolutions*. Chicago: University of Chicago.

Kuhne, G. W., and Quigley, B. A. (1997). Understanding and using action research in practice settings. *New Directions for Adult and Continuing Education, 73*, 23–40.

Kuhne, G. W., et al. (1997). Case studies of action research in various adult education settings. *New Directions for Adult and Continuing Education, 73,* 41–62.

Kutscher, R. (1995). Summary of BLS projections to 2005. *Monthly Labor Review, 118*(11), 3–9.

Laabs, J. (1995). Shrinking pains cause HR to redevelop talents. *Personnel Journal, 74*(8), 78–82.

Labich, K. (1992). The new crisis in business ethics. *Fortune, 125*(8), 167–176.

Lado, A., and M. Wilson. (1994). Human resource systems and sustained competitive advantage: A competency-based perspective. *Academy of Management Review, 19*(4), 699–727.

Langdon, D. (1991). Performance technology in three paradigms. *Performance and Instruction, 30*(7), 1–7.

Langdon, D. (1999). Objectives? Get over them. *Training and Development, 53*(2), 54–58.

Langdon, D. G., Whiteside, K. S., and McKenna, M. M. (eds.) (1999). *Intervention resource guide: 50 performance improvement tools*. San Francisco: Jossey-Bass/Pfeiffer.

Lansbury, R. (1978). *Professionals and management*. St. Lucia, Queensland: University of Queensland Press.

Larimer, L. (1997). Reflections on ethics and integrity. *HR Focus, 74*(4), 5.

Lawrie, J. (1990). Differentiate between training, education, and development. *Personnel Journal, 69*(10), 44.

Lawson, T. (1990). *The competency initiative: Standards of excellence for human resource executives*. Minneapolis, Minn.: Golle and Holmes Custom Education, p. v.

Lawson, T. (1996). Critical competencies and developmental experiences for top HR executives. *Human Resource Management, 35*(1), 67–85.

Leach, J. (1991). Characteristics of excellent trainers: A psychological and interpersonal profile. *Performance Improvement Quarterly, 4*(3), 42–62.

Lee, C. (1985). Human resource development: A useful bit of jargon? *Training, 22*(1), 75–76.

Lee, S. (1994). *A preliminary study of the competencies, work outputs, and roles of human resource development professionals in the Republic of China on Taiwan: A cross-cultural competency study.* Unpublished doctoral dissertation. University Park: Pennsylvania State University.

Lefrancois, G. (1982). *Psychological theories and human learning* (2nd ed.). Monterey, Calif.: Brooks/Cole.

Lei, D., Slocum, J. W., and Pitts, R. A. (1999). Designing organizations for competitive advantage: The power of unlearning and learning. *Organizational Dynamics, 27*(3), 24–38.

Leicester, C. (1989). The key role of the line manager in employee development. *Personnel Management, 21*(3), 53–57.

Levison, H. (1972). *Organizational diagnosis.* Cambridge, Mass.: Harvard University Press.

Lewin, K. (1946). Action research and minority problems. *Journal of Social Issues, 2*(4), 34–46.

Lewin, K. (1948). *Resolving social conflicts.* New York: Harper.

Lewin, K. (1951). *Field theory in social science.* New York: Harper.

Liebig, J. (1994). *Merchants of vision: People bringing new purpose and values to business.* San Francisco: Berrett-Koehler.

Liedtka, J. (1998). Linking strategic thinking with strategic planning. *Strategy and Leadership, 26*(4), 30–35.

Lindholm, E. (1997). IT training companies bulk up. *Inside Technology Training, 1*(8), 12–18, 59.

Lindsey, E., Homes, V. and McCall, M., Jr. (1987). *Key events in executives' lives.* Greensboro, S.C.: The Center for Creative Leadership.

Lippitt, G. and Nadler, L. (1967). Emerging roles of the training director. *Training and Development Journal, 21*(8), 26–31.

Lippitt, R., Watson, J. and Westley, B. (1958). *Dynamics of planned change.* New York: Harcourt Brace.

Lombardo, M. and Eichinger, R. (1989). *Eighty-eight assignments for development in place: Enhancing the development challenge of existing jobs.* Greensboro, N.C.: The Center for Creative Leadership.

Lorange, P. (1996). Strategic planning for rapid and profitable growth. *Strategy and Leadership, 24*(3), 42–48.

Lubin, Bernard, Robinson, Albert J., and Sailors, Jean R. (1992). Burnout in organizations: A bibliography of the literature, 1980 through 1991. *Organization Development Journal, 10*(2), 66–90.

Mager, R. (1992). *What every manager should know about training, or "I've got a training problem"...and other odd ideas.* Belmont, Calif.: Lake Publishing.

Mager, R. and Pipe, P. (1970). *Analyzing performance problems, or `You really oughta wanna'.* Belmont, Calif.: David S. Lake Publisher.

Mager, R., and Cram, D. (1985). The regulators are coming! *Training, 22*(9), 40–45.

Mai-Dalton, R. R., and Barnes, F. B. (1991). The evolution of an employee-training program: A three-year flexible organization development effort. *Group and Organization Studies, 16*(4), 452–471.

Mantyla, K., and Gividen, J. (1997). *Distance learning: A step-by-step guide for trainers.* Alexandria, Va.: The American Society for Training and Development.

Marquardt, M. and Engel, D. (1993a). *Global human resource development.* Englewood Cliffs, N.J.: Prentice-Hall.

Marquardt, M. and Engel, D. (1993b). HRD competencies for a shrinking world. *Training and Development, 47*(5), 59–65.

Marrow, A. (1969). *The practical theorist: The life and work of Kurt Lewin.* New York: Basic Books.

Martell, K., and Carroll, S. (1995). How strategic is HRM? *Human Resource Management, 34*(2), 253–267.

Mathys, N., and Burack, E. (1993). Strategic downsizing: Human resource planning approaches. *Human Resource Planning, 16*(1), 71–85.

Maurer, R., and Mobley, N. (1998). Outsourcing: Is it the HR department of the future? *HR Focus, 75*(11), 9–10.

Mayadas, A. (1997). Online networks build time savings into employee education. *HR Magazine, 42*(10), 31–35.

McAfee, R. B., and Champagne, P. J. (1988). Employee development: Discovering who needs what. *Personnel Administrator, 33*(2), 92–98.

McClenahen, J. (1995). Good enough? *Industry Week, 244*(4), 59–62.

McCune, J. (1994). Measuring the value of employee education. *Management Review, 83*(4), 10–15.

McCune, J. (1995). The consultant quandary. *Management Review, 84*(10), 40–43.

McDermott, L. (1984). The many faces of the OD professional. *Training and Development Journal, 38*(2), 14–19.

McDonald, K., and Wood, G., Jr. (1993). Surveying adult education practitioners about ethical issues. *Adult Education Quarterly, 43*(4), 243–257.

McIlvaine, A. (1998). Work ethics. *Human Resource Executive, 12*(11), 30–34.

McLagan, P. (1989). *Models for HRD practice.* (4 volumes). Alexandria, Va.: The American Society for Training and Development.

McLagan, P. (1989). *The models.* [A volume in *Models for HRD Practice.*] Alexandria, Va.: The American Society for Training and Development.

McLagan, P. (1996). Creating the future of HRD. *Training and Development, 50*(1), 60–65.

McLagan, P. (1996). Great ideas revisited: Competency models. *Training and Development, 50*(1), 60–64.

McLagan, P., and McCullough, R. (1983). *Models for excellence: The conclusions and recommendations of the ASTD training and development competency study.* Washington, D.C.: The American Society for Training and Development.

McLean, G., and Yang, J. (1992). Instructor competencies needed by Korean training and development professionals. In E. Kaynak and T. Chan (eds.), *Proceedings of the 1992 world business congress on international perspectives of management development* (pp. 264–273). Halifax, Nova Scotia: International Development Association.

McMahan, G. C., and Woodman, R. W. (1992). The current practice of organization development within the firm: A survey of large industrial corporations. *Group and Organization Management, 17*(2), 117–134.

McVinney, C. (1999). Dream weaver. *Training and Development, 53*(4), 38–42.

Meade, J. (1998). A solution for competency-based employee development. *HR Magazine, 43*(13), 54–58.

Melcher, R. A. (1999). Education prognosis 1999. *Business Week, 3611,* 132–133.

Merriam, S., and Brockett, R. (1997). *The profession and practice of adult education: An introduction.* San Francisco: Jossey-Bass/Pfeiffer.

Miller, V. (1996). The history of training. In R. Craig (ed.), *The ASTD training and development handbook: A guide to human resource development* (pp. 3–18). New York: McGraw-Hill.

Miller, W. (1996). Leadership at a crossroads. *Industry Week, 245*(15), 42–56.

Minehan, M. (1997). What the future holds for HR. *HR Magazine,* 42(3),116–118.

Miners, I. A. (1994). Organization development impacts interrupted: A multiyear time-serial study of absence and other time uses. *Group and Organization Management, 19*(3), 363–394.

Mintzberg, H. (1993). The pitfalls of strategic planning. *California Management Review, 36*(1), 32–47.

Mintzberg, H. (1994). The fall and rise of strategic planning. *Harvard Business Review, 72*(1), 107–114.

Models for excellence: The conclusions and recommendations of the ASTD training and development study. (1983). Washington, D. C.: The American Society for Training and Development.

Moorby, E. (1991). How to succeed in employee development: The politics. *Leadership and Organization Development Journal, 12*(7), 21–27.

Morgen, S. (1997). *Selling with integrity: Reinventing sales through collaboration, respect, and serving.* San Francisco: Berrett-Koehler Publishers.

Morris, D. (1996). Using competency development tools as a strategy for change in the human resource function: A case study. *Human Resource Management, 35*(1), 35–51.

Murray, D. (1995). The future of Eugene, Oregon. *At Work: Stories of Tomorrow's Workplace, 4* (4), 5–6.

Nadler, D. and Tushman, M. (1977). A diagnostic model for organizational behavior. In J. Hackman, E. Lawler, and L. Porter (eds.), *Perspectives on behavior in organizations*. New York: McGraw-Hill, 1977.

Nadler, L, and Lippitt, G. (1967). The emerging roles of the training director. *Training and Development Journal, 21*(8), 2–10.

Nadler, L. (1962). *A study of the needs of selected training directors in Pennsylvania which might be met by professional education institutions*. Dissertation Abstracts International, *24*(2).

Nadler, L. (1980). Defining the field—Is it HRD or OD, or ? *Training and Development Journal, 34*(12), 66–68.

Nadler, L. and Nadler, Z. (1989). *Developing human resources* (3rd ed.). San Francisco: Jossey-Bass.

Naisbitt, J. (1983). *Megatrends*. New York: Ballantine.

Nasaw, D. (1979). *Schooled to order: A social history of public schooling in the United States*. New York: Oxford University.

Nash, L. (1993). *Good intentions aside: A manager's guide to resolving ethical problems*. Boston: Harvard Business School Press.

Nash, M. (1983). *Managing organizational performance*. San Francisco: Jossey-Bass, p. 4.

National Academy of Public Administration. (1996). *A competency model for human resources professionals*. Washington, D.C.: The National Academy of Public Administration.

Navran, F. (1997). 12 steps to building a best-practices ethics program. *Workforce, 76*(9). 117–122.

Needs assessment for online learning. (1999). *Multimedia and Internet Training, 6*(3), 6–7.

Neilsen, E. (1984). *Becoming an OD practitioner*. Englewood Cliffs, N.J.: Prentice-Hall.

Nelson, R. (1992). Training on ethics: Cummins Engine Company. *Journal of Management Development, 11*(4), 21–33.

Nielsen, R. (1989). Changing unethical organizational behavior. *Academy of Management Executives, 3*(2), 123–130.

Nilson, C. (1992). *How to start a training program in your growing business*. New York, N.Y.: American Management Association.

Odenthal, L., and Nijhof, W. (1996). *HRD roles in Germany*. De Lier: Academisch Boeken Centrum.

Odenwald, S., and Matheny, W. (1996). *Global impact*. Chicago: Irwin.

Ontario Society for Training and Development. (1976). *Competency analysis for trainers: A personal planning guide*. Toronto, Ontario: Ontario Society for Training and Development.

Ontario Society for Training and Development. (1976). *Core competencies for training and development*. Toronto: Ontario Society for Training and Development.

Organization development practitioner: Self development guide. (1983). Alexandria, Va.: American Society for Training and Development

Pace, R. (1983). *Organizational communication: Foundations of human resource development*. Englewood Cliffs, N.J.: Prentice-Hall.

Paine, L. (1994). Managing for organizational integrity. *Harvard Business Review, 72*(2), 106–117.

The paradox principles: How high-performance companies manage chaos, complexity, and contradiction to achieve superior results. 1996. Chicago, Ill.: Irwin Professional Publishing.

Parsons, T. (1960). *Structure and process in modern societies*. New York: The Free Press.

Pastin, M. (1986). *The hard problems of management: Gaining the ethics edge*. San Francisco, Calif.: Jossey-Bass.

Paton, S. M. (1989). Force field analysis proves money isn't everything. *Quality Digest, 9*(4), 21–25.

Pattan, J. (1986). The strategy in strategic planning. *Training and Development Journal, 41*(2), 30–32.

Paul, K. (ed.). (1987). *Business environment and business ethics*. Cambridge, Mass.: Ballinger Publishing.

Peak, M. (1997). Training: No longer for the fainthearted. *Management Review, 86*(2), 23–27.

Peerapornvitoon, M. (1999). *A survey of workplace learning and performance: Competencies and roles for practitioners in Thailand*. Unpublished doctoral dissertation. University Park: The Pennsylvania State University.

Perrottet, C. (1996). Scenarios for the future. *Management Review, 85*(1), 43–46.

Peters, T. and Waterman, R., Jr. (1982). *In search of excellence: Lessons from America's best-run companies*. New York: Harper & Row.

Peterson, L. (1997). Technical trainers predict big changes by the millennium. *Technical and Skills Training, 8*(2), 3–4.

Petrick, J., and Manning, G. (1990). Developing an ethical climate for excellence. *Journal for Quality and Participation, March*, 84–90.

Phillips, J. (1998). The return-on-investment (ROI) process: Issues and trends. *Educational Technology, 38*(4), 7–14.

Piaget, J. (1951). *Play, dreams, and imitations in childhood*. New York: Norton.

Piaget, J. (1972). Intellectual development from adolescence to adulthood. *Human Development, 15*, 1–12.

Picken, J., and Dess, G. (1997). Out of (strategic) control. *Organizational Dynamics, 26*(1), 35–48.

Pieper, R. (1990). O.D. in Germany. *Organization Development Journal, 8*(4), 50–58.

Pink, D. H. (1999). Report from the future: What's your story? *Fast Company*, 21, 32–34.

Pinto, P. and Walker, J. (1978). *A study of professional training and development roles and competencies: A report to the professional development committee*. Madison, Wis.: The American Society for Training and Development.

Piskurich, G. M. (1999). Now-you-see-'em, now-you-don't learning centers. *Technical Training, 10* (1), 18–21.

Piskurich, G. and Sanders, E. (1998). *ASTD models for learning technologies: Roles, competencies, and outputs.* Alexandria, Va.: The American Society for Training and Development.

Pocock, P. (1989). Is business ethics a contradiction in terms? *Personnel Management, 21*(11), 50–63.

Porras, J. I., and Silvers, R. C. (1991). Organization development and transformation. *Annual Review of Psychology, 42,* 51–78.

Posner, B., and Schmidt, W. (1992). Values and the American manager: An update updated. *California Management Review, 34*(3), 80–94.

Post, F. G. (1989). Beware of your stakeholders. *Journal of Management Development, 8*(1), 28–35.

Potter, K. R. (1999). Learning by doing: A case for interactive contextual learning environments. *Journal of Instruction Delivery Systems, 13*(1), 29–33.

Prescott, R. (1999). *The changing role of human resource management: A comparative study of importance factors concerning human resource competencies among general managers.* Unpublished doctoral dissertation. University Park: Pennsylvania State University.

Price, C. (1991). A new national program for consulting. *Journal of Management Consulting, 6*(4), 34–37.

Pruzan, P., and Thyssen, O. (1994). The renaissance of ethics and the ethical accounting statement. *Educational Technology, 34*(1), 23–28.

Puffer, S., and McCarthy, D. (1995). Finding the common ground in Russian and American business ethics. *California Management Review, 37*(2), 29–46.

Putterman, B. (1999). Busy executives want action when they learn. *Training Directors' Forum Newsletter, 15*(3), p7.

Quality circles: Employee development tool. 1989. *Bulletin on Training, 14*(12), 1.

Quigley, B. A. (1997). The role of research in the practice of adult education. *New Directions for Adult and Continuing Education, 73,* 3–22.

Rae, L. (1993). *Evaluating trainer effectiveness.* New York: Business-One.

Raelin, J. (1989). Professional ethics and business ethics. *Management Review, 78*(11), 39–42.

Raimy, E. (1995). 1-800-ETHICS. *Human Resource Executive, 9*(11), 36–39.

Raimy, E. (1995). 'Strat planning' in the trenches. *Human Resource Executive, 9*(6), 1, 20–25.

Raimy, E. (1997). Never a dull moment. *Human Resource Executive, 11*(6), 27–32.

Rand, A. (1996). Technology transforms training. *HR Focus, 73*(11), 11–13.

Raths, L., Harmin, M. and Simon, S. (1966). *Values of teaching.* Columbus, Ohio: Charles E. Merrill, 1966.

Reading, writing, and enrichment. (1999). *Economist, 350*(8102),55–56.

Redding, J. C., and Catalanello, R. F. (1994). *Strategic readiness: The making of the learning organization.* San Francisco, Calif.: Jossey–Bass.

Reid, R. L. (1995). On target: New roles for frontline supervisors. *Technical and Skills Training, 6*(3), 6–8.

Reynolds, A. (1993). *The trainer's dictionary: HRD terms, acronyms, initials, and abbreviations*. Amherst, Mass.: HRD Press.

Rhodeback, M., Ben-Lai, W., and White, L. P. (1990). Ethical consideration in organization development: An empirical approach. *Organization Development Journal, 8*(4), 40–49.

Rice, D., and Dreiling, C. (1990). Rights and wrongs of ethics training. *Training and Development Journal, 44*(5), 103–108.

Richter, A., and Barnum, C. (1994). When values clash. *HR Magazine, 39*(9), 42–45.

Rijk, R., Mulder, M., and Nijhof, W. (1994). *Role profiles of HRD practitioners in Four European countries*. A paper presented in Milan, Italy. Twente: University of Twente.

Ripley, D. (1996). Strategic HR analysis. Unpublished paper. Alexandria, Va.: The Society for Human Resource Management. Presented at www.shrm.org.

Ritchie, D., and Earnest, J. (1999). The future of instructional design: Results of a Delphi study. *Educational Technology, 39*(1), 35–42.

Roberts, G. (1998). Perspectives on enduring and emerging issues in performance appraisal. *Public Personnel Management, 27*(3), 301–320.

Robin, D., and Reidenbach, R. (1989). *Business ethics: Where profits meet value systems*. Englewood Cliffs, N.J.: Prentice-Hall.

Rogers, C. (1969). *Freedom to learn*. Columbus, Ohio: Merrill.

Rokeach, M. (1973). *The nature of human values*. New York: The Free Press.

Rooze, G., and Ishler, R. (1985). Training and development specialists. *Texas Tech Journal of Education, 12*(1), 19–26.

Rose, A. (1996). Group learning in adult education: Its historical roots. *New Directions for Adult and Continuing Education, 71*, 3–13.

Rosenberg, M. (1990). Performance technology: Working the system. *Training, 27*(2), 46.

Rosenberg, M., Coscarelli, W., and Hutchison, C. (1992). The origins and evolution of the field (pp. 14–31). In H. Stolovich and E. Keeps (eds.), *The handbook of human performance technology: A comprehensive guide for analyzing and solving performance problems in organizations*. San Francisco: Jossey-Bass/Pfeiffer.

Rossman, A. B. (1993). Making connections: Organization development and total quality management process. *Organization Development Journal, 11*(1), 51–56.

Rothwell, W. (1994). *Effective succession planning: Ensuring leadership continuity and building talent from within*. New York: AMACOM.

Rothwell, W. (1996). *ASTD models for human performance improvement: Roles, competencies, and outputs*. Alexandria, Va.: The American Society for Training and Development, p. 79.

Rothwell, W. (1999). *The action learning guidebook*. San Francisco: Jossey-Bass/Pfeiffer.

Rothwell, W. (ed.). (1998). *In action: Linking HRD programs with organizational strategy*. Alexandria, Va.: The American Society for Training and Development.

Rothwell, W. and Kazanas, H. (1994). *Human resource development: A strategic approach.* (rev. ed.). Amherst, Mass.: HRD Press, pp. 259–260.

Rothwell, W. and Kazanas, H. (1998). *Mastering the instructional design process: A systematic approach* (2nd ed.). San Francisco: Jossey-Bass.

Rothwell, W., and Kazanas, H. (1994). *Planning and managing human resources: Strategic planning for personnel management* (Rev. ed.). Amherst, Mass.: Human Resource Development Press.

Rothwell, W., and Sensenig, K. (eds.). (1999). *The sourcebook for self-directed learning.* Amherst, Mass.: HRD Press.

Rothwell, W., Prescott, R., and Taylor, M. (1998). *Strategic HR leader: How to prepare your organization for the six key trends shaping the future.* Palo Alto, Calif.: Davies-Black publishing.

Rothwell, W., Prescott, R., and Taylor, M. (1998). *Strategic human resource leader: How to help your organization manage the six trends affecting the workforce.* Palo Alto, Calif.: Davies-Black Publishing.

Rothwell, W., Sanders, E., and Soper, J. (1999). *ASTD models for workplace learning and performance: Roles, competencies, and outputs.* Alexandria, Va.: The American Society for Training and Development.

Rothwell, W., Sullivan, R., and McLean, G. (1995a). *Practicing organization development: A guide for consultants.* San Diego: Pfeiffer and Co.

Rummler, G. (1996). In search of the holy performance grail. *Training and Development, 50*(4), 26–32.

Sabatino, K. (1996). Teaching cognitive strategies to improve performance. *Performance Improvement, 35*(7), 4–7.

Salopek, J. (1998). Arrested development. *Training and Development, 52*(9), 65.

Salopek, J. J. (1999). Stop playing games. *Training and Development, 53*(2), 28–38.

Sanders, E. (1999). Coming to terms with learning technologies. *Technical Training, 10(1)*, 34–35.

Sanders, E. (1999). The golden age of learning. *Technical Training, 10*(2), p. 36.

Sanders, E. S. (1999). *Learning Technologies.* INFO-LINE. Alexandria, Va.: American Society for Training and Development.

Sanzgiri, J., and Gottlieb, J. Z. (1992). Philosophic and pragmatic influences on the practice of organization development, 1950–2000. *Organizational Dynamics, 21*(2), 57–69.

Savicevic, D. (1991). Modern conceptions of androgogy: A European framework. *Studies in the Education of Adults, 23*(2), 179–201.

Schaaf, D. (1998). What workers really think about training. *Training, 35*(9), 59–66.

Schein, E. (1969). *Process consultation: Its role in organization development.* Reading, Mass.: Addison-Wesley.

Schmitt, N., and Borman, W., et al. (1993). *Personnel selection in organizations.* San Francisco: Jossey-Bass/Pfeiffer.

Schmuck, R. and Miles, M. (eds.). (1971). *Organization development in schools.* LaJolla, Calif.: University Associates.

Schoemaker, P. (1995). Scenario planning: A tool for strategic thinking. *Sloan Management Review, 36*(2), 25–40.

Schoemaker, P. J. (1992). How to link strategic vision to core capabilities. *Sloan Management Review, 34*(1), 67–81.

Schriefer, A. (1998). The future: Trends, discontinuities, and opportunities. *Strategy and Leadership, 26*(1), 26–32.

Schriver, R. (1997). Testing employee performance: A review of key milestones. *Technical and Skills Training, 8*(3), 27–29.

Schumpeter, J. (1943). *Capitalism, socialism, and democracy.* London: Allen and Unwin.

Segalla, E. (ed.). (1987). *Ethics education.* Management Development Report, Alexandria, Va.: The American Society for Training and Development.

Seibert, K. W. (1999). Reflection-in-action: Tools for cultivating on-the-job learning conditions. *Organizational Dynamics, 27*(3), 54–65.

Senge, P. (1990). *The fifth discipline: The art and practice of the learning organization.* New York: Doubleday.

Settle, T. (1995). Evolution of a trainer. *Training and Development, 49*(9), 15–16.

Shair, D. (1999). Toolbook II Assistant offers samples, choices, and guides. *HR Magazine, 44*(1), 83–84.

Shakespeare vs. Einstein. (1991, May/June). *National Report on Human Resources,* 3.

Sharpe, C. (ed.). (1999, May). Training telecommuters. *INFO-LINE,* no. 9905.

Shepard, H. (1960). An action research model. In *An action research program for organization improvement.* Ann Arbor: The Foundation for Research on Human Behavior, University of Michigan.

Shepard, K. and Raia, A. (1981). The OD training challenge. *Training and Development Journal, 35*(4), 90–96.

Shepherd, C. (1999). How to manage an online learning project. *Multimedia and Internet Training, 6*(3), 8–9.

Sherry, L., and Wilson, B. (1996). Supporting human performance across disciplines: A converging of roles and tools. *Performance Improvement Quarterly, 9*(4), 19–36.

Sibson, R. (1992). *Strategic planning for human resources management.* New York: AMACOM.

Sims, R., and Sims, S. (1994). *Changes and challenges for the human resource professional.* Westport, Conn.: Quorum Books.

Singer, B. (1996). *Work values.* Durango, Colo.: International Learning Works.

Skinner, B. (1953). *Science and human behavior.* New York: Macmillan.

Sleezer, C. (1990). *The development and validation of a performance analysis for training model.* St. Paul, Minn.: University of Minnesota.

Sleezer, C. (1991). Developing and validating the performance analysis for training model. *Human Resource Development Quarterly, 2*(4), 355–372.

Sleezer, C. (1993). Tried and true performance analysis. *Training and Development, 47*(11). 52–54.

Sleezer, C. (1996). Using performance analysis for training in an organization implementing integrated manufacturing: A case study. *Performance Improvement Quarterly, 9*(2), 25–41.

Smith, T. et al. (1995). *The condition of education.* Washington, D.C.: U.S. Department of Education.

Snell, N. (1999). Pinnacle learning manager. *Inside Technology Training, 3*(3), 48–52.

Society for Human Resource Management. (1997). Demographic profile of the HR profession. *Workplace Visions,* September–October. (1800 Duke St., Alexandria, Virginia 22314-3499; http://www.shrm.org/issues/visions/0997d.htm.)

Solomon, C. (1996). Put your ethics to a global test. *Personnel Journal, 75*(1), 66–74.

Sonnesyn, S. (1991). A question of ethics. *Training and Development Journal, 45*(3), 29–37.

Sorensen, P. F., et al. (1990). Organization development in Denmark. *Organization Development Journal, 8*(4), 28–32.

Sork, T., and Welock, B. (1992). Adult and continuing education needs a code of ethics. *New Directions for Adult and Continuing Education, 54,* pp. 115–122.

Spence, K. (1960). *Behavior theory and learning.* Englewood Cliffs, N.J.: Prentice-Hall.

Sperano, P. (1999). The role of electronic performance support systems (EPSS) in the delivery of just-in-time business training. *Journal of Instructional Delivery Systems, 13*(1), 14–16.

Stadius, R. (1999). *ASTD trainer's toolkit: Job descriptions in workplace learning and performance.* Alexandria, Va.: The American Society for Training and Development.

Stadler, A. (1995). A transformational learning cycle. *At Work: Stories of Tomorrow's Workplace, 4*(4), 9–11.

Stolovich, H., Keeps, E., and Rodrigue, D. (1995). Skills sets for the human performance technologist. *Performance Improvement Quarterly, 8*(2), 40–67.

Stolovitch, H. D., and Keeps, E. (eds.) (1992). *Handbook of human performance technology: A comprehensive guide for analyzing and solving performance problems in organizations.* San Francisco: Jossey-Bass.

Stone, D., and Vllachica, S. (1997). Performance support for knowledge workers: Practical strategies based on research and practice. *Performance Improvement, 36*(3), 6–12.

Storey, W. (1979). *A guide for career development inquiry.* Madison, Wis.: The American Society for Training and Development, pp. 4–5.

Study identifies qualities required for effective workforce development system. 1998. *HR Reporter, 15*(11), 1–7.

Stump, R. (1990). *Your career in human resource development: A guide to information and decision-making.* Alexandria, Va.: The American Society for Training and Development.

Sunoo, B. (1997). When native values drive survival. *Workforce, 76*(2), 59–66.

Swan, W. S.; Margulies, P. (1991). *How to do a superior performance appraisal.* New York, N.Y.: John Wiley & Sons.

Swanson, R. A., and Zuber, J. A. (1996). A case study of a failed organization development intervention rooted in the employee survey process. *Performance Improvement Quarterly, 9*(2), 42–56.

Tannenbaum, S., and Dupuree-Bruno, L. (1994). The relationship between organizational and environmental factors and the use of innovative human resource practices. *Group and Organization Management, 19*(2), 171–202.

Thomas, R. (1996). *Redefining diversity.* New York: AMACOM.

Thompson, B. (1990). Ethics training enters the real world. *Training, 27*(10), 82–94.

Toffler, B. (1986). *Tough choices: Managers talk ethics.* New York, N.Y.: John Wiley & Sons.

Torraco, R., and Swanson, R. (1995). The strategic roles of human resource development. *Human Resource Planning, 18*(4), 10–21.

Tough, A. (1971). *The adult's learning projects.* Toronto: Ontario Institute for Studies in Education.

Tough, A. (1979). *The adult's learning projects* (2nd ed.). Toronto: Ontario Institute for Studies in Education.

Townsend, P., and Gebhardt, J. (1997). *Five-star leadership: The art and strategy of creating leaders at every level.* New York: John Wiley & Sons.

Training and Development Lead Body. (1992). *National Standards for Training and Development.* England: Training and Development Lead Body.

Training budgets. (1997). *Training, 34*(10), 39–42, 44–46.

Training budgets: The national investment in workplace training continues to grow. (1998). *Training, 35*(10), 47–50, 52.

Training by computer. (1998). *Training, 35*(10), 71–74, 76.

Training multimedia buyers' guide. 1999. *Human Resource Executive, 13*(1), 79–80.

Transportation leader Viking Freight takes the high road in employee education. 1996. *Corporate University Review, 4*(5), 13.

Trends. (1995). *Training, 32*(10), 69–74.

Trevino, L., and Nelson, K. (1995). *Managing business ethics: Straight talk about how to do it right.* New York: John Wiley & Sons.

Tschohl, J. (1995). *Cashing in: Make more money, get a promotion, love your job.* Minneapolis, Minn.: Best Sellers.

Tyson, K. (1998). Perpetual strategy: A 21st century essential. *Strategy and Leadership, 26*(1), 14–18.

U.S. Civil Service Commission. (1976). *The employee development specialist curriculum plan: An outline of learning experiences for the employee development specialist.* Washington, D.C.: U. S. Civil Service Commission.

Ulrich, D. (1997). *Human resource champions: The next agenda for adding value and delivering results.* Boston: Harvard Business School Press.

Ulrich, D., Losey, M., and Lake, G. (Eds.). (1997). *Tomorrow's HR management: 48 thought-leaders call for change.* New York: John Wiley & Sons.

Ulrich, D.; Brockbank, W.; and Yeung, A. (1989). HR competencies in the 1990s. *Personnel Administrator, 34*(11), 91–93.

Uncommon good, The. (1995). *Economist, 336*(7928), 55–56.

Unique combination of satellite TV, gamesmanship improves ethics training. (1997). *Training Directors' Forum Newsletter, 13*(5), 5.

Values and ethics. 1987. *HR Reporter Special, 4*(1), 1–4.

Varney, G. (1980). Developing OD competencies. *Training and Development Journal, 34*(4), 30–35.

Varney, G. H. (1990). A study of the core literature in organization development. *Organization Development Journal, 8*(3), 59–66.

Verardo, D. (1997). *Managing the strategic planning process.* INFO-LINE. Alexandria, Va.: The American Society for Training and Development.

Vincola, A. (1998). Work and life: In search of the missing links. *HR Focus, 75*(8), s3–s4.

Vinton, D. (1987). Delegation for employee development. *Training and Development Journal, 41*(1), 65–67.

Vogel, D. (1992). The globalization of business ethics: Why America remains distinctive. *California Management Review, 35*(1), 30–49.

Vogel, D. (1993). Is U.S. business obsessed with ethics? *Across the Board, 30*(9), 30–33.

Von Hoffman, C. (1999). The final rung. *Inside Technology Training, 3*(1), 26–27.

Wagel, W. (1987). A new focus on business ethics at General Dynamics. *Personnel, 64*(8), 4–8.

Wagner, S. (1999). Globalization drives training in Europe. *Training and Development, 53*(2), 59.

Wake up! (and reclaim instructional design). (1998). *Training, 35*(6), 36–42.

Walker, A. (1996). Views from the top. *Human Resource Executive, 10*(1), 26–27.

Wall, S. (1997). Creating strategists. *Training and Development, 51*(5), 75–79.

Wall, S., and Wall, S. (1995). The evolution (not the death) of strategy. *Organizational Dynamics, 24*(2), 6–19.

Walter, K. (1995). Ethics hot lines tap into more than wrongdoing. *HR Magazine, 40*(9), 79–85.

Walter, K. (1995). Values statements that augment corporate success. *HR Magazine, 40*(10), 87–93.

Walton, C. (1988). *The moral manager.* Cambridge, Mass.: Ballinger Publishing.

Warrick, D. and Donovan, T. (1979). Surveying OD skills. *Training and Development Journal, 33*(9), 22–25.

Waste management: Building an ethical culture. 1991. *HR Reporter, 8*(4), 1–3.

Watkins, K. (1990). Tacit beliefs of human resource developers: Producing unintended consequences. *Human Resource Development Quarterly, 1*(3), 263–275.

Watkins, K. (1991). Many voices: Defining human resource development from different disciplines. *Adult Education Quarterly, 41*(4), 241–255.

Watson, R. and Evans, R. (1991). *The great psychologists: A history of psychological thought* (5th ed.). New York: HarperCollins Publishers.

Webber, A. M. (1999). Learning for a change. *Fast Company*, 24, 178–188.

Webster, L. and Henderson, S. (1987). Charting your HRD career. In R. Bard, C. Bell, L. Stephen, and L. Webster (eds.), *The trainer's professional development handbook.* San Francisco: Jossey-Bass.

Weisbord, M. (1976). Organizational diagnosis: Six places to look for trouble with or without a theory. *Group and Organization Studies, 1,* 430–447.

Weiss, A. (1991). Seven reasons to examine workplace ethics. *HR Magazine, 36*(3), 69–74.

Weiss, A. (1997). Slogging toward the millennium. *Training, 34*(4), 51–54.

Wellner, A. (1999). Get ready for Generation Next. *Training, 36*(2), 42–48.

Wells, R. (1999). Back to the (Internet) classroom. *Training, 36*(3), 50–54.

Westera, W. (1999). Paradoxes in open, networked learning environments: Toward a paradigm shift. *Educational Technology, 39*(1), 17–23.

What employers teach. (1997). *Training, 34*(10), 49–50, 52, 54–56, 58.

Who gets trained? Where the money goes. (1998). *Training, 35*(10), 55–56, 58, 60–61.

Whyte, W. and Hamilton, E. (1964). *Action research for management.* Homewood, Ill.: Irwin-Dorsey.

Williams, W. (1985, June 9). White collar crime: Booming again. *New York Times,* p. 4:1.

Willmore, J. (1998). *Scenario planning.* INFO-LINE. Alexandria, Va.: The American Society for Training and Development.

Wills, J. (1997). *The ASTD trainer's sourcebook: Strategic planning.* New York, N.Y.: McGraw-Hill.

Wood, D. (1996). A framework for re-engineering traditional training: Interactive training and electronic performance support. *Performance Improvement, 35*(8), 14–18.

Wood, G., Jr. (1996). A code of ethics for all adult educators? *Adult Learning, 8*(2), 13–14.

Workplace trends. (1997). *Training, 34*(10), 61–65.

Wrege, C. and Perroni, A. (1974, March). Taylor's pig-tale: A historical analysis of Frederick W. Taylor's pig-iron experiments. *American Management Journal, 17,* 6–27.

Wren, D. (1979). *The evolution of management thought* (2nd ed.). New York: Wiley.

Wright, V. (1993). There are case studies...and case studies. *Performance and Instruction, 32*(2), 31–33.

Wyatt, J. (1997). Customer-driven HR. *HR Focus, 74*(2), 3.

Yang, J. (1994). *Perceived competencies needed by HRD managers in Korea.* Unpublished doctoral dissertation. Minneapolis: University of Minnesota.

Yeung, A. (1996). Identifying and developing HR competencies for the future: Key to sustaining the transformation of HR functions. *Human Resource Planning, 19*(4), 48–58.

Yiu, L., and Saner, R. (1998). Use of action learning as a vehicle for capacity building in China. *Performance Improvement Quarterly, 11*(1), 129–148.

Yoo, J. (1999). *Korean human resource development (HRD) practitioners' perceptions of expertise level and importance of workplace learning and performance (WLP) competencies*. Unpublished doctoral dissertation. University Park: Pennsylvania State University.

You, S. (1993). *Perception of Korean human resource development practitioners toward selected roles and competency standards*. Unpublished doctoral dissertation. College Park: University of Maryland.

Young, C. (1993, Fall). Human resource planning: An expatriate process. *HR Horizons*, n114, pp. 27–31.

Zemke, R. and Zemke, S. (1981). Thirty things we know for sure about adult learning. *Training, 18*(6), 45–52.

Zielinski, D. (1995). New world of work demands employees take more ownership of training, career paths. *Training Directors' Forum Newsletter, 11*(9), 1–3.

Zielinski, D. (1995). Study: Growth of self-directed learning changing PC trainers' roles. *Training Directors' Forum Newsletter, 11*(2), 6.

Zinno, V. (1995). A peak development. *Human Resource Executive, 9*(4), 38–41.

APPENDICES

APPENDIX A

Key Journals About WLP and Related Fields

Key journals and periodicals about Workplace Learning and Performance and related fields include:

–A–

Academy of Management Executives
P. O. Box Drawer KZ
Mississippi State, MS 39762

Across the Board
The Conference Board, Inc.
845 Third Ave.
New York, NY 10022

Adult Education Quarterly
American Assoc. for Adult and Continuing
  Education
1201 16th St., NW
Suite 230
Washington, D. C. 20036

–B–

Bulletin on Training
Bureau of National Affairs
1231 25th St., NW
Washington, D.C. 20037

–C–

The Career Center Bulletin
Columbia University
314 Uris
New York, NY 10027

CBT Directions
Weingarten Publications
38 Chauncy St.
Boston, MA 02111

–D–

Data Training
Weingarten Publications
38 Chauncy St.
Boston, MA 02111

–E–

Educational Technology
Educational Technology
720 Palisade Avenue
Englewood Cliffs, NJ 07632

*Educational Technology Research and
   Development*
AECT
1126 Sixteenth St., NW
Washington, D.C. 20036

Executive Development
MCB University Press Ltd.
P. O. Box 10812
Birmingham, AL 35201

–F–

Futurist
World Future Society
4916 St. Elmo Ave.
Bethesda, MD 20814

–G–

Group and Organization Studies
Sage Publications
2111 W. Hillcrest Drive
Newbury Park, CA 91320

–H–

HRD Quarterly
Jossey-Bass
350 Sansome St.
San Francisco, CA 94104

The HRD Review
52-A Phelps Ave.
New Brunswick, NJ 08901

HR Magazine
Society for Human Resource Management
606 N. Washington St.
Alexandria, VA 22314

Human Resource Executive
747 Dresher Road
Suite 500
Horsham, PA 19044

Human Resource Management
Graduate School of Business Administration
University of Michigan
Ann Arbor, MI 48109

Human Resource Planning
The Human Resource Planning Society
P. O. Box 2553
Grand Central Station
New York, NY 10163

–I–

Industrial and Commercial Training
MCB University Press Ltd.
P. O. Box 10812
Birmingham, AL 35201

Info-Line
American Society for Training and
   Development
P. O. Box 1443
1640 King Street
Alexandria, VA 22313

–J–

Journal of Computer-Based Instruction
Miller Hall 409
Western Washington University
Bellingham, WA 98225

Journal of European Industrial Training
MCB University Press Ltd.
P. O. Box 10812
Birmingham, AL 35201

Journal of Instructional Development
Association for Educational Communications
  and Technology
1126 16th St., NW
Washington, D.C. 20036

Journal of Management Development
MCB University Press Ltd.
P. O. Box 10812
Birmingham, AL 35201

–L–

Lifelong Learning
American Assn. for Adult and Continuing
  Education
1201 16th St. NW
Suite 230
Washington, DC 20036

–M–

Management Education
CSML
University of Lancaster
Lancaster, LAI 4YX
England

Management Review
American Management Association
Saranac Lake, NY 12983

Management World
Administrative Management Society
4622 Street Rd.
Trevose, PA 19047

–O–

Organization Development Journal
Organization Development Institute
6501 Wilson Mills Road
Suite K
Cleveland, OH 44143

Organizational Dynamics
American Management Association
Box 408
Saranac Lake, NY 12983

–P–

Performance Improvement
NSPI Publications
4423 East Trailride Road
Bloomington, IN 47408

Performance Improvement Quarterly
NSPI Publications
Learning Systems Institute
406 Dodd
Florida State University
Tallahassee, FL 32306

Personnel
American Management Association
Box 319
Saranac Lake, NY 12983

Personnel Journal
P. O. Box 2440
Costa Mesa, CA 92628

Personnel Management
Personnel Publications Ltd.
57 Mortimer Street
London, WIN 7TD, England

Personnel Psychology
9660 Hillcroft
Suite 337
Houston, TX 77096

Personnel Review
MCB University Press
P. O. Box 10812
Birmingham, AL 35201

Planning Review
Planning Forum
P. O. Box 70
Oxford, OH 45056

Public Personnel Management
International Personnel Management
  Association
1617 Duke Street
Alexandria, VA 22314

–S–

Sales and Marketing Training
Executive Business Media
P. O. Box 1500
Westbury, NY 11590

Successful Meetings
633 Third Avenue
New York, NY 10017

–T–

Technical & Skills Training News
American Society for Training and
  Development
1640 King Street
Alexandria, VA 22314

Tech Trends
AECT
1126 Sixteenth St., NW
Washington, D.C. 20036

Trainer's Workshop
American Management Assn.
Saranac Lake, NY 12983

Training
Lakewood Publications
50 South Ninth St.
Minneapolis, MN 55402

Training and Development Journal
American Society for Training and
  Development
1640 King Street
Alexandria, VA 22314

Training Directors' Forum Newsletter
Lakewood Publications
50 South Ninth St.
Minneapolis, MN 55402

–V–

Vocational Education Journal
American Vocational Association
1410 King St.
Alexandria, VA 22314

Major Professional Associations for WLP and Related Fields

Key associations related to WLP include the following:

American Association for Adult and
   Continuing Education
(AAACE)
1201 16th St., NW
Suite 230
Washington, D.C. 20036

American Association of Community and
   Junior Colleges (AACJC)
National Center for Higher Education
1 Dupont Circle
Suite 410
Washington, D.C. 20036

American Management Association (AMA)
135 W. 50th St.
New York, NY 10020

American Society for Training and
   Development (ASTD)
1640 King Street
Alexandria, VA 22313

American Vocational Association (AVA)
1410 King St.
Alexandria, VA 22314

Association for Continuing Higher
   Education (ACHE)
c/o R. Sublett
College of Graduate and Continuing Studies
University of Evansville
1800 Lincoln Avenue
Evansville, IN 47722

Association for Educational
   Communications and Technology
   (AECT)
1126 16th St., NW
Washington, D.C. 20036

Human Resource Planning Society (HRPS)
P. O. Box 2553
Grand Central Station
New York, NY 10163

International Federation of Training and
  Development Organizations (IFTDO)
c/o Derek Wake
Institute of Management Education
7 Westbourne Rd.
Southport PR 8 2HZ England

International Society for Performance
  Improvement (ISPI)
1126 16th St., NW
Suite 102
Washington, D.C. 20036

APPENDIX C

Internet and Web Sites Useful for WLP

Directions: Simply go to a search engine and type in the name of any of these associations if you are interested in finding out more information.

Associations

Academy of Human Resource Development

American Automobile Manufacturers Association

American Chamber of Commerce-Brazil (AmCham-Brazil)

American Counseling Association

American Management Association International

American Society of Association Executives

American Society of Safety Engineers

American Society for Quality Control

Arabian Society for Human Resource Management (ASHRM)

Association for Educational Communications and Technology

Association for Experiential Education

Australian Human Resources Institute (AHRI)

Australian Institute of Training and Development (AITD)

Battelle Seattle Research Center

Canadian Automotive Parts Manufacturers' Association (CAPMA)

Canadian Centre for Occupational Health and Safety (CCOHS)

Conference Board, The

Consumer Electronics Manufacturers Association

Educom home page

Employment Management Association (EMA)

The Foundation for Enterprise Development

Associations *(continued)*

Human Resource Institute

Human Resources Development Canada (HRDC)

Information Technology Training Association

International Association of Computer Professionals (IACP)

International Association of Facilitators (IAF)

International Federation of Training and Development Organizations (IFTDO)

International HR Information Management Association (IHRIMA)

International Personnel Management (IPM)

International Society for Performance Improvement (ISPI)

International Teleconferencing Association (ITA)

International Personnel Management Association (IPMA)

National Skill Standards Board (NZATD)

New Zealand Association for Training and Development

NPES The Association for Suppliers of Printing and Publishing Technologies

Netherlands Association of Training Professionals (NVvO)

Ontario Society for Training and Development (OSTD)

Singapore Training and Development Association (STDA)

Society for Human Resource Management

Training Forum

Business Sites

Corporate University Xchange

The Electronic Money Tree

Entrepreneur Weekly

Entrepreneurial Edge Online

Internet Public Library

National Small Business United

Partners for Small Business Excellence

Small Business Law Center

U.S. Small Business Administration

Career Resources

America's Job Bank

Career America

CareerMosaic

Careerpath.com

CareerWeb

Corporate Personnel Job Bank

Electronic Recruiting News

Exec-U-Net

jobfind

JOBNET

JobWeb

MonsterBoard

Multimedia Job Bank

Online Career Center

Regional Career Resources

Boston Job Bank

Canada's Job Bank

Career Resource Newsgroups

misc.jobs.contract

misc.jobs.offered

Distance Learning

Thomas Edison State College

Dyro's Web-Based Training Site WBT Information Center

AT&T Center for Excellence in Distance Learning

Distance Education Clearinghouse

National Distance Learning Center: Telnet to:
  ndlc.occ.uky.edu. Type NDLC for UserID. Complete first-time user questionnaire.

Institute for Distance Education—Models

The Teletraining Institute

Distance Learning *(continued)*

University of Wisconsin—Distance Learning Clearinghouse

Distance Education at a Glance

Arizona State University—Distance Learning Technology

Open and Distance Learning Critical Success Factors

Learning Resource Network

Web-based multimedia courseware

Distance Learning Listservs

DEOS-L
  The Distance Education Online Symposium
  listserv@psuvm.psu.edu— info DEOS-L
DEOS-R
  Distance Education Online Research
  listserv@cmuvm.csv.cmich.edu—info DEOS-R
  DEOSNEWS

The Distance Education Online Symposium
  listserv@psuvm.psu.edu—info DEOSNEWS

General HR

Center for Human Resources

HRIMMall . . . Online Human Resource Systems and Services Guide

HRnet

Human Relations

The Human Resource Store

Inside HR

International Workplace Studies Program

People Management

Society for Human Resource Management

WorkIndex Home Page

Business Sites

Corporate University Xchange

The Electronic Money Tree

Entrepreneur Weekly

Entrepreneurial Edge Online

Business Sites *(continued)*

Internet Public Library

National Small Business United

Partners for Small Business Excellence

Small Business Law Center

U.S. Small Business Administration

Internet Search Tips

Tricks and Tips

Search Insider

Free Pint Newsletter

Knowledge Management

Thomas Edison State College

Business Researcher's Interest (BRI) Knowledge Management and Organizational Learning Page

Enabling Technologies

Knowledge, Inc.

Knowledge Management Server

The Knowledge Organisation

New Language for New Leverage: The Terminology of Knowledge Management

The Official Intellectual Capital Home Page

Swedish Community of Practice

Themes in Knowledge Management

Learning Technologies

Thomas Edison State College

Gil Gordon Associates

Presenters' University

CBT Solutions Magazine Online

Computer-Supported Cooperative Work (CSCW) and Groupware Research Laboratory

EDUCOM

TCBWorks Groupware Software

Frontiers in Education (Session papers on multimedia topics)

Learning Technologies *(continued)*

Presenters' University (Multimedia)

Spectrum Virtual University

Management Development

The Conference Board

Performance Improvement

The EPSS Info Site Home Page

EPSS Resources

EPSS Info Site

Epss.com!

International Society for Performance Improvement

Performance Technology

Safety Training

American Society of Safety Engineers

Canadian Centre for Occupational Health and Safety

Occupational Safety and Health Administration

National Institute for Occupational Safety and Health

Frequently Cited OSHA Standards

Ergo Web

UVA's Video Display Ergonomics page

Safety Training Newsgroups

uiuc.misc.safety

sci.engr.safety

Search Engine Help

Search Engine Watch

Choose the Best Search Engine

Understanding Web Search Tools

Skill Standards

National Skill Standards Board
National Health Care Skill Standards Project

Statistics and Surveys

National Adult Literacy Survey
National Household Education Survey (NHES)
Economy at a Glance
Bureau of Labor Statistics

Technical Training Sites

Manufacturing Marketplace

Technical Training Newsgroups

misc.business.consulting
misc.education.adult
misc.education.medical
misc.education.multimedia
misc.industry.utilities.electric
uk.comp.training

Training Basics

The Center for Creative Leadership
Downloadable Internet HR bookmark file
New Horizons for Learning
Training Information Source
TRDEV-L Listserv Home Page

Training Basics: Newsgroups

misc.business.consulting
misc.education
misc.education.adult

U.S. Government

Council of Great Lakes Governors

Department of Education

Department of Labor

FEDWORLD

Manufacturing Extension Partnership

National Institute for Occupational Safety and Health

National Institute of Standards and Technology

Occupational Safety and Health Administration (OSHA)

USAJobs—Office of Personnel Management

U.S. Army Training and Doctrine Command

U.S. Legislative Branch

Specific Web Links *(with selected remarks by authors)*

www.ahrd.org
   Academy of Human Resource Development

www.trainingnet.com
   The TrainingNet

http://www.nwlink.com/~donclark/hrd.html
   Big Dog's Human Resource Development Page

http://www.josseybass.com/hrdq.html
   Human Resource Development Quarterly

http://www.escape.ca/~mhr/
   Measurements for HR

http://www.astd.org
   The American Society for Training and Development (ASTD)

http://tcm.com/trdev/
   Training and Development Resource Centre: Gateway to a "Virtual" gold mine of resources for
   the T&D / HR Community !

http://www.funderstanding.com/about_learning.html
   Learning Theory Funhouse: Funderstanding

Specific Web Links *(with selected remarks by authors)* (continued)

http://www.gwu.edu/~tip/
   Theory Into Practice (TIP)

http://www.tregistry.com/home.htm
   The Training Registry

http://www.ott.navy.mil/
   Naval Operations Training Technology Resource Center

http://mime1.marc.gatech.edu/MM_Tools/
   Multimedia Development Tools

http://www.teambuildersplus.com/links.html
   This site contains a very good list of T&D links.

http://quark.arl.psu.edu/training/tr-menu.html
   Training and Instructional Design

http://www.nwlink.com/~donclark/hrd/glossary.html
   An extensive training and learning glossary of terms.

http://www.peoplesoft.com/peoplepages/c/marcia_conner/learning_exchange/
   A site with FAQs about training and development. It also has references to other resources for T&D.

http://www.siweb.com/staff/dsleight/trainhst.htm
   This site is a copy of the article *A Developmental History of Training in the United States and Europe* by Deborah A. Sleight, M.A., Educational Psychology, Michigan State University, December, 1993.

http://www.tpid.com/~tpike/IDChecklist.html
   An instructional design checklist based on the theories of Robert Mager and written by Thomas Pike.

http://www.ccn.cs.dal.ca/~ac200/DACUM.html
   This site provides information about the DACUM (Develop A CUrriculuM) method.

http://www.seas.gwu.edu/student/tlooms/ISD/isd_homepage.html
   This Web site includes a number of interesting things about Instructional Design, and links to models of various sorts.

Specific Web Links *(with selected remarks by authors)* (continued)

http://www.princeton.edu/%7Ercurtis/aee.html
  Association for Experiential Education

http://www.hmc.psu.edu/edres/hints/intro.htm
  Deals with the how-to of distance education. Primarily text-based.

http://www.seas.gwu.edu/student/sbraxton/ISD/isd_homepage.html
  Instructional Design Methodologies and Techniques (George Washington University)

http://www.ils.nwu.edu/~e_for_e/nodes/I-M-NODE-4121-pg.html
  Engines for Education

http://www.ee.ed.ac.uk/~gerard/MENG/MECD/index.html
  This site deals with facilitation. It discusses groups and group dynamics, as well as the role and competencies of the facilitator.

http://www.topten.org/content/tt.AU20.htm

http://www.imc.org.uk/services/coursewa/ada/ad3.htm#session2

http://www.imc.org.uk/services/coursewa/bmgt/bm8.htm#SESSION3
  These two sites are text-based sessions about presentation skills. They are practical 'how-to' guides for preparing quality presentations.

http://tdg.uoguelph.ca/~pi/pdrc/facbox.html
  The facilitator's toolbox

http://www.users.globalnet.co.uk/~rogg/index.htm
  Guide to active reviewing

http://www.hcc.hawaii.edu/education/hcc/facdev/breakice.html

http://www.cornell.edu/Admin/TNET/Icebreakers/Icebreakers.html
  These pages contain numerous activities to 'break the ice' with new groups of people.

http://www.hrdpress.com/FreeAct.html
  HRD Press—This page contains free training activities, which can be downloaded.

http://www.presentations.com/

http://www.computouch.ca/present.htm

Specific Web Links *(with selected remarks by authors)* (continued)

http://www.access.digex.net/~nuance/keystep1.html

http://www1.tagonline.com/~strategy/resources.html
These sites provide how-to guidance for doing presentations. Particularly helpful for technology-based presentations using LCD displays, laptops, etc. Also provides guidance for selecting technologies.

http://www.esper.com/a_e/
This is a fairly comprehensive site on training evaluation. It includes information about the history of evaluation in training, current practices, the costs of evaluation, and how to move beyond the smile sheet, along with other information.

http://www.uct.ac.za/projects/cbe/mcqman/mcqman01.html
Designing and managing multiple-choice questions

http://halley.pepperdine.edu/studios/etcadre2/bgalde/costtools/index.html
A toolkit for calculating the cost and evaluating the effectiveness of training programs

http://www.ktic.com/TOPIC7/14_BROWN.HTM
This is an article by Stephen M. Brown, Ed.D., Dean of the Center for Adult Learning at Lesley College. It is a good overview of some of the important issues in evaluation.

http://www.fredcomm.com/articles/value/kirkpatr.htm
This is a discussion of Kirkpatrick's Four Levels of Evaluation: reaction, learning, transfer, and business results.

http://www.karinrex.com/tc_evals.html
The Ten Rules for Perfect Evaluations: On Choosing between Training Excellence and Great Evaluations written by Jay McNaught and originally published by Data Training Magazine in May of 1991.

http://cleo.murdoch.edu.au/gen/aset/ajet/ajet5/su89p89.html
Evaluation of training and development programs: A review of the literature

http://www.imc.org.uk/services/coursewa/ada/iad1.htm#session1
This site contains text-based material related to how to develop your own career. It includes suggested questions to ask yourself, and activities to do.

Specific Web Links *(with selected remarks by authors)* (continued)

http://www.tmn.com/odn/index.html
  Organization Development Network (ODN)—ODN is an association of organization development practitioners representing a range of professional roles in a wide variety of organizations. This large site contains OD resources and links, as well as information about ODN.

http://www.cs.ius.indiana.edu/LZ/pmccarth/web_docs/homepage.htm
  The Resource Center/Playground in Industrial and Organizational Psychology

http://gopher.tmn.com:70/0/OrgManTQM/odn94/Sessions/odsk
  This Web page has a list of 220 OD skills. That is all that is on this page, but it is worthwhile.

http://www.ispi.org/
  International Society for Performance Improvement (ISPI)—This site contains various resources related to HPI, including member information and resources, conference information, a job bank, a definition of the field of human performance technology, and publication information.

http://edweb.sdsu.edu/edweb_folder/pt/pt.html
  Performance Technology

http://www.npr.gov/library/resource/measure.html
  Visit this site for help with performance measures. It has links to various sources of information provided by the federal government.

http://www.zigonperf.com/Links.htm
  This web page provides a substantial list of performance-related web resources.

http://www.tcm.com/trdev/harless.htm
  This page contains the summary of an article by Joe Harless, one of the leaders in the field of HPI.

http://users.ids.net/~brim/sdwtf.html
  This site contains the answers to FAQ about teams.

http://rampages.onramp.net/~bodwell/home.htm
  This Web site is a resource for businesses and organizations interested in harnessing the power of teams to achieve business objectives. It addresses team concepts, team building, coaching high performance teams, and other resources.

INDEX: VOLUME I

Index: Volume I